D1633271

The essays collected here relate the writings of Antonio Gramsci and others to the contemporary reconstruction of historical materialist theories of international relations. The contributors analyse the contradiction between globalising and territorially based social and political forces in the context of past, present, and future world orders, and view the emerging world order as undergoing a structural transformation, a 'triple crisis' involving economic, political and 'socio-cultural' change. The prevailing trend of the 1980s and early 1990s toward the marketisation and commodification of social relations leads the contributors to argue that socialism needs to be redefined away from the totalising visions associated with Marxism-Leninism, towards the idea of the self-defence of society and social choice to counter the disintegrating and atomising effects of globalising and unplanned market forces.

Contributors: Giovanni Arrighi, Enrico Augelli, Robert W. Cox, Stephen Gill, Barry K. Gills, Otto Holman, David Law, Craig Murphy, Mark Rupert, Kees van der Pijl.

CAMBRIDGE STUDIES IN INTERNATIONAL RELATIONS: 26

GRAMSCI, HISTORICAL MATERIALISM AND INTERNATIONAL RELATIONS

Cambridge Studies in International Relations is a joint initiative of Cambridge University Press and the British International Studies Association (BISA). The series includes a wide range of material, from undergraduate textbooks and surveys to research-based monographs and collaborative volumes. The aim of the series is to publish the best new scholarship in International Studies from Europe, North America and the rest of the world.

CAMBRIDGE STUDIES IN INTERNATIONAL RELATIONS

Series list continues after index

GRAMSCI, HISTORICAL MATERIALISM AND INTERNATIONAL RELATIONS

edited by
STEPHEN GILL

Professor of Political Science, York University, Toronto

CAMBRIDGE
UNIVERSITY PRESS

Published by the Press Syndicate of the University of Cambridge
The Pitt Building, Trumpington Street, Cambridge CB2 1RP
40 West 20th Street, New York, NY 10011–4211, USA
10 Stamford Road, Oakleigh, Melbourne 3166, Australia

First published 1993
Reprinted 1994

A catalogue record for this book is available from the British Library

Library of Congress cataloguing in publication data

Gramsci, Historical materialism and international relations / edited
by Stephen Gill.
     p.   cm. – (Cambridge studies in international relations ; 26)
Includes bibliographical references and index.
ISBN 0 521 43509 9 (hardback). – ISBN 0 521 43523 4 (paperback)
1. Gramsci, Antonio, 1891–1937. 2. International relations.
3. Communism and international relations. 4. Historical
materialism. I. Gill, Stephen, 1950– . II. Series.
HX289.7.G73G73 1993
327.1′01 – dc20 92–23173 CIP

ISBN 0 521 43509 9 hardback
ISBN 0 521 43523 4 paperback

Transferred to digital printing 2000

CONTENTS

NOTES ON CONTRIBUTORS

Giovanni Arrighi is Professor of Sociology at the State University of New York, Binghamton. He is the author of many books and articles, including *The Geometry of Imperialism* (1976). He writes on international relations and political economy.

Enrico Augelli is an independent scholar and a Senior Economic Officer in the Italian Ministry of Foreign Affairs. His scholarly work concentrates on development and international affairs. He is the co-author, with Craig Murphy, of *America's Quest for Supremacy in the Third World* (1988).

Robert W. Cox is Professor of Political Science and Social and Political Thought at York University, Toronto, Canada. The author of many books and articles, he writes on international relations, political economy and international organisation. He is the author of *Power, Production and World Order: Social Forces in the Making of History* (1987).

Stephen Gill is Associate Professor of Political Science at York University, Toronto, Canada. He has written and edited several books and written many articles on international relations, political economy and US politics and is the author of *American hegemony and the Trilateral Commission* (1990).

Barry K. Gills is Lecturer in East Asian Studies at Newcastle University in England. He writes on political economy and international relations with reference to East Asia.

Otto Holman is Lecturer in International Relations at the Department of International Relations and Public International Law, University of Amsterdam, Netherlands. He writes on international relations and political economy, with special reference to Spain, the Mediterranean and Latin America.

David Law is a Senior Lecturer in Economics at Wolverhampton University in England. He writes on international political economy and development. He is the co-author, with Stephen Gill, of *The Global Political Economy* (1988).

Craig Murphy is a Professor of Political Science at Wellesley College in the USA. He has written a substantial number of books and articles in the fields of international organisation, international political economy and North–South relations.

Mark Rupert is an Assistant Professor of Political Science in the Maxwell School of Citizenship and Public Affairs, Syracuse University, USA. He writes on political economy and international relations theory.

Kees van der Pijl is a Professor of International Relations in the Department of International Relations and Public International Law, University of Amsterdam, Netherlands. He writes on international relations and political economy, and is the author and editor of several books and many articles, including *The Making of an Atlantic Ruling Class* (1984).

ACKNOWLEDGEMENTS

I gratefully acknowledge permission to reprint and edit the original versions of chapters 1, 2, 4 and 6. There were originally published, respectively, as: Stephen Gill, 'Gramsci, Historical Materialism and International Political Economy', in C. Murphy and R. Tooze (ed.), *The New International Political Economy* (London: Macmillan, 1991), pp. 51–75; Robert W. Cox, 'Gramsci, Hegemony and International Relations: An Essay in Method', *Millennium: Journal of International Studies*, 1983, vol. 12, pp. 162–75; Stephen Gill and David Law, 'Global Hegemony and the Structural Power of Capital', *International Studies Quarterley*, 1989, vol. 33, pp. 475–99; Giovanni Arrighi, 'The Three Hegemonies of Historical Capitalism', *Review*, 1990, vol. XIII, pp. 365–408.

In developing some of the ideas in this collection I would like to thank, among others, the following friends and colleagues who have played a role, however indirectly: John Agnew, Rob Albritton, Giovanni Arrighi, Richard Ashley, Enrico Augelli, Steve Burman, Alan Cafruny, David Coates, Robert Cox, Martin Durham, Seiji Endo, Richard Falk, Jeff Frieden, Barry Gills, Eric Helleiner, Otto Holman, Glenn Hook, Makato Itoh, Takehiko Kamo, Robert Keohane, Bradley Klein, David Lake, David Law, Geoff Martin, Craig Murphy, Henk Overbeek, Leo Panitch, Frank Pearce, David Rapkin, Mark Rupert, Yoshikazu Sakamoto, Tim Shaw, Steve Smith, Susan Strange, Roger Tooze, Kees van der Pijl, Douglas Verney, the late John Vincent, Rob Walker and Victor Wolfenstein. I also appreciated the constructive comments of anonymous reviewers. Some of the thoughts for the book were developed at the conventions of the American Political Science Association and at the British and US International Studies Associations.

Both the series editor, Steve Smith, and the editor of social sciences, Michael Holdsworth, at Cambridge University Press, gave valuable editorial comment and support. Melodie Cilio assisted with the preparation of the manuscript and the bibliography, and Randy Persaud with the index.

Financial support came from: Wolverhampton Polytechnic, The British Academy, the University of Manchester (in the context of the Hallsworth Senior Research Fellowship in Political Economy), York University and the Japan Foundation Endowment Committee. I am most grateful for this.

Finally, I am particularly indebted to Robert and Jesse Cox, my mother, Millicent Gill, and David Law, for their inspiration and support, in good times and bad.

It goes without saying that I am responsible for any shortcomings of the final product.

GRAMSCI AND GLOBAL POLITICS: TOWARDS A POST-HEGEMONIC RESEARCH AGENDA

STEPHEN GILL

This book introduces selected new developments in historical materialism. Its central argument is that we need to develop new approaches to international political economy (IPE) and international relations (IR) through the elaboration of historically integrated, dialectical forms of explanation, appropriate to the conditions of the late twentieth century. In this introduction I sketch some of the main ideas, issues and research questions which relate broadly speaking to the reconstruction of historical materialist theories of IR.[1] The contributions to this book offer a range of different approaches within a broadly shared perspective. An anonymous reviewer called the perspective which informs most of the contributions the 'new Italian school' of IR. In chapter 1, I use the epithet 'Italian' with some irony, hesitation and deference to our two Italian contributors (Giovanni Arrighi and Enrico Augelli).

As will become apparent, the essays here are inspired by the problems raised not only in Antonio Gramsci's writings but also those of other authors, such as Karl Marx, Fernand Braudel, Karl Polanyi, Robert Cox, and others, for example, working in the Amsterdam School of International Relations (see the chapters by Otto Holman and Kees van de Pijl). In other words, Gramsci's notes on IR need to be linked to a reconstruction of historical materialist thought in a broad sense, so as to avoid a new intellectual sectarianism. It is important to transcend academic distinctions of limited usefulness, such as that between IR and comparative politics, between political theory and empirical theory, between political sociology and political economy. The reconstruction of historical materialist theory needs to consider epistemological, ontological and methodological questions in the context of past, present and future. Within the writings of Marx a theoretical emphasis was on the idea of an integral, historical society, the analysis of which implied the rejection of reductionism inherent in 'objectivist materialism,

1

mechanicism and empiricism . . . in order to reach a truly realist attitude which is self-consciously a product of thought'.[2]

The problematic of this book can be related to the idea that socialism needs to be redefined away from its association with totalising projects, such as that of Stalinism. In turn, this redefinition and the politics it implies can be linked in part to the idea of the self defence of society against the disintegrating and atomising thrust of globalising, relatively unplanned, market forces.

A GRAMSCIAN SCHOOL OF INTERNATIONAL RELATIONS?

As there is no single school of Marxism (Marx himself denied he was a Marxist) so too is there no single Gramscian or 'Italian' school. Nor is there any consensual interpretation of Gramsci's fragmentary and often contradictory thoughts concerning social theory. Instead, there are clusters of scholars working in ways that address some of the questions raised and posed in Gramscian terms, across different disciplines, in a large number of countries. These scholars have begun to communicate, and to participate in joint conferences, and have thus begun to form the embryo of a global research community. Some research is of practical consequence in so far as it is linked in different ways to supporting the activity of socialist and progressive political parties and social movements.

Some initial work from the neo-Gramscian perspective has entailed a constructive dialogue with, as well as a critique of, different perspectives, including the prevailing, or in Gramscian terms, hegemonic theorisation in the fields of political economy and international relations (e.g. Gill and Law, 1988). The need for this is, in my view, occasioned by at least two important factors. First, whilst Marxism has always offered an integrated approach, in large part because of the orientation and predominance of American theory in the field, historical materialism has tended to become marginalised from many of the major debates in international studies. This marginalisation is occasioned in no small part by the limitations of a rather mechanical and ahistorical application of many Marxist ideas and theories, some of which are linked to a fundamentalist tendency to generate 'ever-increasing expectations of the collapse of capitalism' (whereas Gramsci argued pointedly that there was no necessary relationship between economic and political crisis, or *vice versa*).

This theoretical weakness has led to a lack of plausibility in argument as well as to a diminution in the appeal of historical materialist ideas to new generations of students in Western academies. This also seems to have been the fate of orthodox Marxism in Japan during the last twenty years or so. Particularly in the context of the capitulation of the Leninist and post-Stalinist systems of rule in Eastern Europe, as well as the collapse of dogmatic Marxism-Leninism as a social doctrine, we can perhaps now look forward to the moment when such pathological, mechanical Marxism can be consigned to a place as a macabre exhibit in a museum of twentieth-century history. The latter observation reinforces my second point in favour of dialogue. The 1980s and 1990s have witnessed a secular and in some cases spectacular decline in the salience and theoretical appeal of left-wing ideas. Notwithstanding Western triumphalism and propagandists who proclaim the 'end of history', developments in Eastern Europe and the former Soviet Union have reinforced the claims to credibility, positional power and vigour of the hegemonic discourses in the West. On the question of Russia, and the brittleness of the relations between state and civil society, and thus, the propensity for the state to collapse suddenly, Gramsci had a significant insight. This insight might be applied to the events of 1991–2 as the Soviet Union collapsed:

> In Russia, the State was everything. Civil society was primordial and gelatinous; in the West, there was a proper relation between State and civil society, and when the State trembled, a sturdy structure of civil society was at once revealed. (Gramsci, 1971: 238)

Marxist ideas developed in a theoretical ghetto will suffer from a lack of relevance. There is much to be gained from a constructive dialogue with arguments and theories from different perspectives. This is of crucial importance in order to assess the status of new theoretical ideas: to be persuasive, these ideas must provide more comprehensive, consistent and reflexive explanations than those which predominate (Gill, 1990).

Most of Gramsci's substantive work focused upon the analysis of national social formations in particular historical periods, particularly Italy. Gramsci argued that this was the initial level at which the state and civil society (and its anatomy, the political economy) should be analysed, and where the foundations of social hegemonies were built. This national focus predominates in Gramsci scholarship in not only Japan and Latin America, but also in Western Europe, as reflected in the work of the Birmingham University Centre for Contemporary Cultural Studies (e.g. Hall, 1982; and Larrain, 1983) and in the ongoing debates in *New Left Review* and *Socialist Register* on the nature of culture, ideology, the state, civil society and

3

hegemony in capitalist society. There have also been many discussions in left-wing journals over the question of imperialism, although these have usually been couched in terms of theories of ultra- and super-imperialism, rather than posed in Gramscian terms.

The movement towards the extension of Gramscian ideas to the study of IR and IPE has been slow and recent, and has involved relatively few ambitious studies concerned to define the origins, development and dynamics of the emerging global political economy. None the less, impressive work has begun to emerge on the internationalisation of state and civil society, the international aspects of social hegemony and supremacy, and the transnational class and bloc formations and economic forces, the role of organic intellectuals and of international organisations and other issues which help to define the nature of global politics in the twentieth century (e.g. van der Pijl, 1984; Cox, 1987; Augelli and Murphy, 1988; Gill, 1990; Overbeek, 1990). Important here is the pioneering work of Robert Cox, who published two important essays in *Millennium* in the early 1980s (Cox, 1981; Cox, 1983) the latter of which can be fruitfully read as an introduction to the application of Gramscian concepts at the international level and which is reprinted in this collection.

Thus, whilst many social scientists are aware of the application of Gramscian ideas to the analysis of the role of politics, popular culture and ideological and cultural hegemony at the national level, such awareness is much less apparent in IR and IPE. This may be partly because little of Gramsci's thinking focused on questions of political economy *per se*, mainly because he seems to have worked within classical Marxist assumptions about the political economy of capitalism and feudalism.

In the absence of a satisfactory apparatus for analysing the dynamics of the global political economy in the 1980s, students of IR and IPE have begun to develop their own conceptual apparatuses and ontology (e.g. Cox, 1987; van der Pijl, 1984). It is clear that much work is to be done to develop Gramscian perspectives in ways which can have wider appeal. There are a number of ways that this endeavour can be approached. For example, the Amsterdam school have made the non-teleological concept of socialisation (*Vergesellschaftung*) central to their intellectual endeavour, a concept which is linked to the objective of placing an integral history and social theory at the core of analysis:

> The relation between society and the state, as well as relations between states as a consequence of their social interaction, has to be

placed in the context of socialisation as a pervasive process. The ways in which capital (in the sense of total capital, i.e., a self-sustaining, quasi-totalitarian universe of competitive accumulation of surplus value) acts as the agent of socialisation while simultaneously constraining its potential (both in the sense of the division of labour and in the sense of universal culture/normative structures), has to be clarified and related to other structures of socialisation of a community nature – family, nationality, ethnicity – as well as law and state as formal arrangements constitutive of legal/legitimate agents.[3]

The type of work included here needs to be linked to broader theoretical work so that, for example, studies which have a more 'local' or 'national' focus are linked to 'global' studies. This might permit, then, a new intellectual and practical synthesis. With this in mind, in the rest of this preface I elaborate upon some of the other main themes found in this collection.

THE DIALECTIC OF INTEGRATION-DISINTEGRATION AND WORLD ORDER: THE VIEW FROM THE TOP

One theme of this volume is that of a crisis of post-war hegemony. Part of the explanation for this crisis is attributed to a range of globalising forces which are integrating the material, political, social and cultural life of so many people on the planet, but which are simultaneously disintegrating previously embedded forms of socio-economic and political organisation (this idea partly corresponds to the historical process of *Vergesellschaftung*). This dialectical process is most clearly apparent in Eastern and Central Europe and in the Soviet successor states, but it is also occurring in the so-called Third World as well as in the metropolitan capitalist countries. Indeed, this can be analysed as part of an organic, 'triple crisis' of the post-war world order, which is sketched below. One indicator of these changes is the recent growth in migratory and refugee movements, the 'globalisation' of peoples driven by the restructuring of global production and finance, and more generally by growing disparities in economic and environmental conditions, and by war and political conflict.

By contrast, some neo-realists such as John Mearsheimer (1990) assume a basic continuity in international relations. For them, the condition of anarchy in world politics persists, and the inter-state rivalry and insecurity which goes with this condition will reassert itself now the Cold War is over in Europe. Instability is predicted,

5

since the order-producing superstructure of the Cold War has been removed. Other neo-realists, using rather more nuanced historical analogies (e.g. Lawrence Freedman, Sir Michael Howard) have argued that the end of the Cold War means the resurgence of nationalism and a return to the problems which have plagued European security since the end of the Hundred Years' Peace. In this view, then, what has changed is the East–West security superstructure. With its demise, and the erosion of Soviet power, the basic underlying (anarchic) structure of international relations is once more revealed, and the growing diffusion of global power – in the absence of a stable balance of power – is associated with instability and conflict. The apparently recent growth of inter-communal violence, ethnic tensions, the centrifugal forces in some countries (notably the former USSR and Yugoslavia) provides evidence to support this position.

Accordingly, neo-realists see not only the Group of Seven (G7), but also the UN and the EEC and the process of economic and political union in Western Europe, as well as the possible extension of the EC to include other countries, as simply reflecting a series of inter-state bargains and thus an underlying structure of power between states, rather than a series of structural changes which generate new conditions and promote changing conceptions of interest and identity, for example in the pan-European context.

However, it may well be that the twentieth century has ushered in a new era in global politics, so that it may be more appropriate to begin to speak in terms of a more globally integrated set of structures, or, as David Law and I have called it, a 'global political economy'. Whilst these structures have, at least until the late 1980s, been configured by the dialectical struggles between pre-capitalist, capitalist, and communist socio-economic systems, recent evidence of changes in Eastern and Central Europe, the USSR and China, as well as in countries like Vietnam, suggest that capitalism is once again spreading as the predominant form of socio-economic organisation, not only across states, but also within states as marketisation and commoditisation deepens its social and geographical reach. At the same time a growing planetary consciousness of ecological and environmental questions reflects the complex interlinkages between the cumulative forces of economic development and underdevelopment, the interplay between town and country, rich and poor, and war and peace in the emerging world order.

It is sometimes asserted that the current level of internationalisation of economic activity is less than that which prevailed prior to

1914. Some indicators can be found to support this contention. However, we now live in a world which is characterised by the growing global integration of production and financial structures, complex communications grids, the rapid innovation and diffusion of technology and the possible emergence of associated forms of consciousness, as well as changes in security structures and strategic alignments. Thus, today's emerging global economy implies a system of planetary reach, not just a system of independent national economies primarily co-ordinated through exchange mechanisms and portfolio and speculative capital flows, i.e. the 'international' political economy of the nineteenth century which probably endured until the 1960s – the period which coincided with the onset of massive growth in the Euromarkets, and a substantial growth in the activities of transnational firms in manufacturing as well as in extractive industries.

Despite the emergence of the outlines of an informal global power structure, at least at the elite level, there is a relatively partial development of global civil and political society, and, as a consequence, an underdeveloped internationalisation of political authority. Indeed, whereas there has been a good deal of institutionalisation of global economic and security relations through international organisation and alliances, the locus of political authority is still largely territorially bounded in formally sovereign states, although this situation is changing, as discussed below.

In the context of the tumultous events of 1989–91, what we may be observing, nevertheless, is a kind of 'patterned disorder'. By this I mean a movement at the elite level towards the attempt to consolidate a new form of hegemony within the core of the system, although one with a different social basis to its predecessor, that is from 1945 to about 1970. The discussions at the 15–19 July 1991 G7 summit were of interest, then, partly because of the agenda (which included the restructuring of the USSR; the reconstituting of the United Nations; an abortive ecological initiative, involving a debt-for-nature swap to save the Brazilian rainforests; and questions relating to trade protectionism and macroeconomic relations). Forums like the G7 (and its private counterparts such as the World Economic Forum and the Trilateral Commission) are important also because their existence highlights the vanguard forces, and how they may serve to generate strategic consensus in order to configure what might be called 'the pyramids of privilege' in the world order structures that the G7 rulers seek to bestride. Not least, these forums indicate the conditions of entry into the 'core' institutions in the global political economy.

7

G7 attempts to mobilise allied consensus around President Bush's concept of a 'new world order' reflects the complex interplay between ideas, institutions, and material capacities (production and military power), and how, under certain conditions, these might be synergised into a coherent concept of action. Nevertheless, the post-Cold War discussions also highlight divisions and conflicts within the ranks of the G7 (e.g. on how to respond to Gorbachev's and later Yeltsin's pleas for assistance, with France, Germany and Italy, plus the EC ranged against Canada, Japan, the USA and the UK on the nature and scope of assistance; the USA and the EC disagreements on GATT negotiations). Whilst, however, it could be argued that there has been movement towards the reconsolidation and recomposition of the 'core' of the system, we simultaneously see the break up of previous forms of state, economic and political crisis, war, famine and ecological disaster.

An awareness of some of these problems has recently prompted initiatives on the part of the G7 and the EC, in the wake of the Gulf War, to press for a tighter arms export regime and to provide aid conditions closely linked to 'democratisation' and reduced military expenditures. These initiatives have occurred at the same time as NATO military capacities are being reorganised to allow for a swifter intervention capacity on the part of European members, along the lines of the US Rapid Deployment Force (which was created in the aftermath of the 1979 Iranian Revolution, and which was central to the US military victory in the 1991 Gulf War). Along with market forces, for example relating to supplies of credit, these initiatives indicate a double form of discipline on the part of the G7 relative to Third World development possibilities. New capacities to sustain rapid intervention are coupled with some institutional control over the conditions for the supply of finance and investment (for example, in the Group of Seven, the International Monetary Fund, the World Bank, the newly found European Bank for Reconstruction and Development and, in the central banker's bank, the Bank for International Settlements).

THE VIEW FROM THE BOTTOM AND THE EMERGING WORLD ORDER; GLOBAL POLITICS BEYOND 2000

A given world order has its own specific conditions of existence and dynamics. Because of this, world order cannot be explained adequately by means of abstract structuralism or, perhaps even less, by idealist references to the spirit of history. History is always in the making, in a complex and dialectical interplay between agency, structure, consciousness and action, within what Fernand Braudel (1981: 29), has termed the 'limits of the possible':

> the co-existence of the upper and lower levels [of civilisation] forces upon the historian an illuminating dialectic. How can one understand the towns without understanding the countryside, money without barter, the varieties of poverty without the varieties of luxury, the white bread of the rich without the black bread of the poor?

Then what has really changed in the world order? Implicit in this question are issues of epistemology and ontology. Different positions in the current debates over the emerging world order reflect various approaches to the process of acquiring knowledge, as well as views on how the social world is constituted. In part, then, the theoretical (and practical) debate(s) over world order are concerned with three interlinked issues: how do we understand the nature of social reality, what are its key components and relationships, and how do they change over time? Moreover, since order is a political concept, we need to ask 'order for whom and for what purposes?'.

As suggested above, the emerging world order might be thought of as undergoing a triple crisis, that is a transformation involving three interlinked 'levels': (i) 'economic', including the restructuring of global production, finance and exchange which challenges previous sets of arrangements and forms of economic organisation; (ii) 'political', that is in terms of institutional changes including changing forms of state, the internationalisation, transnationalisation or indeed globalisation of the state, and what Robert Cox (chapter 10) calls the emergence of the 'post-Westphalian' inter-state system, thus indicating a change where neo-realists see an essential continuity; and (iii) 'socio-cultural', that is (in part) the way global restructuring at the political and economic levels also entails challenges to embedded sets of social structures, ideas and practices, thus promoting, as well as constraining the possibilities of change.

Each of these 'levels' abstracts from social structures and social forces which exist, by definition, within and across each level. This crisis has features common to different parts of the world, although its impact is uneven, partly because of the different characteristics of town and country, rich and poor within and across groups of countries. Thus, the categories of 'First', 'Second' and 'Third' worlds are, again, primitive abstractions or ideal types, meant to convey ways in which the nature and scope of the crisis of world order can be conceptualised.

With regard to the question of forms of state, vanguard economic forces, among others, especially the intensification of global innovation and competition in an era of often instant communications, are serving to unravel the social hegemonies, political settlements and the forms of state which have prevailed in both the metropolitan capitalist states of North America and Western Europe (and possibly Japan), and more dramatically, in the social structures and political orders of 'existing socialism'. Similar changes are occurring in many developing nations, for example in Latin America, in so far as traditional statist and mercantilist orders are giving way to a more market-oriented path of development. None the less, the emerging world order is still configured by the division of the globe into political sovereignties, although these may be in the process of being reformulated. This involves the internal and external restructuring of the state and civil society in response to, and as a result of, the impact of globalising social forces.[4] Such changes, it would appear, are central to our understanding of the emerging world order, and call for much more research.

In studying contemporary issues, for example, it may be important to problematise the concepts of the state and (juridical) sovereignty. Redefinitions of sovereignty and constitutional reconsideration are now important political issues in a range of contexts, such as in the European Community, Eastern and Central Europe, Canada, Australia and in many parts of the Third World. Here the question posed might be, 'what kind of sovereignty, for whom, and for what purposes?'

Elsewhere (Gill, 1992) I have written of the discourse of the 'new constitutionalism', that is a doctrine and associated set of social forces which seek to place restraints on the democratic control of public and private economic organisation and institutions. The discourse can be linked to attempts to embed the hegemony of 'disciplinary' neo-liberalism, of the type associated with the attempts to restructure the post-communist states under IMF and Western tutelage. Attempts at the elite level in Europe, for example, have sought to create a form of macro-regionalism premised on liberal economic rationality (e.g. the 1992 programme). Constitutional and political development associated with the Economic and Monetary Union of the EC has involved the idea of 'binding constraints' on the freedom of manoeuvre of (future) member governments to freely make fiscal and monetary policy. These limitations would complement the discipline of market forces to constrain the policy autonomy of governments (see chapter 4 on the power of capital in response to certain types of policies). In addition, the role of the European Parliament as an institution of representative government is underdeveloped, that is, its voice as a sovereign of the European people is severly limited (objections to this limitation are expressed, for example, in the German Social Democratic Party's opposition to aspects of the Maastricht Accords of December 1991 and in the results of the Danish referendum of June 1992, which rejected ratification of the Maastricht Treaty). The European Parliament's powers are mainly consultative: it will have little say in most of the crucial areas of European policy (this has been termed the 'democratic deficit' of the EC). Similarly, the reconstruction of capitalist institutions in Eastern Europe has gone with the insulation of, for example, central banks, from popular accountability. The new constitutionalism is intended to guarantee the freedom of entry and exit of internationally mobile capital with regard to different socio-economic spaces (this is reflected in the widening scope of rules formulated in the GATT Uruguay Round negotiations, and in the US–Canada Free Trade Agreement). The scope of these constraints in an era of substantial mobility for capital mean that political leaders will need to be perhaps as accountable to international market forces as they are to electorates.

Thus sovereignty in both its senses (with regard to the policy autonomy of elected governments, and of the people) is at issue. In this regard, the central position and unique prerogatives of the USA is contradictory for a new constitutionalism on a world-wide basis. The USA is the least likely of any country to submit to the binding constraints of such an order (its politicians prefer to be 'bound to lead' instead of being 'bound to the mast' as Ulysses was, before the temptations of the Sirens). None the less, even the autonomy of the USA in matters of macroeconomic policy is increasingly constrained by the globalisation of finance and production, although larger states and macro-regional political associations (like Japan and the EC) generally have greater room for manoeuvre than small states. Thus, some are more sovereign than others in the emerging world order.

The sovereignty issue involves not only juridical rights and the question of citizenship and accountability, but also the allocation of resources and life chances, in so far as these are associated with the capacity for human autonomy and social choice. Thus, whilst world systems and dependency theorists speak of 'core', 'semi-periphery' and 'periphery' as concepts which reflect the hierarchy of states and stages of socio-economic development (and the constraints and

11

possibilities this entails), we might also emphasise that such concepts might apply within, as well as across, states. Thus in the case of the EC, there is not just uneven socio-economic development across different regions, but also within regions, and even within certain cities: this can be seen clearly in the USA today (not just in the case of rural poverty which is rising), where New York City is a microcosm of these patterns. This point is reinforced if we take into account patterns of internal migration and urbanisation in 'Third World' countries, with cities like Lagos, Rio and Shanghai as good examples. Thus, even if our focus is on the relatively privileged, affluent societies of Western Europe, we can still speak of the 'peripheralisation of the core', and broaden our conceptualisation to include life-chances, questions of personal security and insecurity, and forms of consciousness.

The nature of these developments indicates contradictions between the logic of globalising forces and the political conditions of existence for the operation of those forces. Structural adjustment in Latin America is atomising many state capacities and is generating new social movements and political parties which may in time come to challenge the thrust of neo-liberal orthodoxies, such as the Lula phenomenon in Brazil.[5] In Eastern Europe, the reintroduction of neo-liberal marketisation is generating a combination of widespread disillusionment and resentment, sentiments which are to a certain extent reflected in the resurgence of populism, racism, fascism and gangsterism. In present-day Russia, for example, the concept of marketisation is increasingly associated with desperation, a massive upsurge in crime (the nation's biggest growth industry) and violence (a recent report cited in the article quoted below claimed that there is one murder every twenty-two minutes in Russia). The 'market' is being reintroduced in the context of a general collapse of law and order. A recent account by a Western financial journalist argued that the social and economic conditions during the 900-day siege of Leningrad in 1941 were far better than those in the renamed city of St Petersburg in March 1992.[6] The journalist recounted his experiences at a market adjoining Peace Square Station, in central St Petersburg as follows:

> It would take a Hogarth, Goya or Hieronymous Bosch to depict this desolate 'market' where some 5,000 people were buying and selling . . . The term market conjures up visions of neat stalls and well-displayed products. There were few stalls and Peace Square was ankle-deep in slush and black mud. Those with little to sell stood in lines hundreds long, holding out ration cards, tins of sprats, cans of

the Western dried milk issued to St Petersburg children, a rusty tap or a handful of nails . . . used light bulbs, military decorations, worn fur hats or broken household fittings . . . traders walked around with placards reading: Money changed, Russian or foreign. Drunks slumped against the walls. Everything and everyone is for sale. Barter is a way of life, especially as a new shortage has developed. Unbelievably there are no roubles. Banks are closing their doors, people are not receiving salaries, Western business organizations are going crazy trying to find money to pay local staff . . . 'Where', I ask the businessman, the touts, the police, the banks, 'have all the roubles gone?' Inevitably I receive the same reply, a shrug of the shoulders: 'We do not know. It is another of our great Russian mysteries'.

HISTORICAL CHANGE AND SOCIAL CHOICE

My short discussion of the concepts of sovereignty, periphery and market is meant to highlight the degree to which the making of history is both an intellectual and historical exercise, in the sense that the theorist makes sense of complex historical developments. The making of history involves the interplay between past, present and future. The 1991 Gulf War provides yet another example:

> It is the most recent chapter in the historical struggle between the Arab world and the West, in contemporary times over the control of oil. More fundamentally, however, it partly reflects not simply the struggles between states, central to neo-realist and liberal institutionalist theorising, but also the struggles over the organising principles of society – struggles which began at least as early as the Middle Ages and the era of the crusades – between Western capitalist secular materialism and the metaphysics and social doctrine of Islam, as well as more secular pan-Arabist forces in the shape of the Iraqi regime. In this sense, the Gulf War is rooted in the social struggles and transformations which have occurred in the world over many centuries. (Gill, 1991b: 275)

The Crusades were associated, not only with a clash of religious values, but also with the struggle to extend the economic reach of merchant capitalism, associated with the growth and expansion of such city states as Venice and the early emergence of capitalist socioeconomic forces which partly configured the historical development of the regions surrounding the Mediterranean in the twelfth and thirteenth centuries.

Thus, research from this perspective might relate to the political use (and abuse) of history, and political myth: myths of national origin and identity, and myths about human potential, including that for economic development and international co-operation. This issue broadly involves the relationship between hegemonic discourses and the principles of inclusion/exclusion and supremacy/subordination they contain or imply. In the context discussed in the previous section of this introduction, it raises the questions, not only about the concepts of state, marketisation and political pluralism, but also about education and mass communications. One way to look at these issues is the way in which the existing structures associated with the latter (which have traditionally been to a degree 'nationally' bounded and defined) are being reinforced and/or transformed by the processes of socialisation. Such questions need to be dealt with critically, backed by extensive historical research in order to overcome the simple juxtaposition, for example, of the equation of progress with the spread of liberal, post-enlightenment economic rationality (such as associated with the World Bank's development reports) and the fundamentalisms of 'backwardness' and/or the failures of 'existing socialism'.

In this light it is noteworthy that the political discourse surrounding the immigration question in the EC in the early 1990s, in the context of the rise of racist, fascist and neo-nazi parties (with the French Front National becoming increasingly powerful) is designed to implicitly and explicitly constrain freedom of mobility within labour markets, and to institutionalise hierarchies of legal rights within them. This is linked to debates which seek to determine the principles for inclusion into exclusion from the enlarging socio-ecomomic and political space of a more integrated EC. Apart from flagrant racism and gender discrimination which is widespread (and is to be found in ail major political parties in France, for example), there is a more diffuse discourse of European identity. This is based upon the mythological origins of Europe as recounted in Græco-Roman and Judea-Christian myth and theology, anchored around the historical idea of Christendom. This discourse is meant to exclude immigrants from North Africa, the Middle East and from Asia and those from the lands of Eastern European and Russian Orthodoxy on grounds of their 'otherness' or 'non-Europeanness'.[7] The practical application of this discourse is the construction of a category of 'economic migrants' who are not deemed fit for 'political asylum' and permanent residence in the EC. This despite the fact that the migration issue relates to the restructuring of production and the nature of global inequality. It interacts with and overlays many forms of violence, such as those associated with inter-communal, nationalist reassertion, religious intolerance and persecution. What the changes

14

and political struggles in the Middle East and Europe have in common, then, is that they are bound up with the continuing expansion of a modernist, secular and materialist social system. This has been associated historically with particular, Eurocentric forms of religious and cultural imperialism. Modernist, globalising capitalism is perhaps the key motor force of contemporary history, and it consistently gives rise to contradictory sets of social forces.[8]

Some of the above comments may be suggestive of research which can identify the formation of discourses and of concrete historical blocs which have existed nationally and internationally over time, and under what conditions they are countervailed by opposing discourses and blocs; how they mutate, and are superseded or collapse. Broad-based historical research is needed, not simply focused on the 'first world'. This might start at least since the beginning of the modern world economy, as defined by Braudel (1981), or even earlier (see below, chapter 7 by Barry Gills).

Whether the above hypotheses, arguments and suggestions for research are accepted or not, simply to consider them seriously implies a need consistently to address ontological questions, and their implications for theorising change. This book offers ways, and by no means the only ways, to attempt to explain some of the changes which are taking place in the emerging world order. That it is only one of many such endeavours itself partly reflects the crisis of world order, a crisis which is reflected in changes in the intellectual world, and the challenge to hegemonic discourses in the study of political economy and international relations. Finally, the historical dialectic between economics and politics is changing in the late twentieth century world order, producing new political conditions, only some of which are fully or clearly discernable.

These changes may open up political space for counter-hegemonic movements. For challenges to be meaningful, there needs to be a synergy between progressive social movements and political parties. Amongst other things, this will require tolerance and respect for differences, and a conscious effort to bridge the gap (some might call it a chasm), for example, between historical materialist and feminist projects of emancipation (see Tickner, 1991). In this light, developments in mass communications and education will be crucial, as will, of course, those associated with the broad contours of material life and politics. Humanising control of the globalising forces discussed in this introduction will require, in Gramscian terms, a long and patient 'war of position' whereby progressive forces can cohere into more integral counter-hegemonic blocs, so as to engage in intellectual

15

and political struggle at a variety of levels in the emerging world order: from local to global.

OUTLINES OF A RESEARCH AGENDA

To summarise, then, a new historical materialist research agenda for the study of global politics might consistently and systematically involve at least the following theoretical and practical dimensions:

(1) ongoing attempts to reconsider epistemological and ontological aspects of world order, in the context of past, present and future;

(2) a continuous effort to promote methodological, theoretical and conceptual innovation, so as, for example, to bridge the divide between subjective and objective aspects of analysis (and agent–structure dichotomies). Work should try to generate integrated forms of explanation. This might be pursued, for example, by placing the idea of an integral history, and the related concept of socialisation at the centre of analysis;

(3) the concrete historical study of the emerging world order, in terms of its economic, political, and socio-cultural dimensions, with a view to its emerging contradictions, and the limits and possibilities these imply for different collectivities. This would involve work along the following dimensions:

  (a) analysis of the structures/agents of globalisation (for example in production and finance, migration, communications and culture, ecology, security), and their relations with more territorially bounded social structures and forces;

  (b) this would be linked to the analysis, in various social formations, of the role of and changes in social institutions such as state and civil society, the market and family. For example, the hypotheses concerning 'post-Westphalian' forms of state and the internationalisation of authority, and work on the prospects for a global civil society need further analysis and more research. Some of this work would concentrate on the public/private forums concerned with management of the global economy, such as the G7, World Economic Forum and the Trilateral Commission, and those which might countervail them;

(c) in turn (a) and (b) would be connected to analysis of (the persistence of, and change in) patterns of interest and identity, for example with regard to religion, nationality, ethnicity and gender. In this regard, studies of the political uses of history and the construction of social myths (e.g. of human possibility, economic development and the possibilities for international co-operation) are of substantial importance.

(4) finally, directly addressing and developing related ethical and practical approaches to global problems. This venture would need to be linked to careful analysis of existing and potential forms of political organisation and action, including parties, social movements and informal links at a variety of levels from local to global.

As was noted above, such analysis of politics might be linked, for example, to the idea of the self-defence of society against the disintegrating and atomising thrust of globalising economic forces.

Such work would not only problematise the concepts of sovereignty, state and market, but also would seek to articulate and develop conceptions of citizenship and political accountability consistent with democratic control over economic forces, so as to provide, for example, alternatives to 'the new constitutionalism' and neo-liberal dominance. Such efforts would show respect for differences, avoid ethnocentrism, and might assist the development of (transnational) counter-hegemonic historic blocs. Its politics would be linked to broadening the capacity for social choice within and across different societies.

In other words, this 'post-hegemonic' research agenda can be viewed as generating a perspective which needs to be understood as *a part of* the historical process, that is, its form of engagement involves human knowledge, consciousness and action in the *making* of history and shaping our collective futures.

Notes

1 This introduction draws on Gill (1991a) and Gill (1992).
2 Letter from Alex Fernandez, Otto Holman, Henk Overbeek and Kees van der Pijl to the editor, 10 June 1991.
3 Letter from Fernandez *et al.*, 10 June 1991.

4 On this idea see Cox (1989); and R. W. Cox, 'Production and Security', paper given to 'Conference on Emerging Trends in Global Security', Montebello, Québec, October 1990.

5 The Lula phenomenon refers to the coalition which formed in support of the trades union leader who challenged, and nearly defeated the neo-liberal, Collor de Mello, in the 1990 Brazilian Presidential elections. This coaltion included trades unions, public sector workers, the urban and rural poor, and a range of groups and social movements.

6 Jack Chisholm, 'Where Have all the Roubles Gone?', *Financial Times*, Weekend Supplement, 7–8 March 1992.

7 There are some exceptions to this. Those of Greek Orthodoxy are excepted since Greece is already an EC member. Moreover, people who can prove German descent are constitutionally guaranteed the right to emigrate to Germany.

8 This term is used in the sense of Barraclough (1967). It refers to the social structures and forces which have configured the development of twentieth-century world orders. Barraclough highlights two sets of fundamental changes, those associated with the technological and socio-economic transformations of the second industrial revolution, and a related process of the emergence of mass politics. Both can be traced back to earlier in the nineteenth century, and perhaps even to the Enlightenment. Among other things, these developments contributed to the eclipse of the Eurocentric nineteenth century order, and the rise of the superpowers and the 'revolt of the Third World' (against European domination).

PART I
PHILOSOPHICAL AND
THEORETICAL REFLECTIONS

1 EPISTEMOLOGY, ONTOLOGY AND THE 'ITALIAN SCHOOL'

STEPHEN GILL

This chapter should be read in conjunction with the introduction to this volume.[1] The term 'Italian School' was coined by an anonymous reviewer. The objective of this chapter is to raise a number of epistemological, ontological and practical questions which seem to me to be germane to the chapters which follow and which may be useful in helping to promote theoretical development in this broad field of study. Central to this discussion will be Gramsci's distinction between historical materialism and historical economism, and the attempt to move towards a more historicist, reflexive and dynamic form of political economy explanation.

The approach of this chapter assumes that the central task of social science is to explain social action, social structure and social change. Further, with respect to epistemological questions, it assumes that 'there is no symmetry between the social and natural sciences with regard to concept formation and the logic of inquiry and explanation' (Gunnell, 1969: 168). A further assumption is that there is not, and logically can not be, a single language of scientific explanation. The key contrast between social science and natural science is that the structure of social relationships and the meaning of social events are not principally functions of the scientist's theory, since what the social scientist confronts is 'not a first but a second-order reality'. The 'world' of the social scientist is a second-order one because it has been logically pre-ordered by its participants, 'in whose terms action is conducted and is justified'. As will be argued below, this implies that social scientific explanation entails limited generalisations and a conditional vocabulary (Gunnell, 1968: 179, 180). In order to avoid conceptual reification, this entails continual interaction between social scientific constructs and 'social reality': 'Such a requirement will be viewed as a limitation only if it is assumed that the science of physical mechanics must somehow serve as a standard of all explanation' (Gunnell, 1968: 186).

Underlying this contention is the argument that social science explanation cannot develop either if it rests upon a Cartesian dualism concerning subject and object or if it theorises in terms of cause and effect. Of course, there is no single way in which the Cartesian dichotomy can be overcome. This essay simply introduces one approach: a particular form of historicism associated with Marx and Gramsci, which is limited in space and time in terms of its explanatory power.

The remainder of this chapter discusses some recent literature in IPE and IR, partly to highlight and critique a widespread tendency to use transhistorical theorisations based upon sets of *a priori* categories which appear to take on an ontological autonomy (see chapters 2, 3 and 10 for elaborations). This is a characteristic associated with both neo-realism and mechanical forms of Marxism. Both of these orthodoxies share the problem of being constructed upon subject–object and agent–structure dichotomies. Thus, whilst they may be *socially effective* (in that they inform the construction of the social world and of certain policy initiatives at any given moment) they fail to meet the criteria introduced above: that is they cannot provide social scientific *explanation*.

DIFFERENCES BETWEEN GRAMSCIAN AND POSITIVIST IR AND IPE

How does the Gramscian approach differ from the major traditions and prevailing orthodoxy? Three main differences can be outlined.

First, in international studies the Gramscian approach is an epistemological and ontological critique of the empiricism and positivism which underpin the prevailing theorisations. This is because the Gramscian approach is a specific form of non-structuralist historicism. As Robert Cox (1987) has pointed out, the notion of structure in Gramsci is opposed to the structuralisms of Louis Althusser and Etienne Balibar (1969/79) or, from a different tradition, Kenneth Waltz (1979). Nevertheless, Gramsci's approach is consistent with the idea of historical structures, which are partly constituted by the consciousness and action of individuals and groups. Thus, Gramsci's approach stands in contrast to abstract 'structuralism' in so far as it has a human(ist) aspect: historical change is understood as, to a substantial degree, the consequence of collective human activity.

More specifically, Gramsci's historicism might be said to have three main components: (a) transience, (b) historical necessity, and (c) a dialectical variant of (philosophical) realism (Morera, 1990).

Point (a) implies that history and social change is a cumulative, endless, yet non-repetitive process, with different rhythms and tempos, applying respectively to structural developments and to patterns of apparently discrete events. Thus the critique of political economy for Marx and Gramsci begins with the concept of the historicity, or historical specificity of the capitalist market system, rather than seeing it as natural or eternal (see below, chapter 3, by Mark Rupert).

The idea of historical necessity, point (b), implies that social interaction and political change takes place within what can be called the 'limits of the possible', limits which, however, are not fixed and immutable but exist within the dialectics of a given social structure (comprising the inter-subjective aspect of ideas, ideologies and theories, social institutions, and a prevailing socio-economic system and set of power relations). The dialectical aspect of this is historical: although social action is constrained by, and constituted within, prevailing social structures, those structures are transformed by agency (for example through collective action in what Gramsci called 'the war of position'). Thus, the problem of historical necessity is understood in dialectical terms in ways which challenge the subject/object dichotomy of positivist epistemology. In this sense, Gramscian historical materialism builds upon and extends aspects of the Marxian critique of classical political economy.

Marx, in the *Grundrisse*, showed how, by abstracting from the social relations of production, Ricardo developed an ahistorical and therefore misleading conception of the freedom of the individual:

> In money relationships in the developed exchange system . . . individuals appear to be . . . independent, that is to collide with one another freely and to barter within the limits of this freedom. They appear to do so, however, only to someone who abstracts from the conditions of existence in which these individuals come into contact . . . close investigation to these external circumstances or conditions shows, however, how impossible it is for individuals forming part of a class, etc., to surmount them *en masse* without abolishing them. (Marx, 1971: 83–4)

Gramsci's variant of philosophical realism, point (c), identifies the intellectual process as a creative, practical, yet open-ended and continuous engagement to explain an apparently intractable social reality. This process is, like the processes of change within a given necessity, a dialectical one, and is thus a *part of* the historical process; it does not stand outside it. Indeed, Gramsci developed the unique concept of the 'organic intellectual' to show how the processes of intellectual production were themselves in dialectical relation to the

23

processes of historical change. Intellectual work directed towards social explanation was often directly or indirectly linked to political strategies, themselves developed from different perspectives. Such perspectives exist in political time and space. Thus by linking the theory of knowledge production to a theory of identity and interests, Gramsci was able to show how, at least in this sense, theory is always for someone and for some purpose (for an application of this argument, with respect to the world order concepts associated with, amongst other things, the perspective of transnational capital, see Gill, 1990; for wider arguments see Cox, 1987; Gill and Law, 1988).

This Gramscian viewpoint can be contrasted with the technocratic assumptions which inform the outlook of most professional economists in the West and Japan, and those working in major international economic organisations like the IMF and the World Bank. More generally, these assumptions are associated with those working within the neo-classical tradition in modern political economy, for example Keynesians, with their engineering assumption that the role of the economist is to build a behaviourist apparatus enabling the fine-tuning of the economy. Again, this assumption is founded upon the positivist separation of subject and object.

Second, the Gramscian approach provides a general critique of methodological individualism, and methodological reductionism. The latter, of course, is frequently found in some variants of Marxism, as well as in other traditions. Indeed, analytical Marxism seeks to synthesise methodological individualism and methodological holism, for example in developing a theory of exploitation (Roemer, 1982; for an overview, see Mayer, 1989). In the Gramscian approach, history and political economy are not understood as a sequence or series of discrete events or moments which when aggregated equal a process of change with certain governing regularities: for Gramsci, it is the *ensemble* of social relations configured by social structures ('the situation') which is the basic unit of analysis, rather than individual agents, be they consumers, firms, states or interest groups, interacting in a (potentially) rule-governed way in the 'political market-place' at a given moment or conjuncture, as in modern public choice theory (see Frey, 1984).

Third, the approach insists upon an ethical dimension to analysis, so that the questions of justice, legitimacy and moral credibility are integrated sociologically into the whole and into many of its key concepts. This is reflected in Gramsci's dual conception of politics and the state: on the one hand, there is a classical Marxist concern to analyse the state as a class-based apparatus of rule. On the other is

24

something akin to the Aristotelian view of politics as the search to establish the conditions for the good society, where the state is seen as able at least potentially to be transformed from an apparatus based upon social inequality into an ethical public sphere.

In consequence, unlike the prevailing orthodoxy with its priority given to political order and the pragmatic need for systems management, the normative goal of the Gramscian approach is to move towards the solution of the fundamental problem of political philosophy: the nature of the good society and thus, politically, the construction of an 'ethical' state and a society in which personal development, rational reflection, open debate, democratic empowerment and economic and social liberation can become more widely attainable. It is important to emphasise here that this is a rather negative definition, concerning minimum conditions, of the 'good society', and it offers no promises nor prescriptions for the form that such a society might take: historical structures can be changed by collective action in a 'war of position', but there is no historical inevitability. The key contrast here would be with teleological Marxism, with its promise of possible utopia(s), or Francis Fukayama's much-publicised dystopia of the 'end of history': the eventual unfolding of the logic and spirit of liberal democratic capitalism. In Gramscian terms, *telos* is 'myth':

> From Sorel, [Gramsci] took the notion of social myth (e.g. the modern prince as a myth). Myth presupposes a psychic force, a compelling movement combined with a rejection of the prevailing norms (e.g. as hypocritical, demystified). It is a normative force but not a normative plan or set of normative criteria. It can generate movement but not predict outcome. Thus the normative element is crucial but not as teleology.[2]

To summarise, then, in contrast to the tendency in much of the (American) literature to prioritise systemic order and management, from a vantage point associated with the ruling elements in the wealthy core of the global political economy, the historical materialist perspective looks at the system from the bottom upwards, as well as the top downwards, in a dialectical appraisal of a given historical situation: a concern with movement, rather than management. This highlights the limits of a narrow political economy approach to the analysis of IR. For Gramsci, a broad-based and more integrated perspective is achieved by the elaboration of a historicist version of the dialectical method developed from Hegel and Marx, also influenced by Machiavelli. In the *Prison Notebooks*, this took the form of a critique of and polemic against the German historicists and more specifically, of the Italian idealist, Benedetto Croce.

THE CRITIQUE OF POLITICAL ECONOMY; FOUR ARGUMENTS

Here I attempt initially to identify and develop some of the key theoretical and applied features of a *historical materialist* approach to social and historical explanation, and to contrast them with narrower *materialist* theories, which can be associated with Gramsci's notion of *historical economism*. To indicate initially how Gramscian historical materialism develops concepts to help explain aspects of the normative structure of society we can bear in mind Gramsci's concept of myth (e.g. *telos* as myth), which suggests how apparently normative forces may have the social power normally associated with 'material forces' (such as technology, the forces of production).

A *materialist* theory of knowledge assumes that nothing exists (e.g. God, the idea of liberty, providence) outside and apart from nature and society. In my view, this also implies that no *telos* or spirit exists as a guide to or purpose for that process. Nevertheless, for materialists, metaphysics and idealist thinking are a part of the social reality which is to be explained, since they help to constitute the social outlook and predispositions of individuals and more broadly, groups and movements within social formations. In a recent book on Gramsci's historicism, Esteve Morera (1990: 122) argues that to be a *materialist* theory, at least four conditions need to be met:

(1) Materialism acknowledges the existence of an object of knowledge, independent of a knowing subject, the process of knowledge production and the system of knowledge itself;

(2) the adequacy of the object of knowledge provides the ultimate standard by which the cognitive status of thought is to be assessed;

(3) thought and ideas are recognised as realities in their own right and thus an object of knowledge;

(4) those realities are theorised as not *sui generis* but as the result of causal mechanisms.

I will now attempt to show how conventional materialist epistemology has severe limitations, particularly in its more positivist representation. Here, I will suggest that a creative historical materialist approach transcends rigid theories of causality and moves towards a reflexive and dynamic form of political economy *explanation*. As will be argued below, for example, the concept of mechanical causality is inconsistent with historicism, since historicism is concerned with explanation, rather than causality. This entails the rejection of technological, economic or indeed any form of reductionism. Explanation in this sense is founded in an approach which insists upon the centrality of the interrelationship between the 'subjective' and 'objective' social forces in historical development, for example with its focus upon the social organisation of production and class relations in the state, that is where subjective and objective interpenetrate: the 'second order reality' that Gunnell (1968) identifies as the object of social science. This line of argument relates to the difference between what Gramsci called 'historical economism' and 'historical materialism'.[3]

Beyond the intransigence of 'social reality'

Of course, we can accept that there is a certain intransigent 'reality' to society and nature (which we can never fully know or explain because of its scale and complexity). Therefore, this reality is to a certain extent independent of, but none the less interdependent with, the processes of knowledge production. Further, the 'truth' of social reality is made more intractable because it involves the thought and inter-subjective meanings of individuals who have different forms of self-consciousness and awareness as to the social nature of their action/inaction. The social organisation of production, as an aspect of the social world, is thus necessarily constituted partly by inter-subjective meanings, which can be identified and understood, however imperfectly. Thus our second-order, social 'reality' has different dimensions which cannot be understood fully or completely recorded, although abstractions concerning the structural components of such social reality can and must be intellectually produced for explanation to be possible.

With regard to the interdependence of theory and reality, following Hegel, we can argue that there can be no immediate knowledge, since this would imply that we have no consciousness which mediates with such a reality. Consciousness then, implies an explicit or implicit conceptual apparatus and language. As outlined in the *Grundrisse*, Marx's adaptation (or inversion) of the Hegelian dialectical method (further extended and elaborated by Gramsci) applies a particular materialist approach to society and continually extends, refines and elaborates its conceptual apparatus generating new concepts and discarding others. This occurs in the context of historical explanation which is seen to entail a dialectical process. With regard to concept formation our senses are partly theoreticians; our ideas of what is or can be are produced conceptually and our conceptual frameworks are partly produced by the environment or society.

With regard to the process of knowledge, one version of how the historical dialectic, as I have defined it here, might be approached is through Marx's ideas concerning the 'concrete-real' (which determines theory) and the 'thought-concrete' (which is an understanding of the concrete, or the significance of social action and structure generated by the process of reflection and thought). Implied here is that each conceptual framework produces its own version of 'concrete-real' and 'thought-concrete' (Resnick and Wolff, 1987). For Marx, then, knowledge was the process of change in which the two 'concretes' are interconnected and are mutually transformed to provide a new synthesis.[4]

At this point we can emphasise a key issue which differentiates historical materialism from empiricism and positivism. A change in thinking is a change in the social totality and thus has an impact on other social processes; a change in the social totality will provoke change in the process of thought. Hence, the process of thinking is part of a ceaseless dialectic of social being.

The limits of ontological objectivity

How then are thought-concretes developed and elaborated? The answer to this question may be approached by making an initial distinction between the appearance and essence, or inner and outer manifestations of social reality. Following Marx's method as outlined in *Grundrisse*, this is attempted through an ongoing and endless process of the generation of abstractions and concepts, which are reconstructed and refined as they encounter a mass of data. This method, to use the metaphor of Engels, enables the theorist to approach a more comprehensive and consistent explanation of social reality, rather like the way an asymptote approximates a straight line (an asymptote is a curve which increasingly approximates, but never touches, a straight line stretching to infinity).

This position seems to be superficially similar to that of John Stuart Mill and the skeptical empiricists, who argue that the senses or their surrogates can never yield social knowledge which can truthfully approximate social reality. However, historical materialists take this argument one step further, by arguing that society is a totality or system which is regulated or conditioned by structural relations and can thus never be understood through the method of empiricist atomism. Further, the process of development of thought-concretes is ongoing and is simply arrested and incomplete if it rests with, or is explained through, transhistorical abstractions or theories, such as those associated with the Cassandras of the rise and (inevitable) fall of (Roman, Dutch, British) American hegemony (for an elaboration on this literature see Gill, 1986; Gill, 1988; Gill, 1990). This type of argument was, of course, originally made by Marx when developing his critique of political economy, for example his criticisms of Ricardo and Malthus. This point is further developed below with regard to structuralism and Gramsci's critique of Bukharin.

Thus, whereas much modern IR theory takes the rise and decline of hegemonies and balances of power in the inter-state system as largely given, with its primordial anarchic form constitutive of the development possibilities in international relations since at least the time of Thucydides, historical materialists argue that this structure, in so far as its existence can be substantiated, is a particular configuration of states and social forces, corresponding to a particular epoch and having certain conditions of existence which are corporeal and transitory (for the archetypical realist statement, see Gilpin, 1981: 11). In other words, Marxists stress the conditional and historical application of what for Robert Gilpin seems to operate as a something akin to a sociological abstraction.

By contrast, Robert Cox (1987) suggests that there are different forms of state and world orders, whose conditions of existence, constitutive principles and norms vary over time. These conditions include different social modes of production and social structures of accumulation, with their own characteristic ethics and politics, and which vary in political time and space. Thus, no transhistorical essentialism or homeostasis is imputed to any given social system or world order. Moreover, as Cox is at pains to show, the state itself, and the forms of state action are themselves differentially constituted in complex ways by blocs of socio-economic and political forces which operate within the limits of a given historical necessity.

Indeed, whereas empiricists move towards the understanding of social reality from the perspective of methodological individualism, historical materialists develop a theory based upon social structures as the fundamental unit of analysis. In this sense, although all 'social realities' are theorised, some are more theorised than others. Thus, for Kenneth Waltz (1979), the inter-state system is viewed in individualistic terms, with states as atomised actors interacting within the structure of anarchy: i.e. Waltz, Gilpin, and most of American students of IR and IPE, operate within what Richard Ashley (1988) calls the anarchy *problématique*.

To make some applications of this point clearer, and in a more substantive way, let us sketch some aspects of the post-war system from a historical materialist perspective.

The first, and most fundamental, point is that it is assumed that any historical materialist approach to understanding and explaining a given world order system must analyse it as a whole. The particular ontology used is by no means self-evident and must, on one level, be a theorised one. Synthesising insights of different writers from within this perspective influenced by Gramsci, then, our ontology must be founded upon the idea of a global social formation constituted in part by the degree of integration/disintegration of basic social structures, social forces and what Robert Cox (1987) calls 'forms of state'. This is the fundamental basis for understanding the 'international': that is what is usually seen as a relatively autonomous inter-state system articulated with related forces, mechanisms and institutions of production and exchange at the 'domestic' and 'international' levels.

In other words, our understanding of the dynamics of the political economy is founded upon certain sociological ideas concerning, for example, the degree of 'embeddedness' of world orders in socio-political structures at the national or transnational levels (e.g. Polanyi, 1944). Thus, in the contemporary era (i.e. since 1945), we can call such a historically specific yet changing ensemble of social structures and social forces the global political economy (Gill and Law, 1988).

Thus, since 1945, in the era of the *Pax Americana*, a new world-order structure emerged which was in some ways qualitatively different from its predecessors. However, this new system cannot simply be explained with regard solely to apparently unique features, for example, the existence of weapons of mass destruction or the long-term threats to survival of the species through ecological catastrophe (previous weapons systems caused mass destruction and former civilisations were either displaced or eliminated partly because of adverse environmental and ecological changes). Hence, the conventional focus of much IR theorising, the inter-state system, and the transition from a balance of power/hegemony (Westphalian) international political system towards a post-Westphalian system (Cox, 1990) needs to be explained through the examination of the ways in which social forces and social structures are entering a period of transition so that, in classical Marxist terms, there is both a growing socialisation (universalisation) of aspects of social life, and a disintegration of previous forms of identity and interest: crudely speaking between, for example 'internationalist' and 'nationalist' groups of interest. This transformation and struggle, amongst other things then, involves a dialectical interplay between forces which are relatively cosmopolitan, and others which are more territorially bounded, such as nationalist movements and ideologies, military-security structures, particular linguistic forms and patterns of identity.

In a more specific sense, the formal system of state sovereignty, which was in some ways reinforced and constituted by earlier forms of international economic activity (hence the term the 'international' political economy) appears now to have been cumulatively undermined by more pervasive and deep-rooted economic integration and competition (including inter-state competition to attract supplies of capital and investment from overseas, and to promote the competitiveness of 'home' industries). This has created a new force-field of constraints, opportunities and dangers, i.e. new conditions of existence for all states, groups and classes in the system, as well as extending, albeit in still limited and contradictory ways, a growing structural power for internationally-mobile transnational capital (Gill and Law, 1989).

To continue the Orwellian metaphor, some are more constrained than others in this world-order system. Not only does this new order coincide with a decisive change in the productive powers and balance of social forces within and between the major states, but also state structures in the major capitalist countries have been transformed into different variants of a neo-liberal form, i.e. more oriented to the integration of their economies into the emerging global system of production and exchange, in which knowledge, finance, and information play a more decisive role, when contrasted with the inter-war period. This largely is what Cox (1987) means by the process of the internationalising of the state, involving coalitions, class alliances and historic blocs of social forces across, as well as within, countries.

At the same time, peripheral economies have become more tightly geared to the economic activity of the core, and their developmental rhythms partly subjected to the imperatives of Cold War politics and liberal neo-classical economic doctrines and associated institutions and social forces. They have entered a period of widespread social restructuring as their domestic arrangements have both begun to disintegrate and become ever-more attuned to the growing integration of trade, investment, production and finance. The story of the 1980s attests to some of the social costs of this transformation: a period of arrested development potential, with the Third World debt

31

crisis involving huge transfers of resources from the poorer countries to the richest.

In the emerging post-Westphalian system, then, the cosmopolitanism of international economic forces was accompanied by a disciplining of social groups in the Third World, in order to deepen the structural power of internationally-mobile capital and undermine prevailing mercantilist arrangements. This has occurred, with varying degrees of effectiveness, through a combination of market power and the surveillance of the Bretton Woods international organisations under US leadership (see Augelli and Murphy, 1988).

This capitalist cosmopolitanism is also important in any explanation of the breakdown of the Cold War blocks structure between the USA, USSR and in Europe. Here, changes occurred in large part because of the intensification of technological innovation and military rivalry, especially between the USA and USSR. In the context of a deep crisis in the social structure of accumulation and thus of the productive power of the various nations of the Soviet-led block, the social myth of the communist utopia, which had reached its apogee in an earlier period of history, was vapourised almost completely. This hegemonic, organic crisis of 'actually existing communism' proved to be especially severe in Poland, Romania, East Germany and most important, the USSR. In the context of the brittle (and economistic) legitimacy of the communist states, with the relations between state and civil society co-ordinated by an authoritarian and paternalist structure of political power, the inability of the USSR to respond to the long-term challenges posed within the context of existing forms of post-Stalinist political economy led to its collapse as an alternative social myth (to capitalism).

In the world capitalist order, then, power appeared to be re-concentrated in the metropolitan countries, which were, however, also undergoing substantial transformation in what is, clearly, a global process of restructuring. The social forces and political arrangements associated with what John Ruggie (1982) called 'embedded liberalism' were progressively undermined by the growing extension, resources and power of internationally-mobile forces, undermining the historic blocs of social forces which constituted, at the national level, the structural underpinnings of the post-war international political economy. In Gramscian terms, the ensemble of these blocs and 'welfare-nationalist' forms of state (Cox, 1987) was politically synthesised within the context of the twin pillars of American hegemony (the Cold War structures and the liberalising international economic order) into an *international historic bloc* initially in a transatlantic, then later Trilateral (i.e. including Japan) format. However, the recessions and restructuring of the 1970s and 1980s, allied to the cumulative internationalisation of production, consumption and exchange, and the integration of global economic forces, meant that the integral nature of these historic blocs was undermined, and an underdeveloped, yet clearly emergent *transnational historic bloc of forces* (associated with dominant interests in the metropolitan countries and elsewhere) began to emerge, particuarly during the 1970s and 1980s. The contradictions of this development, which involves a crisis of the old hegemonic structures and forms of political consent, negotiated internationally, are now unravelling the former international historic bloc and are bound up with the new and emergent transnational bloc (Gill and Law, 1989; Gill, 1990).

Even here, however, the contradictions of the system may be intensifying. Developments in the metropolitan heartland of the system, with ripple effects in the Third World, for example as pointed out in Susan Strange's book, *Casino Capitalism* (1986), may be leading to a situation in which production and exchange structures are becoming disarticulated in an era of shortening time-horizons and speculative capitalism (e.g. growing disparities between productive investment, international trade and capital and exchange markets), so that, on one level, the ethical appeals of the social contracts of the era of embedded liberalism are rapidly being laid to waste. As Strange points out, the game of economic life comes to resemble a combination of snakes and ladders and (Russian) roulette.

How are we to begin to explain the nature of these changes? In the conventional literature in IPE, what has just been discussed is usually understood as the disjuncture between 'domestic' and 'international' forces in the international exchange system, along with an international diffusion of inter-state power leading to a move away from the stability of the superpower duopoly towards a more complex plural system. The question then is how is order possible 'after hegemony'? (Keohane, 1984a). Theories have been developed to ascertain how the metropolitan capitalist nations at the centre of the system can co-operate fruitfully in a post-hegemonic world characterised by slower growth and economic instability. Much debate centres on the problem of the highly imperfect co-ordination at the summit of the system, that is how to cope with the complexities of 'two-level' or 'multi-level' or 'mixed' games between larger numbers of national actors, i.e. governments (the pioneer here is Axelrod, 1984). Thus, the question which continues to constitute, and has constituted the research agenda for orthodox IPE theory during the last decade is: 'how can co-operation be achieved under anarchy?'

Another way of looking at this question, however, is to situate a discussion of inter-state forums, international organisations and informal councils like the Trilateral Commission, in the context of the development and application of hegemonic strategies on an increasingly transnational basis. Yet this level of analysis is still insufficient to explain adequately the emergence and salience of these strategies, and the political struggles which are entailed by them. The political gods at the summit of the system, and the various forums in which they interact, such as the Group of Seven summits, operate within the limits of the possible, limits situated within the context of the historical transformations discussed above, as well as the blocs of social forces with which they are associated at the domestic level in their own countries and elsewhere (Gill, 1990).

Given the historical complexity of these forces, the importance of, and interaction within, these elite forums cannot simply be explained with abstract formulations such as the Prisoner's Dilemma (which Axelrod claims can explain biological evolution and trench warfare in World War I equally well). Since such inter-governmental and transnational forums have existed for some time, their growing importance can only be explained historically. Apart from being concrete institutional responses to the crisis or transformation in the post-war world order system, corresponding to an uneven globalisation of the political economy, they are also initiatives which are bound up with the birth and early development of an international political and civil society which is in some respects new and suggestive of a reconfiguration of the world order in the late twentieth century.

From a world systems viewpoint, the above developments would appear to correspond to a situation where power appears to have been reconcentrated in the 'core' states, whilst realists, agreeing to a point, would lament the dissolving of the glue of block structures associated with the balance of terror and the decline of American power and leadership. However, what may be the most important aspect of the current epoch is the fact that social relations and social structure are in a period of extended and deep-seated transformation or crisis, on a global scale: a crisis which is in fact, a crisis of both the existing Cold War and inter- and intra-capitalist order.

In so far as there are leading elements in this process, the principles of organisation of this reconstructed and restructured world order system are increasingly those associated with liberal economic ideas and interests (e.g. transnational capital and the Bretton Woods institutions), which are engaged in a dialectical struggle *vis à vis* embedded mercantilist and statist perspectives (often associated with the public sector, the security complex, and protected industries which are non-competitive internationally). This struggle and transformation involves not only the states in the capitalist core, but also configures the agenda of social transformation in Latin America, in Central and Eastern Europe, and in the successors to the Soviet Union, the Commonwealth of Independent States, formed in December 1991. Both the essays by Giovanni Arrighi (chapter 6) and by Robert Cox (chapter 10) can be read in terms of the transformations in international society understood in terms of (globalising) capitalism and territorialism as opposing logics and forms of the organisation of power.

A good recent example of the globalising thrust of capitalism, and of the internationalisation of political and civil society and, to an extent, of the internationalisation of authority under these new conditions was the way in which the Bretton Woods institutions, the OECD, and metropolitan capitalist governments and a range of private interests (e.g. leading figures from banking and transnational companies, as well as think tanks and private universities) rapidly came together in January 1990 to produce a radical and draconian package of reforms, to transform the Polish economy (in 1991–2 this approach was also applied in Russia, after the collapse of the USSR). The Polish experiment was, as the OECD put it at the time, the launching of an unprecedented strategy of social transformation from a communist, protected and mercantilist society, into a market-based, capitalist society, a 'great transformation' which took at least seventy years to accomplish in nineteenth-century England (Polanyi, 1944). The plan for Poland was itself based upon a learning process amongst capitalist elites in light of the experience of the 1970s and 1980s, and the experiments with the use of IMF/World Bank conditionality. The new strategy applies Kornai's (1986) concept of macro/micro restructuring and the idea of hard budget constraints (on state expenditures and also on individual enterprises) in ways which will extend and deepen the structural power of capital. This strategy, which, to say the least, is by no means certain of success, is none the less not a pure market strategy: there is some political direction and internationalisation of authority in order to prevent the mistakes of the 1970s (over debt recycling) and the 1980s (over the debt crisis) from being repeated. This strategy then, in so far as it has an internal logic, represents the use of direct political power in order to develop the structural power of capital (see chapter 4 for an elaboration).

In this context the ultimate form of 'conditionality' was reflected in the economic, monetary and social unification of East Germany with the Federal Republic started 1 July 1990. This was, of course, soon followed by full political unification on 2 October 1990, when the Volkskammer dissolved itself and a crowd estimated to be over a million people gathered in front of the Reichstag in the old Prussian (now all-German) capital of Berlin. Observers reported that the mood of the vast, emotional crowd was a mixture of joy, bewilderment, anxiety and catharsis. The West German political establishment gathered in the Schauspielhaus and its cocktails were made headier by the echoing 'Ode to Joy' from Beethoven's Ninth Symphony. Not wishing to dampen their euphoria, the normally sober Bundesbank was denying the prospect of economic hopelessness in East Germany. As the Germans celebrated to the words of Schiller and the strains of Beethoven, Mrs Thatcher offered her congratulations after earlier ominous warnings about German dominance in Europe. The Soviet Union announced that unification was caused by the logic of the enlightened policy of perestroika, and the European Commission said that it meant that the process of economic and political unification in Europe would be accelerated (see, for example, *Financial Times*, 3 October 1990).

The structure of necessity and political consciousness

In the above examples, then, the structure of necessity varied partly according to the viewpoint of different agents, be they individuals, unions, firms, government bureaucracies, or international organisations. Further, the nature of this structure changes over time. The post-war changes just described are not simply the result of impersonal cumulative structural transformations, although, following Fernand Braudel (1979), those changes relating to the *longue durée* that is the *gestes répétées* of history, have created the structure of necessity in which the *évènements* or events of history occur in particular conjunctures. Of course, this two-fold chronological rhythm is itself a simplification, although changes of long-standing structural importance in this context are the spreading and deepening of commodification and monetisation of social relations.

Yet social reality involves not only the structural constraints which are often taken as the limits of the possible: it also involves consciousness and thus encompasses philosophical, theoretical, ethical, and common sense ideas. Beethoven, rather than Wagner, was chosen to symbolise the cathartic emotion of the united Germany for its present generation of political leaders. In the case of Gramsci this aspect of society is reflected in his interest in the questions of consciousness and political culture, the role of the intellectuals and philosophy, and the substantive attention given to the superstructures, notably civil society, in his conceptions of hegemony and of the constitution of society:

> Critical understanding of self takes place therefore through a struggle of political 'hegemonies' and of opposing directions, first in the ethical field and then in politics proper, in order to arrive at the working out at a higher level of one's conception of reality. Consciousness of being part of a particular hegemonic force (that is to say political consciousness) is the first stage towards progressive self-consciousness in which theory and practice will finally be one. Thus the unity of theory and practice is not just a matter of mechanical fact, but part of a historical process, whose elementary and primitive phase is to be found in the sense of being 'different' and 'apart', in an instinctive feeling of independence, and which progresses to the level of real possession of a single and coherent conception of the world. This is why it must be stressed that the political development of the concept of hegemony represents a great philosophical advance as well as a politico-practical one. (Gramsci, 1971: 333)

Here, then, Gramsci is arguing that critical understanding is not an automatic process: it involves reflection and effort within oneself, as well as within the context of the wider struggle of ideas and political programmes. 'Progressive self-consciousness' is thus defined developmentally and politically: the awareness of self is reconstituted through an appreciation of prevailing thought-patterns and the nature and distribution of life-chances. Hence, the moment of self-awareness leads to a more complex and coherent understanding of the social world and is a form of historical change (and thus in the balance of social and political forces). The achievement of self-consciousness is understood dialectically. Politics and the individual are central to the definition of structures and of change, and are not abstracted 'falsely' out of a theory of history.

This argument does not imply that Gramsci was an idealist or that he subordinated 'economics' to 'politics'. In his social theory society is conceived, as in classical Marxism, as a totality primarily constituted by modes of production. This can be separated analytically into ideas, institutions and material forces but remains a general, integrated if contradictory entity. Certain systems of thought such as religion or common sense (or philosophies as Gramsci would have it) or social institutions (like the family) can outlive any given mode of production, or social structure of accumulation, and thus there is no necessary congruence between 'base' and 'superstructure'. The same would apply to systems of government and politics more generally: a capitalist mode of production can go with authoritarianism, dictatorship or parliamentary democracy. What is crucial is to place each of these sets of ideas and social institutions in its proper socio-historical context, since their importance and meaning can change over time.

Likewise if we take the case of the revolutions of 1989 in Eastern and Central Europe, a key structural aspect of the explanation of this type of change was an implosion of economic performance and a deep-rooted and long-term crisis in the irrational and embedded social structure of accumulation. 'Actually existing socialism' lost momentum because it could not reconcile its own contradictions. For example, Kornai (1986) shows how, at least in the Hungarian case, the practice of politically allocated but largely open-ended subsidies allied to the system's overall centralisation and the setting of abstract and unrealistic plan targets resulted in an inefficient system of allocation and incentives: there were no real market signals as exist in capitalism, and no financial or market constraints to punish the inefficient. The allocation of labour was distorted (massive underemployment, hoarding of labour and factors of production). The system simply did not provide the goods and services that people either wanted or needed. In Habermasian terms, this represented a deep rationality crisis (Habermas, 1973) of a social system premised upon, as it were, the perfect computation of social needs and economic activity.

This organic crisis was intensified, on the one hand, by the long-term economic challenges being posed by the advanced capitalist countries, and on the other, by the military and economic implications of the strategic challenge of Reaganism to the USSR. The lack of any substantive legitimacy under conditions of declining economic performance merely underlined the increasingly brittle legitimacy of the Stalinist anti-democratic system. This crudely materialist and anti-democratic form of legitimacy was of course made more fragile by the virtual elimination of any autonomous political activity and thus prevented the creation or rebirth of a civil society. Thus, like a snowball gathering size as it rolls down a hill, when it reached its point of destination, the contradictions of the system had reached the scale of an avalanche. Kees van der Pijl (1988) places these developments in the context of what he calls an organic crisis of the Hobbesian, repressive state form. At its worst in Romania, this process (which was condoned if not welcomed during the 1970s and 1980s by Western leaders because of Ceaucescu's opposition to Moscow and his ability to pay his bills to foreign bankers) involved the abuse of political and human rights and the virtual starvation of the population to pay for, amongst other things, a grotesque marble palace for the butcher of Bucharest. Here, the key point is that a Gramscian analysis might have suggested that a Hobbesian state structure is inherently unstable for two reasons; it lacks ethical credibility and, since its political system is not embedded in the 'fortresses and earthworks' of a strong civil society, like Ceaucescu's palace it can be toppled by an insurrectionary form of revolutionary spontaneity.

In van der Pijl's theorisation, then, hegemonic state–civil society complexes in the West have been historically associated with the idea of the 'Lockeian state', that is one in which there is a vigorous and largely self-regulating civil society. This type of state–civil society complex is exemplified by the Anglo-Saxon countries, and to a certain extent, by many of the member states of the European Community. The international counterpart to this type of hegemonic formation is the British Commonwealth, which is rooted in the history of British imperialism and colonialism but represents, at the international level, the transformation of coercion into consent and informal regulation of inter-state relations. Here, the contrast can be made with the usual idea of a strong state found in the bulk of IR theorising, which is often associated with what van der Pijl calls the Hobbesian state form: a strong state which dominates civil society from above, with the political capacity to centralise political power so as to develop and mobilise the national material resources. This type of state form, then, is generally non-hegemonic, since it is not socially embedded in a strong civil society, and by implication has fragile legitimacy. At least in Eastern Europe, this crisis reflects not only the feeble legitimacy of communist rule (e.g. the coming to power of Vaclav Havel as a symbol of the ethico-political rejection of the social myth and concrete form of communist order in Czechoslovakia), but also the cumulative pressure of international forces for each of the countries involved.

Thus, instead of the tendency to reify the state and the interstate system, the Gramscian approach explains the nature of the state in terms of the complexity of state–civil society relations, and shows how the nature of state power is related to the strength of the dynamic synthesis between the key forces in the economy and society, operating politically on an inclusive basis. The synthesis between these forces creates what Gramsci called a historic bloc, which may at times have the potential to become hegemonic. For ethical hegemony to be possible the state must necessarily be constituted primarily by general legitimacy and active consent, which implies inclusion of the interests of the subordinate elements within the system. Precisely what the components are for any particular social formation, of course, needs to be explained by historical analysis. In its most fundamental and complete sense, however, the achievement of hegemony is concerned with the transcendence of narrowly based economistic or corporate perspectives, so that a genuinely universal position, synthesising particular with general interests, could come to prevail.

Pursuing van der Pijl's line of argument we might also compare the revolutions in Eastern and Central Europe (which, with the exception of Romania, were largely peaceful) with the crisis of legitimacy in China, as well as with the decay of state authoritarianism and military dictatorship in Latin America. As I have mentioned, van der Pijl suggests that each of these variants of the Hobbesian state form has undergone or is undergoing a fundamental crisis during the 1970s, 1980s and 1990s. However, the case of China may turn out to be a problematic one for van der Pijl's general thesis. Another problematic case would be the development of Japan since the Meiji Restoration (see chapter 7 by Barry Gills).

To summarise, at the international level, the movement towards a more liberal and integrated global political economy and the beginnings of social reconstruction in Eastern Europe and Latin America are two sides of the same coin of a profound restructuring of the international order. Not only the Hobbesian states, but also many others are moving in a more market-oriented direction and thus towards the internationalisation of something resembling a Lockeian form of self-regulating civil society (although the German model of the social market economy is a key variant in the pan-European context). Despite the contradictions and conflicts involved in the transformation of Eastern and Central Europe, we may see this development, at the European level, sooner, rather than later: the Cold War appears to have been eclipsed. On 6 July 1990, NATO finally announced that it no longer regarded the Warsaw Pact as its enemy, and in early August 1990 Prime Minister Thatcher of Britain was advocating a seat for Mikhail Gorbachev at the next Summit of the Group of Seven in London in 1991. Gorbachev attended the summit, and was then forced to resign as the Soviet Union was formally dissolved. As noted above, some of the members of the CIS, notably

Russia, are embarking on a Polish-type form of draconian economic restructuring, with guidance being given by the IMF and the senior financial and political ministers of the Group of Seven, albeit under rapidly deteriorating economic conditions in the CIS. The 'great transformation' of the former Soviet block may well occur under conditions akin to those of the Great Depression of the 1930s in the West. This can be viewed as an aspect of what Gramsci called 'passive revolution', that is the development of mimetic political and economic structures in less-developed parts of the world (see chapter 9 by Kees van der Pijl on the application of this idea to the Soviet Union).

What seems to characterise the nature of the world-order system of the late twentieth century then, is a series of profound crises of identity, ethics and socio-economic restructuring at the domestic/ international level encompassing all three categories of country we have discussed: in metropolitan capitalism, the communist/post-communist states, and in the Third World (on Latin America, see chapter 8 by Otto Holman). These crises are linked together by the forces at work in the global political economy. From this vantage point, the outcome of these developments is likely to be determined mainly at the domestic level, that is within each of these countries. Nevertheless, the globalisation of the political economy, and the transnationalisation of social and political forces, means that new conditions prevail. These changes cannot be captured simply through a theorisation of historical structures which is static, non-dialectical and premised upon the separation of the 'domestic' and the 'international', the 'economic' and the 'political'.

Historical change and counter-hegemony

It is clear that the achievement of hegemony within a particular social formation is a complex and contradictory process, since counter-hegemonic forces will come to challenge the prevailing institutional and political arrangements. Hegemony is even more difficult to achieve (and therefore much rarer if not theoretically impossible) at the international level, where there is no single world state or a fully developed international civil society, although it can be argued that there is a substantial framework both of international law and of international organisation (and thus a set of international norms, rules and values) which is partly interwoven with an inter-nationalised structure of production and exchange (and thus a complex web of private and informal linkages, some of which involve state agents). International hegemony, as normally defined in the

41

literature, has been associated with the dominance and leadership of a powerful state within the system of international relations, achieving power over other states. However, this is an unsatisfactory definition, since it associates social forces with a territorial entity, whereas the global system needs to be conceived as a totality, and the social forces which operate within that system are not territorially bounded or determined. Thus, as Robert Cox puts it:

> Hegemony is a structure of values and understandings about the nature of order that permeates a whole system of states and non-state entities. In a hegemonic order these values and understandings are relatively stable and unquestioned. They appear to most actors as the natural order. Such a structure of meanings is underpinned by a structure of power, in which most probably one state is dominant but that state's dominance is not sufficient to create hegemony. Hegemony derives from the dominant social strata of the dominant states in so far as these ways of doing and thinking have acquired the acquiescence of the dominant social strata of other states. (Cox, 1990)

Discussing one of the major instances of global hegemony, Giovanni Arrighi (chapter 6) points to some of the reasons why the term 'hegemonic' seemed to apply to the leading strata and dominant social forces emanating from Great Britain during the nineteenth century as industrial and commercial capitalism began to internationalise. Whilst keeping its domestic market relatively open, and with comparative advantage in trade, the UK had substantial control over the world market. It also had a general mastery of the global balance of power, and a 'close relationship of mutual instrumentality with *haute finance*' (and thus the ability to manage the international monetary system under the Gold Standard). This enabled the United Kingdom to govern the interstate system 'as effectively as a world-empire', and thus helping to sustain the unprecedented 100 years' peace among the great powers. Material power was not a sufficient condition for this to be possible. According to Arrighi, the key to British hegemony was:

> the *capacity to claim with credibility* that the expansion of the power of the United Kingdom served not just its national interest but a 'universal interest' as well. Central to this hegemonic claim was a distinction between the power of rulers and the 'wealth of nations' subtly drawn in the liberal ideology propagated by the British intelligentsia . . . presented as the motor force of the universal expansion. Free trade might undermine the sovereignty of rulers but it would be at the same time expand the wealth of their subjects,

> or at least their propertied subjects. (This volume, p. 174; my emphasis)

Thus the combination of material, coercive and hegemonic capacities created the possibility for, and reality of British supremacy, particularly in the middle decades of the nineteenth century. This enabled an extraordinary and generally legitimate (at least among the ruling elements in the most developed European countries) capacity to restructure the world to suit British national interests. However, this was not hegemony in a fundamentally Gramscian sense, although Arrighi's analysis shows how a 'situation', that is, the intersection and interaction of sets of social forces which produce a synthesis of interests, explains the *credibility* of British leadership in the international economy of the nineteenth century. What would strengthen this account is reference to the fact that the Gold Standard and its operation was constituted by, and depended heavily upon, the co-operation of other European states, and in this sense was a European system. The key element here is that for British hegemony to have been possible, it presupposed the consent of leading elements within the metropolitan states. Moreover, in a global sense, the costs of adjustment under the Gold Standard tended to be borne most heavily by the poorer colonies under the control of each of the imperial, metropolitan European nations, and as such was by no means globally embedded nor consensual (Polanyi, 1957), a fact which Arrighi notes in his remarks concerning the siphoning of 'tribute' by the British state from the Indian sub-continent.

Thus social change, and in the above case, international political stability, at any historical moment is the result of the interaction of structural, or relatively permanent aspects of social reality, and specific conjunctures of events, that is the product of synchronic and diachronic forces. Hegemony, in other words, can never be the simple product of the preponderance of a single state or grouping of states exerting power over other states. This is, of course, partly because human beings have consciousness and a degree of free will or agency within the limits of the possible.

Any attempt, therefore, to construct a hegemonic system of rule will tend to generate, dialectically, a set of counter-hegemonic forces, which may or may not be progressive. The corpse of *Pax Brittanica* was buried in the trenches of Ypres and the Somme. The theoretical point here is that the social world is a qualitatively different, 'second-order' reality from that explained by the natural sciences (which can be likened to elaborating systems of causal regularity). Hence,

43

mechanical theories such as the neo-realist theory of hegemonic stability have limited scientific validity, as well as a lack of plausibility in explainaing complex social transformations and the constituents of world orders. Social crisis, and social transformation in this sense, is in large part explicable by the disintegration of social hegemonies, and the formation of counter-hegemony in the global political economy, rather than by 'long waves' of capitalist development.

Finally, no unilinear concept of time can be applied to understand and explain plausibly constellations of social forces and historical conjunctures. Social structures and social events, are partly constituted by processes which reflect different rhythms and historical tempos. Here Gramsci's analysis is similar to that of Braudel (1981) and the *Annalist* historians. As Braudel argued, with respect to historical time, the first dimension is that which changes very slowly, like the topological relationship between continental plates, between humankind and its geography (geographical time). The second dimension, with a faster rhythm than the first, was that of change in fundamental social structures: the *longue durée* (social time). The third rhythm, the most rapid, was that which focused on individuals, events and specific conjunctures: *l'histoire évènementielle* (individual time). Any historical analysis (and by implication any study of the global political economy) should be sensitive at the very least to the dimensions of these temporal rhythms.

BEYOND VULGAR MARXISM AND THE ORTHODOX DISCOURSES

I have not yet addressed in detail the problem of how to go beyond these epistemological questions and move in a more detailed way towards an ontology, social theory and analytical method which avoid the lapse into arguments concerning the determinancy of either 'politics' or 'economics', or some underlying or ultimate causality, although my position on this question is implicit in much of the above. Chapter 3 by Mark Rupert discusses aspects of Marxian/ Gramscian ontology, as do chapters 2 and 10 by Robert Cox and chapter 9 by Kees van der Pijl. Indeed, the longer works of both Cox (1987) and van der Pijl (1984) can be fruitfully consulted on this matter since each develops a rather sophisticated historical materialist ontology, and each applies his own unique method to what David Law and I (Gill and Law, 1988) call the global political economy. The latter concept implies an integrated system of knowledge, production and exchange, and includes the dialectical relations between capitalist and non-capitalist systems and states, and ecological, ethical and other aspects of the whole.

However we develop a given social ontology, it is crucial to remember the abstract, momentary and necessarily incomplete nature of all thought-processes and knowledge systems. Thus, we should heed Marx's warning in his admonition of the classical political economists:

> The vulgar mob [i.e. the classical economists] has therefore concluded that theoretical truths are abstractions which are at variance from reality, instead of seeing, on the contrary that Ricardo does not carry true abstract thinking far enough and is therefore driven into false abstraction. (Marx, *Theories of Surplus Value*, vol. II, cited in Resnick and Wolff, 1987: 58, note 44)

Here, falseness is not simply equated with the approximation of an abstraction to some independent reality, since both Marx and Ricardo conceptualise the relation of thought to the 'concrete real' quite differently. At issue is how and why and with what consquences the classical economists and Marxists arrive at their different 'thought-concretes' (Resnick and Wolff, 1987). Two points seem relevant here. First, there is a relativity in the claim to truth. Second, social conditions interact with and influence the survival, 'scientific' status and consquences of rival social theories: knowledge is also a process of social struggle, again between hegemonic and counter-hegemonic perspectives and principles. Thus, from this point of view, the hegemonic perspectives within IPE and IR can be criticised for not probing deeply enough into the complex role of ideas and consciousness and the interaction of knowlege systems with the rest of the historical process: an extreme example of what Marx calls 'false abstraction', that is abstractions which are not grounded concretely in history. Many Marxists also fall prey to this methodological error.

For example, Gramsci showed how Nicolai Bukharin's *Theory of Historical Materialism: A Popular Manual of Marxist Sociology* eliminated the dialectical standpoint and introduced a 'metaphysical materialism' or 'idealism upside down' (Gramsci, 1971: 437). The search for single, last-instance causes reduced 'the philosophy of *praxis*' to something akin to the search for God, and the philosophical process to social mechanics:

> The philosophy implicit in the *Popular Manual* could be called a positivistic Aristotelianism, an adaptation of formal logic to the methods of physical and natural science. The historical dialectic is replaced by the law of causality and the search for regularity,

> normality, and uniformity . . . In mechanical terms, the effect can never transcend the cause or the system of causes, and therefore can have no development other than the flat vulgar development of economism. (Gramsci, 1971: 437)

Similar criticisms can be made of the dominant neo-realist rational choice approaches to the study of IPE, for example, its ahistorical nature; its lack of a dynamic, dialectical quality; the narrowness and incompleteness of its abstractions which are confined, almost tauto-logically, to the relations between theoretical abstractions (i.e. unitary rational actors called states); the tendency to extreme parsimony in explanation relative to the infinite complexity of its object of analysis, i.e. the international system.[5]

Given the preceding arguments and observations, the persistence of the prevailing American approaches would appear to be surprising were we living in a rational scientific world where, following the injunctions of Karl Popper, those theories which are internally inconsistent and/or are refuted by the evidence, are consigned to the intellectual scrapheap. I make this point simply because Popper has been very influential in the formulation of research programmes in American social science, not because I accept or advocate his positions. How then, do we explain the neo-realist perspective among US students of IPE? In my view, it can be explained in two ways. Despite its limitations it has a degree of *practical effectiveness* which partly stems from its parsimony and surface plausibility: it provides a framework for an instrumentalist social science to develop policy-frameworks. And, to a degree, its use has corresponded with the rise of American globalism, bound up with the tremendous dynamism of capitalist development in the USA. This is not to suggest that American policy-makers accept uncritically either its framework or its policy recommendations. Senior figures in the American political establishment are often more subtle and prag-matic. More important perhaps is that particular policies and initia-tives can be articulated and justified through the use of these ideas, in so far as they correspond to 'common sense', and are reinforced by an appeal to 'authority' (in the sense of learning, wisdom) and to 'tradition' or the advocacy of a particular 'way of life'. There are at least two elements which help to explain this practical effectiveness.

First, the plausibility of neo-realist rational choice approaches corresponds to the predominance of positivist and behaviourist traditions in Anglo-Saxon academia. These traditions have served to constitute the bulk of American social science, and are rooted deeply. They go back a long way in the short history of the United States.

The resonance of this perspective is amplified by the substantial scope and weight of the largest and best-funded academic community in the world. Of course, many academics from other countries receive graduate training in the USA, which has many of the world's leading research universities and think-tanks. The effect of this pattern of academic development is both to insulate the perspective from fundamental attack, especially within the USA itself, and to diffuse its impact on a global scale. This argument can be related to the social basis and funding of research in the USA, where there is widespread privatisation of research initiatives and programmes. Research and publications informed by neo-realist rational choice approaches filter through into public debates and policy formulation. This is not to imply, however, that there is any simple input-output linear programming of policy. The American political system is one of the most complex in the world.

Second, and at a broader social level, as Enrico Augelli and Craig Murphy (1988) illustrate acutely, the abstract application of this discourse, with its substantive liberal capitalist and imperialist bias gains strength from and sits well with deep-rooted elements in America's manichean political culture (see also Gill, 1986b). Two aspects seem important here: American anti-intellectualism and pragmatism (which includes an attraction to simple, parsimonious theories and to detailed empirical work) and, perhaps as fundamental, the pervasive metaphysics of denominational religion, with its ideas concerning Manifest Destiny, evangelism and crusaderism, which evoke a twin sense of mission and responsibility to save the rest of the world from itself. Moreover, I would add, the isolationist tradition, like its schizophrenic counterpart, messianic imperialism (both premised on the opposition between 'us and them') parallels the radical separation of subject and object in positivist thought.

These, then are aspects of both the practical effectiveness and the social myth of American liberalism. Here there is a correspondence with the pseudo-religion of Soviet Marxism. In both there is a tendency to protect a standard theorisation in a process which helps to constitute the limits of the possible in terms of academic innovation. In the US academic industry, at least in the fields of IR and IPE, hundreds of PhD theses, and thus many careers, have been built around regime theory and the Theory of Hegemonic Stability. This is one instance of how the American positivist paradigm is consolidated. A process of social and intellectual enclosure ensures that adherents and their theorisations are insulated from critical dialogue with those of contending perspectives or paradigms. The dominant

47

paradigm, for its adherents, assumes the mantle, as it were, of near, if not absolute, truth.

Notes

1 This chapter is a revised version of Gill (1991a). I am grateful to Robert Cox for highlighting the importance of Gramsci's conception of myth, and to Frank Pearce for clarifying questions relating to Marxist structuralism.

2 Note from Robert Cox to the author, 29 September 1990.

3 I am grateful to Robert Cox for emphasising this point.

4 Here we might distinguish between logical contradiction, of the type which characterises formal logic and mathematics (e.g. as discussed in Hegel's *Science of Logic*) and historical contradictions, which occur partly as a result of human collectivities acquiring self-consciousness and a capacity to conceptualise and understand and act upon historical forces. Of course, there is thus no single or straightforward way to define or elaborate the nature of historical contradictions. To do so necessarily implies the construction of ontological abstractions and categories. In the preface to this collection I made an initial sketch of the contemporary historical dialectic of integration-disintegration world order, that is the historical transformation in world order which was being brought about by the contradictions between the globalising thrust of internationally mobile capital and the more territorially bounded nature of political authority and legitimacy in the late twentieth century.

5 For an elaboration of these points, see C. Murphy and R. Tooze, 'Introduction' and 'Getting Beyond the "Common Sense" of the IPE Orthodoxy' (Murphy and Tooze, 1991: 1–32).

2 GRAMSCI, HEGEMONY AND INTERNATIONAL RELATIONS: AN ESSAY IN METHOD

ROBERT W. COX

Some time ago I began reading Gramsci's *Prison Notebooks*. In these fragments, written in a fascist prison between 1929 and 1935, the former leader of the Italian Communist Party was concerned with the problem of understanding capitalist societies in the 1920s and 1930s, and particularly with the meaning of fascism and the possibilities of building an alternative form of state and society based on the working class. What he had to say centred upon the state, upon the relationship of civil society to the state, and upon the relationship of politics, ethics and ideology to production. Not surprisingly, Gramsci did not have very much to say directly about international relations. Nevertheless, I found that Gramsci's thinking was helpful in understanding the meaning of international organisation with which I was then principally concerned. Particularly valuable was his concept of hegemony, but valuable also were several related concepts which he had worked out for himself or developed from others. This essay sets forth my understanding of what Gramsci meant by hegemony and these related concepts, and suggests how I think they may be adapted, retaining his essential meaning, to the understanding of problems of world order. It does not purport to be a critical study of Gramsci's political theory but merely a derivation from it of some ideas useful for a revision of current international relations theory.[1]

GRAMSCI AND HEGEMONY

Gramsci's concepts were all derived from history – both from his own reflections upon those periods of history which he thought helped to throw an explanatory light upon the present, and from his personal experience of political and social struggle. These included the workers' councils movement of the early 1920s, his participation in the Third International and his opposition to fascism. Gramsci's ideas have always to be related to his own historical context. More than that, he was constantly adjusting his concepts to specific

49

historical circumstances. The concepts cannot usefully be considered in abstraction from their applications, for when they are so abstracted different usages of the same concept appear to contain contradictions or ambiguities.[2] A concept, in Gramsci's thought, is loose and elastic and attains precision only when brought into contact with a particular situation which it helps to explain – a contact which also develops the meaning of the concept. This is the strength of Gramsci's historicism and therein lies its explanatory power. The term 'historicism' is however, frequently misunderstood and criticised by those who seek a more abstract, systematic, universalistic and non-historical form of knowledge.[3]

Gramsci geared his thought consistently to the practical purpose of political action. In his prison writings, he always referred to Marxism as 'the philosophy of praxis'.[4] Partly at least, one may surmise, it must have been to underline the practical revolutionary purpose of philosophy. Partly too, it would have been to indicate his intention to contribute to a lively developing current of thought, given impetus by Marx but not forever circumscribed by Marx's work. Nothing could be further from his mind than a Marxism which consists in an exegesis of the sacred texts for the purpose of refining a timeless set of categories and concepts.

ORIGINS OF THE CONCEPT OF HEGEMONY

There are two main strands leading to the Gramscian idea of hegemony. The first ran from the debates within the Third International concerning the strategy of the Bolshevik Revolution and the creation of a Soviet socialist state; the second from the writings of Machiavelli. In tracing the first strand, some commentators have sought to contrast Gramsci's thought with Lenin's by aligning Gramsci with the idea of a hegemony of the proletariat and Lenin with a dictatorship of the proletariat. Other commentators have underlined their basic agreement.[5] What is important is that Lenin referred to the Russian proletariat as both a dominant and a directing class; dominance implying dictatorship and direction implying leadership with the consent of allied classes (notably the peasantry). Gramsci, in effect, took over an idea that was current in the circles of the Third International: the workers exercised hegemony over the allied classes and dictatorship over enemy classes. Yet this idea was applied by the Third International only to the working class and expressed the role of the working class in leading an alliance of workers, peasants and perhaps some other groups potentially supportive of revolutionary change.[6]

Gramsci's originality lies in his giving a twist to this first strand: he began to apply it to the bourgeoisie, to the apparatus or mechanisms of hegemony of the dominant class.[7] This made it possible for him to distinguish cases in which the bourgeoisie had attained a hegemonic position of leadership over other classes from those in which it had not. In northern Europe, in the countries where capitalism had first become established, bourgeois hegemony was most complete. It necessarily involved concessions to subordinate classes in return for acquiescence in bourgeois leadership, concessions which could lead ultimately to forms of social democracy which preserve capitalism while making it more acceptable to workers and the petty bourgeois. Because their hegemony was firmly entrenched in civil society, the bourgeoisie often did not need to run the state themselves. Landed aristocrats in England, Junkers in Prussia, or a renegade pretender to the mantle of Napoleon I in France, could do it for them so long as these rulers recognised the hegemonic structures of civil society as the basic limits of their political action.

This perception of hegemony led Gramsci to enlarge his definition of the state. When the administrative, executive and coercive apparatus of government was in effect constrained by the hegemony of the leading class of a whole social formation, it became meaningless to limit the definition of the state to those elements of government. To be meaningful, the notion of the state would also have to include the underpinnings of the political structure in civil society. Gramsci thought of these in concrete historical terms – the church, the educational system, the press, all the institutions which helped to create in people certain modes of behaviour and expectations consistent with the hegemonic social order. For example, Gramsci argued that the Masonic lodges in Italy were a bond amongst the government officials who entered into the state machinery after the unification of Italy, and therefore must be considered as part of the state for the purpose of assessing its broader political structure. The hegemony of a dominant class thus bridged the conventional categories of state and civil society, categories which retained a certain analytical usefulness but ceased to correspond to separable entities in reality.

As noted above, the second strand leading to the Gramscian idea of hegemony came all the way from Machiavelli and helps to broaden even further the potential scope of application of the concept. Gramsci had pondered what Machiavelli had written, especially in *The Prince*, concerning the problem of founding a new state. Machiavelli, in the fifteenth century, was concerned with finding the leadership and the supporting social basis for a united Italy; Gramsci, in the twentieth century, with the leadership and supportive basis for an alternative to fascism. Where Machiavelli looked to the individual Prince, Gramsci looked to the Modern Prince: the revolutionary party engaged in a continuing and developing dialogue with its own base of support. Gramsci took over from Machiavelli the image of power as a centaur: half man, half beast, a necessary combination of consent and coercion.[8] To the extent that the consensual aspect of power is in the forefront, hegemony prevails. Coercion is always latent but is only applied in marginal, deviant cases. Hegemony is enough to ensure conformity of behaviour in most people most of the time. The Machiavellian connection frees the concept of power (and of hegemony as one form of power) from a tie to historically specific social classes and gives it a wider applicability to relations of dominance and subordination, including, as shall be suggested below, relations of world order. It does not, however, sever power relations from their social basis (i.e., in the case of world order relations by making them into relations among states narrowly conceived) but directs attention towards deepening an awareness of this social basis.

WAR OF MOVEMENT AND WAR OF POSITION

In thinking through the first strand of his concept of hegemony, Gramsci reflected upon the experience of the Bolshevik Revolution and sought to determine what lessons might be drawn from it for the task of revolution in Western Europe.[9] He came to the conclusion that the circumstances in Western Europe differed greatly from those in Russia. To illustrate the differences in circumstances, and the consequent differences in strategies required, he had recourse to the military analogy of wars of movement and wars of position. The basic difference between Russia and Western Europe was in the relative strengths of state and civil society. In Russia, the administrative and coercive apparatus of the state was formidable but proved to be vulnerable, while civil society was undeveloped. A relatively small working class led by a disciplined avant-garde was able to overwhelm the state in a war of movement and met no effective resistance from the rest of civil society. The vanguard party could set about founding a new state through a combination of applying coercion against recalcitrant elements and building consent among others. (This analysis was partly apposite to the period of the New Economic Policy before coercion began to be applied on a larger scale against the rural population.)

In Western Europe, by contrast, civil society, under bourgeois hegemony, was much more fully developed and took manifold forms. A war of movement might conceivably, in conditions of exceptional upheaval, enable a revolutionary vanguard to seize control of the state apparatus; but because of the resiliency of civil society such an exploit would in the long run be doomed to failure. Gramsci described the state in Western Europe (by which we should read state in the limited sense of administrative, governmental and coercive apparatus and not the enlarged concept of the state mentioned above) as 'an outer ditch, behind which there stands a powerful system of fortresses and earthworks'.

> In Russia, the State was everything, civil society was primordial and gelatinous; in the West, there was a proper relation between State and civil society, and when the State trembled a sturdy structure of civil society was at once revealed. (Gramsci, 1971: 238)

Accordingly, Gramsci argued that the war of movement could not be effective against the hegemonic state-societies of Western Europe. The alternative strategy is the war of position which slowly builds up the strength of the social foundations of a new state. In Western Europe, the struggle had to be won in civil society before an assault on the state could achieve success. Premature attack on the state by a war of movement would only reveal the weakness of the opposition and lead to a reimposition of bourgeois dominance as the institutions of civil society reasserted control.

The strategic implications of this analysis are clear but fraught with difficulties. To build up the basis of an alternative state and society upon the leadership of the working class means creating alternative institutions and alternative intellectual resources within existing society and building bridges between workers and other subordinate classes. It means actively building a counter-hegemony within an established hegemony while resisting the pressures and temptations to relapse into pursuit of incremental gains for subaltern groups within the framework of bourgeois hegemony. This is the line between war of position as a long-range revolutionary strategy and social democracy as a policy of making gains within the established order.

PASSIVE REVOLUTION

Not all Western European societies were bourgeois hegemonies. Gramsci distinguished between two kinds of society. One kind had undergone a thorough social revolution and worked out fully its consequences in new modes of production and social relations. England and France were cases that had gone further than most others in this respect. The other kind were societies which had so to speak imported or had thrust upon them aspects of a new order created abroad, without the old order having been displaced. These last were caught up in a dialectic of revolution-restoration which tended to become blocked as neither the new forces nor the old could triumph. In these societies, the new industrial bourgeoisie failed to achieve hegemony. The resulting stalemate with the traditionally dominant social classes created the conditions that Gramsci called 'passive revolution', the introduction of changes which did not involve any arousal of popular forces.[10]

One typical accompaniment to passive revolution in Gramsci's analysis is caesarism: a strong man intervenes to resolve the stalemate between equal and opposed social forces. Gramsci allowed that there were both progressive and reactionary forms of caesarism: progressive when strong rule presides over a more orderly development of a new state, reactionary when it stabilises existing power. Napoleon I was a case of progessive caesarism, but Napoleon III, the exemplar of reactionary caesarism, was more representative of the kind likely to arise in the course of passive revolution. Gramsci's analysis here is virtually identical with that of Marx in *The Eighteenth Brumaire of Louis Bonaparte*: the French bourgeoisie, unable to rule directly through their own political parties, were content to develop capitalism under a political regime which had its social basis in the peasantry, an inarticulate and unorganised class whose virtual representative Bonaparte could claim to be.

In late nineteenth-century Italy, the northern industrial bourgeoisie, the class with the most to gain from the unification of Italy, was unable to dominate the peninsula. The basis for the new state became an alliance between the industrial bourgeoisie of the north and the landowners of the south – an alliance which also provided benefits for petty bourgeois clients (especially from the south) who staffed the new state bureaucracy and political parties and became the intermediaries between the various population groups and the state. The lack of any sustained and widespread popular participation in the unification movement explained the 'passive revolution' character of its outcome. In the aftermath of the First World War, worker and peasant occupations of factories and land demonstrated a strength which was considerable enough to threaten yet insufficient to dislodge the existing state. There took place then what Gramsci called a 'displacement of the basis of the state'[11] towards the petty bourgeoisie, the only class of nation-wide extent, which became the anchor of fascist power. Fascism continued the passive revolution, sustaining the position of the old owner classes yet unable to attract the support of worker or peasant subaltern groups.

Apart from caesarism, the second major feature of passive revolution in Italy Gramsci called *trasformismo*. It was exemplified in Italian politics by Giovanni Giolitti who sought to bring about the widest possible coalition of interests and who dominated the political scene in the years preceding fascism. For example, he aimed to bring northern industrial workers into a common front with industrialists through a protectionist policy. *Trasformismo* worked to co-opt potential leaders of subaltern social groups. By extension *trasformismo* can serve as a strategy of assimilating and domesticating potentially dangerous ideas by adjusting them to the policies of the dominant coalition and can thereby obstruct the formation of class-based organised opposition to established social and political power. Fascism continued *trasformismo*. Gramsci interprets the fascist state corporatism as an unsuccessful attempt to introduce some of the more advanced industrial practices of American capitalism under the aegis of the old Italian management.

The concept of passive revolution is a counterpart to the concept of hegemony in that it describes the condition of a non-hegemonic society – one in which no dominant class has been able to establish a hegemony in Gramsci's sense of the term. Today this notion of passive revolution, together with its components, caesarism and *trasformismo*, is particularly apposite to industrialising Third World countries.

HISTORIC BLOC (BLOCCO STORICO)

Gramsci attributed the source of his notion of the historic bloc (*blocco storico*) to Georges Sorel, though Sorel never used the term or any other in precisely the sense Gramsci gave to it.[12] Sorel did, however, interpret revolutionary action in terms of social myths through which people engaged in action perceived a confrontation of totalities -- in which they saw a new order challenging an established order. In the course of a cataclysmic event, the old order would be overthrown as a whole and the new be freed to unfold.[13] While Gramsci did not share the subjectivism of this vision, he did share the view that state and society together constituted a solid structure and that revolution implied the development within it of another structure strong enough to replace the first. Echoing Marx, he thought this could come about only when the first had exhausted its full potential. Whether dominant or emergent, such a structure is what Gramsci called an historic bloc.

For Sorel, social myth, a powerful form of collective subjectivity, would obstruct reformist tendencies. These might otherwise attract workers away from revolutionary syndicalism into incrementalist trade unionism or reformist party politics. The myth was a weapon in struggle as well as a tool for analysis. For Gramsci, the historic bloc similarly had a revolutionary orientation through its stress on the unity and coherence of socio-political orders. It was an intellectual defence against co-optation by *trasformismo*.

The historic bloc is a dialectical concept in the sense that its interacting elements create a larger unity. Gramsci expressed these interacting elements sometimes as the subjective and the objective, sometimes as superstructure and structure.

> Structures and superstructures from an 'historic bloc'. That is to say the complex contradictory and discordant *ensemble* of the superstructures is the reflection of the *ensemble* of the social relations of production. (Gramsci, 1971: 366)

The juxtaposition and reciprocal relationships of the political, ethical and ideological spheres of activity with the economic sphere avoids reductionism. It avoids reducing everything either to economics (economism) or to ideas (idealism). In Gramsci's historical materialism (which he was careful to distinguish from what he called 'historical economism' or a narrowly economic interpretation of history), ideas and material conditions are always bound together, mutually influencing one another, and not reducible one to the other. Ideas have to be understood in relation to material circumstances. Material circumstances include both the social relations and the physical means of production. Superstructures of ideology and political organisation shape the development of both aspects of production and are shaped by them.

An historic bloc cannot exist without a hegemonic social class. Where the hegemonic class is the dominant class in a country or social formation, the state (in Gramsci's enlarged concept) maintains cohesion and identity within the bloc through the propagation of a common culture. A new bloc is formed when a subordinate class (e.g., the workers) establishes its hegemony over other subordinate groups (e.g., small farmers, marginals). This process requires intensive dialogue between leaders and followers within the would-be hegemonic class. Gramsci may have concurred in the Leninist idea of an avant-garde party which takes upon itself the responsibility for leading an immature working class, but only as an aspect of a war of movement. Because a war of position strategy was required in the western countries, as he saw it, the role of the party should be to lead, intensify and develop dialogue within the working class and between the working class and other subordinate classes which could be brought into alliance with it. The 'mass line' as a mobilisation technique developed by the Chinese Communist Party is consistent with Gramsci's thinking in this respect.

Intellectuals play a key role in the building of an historic bloc. Intellectuals are not a distinct and relatively classless social stratum. Gramsci saw them as organically connected with a social class. They perform the function of developing and sustaining the mental images, technologies and organisations which bind together the members of a class and of an historic bloc into a common identity. Bourgeois intellectuals did this for a whole society in which the bourgeoisie was hegemonic. The organic intellectuals of the working class would perform a similar role in the creation of a new historic bloc under working class hegemony within that society. To do this they would have to evolve clearly distinctive culture, organisation and technique and do so in constant interaction with the members of the emergent block. Everyone, for Gramsci, is in some part an intellectual, although only some perform full-time the social function of an intellectual. In this task, the party was, in his conception, a 'collective intellectual'.

In the movement towards hegemony and the creation of an historic bloc, Gramsci distinguished three levels of consciousness: the economico-corporative, which is aware of the specific interests of a particular group; the solidarity or class consciousness, which extends to a whole social class but remains at a purely economic level; and the hegemonic, which brings the interests of the leading class into harmony with those of subordinate classes and incorporates these other interests into an ideology expressed in universal terms (Gramsci, 1971: 180–95). The movement towards hegemony, Gramsci says, is a 'passage from the structure to the sphere of the complex superstructures', by which he means passing from the specific interests of a group or class to the building of institutions and elaboration of ideologies. If they reflect a hegemony, these institutions and ideologies will be universal in form. i.e., they will not appear as those of a particular class, and will give some satisfaction to the subordinate groups while not undermining the leadership or vital interests of the hegemonic class.

HEGEMONY AND INTERNATIONAL RELATIONS

We can now make the transition from what Gramsci said about hegemony and related concepts to the implications of these concepts for international relations. First, however, it is useful to look at what little Gramsci himself had to say about international relations. Let us begin with this passage:

> Do international relations precede or follow (logically) fundamental social relations? There can be no doubt that they follow. Any organic innovation in the social structure, through its technical-military expressions, modifies organically absolute and relative relations in the international field too. (Gramsci, 1971: 176)

By 'organic' Gramsci meant that which is structural, long-term or relatively permanent, as opposed to the short-term or 'conjunctural'. He was saying that basic changes in international power relations or world order, which are observed as changes in the military-strategic and geo-political balance, can be traced to fundamental changes in social relations.

Gramsci did not in any way by-pass the state or diminish its importance. The state remained for him the basic entity in international relations and the place where social conflicts take place – the place also, therefore, where hegemonies of social classes can be built. In these hegemonies of social classes, the particular characteristics of nations combine in unique and original ways. The working class, which might be considered to be international in an abstract sense, nationalises itself in the process of building its hegemony. The emergence of new worker-led blocs at the national level would, in this line of reasoning, precede any basic restructuring of international relations. However, the state, which remains the primary focus of social struggle and the basic entity of international relations, is the enlarged state which includes its own social basis. This view sets aside a narrow or superficial view of the state which reduces it, for instance, to the foreign policy bureaucracy or the state's military capabilities.

From his Italian perspective, Gramsci had a keen sense of what we would now call dependency. What happened in Italy he knew was markedly influenced by external powers. At the purely foreign policy level, great powers have relative freedom to determine their foreign policies in response to domestic interests; smaller powers have less autonomy (Gramsci, 1971: 264). The economic life of subordinate nations is penetrated by and intertwined with that of powerful nations. This is further complicated by the existence within countries of structurally diverse regions which have distinctive patterns of relationship to external forces (Gramsci, 1971: 182).

At an even deeper level, those states which are powerful are precisely those which have undergone a profound social and economic revolution and have most fully worked out the consequences of this revolution in the form of state and of social relations. The French Revolution was the case Gramsci reflected upon, but we can think of the development of US and Soviet power in the same way. These were all nation-based developments which spilled over national boundaries to become internationally expansive phenomena. Other countries have received the impact of these developments in a more passive way, an instance of what Gramsci described at the national level as a passive revolution. This effect comes when the impetus to change does not arise out of 'a vast local economic development . . . but is instead the reflection of international developments which transmit their ideological currents to the periphery' (Gramsci, 1971: 116).

The group which is the bearer of the new ideas, in such circum- stances, is not an indigenous social group which is actively engaged in building a new economic base with a new structure of social relations. It is an intellectual stratum which picks up ideas originating from a prior foreign economic and social revolution. Consequently, the thought of this group takes an idealistic shape ungrounded in a domestic economic development; and its conception of the state takes the form of 'a rational absolute' (Gramsci, 1971: 117). Gramsci criticised the thought of Benedetto Croce, the dominant figure of the Italian intellectual establishment of his own time, for expressing this kind of distortion.

HEGEMONY AND WORLD ORDER

Is the Gramscian concept of hegemony applicable at the international or world level? Before attempting to suggest how this might be done, it is well to rule out some usages of the term which are common in international relations studies. Very often 'hegemony' is used to mean the dominance of one country over others, thereby tying the usage to a relationship strictly among states. Sometimes 'hegemony' is used as a euphemism for imperialism. When Chinese political leaders accuse the Soviet Union of 'hegemonism' they seem to have in mind some combination of these two. These meanings differ so much from the Gramscian sense of the term that it is better, for purposes of clarity in this paper, to use the term 'dominance' to replace them.

In applying the concept of hegemony to world order, it becomes important to determine when a period of hegemony begins and when it ends. A period in which a world hegemony has been established can be called hegemonic and one in which dominance of a non-hegemonic kind prevails, non-hegemonic. To illustrate, let us consider the past century and a half as falling into four distinguishable periods, roughly, 1845–1875, 1875–1945, 1945–1965 and 1965 to the present.[14]

The first period (1845–75) was hegemonic: there was a world economy with Britain as its centre. Economic doctrines consistent with British supremacy but universal in form – comparative advantage, free trade and the gold standard – spread gradually outward from Britain. Coercive strength underwrote this order. Britain held the balance of power in Europe, thereby preventing any challenge to hegemony from a land-based power. Britain ruled supreme at sea and had the capacity to enforce obedience by peripheral countries to the rules of the market.

In the second period (1875–1945), all these features were reversed. Other countries challenged British supremacy. The balance of power in Europe became destabilised, leading to two world wars. Free trade was superseded by protectionism; the Gold Standard was ultimately abandoned; and the world economy fragmented into economic blocs. This was a non-hegemonic period.

In the third period, following the Second World War (1945–65), the United States founded a new hegemonic world order similar in basic structure to that dominated by Britain in mid nineteenth century but with institutions and doctrines adjusted to a more complex world economy and to national societies more sensitive to the political repercussions of economic crises.

Sometime from the later 1960s through the early 1970s it became evident that this US-based world order was no longer working well. During the uncertain times which followed, three possibilities of structural transformation of world order opened up: a reconstruction of hegemony with a broadening of political management on the lines envisaged by the Trilateral Commission; increased fragmentation of the world economy around big-power-centred economic spheres; and the possible assertion of a Third-World-based counter-hegemony with the concerted demand for the New International Economic Order as a forerunner.

On the basis of this tentative notation, it would appear that, historically, to become hegemonic, a state would have to found and protect a world order which was universal in conception, i.e., not an order in which one state directly exploits others but an order which most other states (or at least those within reach of the hegemony) could find compatible with their interests. Such an order would hardly be conceived in inter-state terms alone, for this would likely bring to the fore oppositions of state interests. It would most likely give prominence to opportunities for the forces of civil society to operate on the world scale (or on the scale of the sphere within which hegemony prevails). The hegemonic concept of world order is founded not only upon the regulation of inter-state conflict but also upon a globally-conceived civil society, i.e., a mode of production of global extent which brings about links among social classes of the countries encompassed by it.

Historically, hegemonies of this kind are founded by powerful states which have undergone a thorough social and economic revolution. The revolution not only modifies the internal economic and political structures of the state in question but also unleashes energies which expand beyond the state's boundaries. A world hegemony is thus in its beginnings an outward expansion of the internal (national) hegemony established by a dominant social class. The economic and social institutions, the culture, the technology associated with this national hegemony become patterns for emulation abroad. Such an expansive hegemony impinges on the more peripheral countries as a passive revolution. These countries have not undergone the same thorough social revolution, nor have their economies developed in the same way, but they try to incorporate elements from the hegemonic model without disturbing old power structures. While peripheral countries may adopt some economic and cultural aspects of the hegemonic core, they are less well able to adopt its political models. Just as fascism became the form of passive revolution in the Italy of the inter-war period, so various forms of military-bureaucratic regime supervise passive revolution in today's peripheries. In the world-hegemonic model, hegemony is more intense and consistent at the core and more laden with contradictions at the periphery.

Hegemony at the international level is thus not merely an order among states. It is an order within a world economy with a dominant mode of production which penetrates into all countries and links into other subordinate modes of production. It is also a complex of international social relationships which connect the social classes of the different countries. World hegemony is describable as a social structure, an economic structure, and a political structure; and it cannot be simply one of these things but must be all three. World hegemony, furthermore, is expressed in universal norms, institutions and mechanisms which lay down general rules of behaviour for states and for those forces of civil society that act across national boundaries – rules which support the dominant mode of production

THE MECHANISMS OF HEGEMONY: INTERNATIONAL ORGANISATIONS

One mechanism through which the universal norms of a world hegemony are expressed is the international organisation. Indeed, international organisation functions as the process through which the institutions of hegemony and its ideology are developed. Among the features of international organisation which express its hegemonic role are the following: (1) they embody the rules which facilitate the expansion of hegemonic world orders; (2) they are themselves the product of the hegemonic world order; (3) they ideologically legitimate the norms of the world order; (4) they co-opt the elites from peripheral countries and (5) they absorb counter-hegemonic ideas.

International institutions embody rules which facilitate the expansion of the dominant economic and social forces but which at the same time permit adjustments to be made by subordinated interests with a minimum of pain. The rules governing world monetary and trade relations are particularly significant. They are framed primarily to promote economic expansion. At the same time they allow for exceptions and derogations to take care of problem situations. They can be revised in the light of changed circumstances. The Bretton Woods institutions provided more safeguards for domestic social concerns like unemployment than did the Gold Standard, on condition that national policies were consistent with the goal of a liberal world economy. The current system of floating exchange rates also gives scope for national actions while maintaining the principle of a prior commitment to harmonise national policies in the interests of a liberal world economy.

International institutions and rules are generally initiated by the state which establishes the hegemony. At the very least they must have that state's support. The dominant state takes care to secure the acquiescence of other states according to a hierarchy of powers within the inter-state structure of hegemony. Some second-rank countries are consulted first and their support is secured. The consent of at least some of the more peripheral countries is solicited. Formal participation may be weighted in favour of the dominant powers as in the International Monetary Fund and World Bank, or it may be on a one-state-one-vote basis as in most other major international institutions. There is an informal structure of influence reflecting the different levels of real political and economic power which underlies the formal procedures for decisions.

International institutions perform an ideological role as well. They help define policy guidelines for states and to legitimate certain institutions and practices at the national level. They reflect orientations favourable to the dominant social and economic forces. The OECD, in recommending monetarism, endorsed a dominant consensus of policy thinking in the core countries and strengthened those who were determined to combat inflation this way against others who were more concerned about unemployment. The ILO, by advocating tripartism, legitimates the social relations evolved in the core countries as the desirable model for emulation.

Elite talent from peripheral countries is co-opted into international institutions in the manner of *trasformismo*. Individuals from peripheral countries, though they may come to international institutions with the idea of working from within to change the system, are condemned to work within the structures of passive revolution. At best they will help transfer elements of 'modernisation' to the peripheries but only as these are consistent with the interests of established local powers. Hegemony is like a pillow: it absorbs blows and sooner or later the would-be assailant will find it comfortable to rest upon. Only where representation in international institutions is firmly based upon an articulate social and political challenge to hegemony – upon a nascent historic bloc and counter-hegemony – could participation pose a real threat. The co-optation of outstanding individuals from the peripheries renders this less likely.

Trasformismo also absorbs potentially counter-hegemonic ideas and makes these ideas consistent with hegemonic doctrine. The notion of self-reliance, for example, began as a challenge to the world economy by advocating endogenously determined autonomous development. The term has now been transformed to mean support by the agencies of the world economy for do-it-yourself welfare programmes in the peripheral countries. These programmes aim to enable the rural populations to achieve self-sufficiency, to stem the rural exodus to the cities, and to achieve thereby a greater degree of social and political stability amongst populations which the world economy is incapable of integrating. Self-reliance in its transformed meaning becomes complementary to and supportive of hegemonic goals for the world economy.

Thus, one tactic for bringing about change in the structure of world order can be ruled out as a total illusion. There is very little likelihood of a war of movement at the international level through which radicals would seize control of the superstructure of international institutions. Daniel Patrick Moynihan notwithstanding, Third World radicals do not control international institutions. Even if they did, they could achieve nothing by it. These superstructures are inadequately connected with any popular political base. They are connected with the national hegemonic classes in the core countries and, through the intermediacy of these classes, have a broader base in these countries. In the peripheries, they connect only with the passive revolution.

THE PROSPECTS FOR COUNTER-HEGEMONY

World orders – to return to Gramsci's statement cited earlier in this essay – are grounded in social relations. A significant structural change in world order is, accordingly, likely to be traceable to some fundamental change in social relations and in the national political orders which correspond to national structures of social relations. In Gramsci's thinking, this would come about with the emergence of a new historic bloc.

We must shift the problem of changing world order back from international institutions to national societies. Gramsci's analysis of Italy is even more valid when applied to the world order: only a war of position can, in the long run, bring about structural changes, and a war of position involves building up the socio-political base for change through the creation of new historic blocs. The national context remains the only place where an historic bloc can be founded, although world-economy and world-political conditions materially influence the prospects for such an enterprise.

The prolonged crisis in the world economy (the beginning of which can be traced to the late 1960s and early 1970s) is propitious for some developments which could lead to a counter-hegemonic challenge. In the core countries, those policies which cut into transfer payments to deprived social groups and generate high unemployment open the prospects of a broad alliance of the disadvantaged against the sectors of capital and labour which find common ground in international production and the monopoly-liberal world order. The policy basis for this alliance would most likely be post-Keynesian and neo-mercantilist. In peripheral countries, some states are vulnerable to revolutionary action, as events from Iran to Central America suggest. Political preparation of the population in sufficient depth may not, however, be able to keep pace with revolutionary opportunity and this diminishes the prospect for a new historic bloc. An effective political organisation (Gramsci's Modern Prince) would be required in order to rally the new working classes generated by international production and build a bridge to peasants and urban marginals. Without this, we can only envisage a process where local political elites, even some which are the product of abortively revolutionary upheavals, would entrench their power within a monopoly-liberal world order. A reconstructed monopoly-liberal hegemony would be quite capable of practising *trasformismo* by adjusting to many varieties of national institutions and practices, including nationalisation of industries. The rhetoric of nationalism and socialism could then be brought into line with the restoration of passive revolution under new guise in the periphery.

In short, the task of changing world order begins with the long, laborious effort to build new historic blocs within national boundaries.

Notes

1 This essay was originally published in *Millennium*, (1983) 12 (2):162–75. I refer in citation to Gramsci (1971), herafter cited as *Selections*. The full critical edition is Gramsci (1975), hereafter cited as *Quaderni*.

2 This seems to be the problem underlying Anderson (1976–77) which purports to find inconsistencies in Gramsci's concepts.

3 On this point see Thompson (1978), which contrasts a historicist position analogous to Gramsci's with the abstract philosophical structuralism of Althusser. See 'Marxism is not Historicism', in Althusser and Balibar (1979).

4 It is said that this was to avoid confiscation of his notes by the prison censor who, if this is true, must have been particularly slow-witted.

5 Buci-Glucksmann (1975) places Gramsci squarely in the Leninist tradition. Portelli (1972) and Macciocci (1973) both contrast Gramsci and Lenin. Buci-Glucksmann's work seems to me to be more fully thought through. See also Mouffe (1979) and Showstack-Sassoon (1982).

6 This notion fitted well with Gramsci's assessment of the situation in Italy in the early 1920s; the working class was by itself too weak to carry the full burden of revolution and could only bring about the founding of a new state by an alliance with the peasantry and some petty bourgeois elements. In fact, Gramsci considered the workers' council movement as a school for leadership of such a coalition and his efforts prior to his imprisonment were directed toward building this coalition.

7 See Buci-Glucksmann (1975: 63)

8 Machiavelli (1977: 49–50); Gramsci (1971: 169–90).

9 The term 'Western Europe' refers here to the Britain, France, Germany and Italy of the 1920s and 1930s.

10 Gramsci borrowed the term 'passive revolution' from the Neapolitan historian Vincenzo Cuocco (1770–1823) who was active in the early stages of the Risorgimento. In Cuocco's interpretation Napoleon's armies had brought passive revolution to Italy.

11 Buci-Glucksmann (1975: 121).

12 Gramsci, *Quaderni* (1975: 2,632).

13 See Sorel's discussion of myth and the 'Napoleonic battle' in the letter to Daniel Halevy (in Sorel, 1961).

14 The dating is tentative and would have to be refined by enquiry into the structural features proper to each period as well as into factors deemed to constitute the breaking points between one period and another. These are offered here as mere notations for a revision of historical scholarship to raise some questions about hegemony and its attendant structures and mechanisms.

Imperialism, which has taken different forms in these periods, is a closely related question. In the first, *Pax Britannica*, although some territories were directly administered, control of colonies seems to have been incidental rather than necessary to economic expansion. Argentina, a formally independent country, had essentially the same relationship to the British economy as Canada, a former colony. This, as George Lichtheim noted, may be called the phase of 'liberal imperialism'. In the second period, the so-called 'new imperialism' brought more emphasis on direct political controls. It also saw the growth of capital exports and of the finance capital identified by Lenin as the very essence of imperialism. In the third period, which might be called that of the neo-liberal or monopoly-liberal imperialism, the internationalising of production emerged as the pre-eminent form, supported also by new forms of finance capital (multinational banks and consortia). There seems little point in trying to define some unchanging essence of imperialism but it would be more useful to describe the structural characteristics of the imperialisms which correspond to successive hegemonic and non-hegemonic world orders. For a further discussion of this as regards *Pax Britannica* and *Pax Americana*, see Cox (1983).

3 ALIENATION, CAPITALISM AND THE INTER-STATE SYSTEM: TOWARDS A MARXIAN/GRAMSCIAN CRITIQUE

MARK RUPERT

This chapter presents an interpretation of the radicalised historical ontology characteristic of Marx and Gramsci, and argues that it is possible to understand both the system of sovereign states and the capitalist world economy in non-reductionist ways if the theory of IR/IPE is reconstructed on the basis of a Marxian/Gramscian social ontology. Building upon such a foundation, I will suggest an interpretation of the *political* relations which underlie the capitalist organisation of production, as well as the inter-state system, and which allow us to understand the historical construction of these relations without *a priori* reducing one to the other. Viewed from such a perspective, relations among sovereign states can be critically understood as relations of *alienation*, historically constructed among political communities (states/societies) which are themselves constructed on the basis of relations of alienation (i.e., the corresponding separations of the producer from the means of production, of political from economic relations, etc.).

Marx and Gramsci may be said to have shared a common political commitment which permeated their practices of social inquiry and which constitutes, for me, their primary legacy. Both were engaged in a practice of *critique* which aimed at uncovering and making explicit a social ontology – a process of social self-creation – which underlies and makes possible the capitalist mode of production, but which is systematically distorted and hidden from view by the characteristic institutional forms and social practices of capitalism. In the process of constructing this critique of capitalist social reality, ontology itself is radicalized; no longer viewed *a priori*, i.e., as prior to and constitutive of the reality which we can know, it becomes instead an ongoing social product, historically concrete and contestable.[1] This contrasts, therefore with the dominant discourse in North American studies of IPE/IR, neo-realism.[2]

67

For Marx and for Gramsci the construction of a social ontology was integral to the project of uncovering and actualising latent revolutionary possibilities. The social ontology of Marx and Gramsci, then, is as much a concrete and practical political project as a philosophy of social being. To separate and reify these aspects of life (i.e., politics and theory or philosophy) and to emphasise the latter while neglecting the former would be to abstract the theoretical writings of Marx and Gramsci from their historical and political context, to do violence to the integrity of their work and their lives and – most importantly, I think – to lose the vital and practical aspects of their legacy which may be most relevant to our own lives and the historical possibilities which have yet to be determined.

In the two subsections below, I attempt to reconstruct the social ontologies of Marx and Gramsci, and to situate these in their socio-political context of critique. The point here is not to account for all the myriad nuances and contradictions of their life's work (as might an intellectual historian) or to understand the original system of meanings within which the author wrote his texts (as might a hermeneutic interpreter). Rather, the interpretation which follows represents an appropriation and reconstruction of the texts of Marx and Gramsci motivated by particular interests in the present. The purpose is to provide a basis on which to pose the central question of this paper: how might a vision of the Marxian tradition inform a critical understanding of IR and IPE and at the end of the twentieth century?[3]

MARX: NATURE, HUMAN SOCIAL LIFE, AND THE CRITIQUE OF ALIENATION

From the perspective of a radicalised Marxian ontology, the historically developing *internal relation*[4] of society and nature is central to a critical understanding of human social life under capitalism and its unrealised possibilities. Instead of conceiving nature and society as discrete entities, related to one another only externally, Marx understood them as aspects of a single process. For Marx, nature and society are continually mediated through the characteristically human practice of *objectification*, i.e., the conscious creation of a world of objects through socially organised productive activity in which human beings, their social lives and their natural environment are together transformed. In this process, at once social and natural, human beings develop manifold needs and sensibilities as well as new productive powers. Hence, through productive activity human beings socially objectify themselves and may consciously transform their own 'human nature' along with their social and natural circumstances (cf. e.g., Marx and Engels, 1970: 48–52, 59–64; Marx, 1975a: 322–34, 349–50, 355–8, 389–91; Marx, 1977a: 133–4, 173). Stressing the essential connection and ongoing interchange between human social life and a natural environment which is apparently separate from and external to human beings, Marx in his *Economic and Philosophical Manuscripts* refers to nature as 'man's inorganic body' (1975a: 328). The process of objectification and the continual reconstruction of the nature/society relation are ontologically primary and account for the nature of human social beings in any given historical epoch.

At the most general level of abstraction from our own historial experience, Marx suggested that human beings are naturally social, and socially natural, insofar as social interaction with nature (i.e., objectification, the labour process) is a necessary condition for the reproduction of all human life.

> The labour process . . . is purposeful activity aimed at the production of use-values. It is an appropriation of what exists in nature for the purposes of man. It is the universal condition for the metabolic interaction between man and nature, the everlasting nature-imposed condition of human existence, and it is therefore independent of every form of that existence, or rather it is common to all forms of society in which human beings live. (Marx, 1977a: 290).

The ways in which productive activity is organised and carried out cannot be determined *a priori*. The social conditions of productive activity are variable – continually being reproduced or transformed in the productive practices of human beings – and thus historically specific, enmeshed in particular forms of social life and the kinds of practices which they support.

It is on this basis that Marx criticises the representation of social relations specific to capitalism as if they were immediately natural and universal, rather than viewing them as the product of the active mediation of human social relations and nature through productive activity, i.e., as socially produced and historically mutable. In the representation of (capitalist) social reality as if it were natural and universal, Marx sees a self-limiting form of human understanding in which objects – human social products – are abstracted from the process of their creation, and thus are attributed an autonomy and an effective power over human social life which they have by no intrinsic nature. To the extent that human beings envision their products as taking on a life of their own, humans surrender their own social powers of objectification and are increasingly 'subjected to the violence of things' (Marx and Engels, 1970: 84). Human social life is then governed by the objects it has created, and the mystified forms in which it understands those objects. Social life can take on the appearance of the objective, in so far as human beings are subordinated to the objects they have produced, and in that sense are themselves objectified.[5] Marx refers to this distorted, inverse relation of objectification in terms of 'alienation' or 'fetishism'.[6]

Not reducible to simple cognitive error or misperception, alienation and fetishism are rooted in the material practices of capitalist social life. Under the *specific historical conditions* of capitalism, the ontologically central process of objectification takes the form of alienation. The necessary and ongoing process of mediating human beings and nature is itself mediated by the social organisation of capitalist production. The internal relations between human beings and their natural and social circumstances appear as external relations of opposition: human needs and powers, nature and society, are practically separated from the human producers and confront them as alien and hostile forces. It is in terms of this 'alien mediator' that capitalism becomes the main object of Marx's critique.[7]

The means of production (instruments, raw materials and other objective requirements for the objectification of labour) are privately owned under capitalism. Separated from the necessary means of production, workers must contact with someone who owns the means of production (a capitalist) in order to produce anything. The worker is forced to sell his or her capacity to work (in the language of *Capital*, 'labour-power') to a capitalist in order to secure the means simply to survive, i.e., a wage. As part of this bargain, the product of the worker's labour becomes the property of the capitalist. This process of alienated labour formed the central vantage point for Marx's critical analysis of capitalism. (Ollman, 1990) A multifaceted relation, several aspects of estranged labour are explicitly distinguished by Marx (see especially 1975a: 324–34; also Marx and Engels, 1970: 52–4).

First, in so far as the product of alienated labour belongs not to its producer but to the capitalist, and serves only to increase the mass of capital which the worker must confront in the process of labour, 'the object that labour produces, its product, stands opposed to it as *something alien*, as a *power independent* of the producer' (Marx, 1975a: 324). The process of alienated labour thus entails the estrangement of the producer from his or her product, from the world of objects created by labour, and therefore from 'the sensuous external world', i.e., nature itself. Just as capitalism generates vast new wealth through the ever increasing mastery of nature, workers are excluded from the objective world their labour has created in so far as it becomes the private property of another.

A second aspect of alienated labour is the estrangement of the worker from his or her own life-activity, the process of self-objectification. 'So if the product of labour is alienation, production itself must be active alienation, the alienation of activity, the activity of alienation' (Marx, 1975a: 326). Productive activity which could be intrinsically satisfying, a process of self-development, an end in itself, becomes little more than a means to the minimal end of physical survival. Instead of being an activity of self-affirmation and self-realisation, the worker's labours belong to another whose purposes are alien and antagonistic to the worker. Work, then, amounts to a continuing loss of self for the worker, self-estrangement. In the very process of developing unprecedented social powers of production, workers contribute to the accumulation of capital, reproduce the capital/labour relation to which they are subordinated, and thereby actively estrange themselves from themselves.

Another major aspect of Marx's concept of estranged labour involves the alienation of human beings from one another, and of the individual from the species. For the worker, productive activity is reduced to a mere means to secure from the capitalist the necessities of survival. Under such conditions, other humans appear externally related to the worker and to the activity of work. As capitalism brings people increasingly into a single division of labour and a world market, human relations which could be self-consciously cooperative and socially creative instead become individually instrumental and thus negate the sociality of productive activity and of human life. Rather than calling forth the free development of social powers of production and a richness of sensibilities, human needs become an individual vulnerability which can be instrumentally manipulated by others.

This critique of alienation is not based on abstract moral principles or some transhistorical conception of essential human nature which is violated by capitalism; rather, Marx's critique is aimed at the contradiction between the *historical possibilities* and the *historical actuality* which capitalism has brought into being. It is in this sense an immanent critique of the historical irony of capitalist social life, stressing latent possibilities which present themselves to us in distorted, mystified and self-limiting form. The critical leverage of Marx's theory, then, comes from the contradictory existence *within*

71

the same historical reality of objectification (the ontologically primary and open-ended mediation of human social beings and nature) and alienation (the second-order mediation, i.e., the self-limiting form of objectification through the 'alien mediator' of capital). This implies that it may be possible to overcome some problems of alienation by transcending capital.

While a fully developed defence of this thesis is outside the scope of this chapter, I offer here three sorts of evidence in support of this interpretation. (1) Most significantly, Marx's entire critique of capitalism, from the Paris manuscripts of 1844 to *Capital*, was constructed from the perspective of estranged labour, i.e., from within the labour/capital relation, and not from a vantage point external to the historical reality of capitalism. (2) In those texts where the contours of historical materialism are sketched out, such as *The German Ideology* (Marx and Engels, 1970: esp. 42–52, 58–9, 60–4) and the *Theses on Feuerbach* (Marx, 1975d), Marx is at pains to make it clear that 'human essence' is produced through social relations, and hence changes historically along with those relations. To the extent that there is a conception of human nature in Marx, it appears as an open-ended – and hence, in the abstract, indeterminate – capacity for social self-production through objectification, and can only be more fully specified from a particular historical vantage point. Even in the Paris manuscripts (1975: 280–400), where Marx's problematic of alienation is first developed, and is expressed in philosophical language adapted from Hegel and Feuerbach, Marx explicitly states that no transhistorical vantage point is available to him, or to us. As historically situated beings, Marx argues, we are not able meaningfully to discuss either the absolute beginning or end of the historical process mediating human beings and nature. 'If you ask me about the creation of nature and of man, then you are abstracting from nature and from man . . . [Y]our *abstraction* from the existence of nature and man has no meaning' (1975: 357). We know ourselves through the process of objectification in which human social life and nature are mediated, and hence we can have no perspective outside of our own historical situation within that process. Thus the problematic which Marx first constructs in the 1844 manuscripts centres on the labour/capital relation and the self-estrangement of human productive activity which is narrowly understood as 'labour' in the context of the capitalist economy.[8]

Another vantage point from which Marx viewed capitalism was that of the relation of state and civil society, or of politics and economics. The separation of politics and economics has an important role to play in the historically specific mode of exploitation under capitalism, for it allows this exploitation to take on a distinctively 'economic' semblance. In the historical development of capitalism, the 'formal subsumption of labour under capital' represents a crucial point of transition for Marx. Labour is simultaneously 'freed' from its feudal integuments (relations of serfdom or guild) and separated from the means of production, and hence must enter into an 'economic' relationship with capital in order to secure the means of physical survival. With this development, the labour process (objectification) is subordinated to the accumulation of capital (the 'valorisation process', entailing manifold relations of alienation). Surplus labour is now extracted from the producers through the purchase of their labour-power in the market (and its subsequent employment in the labour process which is controlled and directed by the capitalist class, due to their ownership of the means of production). No explicitly political coercion need enter directly into the capitalist exploitation of labour, for it appears as a simple exchange of commodities in the market: labour-power is exchanged for a wage.[9] 'Extra-economic coercion' of the sort wielded by feudal ruling classes is unnecessary because producers (workers) are no longer in possession of the means of production. They are compelled to sell their labour-power in order to gain access to those means of production, and to acquire the means to purchase the necessities of life. The dominance of capital is mediated through the 'impersonal forces of the market', and appears to the individual producer as the ineluctable operation of 'natural' economic laws.[10] To the extent that capitalism is supported by an explicitly coercive power, that power is situated in the putatively communal sphere occupied by the state, and appears as law and order enforced in the public interest.

This is not to say that state power or capitalist class power have no effective presence in the economy. Both are important, but neither has an explicitly 'political' presence in the routine functioning of the capitalist economy. (1) Capitalist class power – 'economically' based in the ability of this class to control access to the necessary means of production – plays a direct role in the labour process. Here the variable amount of surplus value is continually at issue, and the degree of capitalist control over the labour process is an object of ongoing struggle (Marx, 1977a: Marx 1977b). (2) The state defines the juridical conditions of private property, contract and exchange, thus entering implicitly into the constitution and reproduction of the economic sphere, as well as the class powers which reside in that sphere (see, e.g., Marx, 1977a: chapter 10). Further, the state itself can be a terrain of political class struggle and may be explicitly recognised as such. To the extent that class struggles come to be understood in explicitly political terms and encompass the state as well as the economy, they call into question the reproduction of the reified politics/economics dichotomy which is central to capitalism. In this sense, explicitly political class struggle has potentially revolutionary implications.

Reproduction of capitalist social relations and the process of exploitation thus presupposes the formal separation of politics and economics, such that the two spheres seem to be only externally related, and their internal relation is submerged and hidden from view. Complementary to, but far less well developed than, Marx's analysis of the labour/capital relation, is his critique of the modern 'political' state, in which he suggested that this form of state was premised upon capitalism's abstraction of politics from the real material life of the community (i.e., objectification), and the implicit domination of politics by the class which controls that material life (Marx and Engels, 1970: 53–4, 57–8, 79–81, 83; Marx, 1975a: 369; Marx, 1977a: 874–5; Marx 1977b: 1,027).[11]

As a system centred upon the commodification and alienation of labour and, correspondingly, upon the private ownership of the means of production and appropriation of its product, capitalism presupposes the creation of a social space in which the individual's right to own and to alienate property can reside, a space in which capital and labour can meet as buyers and sellers of commodities. The creation of such a space entailed a two-fold historical development in which feudalism's characteristic fusion of economic and political relations was sundered. On the one hand, the emergence of capitalism involved the historical creation of a 'private' sphere in which individuals could be understood in abstraction from the society in which they were embedded, and thus be enabled to conceive and pursue their own selfish economic interests.[12] Following Hegel, Marx referred to this sphere of apparently isolated, egoistic individuals as 'civil society'. The economy (in its modern sense) is situated within the individualistic realm of civil society. Corresponding to this private sphere is a public one in which the communal lives of capitalism's abstract individuals can be expressed (typically through formal procedures and systems of legal order). The same process of abstraction which separated the individual and his private property from the community, and thus created civil society as an intelligible social space, also generated the possibility of a communal space distinct from civil society. The modern political state, with all its Weberian institutional trappings, is distinguished precisely by its historical construction within this public sphere.[13] So, as Derek Sayer (1985: 233) stresses, 'Formation of the political state and de-politicisation of civil society are two sides of the same coin'. In this sense, the state is internally related to the class-based organisation of production in civil society: they are complementary aspects of the same historical social reality.

> This point is of capital importance, for it implies that the state is emphatically a *historical category*, in other words the concept is not a synonym for any and all forms of government (or ways in which ruling classes rule) but describes a definite and historically delimited *social form*: the social form, specifically, of *bourgeois* class rule. (Sayer, 1985: 231)

The modern political state developed within and is integral to a political/economic system of class rule – a state/society complex in which property is assigned to the private sphere as a primordial individual right, and hence is exempted from ongoing political dialogue in the public sphere. In a fully developed bourgeois republic, explicit class relations are banished from the public sphere, as all citizens are recognised for political purposes to be formally equal individuals. Further, in so far as the modern state presupposes the very separation of politics and economics upon which bourgeois property depends, it cannot fundamentally challenge that separation without undermining the preconditions of its own existence. Thus insulated from explicitly communal and political concerns, the 'private' powers of capital are ensconced in the sanctuary of civil society, and from there implicitly permeate the public sphere, rendering it a partial, distorted and self-limiting form of community, a 'false universality'. From a Marxian perspective, then, state power and bourgeois class power are in some real historical sense interdependent.[14] Marx and Engels (1970: 80) summarise this relation in the following terms:

> Through the emancipation of private property from the community, the state has become a separate entity, beside and outside civil society; but it is nothing more than the form of organization which the bourgeois necessarily adopt both for internal and external purposes, for the mutual guarantee of their property and interests.

To the extent that the modern political state is historically embedded in, and internally related to, the relations of alienation which underlie capitalism, the state may be said to embody alienation, to be its specifically political form. In general, capitalist alienation involves the creation of new social powers at the same time that it individualises human beings, estranging them from their own social powers and precluding the self-conscious social control of those powers. As the political expression of this estrangement, the state may aggregate individual preferences and interests but it cannot transcend them: it becomes the instrument of some particular interests and an externally imposed obstacle to others. It can neither overcome the fundamental isolation of individuals under capitalism, nor can it serve as a vehicle for the communal control of the new social powers of production which capitalism creates. The very existence of the state as a specialised political entity testifies to the estrangement of community and communal powers from the daily lives and productive activities of people within capitalist social reality. The politics expressed in the modern state is impoverished by its abstraction from the *whole* process of social reproduction, including those aspects situated in the economy; and it is distorted by the concentrations of 'private' power which exist outside the domain of 'politics' as it is understood in capitalist societies. In these senses, then, the modern political state is premised upon, is integral to, and contains within itself relations of alienation.

In sum, Marx's radical social ontology allows us to interpret as historically specific instances of alienation, not just the capitalist 'economy', but the whole complex of social relations in which it is embedded, including the formal separations of public/private, politics/economics, and state/society. His critique implies that these alienated relations are fundamentally contradictory, in the sense that they bring into being the preconditions for their own transcendence. It was precisely the theoretical and practical transcendence of these historical relations of alienation – especially the related dichotomies of state and society, of dominant class and subordinate groups – which preoccupied Gramsci.

GRAMSCI: PHILOSOPHY OF PRAXIS, HEGEMONY AND HISTORIC BLOC

Gramsci's Marxism emerged out of his critique of the idealist currents in Italian philosophy as well as the crudely materialist, positivistic, and mechanically economistic interpretations of Marxism then widespread in the international socialist movement. Explicitly preoccupied with the unification of theory and practice, Gramsci reconstructed Marx's radicalised social ontology and developed within the context of this reactivated 'philosophy of praxis' an understanding of revolutionary political action in the advanced capitalism of the twentieth-century West. Integral to this project was a 'dual perspective' on *social politics* encompassing (as internally related dialectical moments) state and society, coercive and consensual forms of power, military and cultural aspects of struggle. His practical political commitment pervades Gramsci's theoretical work and is reflected in his distinctive conceptions of politics and of the state under advanced capitalism (Gramsci, 1971: Gramsci, 1988).[15]

In his *Prison Notebooks*, Gramsci sketches a radical social ontology strikingly similar to that in terms of which I have tried to understand Marx. As did Marx, Gramsci insists that human beings must not be thought of as monads isolated from society and nature, nor as having any fixed or trans-historical essence. Rather, he consistently argues for a more empowering self-understanding in which humans are actively self-constitutive in the process of consciously reconstructing their internal relation with society and nature.

> [O]ne must conceive of man as a series of active relationships (a process) in which individuality, though perhaps the most important, is not, however, the only element to be taken into account. The humanity which is reflected in each individuality is composed of various elements: 1. the individual; 2. other men; 3. the natural world. But the latter two elements are not as simple as they might appear. The individual does not enter into relations with other men by juxtaposition, but organically, in as much, that is, as he belongs to organic entities which range from the simplest to the most complex. Thus man does not enter into relations with the natural world just by being himself part of the natural world, but actively, by means of work and technique. Further: these relations are not mechanical. They are active and conscious. They correspond to the greater or lesser degree of understanding that each man has of them. So one could say that each one of us changes himself, modifies himself to the extent that he changes and modifies the complex relations of which he is the hub. (1971: 352).
>
> The discovery that the relations between the social and natural order are mediated by work, by man's theoretical and practical activity, creates the first elements of an intuition of the world free from all magic and superstition. It provides a basis for the subsequent development of an historical, dialectical conception of the world, which understands movement and change . . . and which conceives the contemporary world as a synthesis of the past, of all past generations, which projects itself into the future. (Gramsci, 1971: 34–5)

So, much like Marx's concept of objectification, Gramsci holds that 'reality is a product of the application of human will to the society of things' (1971: 171), and that this process of producing reality entails the historical transformation of human beings and their social lives, as well as nature. Further, humans are potentially capable of self-consciously guiding this activity and thus can determine their own process of *becoming* (see 1971: esp. 9, 34–5, 133–4, 323–5, 332–4, 344, 351–7, 360–1, 445–6).

This process cannot take place in a vacuum of abstraction, however, but only under specific historical circumstances.[16] For Gramsci, historically concrete struggles to determine the social process of becoming are the essence of politics. As did Marx, Gramsci stresses the contradictory relation of historical actuality and latent possibilities which together constitute the nexus in which political praxis can occur.

> The active politician is a creator, an initiator; but he neither creates from nothing nor does he move in the turbid void of his own desires and dreams. He bases himself on effective reality, but what is effective reality? Is it something static and immobile, or is it not rather a relation of forces in continuous motion and shift of equilibrium? If one applies one's will to the creation of a new equilibrium among the forces which really exist and are operative – basing oneself on the particular force which one believes to be progressive and strengthening it to help it to victory – one still moves on the terrain of effective reality, but does so in order to dominate and transcend it (or to contribute to this). What 'ought to be' is therefore concrete; indeed it is the only realistic and historicist interpretation of reality, it alone is history in the making and philosophy in the making, it alone is politics. (1971: 172).

The conflict of historical forces, the fluid political reality with which Gramsci is chiefly concerned, is the political and ideological struggle in the advanced capitalist societies of the West – where civil society is highly developed and capitalist class power has permeated and shaped the cultural institutions of society as well as residing, ultimately, in the political state and its coercive apparatus (1971: 12, 54, 235–9, 242–3, 244, 258–63).

It is important to note at this juncture that Gramsci used such key concepts as 'ideology', 'civil society' and 'state' in somewhat broader ways than did Marx. Expanding beyond Marx's predominantly negative images of ideology as the distorted, inverted and self-limiting forms of consciousness which characterise capitalist social relations, Gramsci's vision entailed explicitly positive and enabling aspects of ideology as a potentially revolutionary terrain of struggle (1971: 164–5, 326, 328, 375–7). In accordance with this 'dual perspective', centring on the internal relation of coercion and consent in the political struggles of advanced capitalism, Gramsci understands 'civil society' as internally related to 'political society'. Whereas the latter designates the coercive apparatus of the state more narrowly understood (i.e., what we would recognise as its classically Weberian aspect), the former represents the realm of cultural institutions and practices in which the hegemony of a class may be constructed or challenged. Gramsci uses civil society to designate an area of cultural and ideological linkage between class relations in the economy and the explicitly political aspect of the state. Civil society would then include parties, unions, churches, education, journalism, art and literature, etc. Together, political society and civil society constitute Gramsci's *extended* or *integral state*, the unified site in which Western bourgeois classes have established their social power as 'hegemony protected by the armour of coercion' (1971: 263). In this broader (integral) sense, then, 'the State is the entire complex of practical and theoretical activities with which the ruling class not only justifies and maintains its dominance, but manages to win the active consent of those over whom it rules.' (1971: 244; see also pp. 12–13, 239, 257–63, 268). Gramsci's apparently idiosyncratic usage of such concepts as these must be understood in the context of his comprehensive vision of social politics in the capitalist societies of the twentieth-century West, and his strategy for the revolutionary transformation of such societies through 'war of position' and the construction of a proletarian counter-hegemony (1971: 229–39, 242–3).[17]

His main political objective is to bring about a transformative process, a unification of theory and practice, which will transcend the division of capitalist society into rulers and ruled, dominant classes and subaltern groups, state and society (1971: 139–40, 144–57, 253, 258–60, 263, 267, 332–5, 350–1, 382, 418). While such a struggle – eventuating in a 'regulated society', i.e., socialism – will necessarily entail the transformation of the capitalist economy, it is neither determined by 'causes' originating in that economy, nor are its implications limited to economic changes (1971: 158–68, 175–85, 229–39, 257–60, 381–2, 407–9). Gramsci's radical politics envisions a comprehensive transformation of social reality through the creation of an effective counter-culture, an alternative world view and a new form of political organisation in whose participatory and consensual practices that world view is concretely realised. Ultimately Gramscian politics aims to produce a qualitatively new form of 'state', a genuinely *self-determining* community bearing little resemblance to the self-limiting 'political' form of state integral to capitalist social reality. In this vision of revolutionary political practice, then, the whole of

79

advanced capitalist society becomes a terrain of struggle on which subordinate groups can challenge bourgeois hegemony and thus begin to actualise real historical possibilities which have been systematically obscured.

Thus I would suggest that Gramsci shares with Marx (including the Marx of the early writings) a common focus on the contradiction between historical actuality and historical possibilities *within capitalist social reality*. In that sense, it may be said that Gramsci, too, was concerned with alienation, even though he did not use that term.[18] I interpret in this light Gramsci's critique of such historically self-limiting forms of theory/practice as 'economism' (971: 158–68, also 175–85, 229–39, 407) and 'statolatry' (1971: 268), as well as his arguments about the actuality of 'contradictory consciousness' among the masses of people in capitalist society (1971: 333) and the possibility for them to develop a more critical self-understanding and thus to actualise their capacities as practical philosophers, self-consciously determining their own economic/political/cultural relations and activities (1971: 9, 323–5, 332–5, 344). It is precisely this task of critical education which distinguishes Gramsci's revolutionary party and its hegemonic project from those of the bourgeoisie.

This moral-political project involves the creation of a new 'historic bloc' in which proletarian leadership of the various classes and groups subordinated under capitalism could be organised and expressed. The construction of an historic bloc is a precondition for the exercise of hegemony in the Gramscian sense, and entails a *reconstruction of state/society relations* through organically related processes of political, economic and cultural change. Gramsci's concept of historic bloc bridges the structured separation of state and society in capitalist social formations, in so far as the ideological leadership of a class or class fraction provides a measure of coherence to a range of apparently disparate social practices (cultural, political, economic). To the extent that a class or fraction is able to articulate a unifying ideology which presents itself as universal, which can elicit the consent of subordinate groups and structure their participation in a variety of social practices, it may create the basis of hegemonic leadership in both state and civil society – that is, in Gramsci's expanded or integral state (cf. 1971: 12, 239, 244, 257–63, see also chapter 2 in this volume).

While stressing that changes in the organisation of productive practices and class domination are organic to the consolidation of such an historic bloc, Gramsci consistently and rigorously maintains that neither political nor cultural practices are reducible to 'economic' forces or interests (see, e.g., 1971: 407). Indeed, a necessary condition for the attainment of hegemony by a class or class fraction is the supersession of their narrow, economic interests (what Gramsci called the 'economic-corporate') by a more universal social vision or ideology, and the making of concrete concessions to subordinate groups in the process of securing their participation in the social vision of the leading class or fraction (1971: 12, 136–7, 161, 167–8, 180–3, 365–7, 375–7, 418; 1988: 190–200).

For Gramsci, an historic bloc is more than a simple alliance of classes or class fractions. It encompasses political, cultural, and economic aspects of a particular social formation, uniting these in historically specific ways to form a complex, politically contestable and dynamic ensemble of social relations.[19] An historic bloc articulates a world view, grounded in historically specific socio-political conditions and production relations, which lends substance and ideological coherence to its social power. It follows, then, that hegemonies and historic blocs have specific qualities relating to particular social constellations, their underlying class forces and productive relations. They can be conservative or revolutionary.

Bourgeois hegemony presupposes the dichotomy of leaders and led, of dominant and subordinate classes, and strives to reproduce this condition in the economy, in the political state and in the cultural institutions of civil society. 'Passive revolution' – in which the dominant group takes the initiative in making limited concessions (of an 'economic-corporate' type) to subordinate classes, thereby forestalling more comprehensive challenges from them – may serve to disable effective social action on the part of the subaltern groups and hence to reproduce the conditions of capitalist domination.

Working-class hegemony, on the other hand, strives toward the dissolution of the dichotomy of leaders and led (as well as the reified separations of politics/economics, state/society, etc.) through the active participation of all subordinate groups within a unified revolutionary movement. This means that the hegemony of the working class cannot be based on piece-meal economic-corporate concessions to other subordinate groups, but entails a transformative process through which these various groups are enabled to participate actively and directly in the reconstruction of the social world. The fundamental project of the working class – building a participatory community in which social powers of self-production are commonly and consensually regulated – cannot proceed without them for, were it to do so, it would simply reproduce the dichotomy of leaders/led. Ultimately, the political party of the philosophy of *praxis* will be self-

81

liquidating in so far as it succeeds in he'ping the masses to become masters of their own collective destiny, and hence eliminates the need for leadership organised in a political party, or for a specialised coercive state (1971: 144, 152, 253, 258–60, 263, 267, 332–5, 382).

In this sense, the class forces, political organisation and historical objectives of an historic bloc are all internally related. It is this broader conception of *social politics* encompassing the state, the economy, and cultural spheres of a social formation which distinguishes Gramsci from more positivistic and economistic theorists of Marxism, and which directs inquiry towards the processes of socio-political struggle through which historic blocs and their hegemonies are constructed in states/societies.

I conclude this interpretive exercise by suggesting that both Gramsci and Marx understood the separations of politics/economics and state/society to be historically real; but not to be an essential part of human social existence, i.e., not to be real in any transhistorical sense. These oppositions were seen to have been historically produced – and open to historical transcendence – through social processes of objectification. An integral part of this social transformation, although by no means the whole of it, will involve the elimination of the capitalist organisation of production which is internally related to these distinctly modern antinomies.

PRAXIS, CAPITALIST ALIENATION, AND THE CRITIQUE OF IPE/IR

Marxian analysis has traditionally been on the margin of IR/IPE, and is widely seen as incapable of adequately conceptualising the realities of a system of autonomous, power-wielding, fundamentally coercive administrative organisations such as sovereign states. (cf. Skocpol, 1979: 26–31; Giddens, 1985; Linklater, 1986). In this vein, Gilpin (1987: 26–33) equates Marxism with economism; and Keohane (1986) suggests that Marxist writers often resort to the implicit use of 'realist' concepts in attempting to come to grips with the international, and thereby demonstrate not just the shortcomings of Marxian analysis but also the superior analytical power and basic validity of the realist model of IR. In this section, I hope to raise doubt about whether Marxism's relevance for IR/IPE is indeed closed.

I argued above that the core of a Marxian dialectical approach to social inquiry is an ontology of *praxis*, an understanding of social reality in terms of the process of producing a world of objects, social relations and identities through the self-conscious activities of human social beings. This allows us to view ourselves and the world around us in relation to our own productive activities, the historically specific ways in which these are socially organised, and the transformative possibilities implicit within that organisation.

Under conditions of capitalist production, producers are alienated. These relations of alienation are multi-faceted: commodified labour, capital, the isolated and self-interested individual of civil society, the economy, the modern political state, all are aspects of alienated social life under capitalism. They appear as things given by nature and, as such, universal and necessary. Thus obscured from view are the relations which make possible the specific institutional forms of capitalist society, as well as the social processes by which these characteristic forms have been produced and reproduced and through which historical social reality may be changed. Illumination of these relations and processes – as a necessary part of the transformation of alienated, capitalist society – is the objective of critique. What I want to argue now is that the project of critique and transformation *encompasses, entails* the critique of IR and IPE. Both the system of sovereign states and the global division of labour – taken as ontologically primitive units by neo-realism and world-system theory, respectively – may instead be understood as aspects of the historically specific social organisation of productive activity under capitalism, as embodying relations of alienation, and as potentially transcendable.

In order to construct a radical critique it is first necessary to broaden our conception of world politics so as to accommodate a meaningful notion of transformative *praxis*. Accordingly, it will be necessary to abandon the characteristic neo-realist premise that the fundamental reality of world politics – everywhere and always – is power struggle among autonomous states in a context of anarchy. Here, I do not wish to be understood as suggesting that the neo-realist vision of world politics is simply wrong, that it is an illusion of 'false consciousness'. Rather, it is an historically real and effective but none the less self-limiting form of theory/practice. Neo-realism, like any ideology, is grounded in practical experience and hence must have some measure of what Derek Sayer (1983: 8) refers to as 'practical adequacy' – 'It must, in other words, allow men and women to conduct and make sense of their everyday activity'. But the way in which it allows them to make sense of their world also has the effect of portraying as natural and universal a set of social relations which are historically specific and socially mutable. It does this by abstracting these relations from the processes which produced them and through which they may be transformed. While analytical distinctions may be made between the 'global' and 'domestic', neo-realism's reification of these 'levels of analysis' fragments the field of political action, disabling critique and *praxis*. Alternatively, national and international should be construed as two aspects of an internally related whole, a whole which is in some sense capitalist and alienated. In place of the neo-realist 'presumption of anarchy' (as Hayward Alker has dubbed it), a Marxian/Gramscian critique would take as its point of departure the proposition that international politics as we know it is *historically embedded* in, and *internally related* to, capitalist social relations.

In so far as the formal separations of state and society, of public and private, of the political and the economic aspects of life, are integral to the historical reality of capitalism, we may say that capitalism and its manifold relations of alienation are the necessary context within which the historical construction of sovereign states – understood in the modern sense as functionally specialised administrative/coercive, i.e. 'political', organisations – becomes possible. The very existence of the kind of states portrayed by neo-realist theory presupposes relations of alienation in which 'politics' assumes an identity distinct from 'economics' and attains its own institutional form of expression. The alienation of the individual from the community and the abstraction of politics from individualised productive life are conditions of possibility for *both* capitalist production and the modern political state.

International politics may then be critically understood as a kind of second-order alienation. That is, international politics concerns itself with the mutual estrangement of political communities which are themselves constructed within relations of alienation.[20] The first-order alienation occurs as the modern political state mediates between, on the one hand, capitalist objectification, i.e., the productive life of the community as lived in the civil society of individuals, and on the other hand, its explicitly communal life in the public sphere. The state is situated as an alien mediator between society as a collection of self-interested individuals, and society as a potentially self-determining political community. It mediates, that is, between capitalist society and itself, its own alienated political life. But the modern political state also mediates between that alienated community and other historically constructed communities. In this sense – i.e., viewed critically from within capitalist social reality – the system of states which emerged historically along with capitalist production represents another facet of the complex of social relations which embody alienation, and must therefore be part of any concrete political strategy aimed at overcoming those relations of alienation. I believe this is what Gramsci had in mind when he wrote:

> according to the philosophy of *praxis* (as it manifests itself politically) . . . the international situation should be considered in its national aspect. In reality, the internal relations of any nation are the result of a combination which is 'original' and (in a certain sense) unique: these relations must be understood and conceived in their originality and uniqueness if one wishes to dominate them and direct them. To be sure, the line of development is toward internationalism, but the point of departure is 'national' – and it is from this point of departure that one must begin. Yet the perspective is international and cannot be otherwise. (Gramsci, 1971: 240)

Clearly, Gramsci assigns an active priority to those aspects of social reality which are produced within the bounds of the 'national' political community. But followers of Gilpin and Waltz should not be too quick in their condemnations; for this is no one-way causality, no crude and ahistorical economistic reduction. Instead, Gramsci is arguing that a *praxis*-based approach must understand international politics from the perspective of the production and reproduction of social life, and that such a practical understanding cannot proceed in abstraction from specific constellations of factors (the interaction of local and global) which have shaped the historical production of particular states and the relations among them. For Gramsci, international relations cannot be merely epiphenomenal. He is clearly indicating in the second passage quoted that IR shapes 'both passively and actively' the development of socio-political relations within particular states. Indeed, a Marxian/Gramscian vision of IR could not resort to economistic reductions without vitiating its fundamental commitment to a philosophy of *praxis*. Such an interpretation, I therefore suggest, entails a critical reconstruction of the *historical interplay* between socio-political processes within particular states, and global relations and processes.

From this general perspective, it appears that the second-order alienation of the inter-state system has reproduced at a global level aspects of the more fundamental, first-order alienation. In particular, the system of political states has reproduced institutions and practices which abstract politics from productive life, and hence preclude explicit communal self-determination directly within productive activity. Instead, productive activity is organised in a world 'economy', a global division of labour governed by world market forces and seemingly beyond the reach of any form of communal control.[21]

Correspondingly, 'politics' is understood in terms of the instrumental interactions of individualised political actors, struggling to exert some control over their social and economic circumstances. The extension of Marx's notion of alienation to encompass global social relations helps to explain the common preoccupation of neo-realism and world-system theory (each from its own point of view) with the construction of political hierarchies superimposed upon the world economy. The perspectives of both neo-realism and world-system theory are produced by abstracting one or the other aspect of this alienated relation of politics/economics, and then constructing abstract causal explanations in terms of this favoured primitive unit.

Instead of beginning with sovereign states or the world-system as a theoretical point of departure, Marx and Gramsci can be interpreted as suggesting another vantage point from which to view IR/IPE. From this perspective, IR/IPE can be understood in terms of the process of objectification as it is organised under capitalism, i.e., as part of capitalism's global aspect. In no way does this imply that political dynamics are wholly understandable in terms of 'economic' causes. Rather, it implies that all social relations – including the system of states and the world economy – are historically produced and politically contestable. Such contests are fought out among various historically specific social forces and actors (e.g., functionaries of the political state, classes or class fractions, historic blocs, subaltern groups). The particular form taken by the relation of politics/economics or national/international is then seen as being determined by the outcomes of these historical struggles. Thus, for example, it is entirely consistent with this perspective to argue that inter-state competition and warfare have had historically significant effects on the relation of capital and labour in the sphere of production, as well as upon state/society relations. Indeed, I have argued that this was the case in the United States during both world wars of this century (Rupert, 1990). The point, then, is not to attribute universal causal efficacy to 'economic' forces or 'domestic' factors, but to understand how the processes of capitalist objectification (global as well as domestic, political as well as economic) have produced contemporary social reality, and how the relations of alienation which inhere in that reality may be overcome.

This raises the question of *praxis*. How can we think about an emancipatory project which is global in its scope? It is certainly not easy to be optimistic here: for example, Berki (1984) and Wallerstein (1984a) both suggest that a class-based emancipatory project will be contained within national boundaries, and will therefore be unable to address more global aspects of alienation. Once again, however, Gramsci's novel theoretical contributions may help us to conceptualise this difficult problem in new and enabling ways; for Gramsci's emancipatory project, his notions of civil society and of the hegemony which may be constructed in that site, are not necessarily circumscribed by the boundaries of nation-states. A progressive historic bloc aims at the construction of a participatory movement in which the dichotomies of leaders/led, etc., are dissolved. This process entails the dissolution of the bourgeois state in which the coercive power of the dominant class is institutionalised. Thus, for Gramsci, transformative praxis need not stop at the border of the state, for the state itself is being transformed as the new hegemony is being constructed and new ways of organising social relations are being learned. 'Every relationship of "hegemony" is necessarily an educational relationship and occurs not only within a nation, between the various forces of which the nation is composed, but in the international and world-wide field, between complexes of national and continental civilizations' (Gramsci, 1971: 350, see also 240–1). What is implied here is a radical political strategy which overturns the hegemony of state-based conceptions of politics (first- and second-order alienation), mediates between various 'national' groups whose political practices had been contained within such conceptions, and enables their active participation in the construction of a global political community.

All this may well seem utopian. What grounds do we have for believing that such a project is historically possible? In this century, the reorganisation of capitalist production on a global scale, and the socio-political developments associated with this transformation, could together make possible new kinds of *praxis* which explicitly transcend national boundaries. Beginning in the United States, especially in the first decades of the twentieth century, manufacturers began to intensify their control over the labour process and to impose upon workers a heightened division between mental and manual labour, planning and execution. Once the resistance of workers was overcome and their consent elicited (the magnitude of this accomplishment should not be underestimated; see Rupert, 1990), this facilitated the breaking down of production processes into a series of discrete steps and specialised tasks. These steps might be integrated into a single mass-production facility, as in Ford's pioneering River Rouge complex where raw materials entered at one end and automobiles emerged at the other; or, as in the last few decades, they could be distributed in ways which rationalise the production process on as large a geographic scale as necessary. In the context of the post-war global order, the growth of transnational production and intra-firm exchange has to a significant degree displaced international trade (Hymer, 1979; Cox, 1981: 146–7; Cox, 1987: 244–53; Gill, 1990: 90–3). Today, vast multinational firms orchestrate their production and trade on a world scale, and render increasingly quaint Marx's (1977a: 470–80) distinction between 'division of labour in the work-shop' – in which the power of the capitalist enforces rationalization of the labour process at the micro level – and 'division of labour in society' – in which the market mediates between producers, and no conscious macro-level social coordination prevails. The mystifying effect of the market (which disguises relations of class power as impersonal, naturalised market forces confronting individuals) may then be lessening as huge firms more directly manage production and exchange world-wide and the social power of capital becomes less opaque. Corresponding with this internationalisation of production has been an internationalisation of Gramsci's extended state (Cox, 1981: 144–6; Cox, 1987: 253–65) and the more explicit development of a global civil society through which the hegemony of international capital has been organised in the post-war world (van der Pijl, 1984; van der Pijl, 1989; Gill, 1990). While these long-term tendencies may have encouraged some fragmentation of the working class (e.g., between workers in globally oriented industries versus those which are more nationally based), now more than ever it is possible to speak realistically about a global class structure, and the possibility of explicitly political struggles which may challenge it.

In the context of this transnationalisation of capitalist production, a transformative critique makes it possible to envision a globally radical political *praxis* emerging even within the industrial workplaces of the North and, in particular, in the USA. In an era when production and jobs are globally mobile, it becomes increasingly difficult for these relatively privileged workers to take for granted the standard of living they have enjoyed. Multinational firms seeking to minimise overall costs may impose draconian wage or benefit cut-backs upon these workers, may try to break their unions, or may simply pack up and move to a more 'hospitable business climate', i.e., one with a compliant, non-unionized, low-wage work force (Bluestone and Harrison, 1982). This in turn could lead to the explicit politicisation of class conflict and open up new horizons of political action which need not be limited by conventional boundaries of political/economic, state/society, domestic/international. Such a struggle could extend to the construction of transnational coalitions among workers and other subaltern groups to confront their exploiters, exert collective control over their lives, and explore new modes of social life. Of course, such conditions could also foster resurgent xenophobia, racism and jingoism among Northern or American workers.

I cannot be confident of the more progressive outcome. Yet, it seems to me that it is precisely this historical openness, this absence of guarantee, which makes it so important for a critical IR/IPE to point toward the *possibilities* for progressive social change which inhere in the social relations we so often take for granted, the historical processes which we tend to accept the same way we resign ourselves to the onset of inclement weather.

We cannot know *a priori* whether or how a global project of emancipation will be effectivly actualised, for this will depend upon what Thompson (1978: 49) refers to as 'the *praxis* of eventuation'. Yet I hope to have persuaded the reader that IR/IPE can and should strive to make explicit the transformative possibilities which we have brought into being in the historical production of global capitalism.

Notes

1 This ontological problem has been cogently summarised by Alex Wendt (1987) in terms on the relation of agents and structures in IR theory, and the epistemological presuppositions of an adequate understanding of these relations. Nevertheless, I have reservations about any attempted resolution of the ontological problem of agents and structures in terms of a scientific realist epistemology or a transhistorical ontology of structuration. I find more satisfying a vision of theory and practice as internally related aspects of the process of social self-production, i.e., a radicalised social ontology of *praxis*. This view emphasises *praxis* as the ground of experience and knowledge, and situates epistemological commitments within a concrete socio-political context, such as the critique of capitalism and its historically specific ontology of alienation. This need not be inconsistent with scientific realism. For arguments which suggest that a Marxian critique of capitalism may entail some sort of scientific realist epistemology (cf. Keat and Urry, 1982: ch. 5; Callinicos, 1983: ch. 5; Sayer, 1983; and Isaak, 1987). However, I would suggest that the reverse claim (that scientific realism entails a critique of capitalism, or of any other historical relations of inequality or domination) does not follow from these arguments. For an argument which is critical of Wendt's version of realist/structuration theory, but which does not necessarily embrace a Marxian conception of *praxis*, see Milliken (1990).

2 I use 'neo-realism' to denote a family of arguments which share a commitment to an atomistic ontology (abstract individualism) and empi-

ricist epistemology. For a critique which attempts to situate neo-realist IPE in a tradition of abstract individualism stretching back to Hobbes and Smith, see Inayatullah and Rupert (1990). On the ontology of abstract individualism and its relation to the whole tradition of Western liberalism see Arblaster (1984: esp. chs. 2–4).

3 This interpretation should not be taken to represent the whole of the Marxian tradition or even a sort of 'central tendency' within it. Marxian thought is so rich and complex as to defy simple summary or schematic overview. None the less, there are works which attempt to provide the reader with some sense of the general contours of this terrain. Kolakowski's *Main Currents of Marxism* (1981) is extraordinarily comprehensive. Other works which deal more specifically with the multi-faceted tradition of Western Marxism – within which Gramsci is often situated – include Anderson (1976), Jacoby (1981), Callinicos (1983: esp. ch. 3), and Jay (1984).

4 A concept of internal relations is central to dialectical method. An internal relation is one in which the inter-related entities take their meaning from (or are constituted within) their relation, and are unintelligible (or non-existent) outside of the context of that relation. Classic examples include master/slave, parent/child and teacher/student relations. Internal relations are contrasted with external relations, 'in which each *relatum* is taken as a separate self-subsistent entity, which exists apart from the relation and appears to be totally independent of it' (Gould, 1978: 38). On this, see Ollman, 1976: 12–40, 256–76; Ollman, 1990: 36–40; Gould, 1978: 37–9, 184 n. 22); and Sayer, 1987: 18–23.

5 Under capitalist relations of production, that is, human beings become objects *in relation to their products*, which are separated from the producers and attributed with autonomous powers as capital, and thus may be said effectively to act upon their human producers.

6 On 'alienation', see Marx and Engels, 1970: 52–4, 84, 91–3; Marx, 1975a: 322–79, Marx, 1977b: 990, 1,002–18, especially pp. 1,003–4, 1,016, 1,054, 1,058. For discussions of the related notion of 'fetishism', see Marx, 1977a: ch. 1, especially pp. 164–5, 167–8, 174–5; also Marx, 1977b: 980–90, 998, 1,003, 1,005–8, 1,052–8. For secondary works which stress the centrality of these themes throughout Marx's work, cf. Avineri, 1968; Bernstein, 1971: 11–83; Colletti, 1975; Meszaros, 1975; Ollman, 1976; Ollman, 1990; Gould, 1978; Sayer, 1983; Sayer, 1985; Sayer, 1987, and Arthur, 1986. Influenced by Althusser, Callinicos (1983: chapter 2) is rather more ambivalent.

7 On this interpretation of alienation as a 'second order mediation' of human beings and nature, see esp. Meszaros (1975: 78–84) and Arthur (1986: 5–19).

8 For other interpretations which entail similar implications about Marx's critique of alienation, see Kolakowski (1968), Bernstein (1971: esp. pp. 66–70), Meszaros (1975: esp. 63–5, 114–19, 162–86), Ollman (1976), Ollman (1990), Petrovic (1983), Sayer (1983), Sayer (1987), and Arthur (1986: esp. 39–41, 117–21, 145–6).

9 According to Marx's (1977a) analysis of the two-fold character of commodities in capitalist society, 'labour-power' denotes the abstract, commodified form of labour – i.e., the capacity to work – which is sold at its 'exchange value' for wages. This is rigorously distinguished from 'labour' which denotes the actual work performed for the wages paid by the capitalist. Labour is then the 'use value' which the capitalist may derive from his purchase of labour-power. In Marx's theory of value, human labour-power is unique among commodities in that the value of the commodities generated by labour is potentially much greater than the value of labour-power itself (that is, the labour *time* socially necessary to produce the workers' means of subsistence and reproduce labour-power). The use value of labour-power, then, is greater (by some variable magnitude) than its exchange value. It is this difference – 'surplus value', the product and in turn a precondition of the process of alienated labour – which serves as the centrepiece of Marx's theory of exploitation in capitalist society, and which represents the daily reality of class struggle.

10 Capitalists, too, are governed by the operation of seemingly objective economic laws, and in this sense may be understood as experiencing their own kind of alienation (see, e.g., Marx, 1977b: 990). They confront the market as individuals in competition with one another, and hence are driven to intensify the extraction of surplus value by increasing their control over the organisation and performance of work. Marx refers to this conquest of the labour process as the 'real subsumption of labour' under capital (1977b: 1,023–5 1,034–8; also 1977a: part 4). It is this conquest which enables the continual incorporation of new technologies and processes into the labour process, and which underlies the unique economic dynamism of capitalist social formations. On social relations as 'forces of production' in Marxist theory, see Brenner (1986), and Sayer (1987: ch. 2).

11 There are continuities in Marx's critical treatment of the state before and after his development of the problematic of estranged labour in the 1844 Manuscripts. Illuminating early discussions of the state/civil society relation may be found in 'Critique of Hegel's Doctrine of the State' (Marx, 1975b: 57–198), and 'On the Jewish Question' (Marx, 1975c: 211–41). Commentaries which help to situate these early works in terms of their relation to Marx's subsequent critique of capitalism include: Avineri (1968), McGovern (1970), Wood (1981), Jessop (1982: 1–31), and Sayer (1985).

12 The historical grounding of the Smithian competitive market and its egoistic individual in capitalist relations of production is a central theme in the works of Brenner (1977; 1986).

13 Compare, for example, Weber (1946), Poggi (1978), Wood (1981), and Sayer (1985; 1987: ch. 4), each of which, from a somewhat different perspective, touches upon the significance of these separations (i.e., public/private, economic/political, etc.) for the character of the modern state.

14 The manner of this interdependence is a matter of vigorous debate among

Marxian political theorists. Provocative early contributions include Miliband (1969), Poulantzas (1969), and their subsequent exchanges in the pages of *New Left Review*. Helpful overviews include Laclau (1975), Jessop (1982), and Carnoy (1984).

15 Among those commentaries which inform the reconstruction offered here, are: Texier (1979), Adamson (1980), Jessop (1982: 142–52), Buci-Glucksmann (1982), Sassoon (1982; 1987), Cox (1983), and Jay (1984: ch. 4).

16 Gramsci clearly implies that the philosophy of *praxis* can claim no validity as absolute, transhistorical truth, but is rather specific to a particular historical social reality and will itself be transcended along with that reality (1971: 404–7; see also p. 364–6, 446 on the historical embeddedness of knowledge).

17 Especially helpful in understanding these aspects of Gramsci are Texier (1979), Adamson (1980: 215–28), Sassoon (1982; 1987; 109–14), and Larrain (1983: chs 1–2).

18 My interpretation here diverges from Adamson (1980: esp. 108–9, 130–5), who views Marx's early works as embodying an 'anthropological dialectic' of human essence and species being, and who contends that Gramsci's concrete 'pragmatological dialectic' could hardly accommodate such notions as alienation. Further, Adamson asserts, Gramsci 'almost entirely lacked the reification problematic that Marx developed on the basis of these concepts' (1980: 132).

19 This point is stressed by Adamson (1980: 178) and Sassoon (1987: 121–22). For more general discussions of Gramsci's understanding of the internal relation of politics and culture to the class-based organisation of production in capitalism, see Texier (1979), Buci-Glucksman (1982) and Sassoon (1982).

20 This argument draws inspiration, but departs substantially, from Berki (1984) and Der Derian (1987).

21 In the context of Wallerstein's world-system theory, the separation of politics (constrained within the individual polities of the inter-state system) and economics (the encompassing global division of labour) is constitutive of the capitalist world-economy and is a functional requirement for its reproduction (cf. 1979: 6, 24, 32, 66; 1984a: 7–12, 33–6, 50, 130).

4 GLOBAL HEGEMONY AND THE STRUCTURAL POWER OF CAPITAL

STEPHEN GILL AND DAVID LAW

In this chapter we distinguish between direct and structural forms of power.[1] We relate these to the concepts of hegemony, historic bloc and the 'extended' state, in our analysis of present-day capitalism. In so doing we seek to meet two major challenges. The first is to integrate better 'domestic' and 'international' levels of analysis. The second, related challenge, is to theorise the complementary and contradictory relations between the power of states and the power of capital.

Unlike Classical Marxists, who emphasise instrumentalism and economism of the Classical Marxists, some contemporary Marxists take their inspiration from the ethical rationalism of Antonio Gramsci. Gramsci's (1971) concept of hegemony differs from the orthodox Realist usage. The latter refers to the dominance of one state over other states and is largely a case of what we call the direct exertion of 'power over,' in the sense used by Max Weber. For Gramsci, hegemony was a concept used to analyse the relation of forces in a given society. A hegemonic order was one where consent, rather than coercion, primarily characterised the relations between classes, and between the state and civil society.

The concept of the state used in Gramsci is an 'extended' and integral one, which reflects the fact that, under certain conditions (for example in Anglo-Saxon countries) there was often an organic fusion between state and civil society (Gramsci, 1971: 12). This concept of the state contrasts with the rather narrowly defined 'nightwatchman' state of liberal economists and the 'interventionist' state associated with Bismarck (Gramsci, 1971: 257-63).

The power of the ruling class, or class fraction over others, was partly exercised through the state. It was not simply a case of dominance through sanctions, punishments or inducements: it also involved 'intellectual and moral leadership' (Gramsci, 1971: 182, 269). Hegemony was exercised within a wider social and political constellation of forces, or 'historic bloc'. The latter concept refers to a

historical congruence between material forces, institutions and ideologies, or broadly, an alliance of different class forces. Thus, a historic
bloc was the 'organic' link between 'political' and 'civil society', a
fusion of material, institutional, inter-subjective, theoretical and
ideological capacities. (Gramsci, 1971: 366) A successful bloc was
politically organised around a set of hegemonic ideas which give
some strategic direction and coherence to the constituent elements.
For a new historic bloc to emerge, its leaders must engage in
'conscious, planned struggle'. This was not simply an issue of the
power of ideology or indeed of 'capturing' the state. Any new historic
bloc must have not only power within the civil society and economy,
it also needs persuasive ideas and arguments (involving what Gramsci called the 'ethico-political' level) which build on and catalyse its
political networks and organisation. According to Gramsci, the cata-
lyst is provided by, 'An appropriate political initiative [which] is
always necessary to liberate the economic thrust from the dead
weight of traditional policies [and ideas] – i.e. to change the political
direction of certain forces which have to be absorbed if a new,
homogeneous politico-economic historical bloc, without internal contradictions, is to be successfully formed'. (Gramsci, 1971: 168)

This aspect of Gramsci's thought provides an inspiration for this
essay because it has potentially far-reaching implications for a new
approach to the study of international relations as Cox (1983) has
demonstrated. It implies the necessity of considering global structural
change and world orders in terms of the dialectics of their normative
(ethical, ideological, practical) as well as material dimensions.

Our contribution here mainly concerns the theory of power. We
assume that theories of power and hegemony must subsume both
normative and material, structural and existential (behavioural, rela-
tional) dimensions of social relations. Part of the richness of Gramsci's
concepts is that they combine these elements. Because of this, they
offer clues for overcoming the gulf between structure and agency.
We believe a possible key to the resolution of the structure–action
problem in social theory more generally, and international relations
theory in particular may be through the development of mediating
concepts such as structural power and historic bloc.[2]

HISTORIC BLOCS AND REGIMES OF ACCUMULATION

Some recent writers have suggested that capitalism is entering into a transnational, post-Fordist stage, which, in significant
respects, differs from the imperialist/welfare nationalist (national

94

capitalist), Fordist stage analyzed by Classical Marxists (see Brewer, 1980: 79-130). Applying Gramsci's ideas internationally, and to this particular stage, Cox (1987: 355–98) has demonstrated that it is possible to conceive of new forms of state, hegemony and the formation of historic blocs on a world scale.

It can then be theorised what role such blocs might play in promoting broad changes in the process of capitalist development. This includes shifts from one type of *social structure of accumulation* to another within the broader confines of a particular *mode of production* (Cox, 1987: 17–34, 309–53, and his two chapters in this volume). Cox's concept of social structure of accumulation is paralleled by that of a *regime of accumulation*, used by the French Regulationist School (Noel, 1987; Jessop, 1988). We assume that such a regime involves class and intra-class relations. This includes the mode of life and composition of the labour force, its political organisation, the labour process (in its technical, organisational and human aspects) and legal regulation of work. It also involves 'forms of regulation' concerning the scope of markets and the freedom of enterprise at both national and global levels. A regime therefore broadly encompasses the forms of socio-economic reproduction which together constitute the conditions of existence of economic development in a particular historical period or epoch. As such there may be different regimes of accumulation (e.g. capitalist or that of 'existing socialism') coexisting at any point in time. Where Cox's concept differs from that of most of the regulationists is that it is less state-centric and is thus more flexible in allowing for changing forms of politics and the state, including the internationalisation or globalisation of the state (see his concluding essay to this collection)

De Vroey (1984) sketches out two dominant regimes of accumulation which have characterised modern capitalism. The first, 'extensive regime' (roughly encompassing the first three-quarters of the nineteenth century) was associated with relatively competitive industrial structures and less capital-intensive forms of production than in the later, 'intensive' regime, which more fully emerged in the twentieth century. The first regime was associated with a rather narrow domain of state intervention and, to a certain extent, a doctrine of economic liberalism. Moreover, political democracy and workers' organisations were very underdeveloped. The second, and somewhat more democratic regime, was characterised by more capital intensive, mass production systems and a gradual rise in real wages. It was accompanied by wide-ranging state intervention, especially as regards monetary and macroeconomic management, and the promotion of education, training, research and development. It was also associated with the widespread growth of trade unionism, left-wing political parties, corporatist planning, and the consolidation of the welfare state. Charles Maier (1988) has called this complex of policies and class compromises the 'politics of productivity'. At the international level, these two regimes of accumulation coincided, respectively, with a period of British hegemony and the Gold Standard and an international balance of power, and the second after 1945 with American globalism, integral or organic alliances between the USA and the other major metropolitan capitalist states, and the Bretton Woods system, counterpoised to the Soviet bloc of 'existing socialism' and China.

What were the key international elements in the post-1945 regime of accumulation which generated uniquely rapid economic growth throughout the industrialised capitalist world? We would suggest at least four. The first was the construction of a US-centred economic, security and political structure for the non-communist world, ensuring peaceful conditions at the capitalist core (in sharp contrast to the 1914–45 years). The second, closely related element, was the ability of the US to maintain the growth of global aggregate demand through its balance of payments deficits, partly generated by heavy overseas military expenditures. The third element was the substantial congruence of ideas, institutions and policies among the leading capitalist nations, in a system of 'embedded liberalism' (Ruggie, 1982). This involved the emergence and consolidation of ideology of the 'mixed economy.' Along with the rise of the Cold War, this was important in the reconstitution (or creation) of the legitimacy of the liberal-democratic form of rule in the West and in Japan. A fourth element was the cheap and plentiful supply of raw materials, especially oil.

Cementing this order was what we term a new *international historic bloc* of social forces, centred in the USA, which came to be the socio-political centrepiece of the post-war organic alliance in the 'West'. This bloc originated in the outward expansion of emerging social forces within the USA. The leading elements in this constellation sought to internationalise New Deal principles and associated forms of Fordist capital-intensive, mass-consumption accumulation, and to extend opportunities for exports and/or foreign direct investment, both in manufacturing and extractive industries, notably in oil. The bloc also encompassed financial interests on Wall Street which sought wider investment opportunities overseas and a more comprehensive international role for the dollar. However, this bloc brought together not only fractions of productive and financial capital, but also

96

elements in the state apparatuses, centrist political parties and non-communist organised labour in the major capitalist nations. Forces associated with the bloc in the US were able to forge links consciously with counterparts in Europe, to form a concept of a transatlantic political community (van der Pijl, 1984; Gill, 1990).

What needs to be emphasised here, therefore, is that the concept of an international historic bloc means much more than an alliance of capitalist interests across national boundaries. It implies that elements of more than one class were involved, its basis was more organic and rooted in material and normative structures of society, that is, 'in the governmental and social institutions and civil societies of a number of countries, including weak states . . . [Hence] the alliance of social forces it comprises is seen as "natural" and legitimate by most of its members'. (Gill, 1986a: 211)

Viewed from this perspective, the post-war mix of social democracy, and the 'mixed economy' incorporated a range of class interests which sustained the emerging liberal international economic order. This maintained its coherence and continuity for approximately twenty-five years after 1945, although the appearance of continuity in this period can be considered to be deceptive, since certain contradictory forces were at work which would, in the long-term, erode the basis of the regime of accumulation and the integral nature of the associated international historic bloc. Examples of such forces were the growing knowledge-intensivity of production and organisational systems and the related gradual rise in the importance of transnational capital, especially financial capital, highlighted in the growth of the Euro-markets since the 1960s. At the same time, the scale and scope of welfare expenditures were also growing, as were state expenditures as a proportion of GNP.

In a structural sense, what was occurring in the post-war period was the emergence of a globally integrated economy whilst political regulation at the domestic level was becoming ever-more comprehensive. We discuss this below, in terms of the simultaneous and in some ways contradictory growth in the 'power' of both states and markets.

STATES, MARKETS AND THE POWER OF CAPITAL

Both markets and states long preceded industrial capitalism. However, the latter was historically associated with the growth of integrated capital markets. Whilst Marxist writers have typically stressed the emergence of wage labour markets as a defining feature of capitalism we suggest that the emergence of elaborate capital markets is at least as important, and we concentrate on this below.

Markets have normally required some form of political organisation and protection, usually provided by the state. By the same token, governmental institutions require finance. This need creates an added interest in both facilitating and regulating markets, for example to obtain taxes. However, extensive regulations and restrictions often lower profits and breed forms of evasion (e.g. smuggling, black markets, financial 'innovation'). The incentive for capital to evade controls is greater if national regulations vary, especially if technical obstacles in transport and communications are reduced, that is as capital becomes more mobile. The growth in the Euromarkets since the 1960s is an important example of this, one which we relate below to the structural power of capital. Just as capital seeks the most propitious conditions for investment, states compete to attract capital flows and direct investments. Under the recessionary conditions of the 1980s, this gave rise to *competitive deregulation* of different national capital markets. Competitive deregulation is a misnomer, however, since it went with attempts to redefine market rules under new conditions. However, most crucial was that the process progressively reduced the barriers to the international mobility of financial capital, creating a more integrated and global capital market.

In this sense, there is an evolving dialectical relationship between the nature and scope of markets, and the forms of state regulation, especially as knowledge, technology and transportation change. The dialectic involves both domestic and international dimensions of state activity, which seek to reconcile the potentially global reach of economic activity with the socially and territorially specific aspects of political rule. The latter is circumscribed by the problems of legitimation, mobilisation and communication in political time and space. Thus *capital as a social relation, depends on the power of the state to define, shape and be part of a regime of accumulation.* By capital as a social relation we have in mind the contrast between those with a substantial or even privileged ownership, control or access to both financial and/or physical assets, in contrast to the bulk of the remainder of society (most of labour and their dependents).

The form of different regimes of accumulation provides the wider context for our discussion of contemporary state-capital relations and the question of the structural power of markets. We will argue that the widening of the scope of the market, in the 1980s and probably during the 1990s, along with certain changes in technology and communications, contributes to the rising structural power of internationally-mobile capital. By contrast, the state (as an institutional and social entity) also creates the possibility for the limitation of such structural power. This is partly because of the political goods and services which it supplies to capitalists and because of the institutional autonomy it possesses. The stance of the state towards freedom of enterprise, in a given regime of accumulation, is at the heart of this issue.

At the domestic level, the distinction between direct and structural forms of the power of capital or of 'business', has already been well-developed (see note 2). Direct aspects of business power and influence, relative to labour, include its financial resources, expertise, contacts with government and control over much of the media. Business has a privileged ability to influence governments, for example through lobbying. Moreover, in oligopolistic industries, large firms possess some *market power* over prices and perhaps wages. This can be contrasted with the case of highly competitive markets where both buyers and sellers are subject to the *power of the market*. An instance of the latter case is the behaviour of highly competitive financial markets (in which governments borrow regularly). In this type of conceptualisation, much of it inspired by Lindblom (1977), business (and capital) is viewed as a type of privileged vested interest in a more-or-less pluralist (polyarchical) political system. By contrast, Marxists associate business with capital as a class. As such, analysis of its power implies a deeper, socio-structural dimension, inherent in the capitalist system. None the less, the power of capital in general needs to be distinguished from the power and influence of particular fractions of capital.

Here, our chief concern is to analyse the power of those fractions of capital which are both large-scale and internationally-mobile. This category includes both some fractions of 'productive capital' (in manufacturing and extraction) and 'financial capital' (e.g. financial services, such as banking, insurance and stockbroking). The power of capital in general partly rests upon the degree of division which exists between different fractions of capital, or what Lindblom would call different sections of business. At the same time, of course, competitive pressure may mean that co-operation between capitalists within different fractions is difficult or even impossible to achieve. None the less, in virtually all analysis of the conflicts and divisions which divide capitalists, the concept of power used is a behavioural one. Thus the focus is on the way a given group of capitalists seeks to exert direct power and influence over others or the state apparatus.

Whilst this dimension is essential, it needs to be combined with an investigation of structural power. Indeed, the more striking are the divisions within its ranks, the more crucial the structural aspect of capital's power becomes.

This structural aspect is associated with both material and normative dimensions of society (such as market structures and the role of ideology). These may or may not be mutually reinforcing. The tenacity of normative structures is illustrated by how, in modern economies, consistently higher priority is given to economic growth relative to other goals (such as conservation). Another illustration of this concerns the assumptions and claims made about the conditions for the achievement of growth. With respect to capitalist economies, Lindblom (1977: 170-88) suggests that businesspeople are able to claim an expertise of public value, partly because there is widespread acceptance of the view that economic growth is fundamentally dependent on investment and innovation by private enterprise.

Acceptance of these assumptions and claims by politicians and the public means that governments have to be concerned with the cultivation of an appropriate 'business climate', or else investment might be postponed, and a recession might be precipitated. An elected socialist party, with a radical programme, would therefore be constrained in its policy choices by the nature of the 'business climate', not least because it would need tax revenue (and/or loans) to finance its ambitious spending plans.[3] An assumption behind these arguments is that there is a market for capital, enterprise and inventiveness, and the supply of these will be reduced by higher taxation. Indeed, such arguments are the essence of so-called 'supply-side' economics which became influential in the USA in the 1980s.[4]

There is a striking contrast between the ability of capital and labour to shape policy in the long-term under capitalist conditions. Whereas an 'investment strike' by business may occur spontaneously if the business climate deteriorates, labour, in order to exert corresponding influence, would have to directly organise a wide-ranging or even general strike. The example of an 'investment strike' is a case of structural power, uniquely available to business. This power works primarily through the market mechanism in capitalist economies. Whereas a reduced willingness to invest for productive purposes usually comes about gradually, the supply of finance to governments through the purchase of government bonds and bills may decline very rapidly. This might result in the government being unable to finance its current activity unless it resorted to monetary inflation.

100

Such inflation would, from the point of view of business, cause the 'investment climate' to further deteriorate, so prolonging he 'investment strike'. Thus capital, and particularly the financial fractions of capital, may have the power to indirectly discipline the state. In so far as many of the top financiers have access to the government leaders, this indirect power may be supplemented by direct use of power, e.g. lobbying, and 'gentlemanly' arm-twisting. However, such arm-twisting is secondary to what can be termed the 'power of markets', notably the financial markets. This power constrains the participants in the market, including the government when it needs to raise finance.

Some of the points made above fit in with the notion of a hegemonic ideology which serves the class interests of capital relative to those of labour. At the heart of this are the ideas that private property and accumulation are sacrosanct, and that without the private sector growth would be endangered. A specific case of the force of such ideas was the way in which monetarist ideas about the need to control inflation became widely accepted and embodied in deflationary policies, in the Western countries during the late 1970s and early 1980s. This commitment was reflected, for example, in discussions during and communiqués of the seven-power Economic Summits (Putnam and Bayne, 1984). The late 1970s was, of course, before conservative governments were in power in most of the Summit nations. None the less monetary targets rapidly became commonplace, mandating 'discipline' in goods and labour markets. Either wages had to be restrained, or, according to the logic of these policies, workers would 'price themselves out of jobs'.

In Britain, Thatcherism involved not just a change in policies but a conscious effort to change ideas and expectations about the appropriate role of government, the importance of private enterprise and the virtues of markets. The aim has been to convince voters that 'there is no alternative' to Thatcherism (if they wish to grow steadily more prosperous). It can thus be argued that a Gramscian form of hegemony favouring capital was being reconstructed.[5] However, this polarised labour–capital analysis can itself be criticised as over-simplified, particularly as it fails to distinguish between transnational and national fractions of capital, and says little about the political and ideological contradictions associated with Thatcherism, which entailed jingoism and racism whilst encouraging Japanese foreign direct investment, and the use of economic and physical violence to defeat selected political opponents (as in the 1984–5 mining dispute) whilst the bulk of the mainstream of the Conservative Party still spoke in terms of 'One nation' Toryism.

THE BEHAVIOURAL POWER OF CAPITAL: THE GLOBAL DIMENSION

Turning now to the world level, given the rise of transnational corporations and of international capital mobility, monetary and information flows and communications links, a *global* analysis of the power of capital is essential (Gill and Law, 1988; United Nations, 1988).[6] Realist analysis is backward here, although some writers on interdependence (e.g. Keohane and Nye, 1977) have shown an awareness of international capital mobility. Neo-classical economists have examined the bargaining power of transnational corporations, and the determinants and policy consequences of short-term capital flows, but have neglected the institutional and ideological aspects of power. This shortcoming also applies to many Marxists (e.g. Radice, 1975).

With respect to direct, behavioural forms of power, while Lindblom has distinguished between authority (associated with governments) and markets (associated with private enterprise) at the national level, it is also the case that transnational corporations exert authority across national boundaries when they allocate resources internationally. Corporate headquarters often decides on the geographical location of production. Transnationals make investment decisions on a global scale, shifting funds from one country to another. Certain subsidiaries are kept from exporting their production, since others are allocated that function. Different subsidiaries engage in intra-firm trading at 'transfer', rather than 'arms length' prices. This means that, to some extent, the output of their subsidiaries (which may be vast, and collectively perhaps greater than the GNP of many countries) is taken out of the market-place, and is allocated, in Lindblom's terms 'authoritatively' within a single transnational firm. This implies that it is allocated consciously, and politically. A dramatic instance of this intra-firm power is when a factory is opened in one country, at the same time as one performing the same functions, is closed or not built in another. Of course, the scope for the use of this type of power is constrained by political pressures and competition from other firms. The fewer the number of competitors, the less the constraints are likely to be. Indeed, if there are only a few firms, oligopolistic collusion is much more likely, producing similar patterns of behaviour on the part of several firms.

The market power of oligopolistic firms in certain industries operates at an international level. The classic case is that of the so-called 'Seven Sisters' in the international oil industry (Sampson, 1975). The seven oil 'majors' (five American-owned, one British, and one Anglo-Dutch) dominated the world oil industry from the 1920s until the end of the 1960s. Posted prices were fixed at agreed levels between the companies. This meant that differences in marginal and transport costs were not consistently reflected in prices. This led to a situation where the oil companies were able to exert power over many parts of the Third World. This case also illustrates the interrelatedness of direct forms of economic and military power. The inroads of Western, especially British, oil firms in the Middle East between 1900–40 were built upon British military power in the region. The profit-making interests of British Petroleum and Shell, and the security interests of the British Empire went hand-in-hand. BP lobbied the British government for military action when its Iranian assets were nationalised in 1953. The British government then turned to the US CIA to secure the return to power of the Shah. Denationalisation followed with BP regaining some of its former stake, the rest going to American majors (Blair, 1976).

So far we have referred to transnational corporations lobbying their parent governments in order to obtain policies favourable to their operations overseas. Such lobbying also takes place with regard to host governments, as well as international organisations, such as the World Bank (Payer, 1982). Transnational financial networks are particularly well-developed, and links between commercial banks, central banks, the IMF and World Bank are illustrated in a number of international forums: for example, the Bank for International Settlements.

The international patterns of elite interaction – between business, state officials, bureaucrats, and members of international organisations – and the networks they generate, have not been thoroughly researched or understood, at least in comparison with domestic networks. However, some organisations such as the Bilderberg meetings (which began in 1954), and the Trilateral Commission (formed in 1973) are explicitly concerned to foster social interaction, networks and a shared outlook amongst the international establishments of the major capitalist countries. Similar interaction is found within intergovernmental organisations such as the OECD, which organises conferences and research initiatives. What is crucial to note is that there are elements of a common perspective, at least with respect to the role of international business and private enterprise, which cuts across all of these institutional forums. Whilst research on aspects of strategic consciousness and ideology-formation at the elite level is in its infancy, some work has identified the way in which the business and government leaders of different countries seek to develop a common outlook on the general conditions of existence of the international order, although not one which is homogeneous on all issues. There is much debate over a number of key questions, such as the welfare state, East–West relations and the regulation of global capital and exchange markets (Gill, 1990). What we are suggesting, however, is that during the 1970s and 1980s, the emphasis, certainly with regard to economic policy, has shifted towards a definition of questions and concepts which is more congruent with the interests of large-scale, transnational capital.[7]

The people active in transnational networks are increasingly well-served by a range of international periodicals, such as *The Financial Times*, *The Economist*, *The Far Eastern Economic Review* and the *Wall Street Journal*. The process of elite interaction and network-building helps to shape the agenda for those state policies which affect the operation of transnational capital. In so far as international organisations accept a framework of thought that serves the interests of capital, they are likely to exert influence and sometimes even pressure (for example in IMF loan conditions) on national governments of a sort which is congruent with that exerted by business. Several writers have suggested that the elements mentioned above are coming together to produce a 'transnational' capitalist class or class fraction, with its own particular form of 'strategic' class consciousness (Cox, 1979; van der Pijl, 1984; Gill, 1990). This consciousness involves a long-term time horizon, and consideration of the general conditions under which transnational capital operates, as well as of more specific, immediate and 'crisis management' issues. However, the time horizons of fractions of transnational capital vary, with private financial capital often displaying a more short-term outlook, one which is perhaps less 'strategic'. A plausible example of the latter was the way in which leading commercial banks, in their efforts to recycle surplus petrodollars, rushed into making loans to less-developed countries in the mid-1970s. However, it is questionable whether governments of the leading capitalist countries were much more aware of the dangers of such loans than were the banks (Frieden, 1981; see also Lipson, 1981; Pfister and Suter, 1987).

THE STRUCTURAL POWER OF CAPITAL: THE GLOBAL DIMENSION

We noted earlier the importance of the business or investment climate and the concept of business confidence. Today, capital is so internationally mobile, especially between the major capitalist economies, that the 'investment climate' of one country will be judged by business with reference to the climate which prevails elsewhere. Transnational corporations routinely appraise the legal freedoms (e.g. to remit profits), production costs, labour relations, political stability, and financial concessions offered by many different countries. This is popularly known as 'political risk analysis' (Schollhamer, 1978). They also examine the size and growth potential of a country's market. As a result, governments are increasingly constrained in their freedom of manoeuvre by the economic policies of other states, as well as the investment decisions of internationally mobile capital. Indeed, such appraisals are made on a daily or even hourly basis by market analysts and investors in the financial sectors (Frieden, 1987).

French attitudes to foreign investment have tended to be highly nationalist, especially under de Gaulle. During the 1960s, a tough stance was taken with regard to the entry of foreign businesses, notably American ones. The fear was that US transnationals would be a Trojan horse to undermine French economic sovereignty. None the less, by the end of that decade, the French government felt it wise to adopt a more welcoming and flexible position with regard to foreign firms in high-technology industries. Exclusion of such firms from France simply resulted in them locating in a neighbouring member of the European Community (EC), from where they could avoid tariff barriers and supply the French market. Under the socialist government of President Mitterand in the 1980s, French attitudes became more 'flexible', even to the extent of welcoming some Japanese firms, after years of complaining of Japanese inroads. Similar flexibility was also shown in a range of other nationalist, mercantilist, and even communist countries, such as in China, and in much of the developing world (United Nations, 1988). Such flexibility makes it all the easier for transnationals to play-off one government against another in their search for concessions. Indeed, in some countries, different regions often compete to win such foreign investment. This phenomenon is visible in countries as diverse in character as the USA, Britain and China. At the national level, a key question for research is how far can and will the central government regulate the competition for foreign investment by different regions (and their state or local administrations). For example, in the US case the institution of federalism makes the creation and implementation of a unified nation-wide policy very difficult. In turn, this situation makes it easier for foreign (as well as domestic) capital to play off one state against another and increase its relative bargaining power.

At the international level, the bargaining power of transnational corporations would be reduced if most national governments were able to co-ordinate their regulations and financial concessions. However, even supposedly like-minded, and wealthy countries, bound together in a collective economic organisation like the EC have not been able to seriously discuss, let alone achieve this goal. Even if governments of some member states were so inclined, given the EC voting rules, there would almost certainly be others (such as Britain) who would oppose such measures, and veto any such policy initiative. It remains to be seen whether the process of EEC political and economic union will change this situation (Gill, 1992). In an age of transnational firms states may be forced to adopt neo-mercantilist policies in order to compete better to attract foreign direct investment, in order to obtain the sinews of power (skills, capital and technology). This reinforces the structural power of transnational corporations, in contrast to national firms, a power which owes much to the division of the world into many states. Thus the threat of nationalisation is less crushing to a transnational company, since it is likely that only a small proportion of its assets would be expropriated by a single country. The purely national firm is more at the mercy of its own government.

We have already seen how business confidence in a government may depend on its economic policies, including its macroeconomic policies. Ideas about 'sound finance' and 'fighting inflation' constrain governments. Such ideas may spread from one country to another. The pursuit of such policies is likely to attract more foreign investment (other things being equal). The response of firms to such policies and other determinants of the investment climate is often gradual, and spread over a number of years. As has been noted, financial capital can react to government policies, or expected policies, much more rapidly than productive capital. With the liberalisation of capital flows between the major capitalist economies (and some less-developed countries) the reaction of financial capital need not be one of postponement of investment (as in an 'investment strike'). Instead, huge sums of money can quickly flow out of a country to more attractive havens. The result of this can be a balance of payments crisis under fixed exchange rates, or a foreign exchange crisis (fall in the exchange rate), under floating exchange rates. A falling exchange rate brings with it increased risks of rising inflation, especially for a small, open economy. Hence, the international mobility of financial capital can swiftly force governments which deviate from policies seen as suitable by the 'market' to change course. For example, governments may be driven to raise interest rates, tighten monetary policy, and thus create a rise in unemployment to offset a currency, or payments crisis. This is in fact precisely what occurred in Britain in 1976, although in this case, the Labour government was able to blame the IMF (the media generally blamed the unions) for imposing its austerity policies. The point was, however, that against a background of high inflation, Britain would have had to change its policies in this direction anyway or there would have been a further collapse in the international value of sterling. The socialist French government changed course after 1981 because of the same types of international pressures (Cobham, 1984).

From the above example, it is tempting to reinterpret the Thatcher slogan, so that it would become 'there is no alternative', in the long-term to providing a business climate, attractive by international standards. In other words the conquest of inflation would be just one aspect of a wider doctrine. We have already noted how the major capitalist states adopted macroeconomic policies premised on the 'war on inflation' from the late 1970s to the mid-1980s. One explanation of the adoption of such policies is, of course, because of the power of markets. However, there is nothing inevitable or automatic about a particular policy response to changes in market conditions, or to the business climate. What may have been crucial in the adoption of monetarist policies was the growing acceptance of a policy outlook amongst political leaders, as well as central and private bankers, which meant that no significant alternative (to market monetarism) was actually contemplated, except in one or two major capitalist states, such as France (see OECD, 1977; Pinder et al., 1979; Putnam and Bayne, 1984; Volcker, 1985). Where such policies are adopted, with little reflection on, or more realistically, belief in the credibility of possible alternatives, the power of capital attains a hegemonic status. Outside the US, of the major capitalist states, this process may have gone furthest in the socio-economic laboratory of Thatcher's Britain, although even here, the attachment to, for example, the National Health Service, is considerable (Grant with Sargent, 1987). We are not suggesting that a transnational hegemony has been attained, or is likely to be in this century. However, the social forces making for such a hegemony, based on free enterprise and open markets, have become more prominent in the 1980s. At this point, however, the question arises, who benefits from such a hegemony?

The impact of increased capital mobility, and also of recessions, has worked to the advantage of large-scale transnational capital, relative to national capital. Transnational capital is not entirely dependent on the business conditions of one country, in the way that purely national firms obviously are. When a recession in one country occurs, it will be easier for transnational corporations to survive or prosper than it is for national firms. A notable example of this was the ability of Ford Motor Company to survive large losses in its US operations during the recession of the early 1980s through drawing on the profits of overseas subsidiaries, a trend which has continued. Indeed, the process of restructuring, whereby weak firms are either made bankrupt, or else taken over by the stronger survivors, is likely to work systematically to the advantage of transnational capital, particularly in the manufacturing sector (United Nations, 1988). Britain in the 1980s provided a clear example of this process (Young et al., 1988).

While the structural power of transnational capital has risen relative to that of governments since World War II (except perhaps in primary industries), it has also risen relative to that of organised labour.[8] Transnational, but not national firms, can threaten unions with plant closures and relocation of investment to other countries. Countries with relatively weak, or politically controlled labour movements, will, other things being equal, tend to attract investment at the expense of countries with strong, independent labour movements. For example, part of the American electronics industry shifted to Asian countries like Singapore and Taiwan in the 1960s. Such tendencies have also been at work *within* particular capitalist countries, for example in the USA over the last two decades, with a shift of manufacturing towards the relatively non-unionised ('sun-belt') states of the South and West, away from the ('rustbelt') North-East and Mid-West, where unionisation was traditionally strong. The wider point to be made here is that the 'new international division of labour', where some manufacturing has been selectively located in the Newly-Industrialising Countries (NICs), is merely one of various manifestations of the rising power of transnational capital, relative to national capital, and to labour, especially in the core capitalist states.

On the other hand, it might be noted that some of the most

successful firms from the NICs have themselves gone transnational and invested in the core capitalist countries (United Nations, 1988: 2). It is important not to overstate the exodus of manufacturing from the core: there has been some internationalisation, but it has frequently been exaggerated (Gordon, 1988). This may be because much potential foreign direct investment is discouraged by adverse political, as well as economic conditions. There is also recent evidence that changes in communications, production technologies and organisational systems, as well as a need for a base in each of the three largest market areas are causing production to shift back to the US, the EC and the Pacific Rim (United Nations, 1988). The general point is not that capital will flee to the NICs in the face of labour militancy, but that it will move to other countries, often ones within the capitalist core.

In the past, the power of capital implied in the 'new international division of labour' might have been countervailed to a certain extent. In the 1950s and 1960s organised labour was relatively stronger in the core states and appeared to have the potential to organise internationally. By the 1980s, such a potential was substantially undermined. Unionised workers of different states found themselves in a similar position to that of their national governments: that is, competing to attract foreign investment. Much higher levels of unemployment put them on the defensive (Gordon, 1988). In Britain, after union resistance to workplace reorganisation declined in the 1980s, there was an influx of foreign direct investment, much of it from Japan and the USA. Some of this was motivated also by companies wishing to gain a stronger foothold in a politically hospitable EC member before the creation of an integrated internal market in 1992. There was also some 'return' of the US electronics industry partly because American unions were weakened, partly because of the introduction of new organisational and production/distribution systems, such as just-in-time (JIT) inventory systems which require component suppliers to be close to assemblers and final markets (United Nations, 1988: 8–9).

With regard to the structural power of capital, the key contrast at the international level is the relative mobility of capital, and the relative immobility of labour in most sectors of activity. However, it is important to qualify this point in respect of skilled, knowledge-intensive labour. This is often internationally-mobile, at least between capitalist countries. In certain high-technology industries (where transnational corporations often predominate), the USA has been able to draw talent (scientists, engineers, managers) from many other countries. The same applies to that most knowledge-intensive 'industry', academia. Such skilled labour is crucial to the economic strength of both countries and transnationals. To date, the most knowledge-intensive activities (e.g. research and development) have tended to be carried out mainly in the parent country of the transnational company. As a result, some national characteristics have continued to feature in the corporate culture of many of these firms. As Robert Cox (1983) has suggested, the incorporation of these skilled workers is vital to the achievement of a transnational historic bloc, that is the forging of links across not only national boundaries, but also classes, to create the conditions for a hegemony of transnational capital. Crucial in this context are what Gramsci called 'organic intellectuals', i.e., those able to theorise the conditions of existence of the system as a whole, suggest policies and justifications for such policies and, if need be to apply them. Such intellectuals need to synthesise both a strategic vision with the technical and political ability to realise it in practice (Gill, 1986a: 210–16).

These changes can be interpreted as signs of the emergence of a new regime of accumulation. In Britain change was accompanied by trade union legislation, as well as a demonstration of the resolve of the government to defeat organised labour during the prolonged 1984-5 miners' strike. The government sought to alter the attitudes of the unions towards a 'new realism' (Crick, 1985). Differences over the desirability of (growing) single union and no-strike deals resulted in splits within the labour movement. Similar splits also emerged in American labour unions, with a two-tier wages system in several industries. New workers have lower pay and less job security than established workers doing identical work (Dodsworth, 1983). The position of organised labour in these countries contrasted with that elsewhere in Western Europe, where unions often fared better.

Although the position of traditional organised labour appears reduced in the emerging transnational historic bloc, this may not necessarily imply a much narrower bloc than that of the post-war boom years. The decline cf unions in the last twenty years has been associated, not just with the internationalisation of production, but with a sectoral shift away from 'traditional' manufacturing towards services. Indeed, this sectoral shift is 'The most important change in international direct investment in the past 10–15 years. While only one-quarter of FDI [foreign direct investment] was in the services sector at the beginning of the 1970s, this share had risen to 40 per cent ($300 billion) of the world stock and some 50 per cent ($25 billion) of annual flows by the mid-1980s) . . . concentrated on the developed market economies' (United Nations, 1988: 42).

Whilst this sectoral shift and the international transformation it is linked to would appear to have set back the prospects for international trade unionism based upon traditional workers' organisations, it opens up the prospect of a wider incorporation of workers and other interests, including foreign governments, into a transnational historic bloc. This is for four main reasons. First, many service subsidiaries, because of the intangible and perishable nature of service activity, carry out similar activities to those of the parent company and offer higher rates of pay than their national competitors, that is skill levels are not centralised in parent companies. Second, skill levels spread to host countries and represent a considerable transfer of skills and technology. Third, transnationals are rapidly building affiliate networks. Finally, these activities appear to offer considerable growth in employment opportunities for the future (United Nations, 1988: 45–7).

At the same time, the proportion of female workers in the labour force has drastically increased. Apart from highly-skilled labour, these and many other manufacturing workers may yet be incorporated into the new bloc. This can happen, for example, through their links to, or involvement in, small family businesses and home-based contractual work in a new type of putting-out system. Control over such a system if facilitated by new communications and information technologies, and can be linked to the use of JIT inventory systems, pioneered by Japanese automobile producers.

At the ideological level, a struggle is under way for 'the hearts and minds' of the growing numbers of non-traditional members of the working class: they may see themselves as middle class, even though most of their current income comes from the application of their labour-power, rather than from property and financial assets. An implication of the above points is that far more needs to be known about the political impact of changes in industrial structure, the labour process, and the degree of labour mobility. These changes need to be related to the consolidation of an individualist consumer culture and the possibilities for collective action on the part of workers and consumers. Specifically, it seems likely that the emerging regime of accumulation will be dominated by information- and knowledge-intensive industries. Thus the organisation of the labour process, geographical location and ideological outlook of key workers in these fields is crucial to any kind of major change. Any successful transnational historic bloc would need to have comprehensively incorporated these relatively privileged workers.

Therefore, to conceive of historic blocs in purely material terms would be a fundamental mistake, since the broad contours of any new regime of accumulation will be partly shaped by the ideological climate at the national and global levels. Hence, developments in the media and in education may prove to be of major long-term importance. Apart from allowing for the generation of technologies and knowledge which allow for the co-ordination of economic and political activity, these sectors of activity also embody both ideological and material structures which operate increasingly on a world-wide basis, such as in advertising and sponsorship, which involves both professional and amateur sporting and cultural pursuits.

In the media and education, institutions have usually been under national control. Indeed, many centres of higher education, as well as telecommunication and radio and television companies have historically been in the public sector. However, given new technological developments (e.g. satellites, cable links for information processing), these sectors are likely to develop much more globally. Economies of scale in the production of television programmes, have put Western, especially American media corporations, at a competitive advantage to such a degree that the soap operas *Dynasty* and *Dallas* were shown in 108 countries in 1988. The importance of such scale economies may increase with the growth of satellite broadcasting. The cost of constructing and launching satellites is so great that costs are often shared through international business consortia, a trend which is interrelated with that developing in other sectors where consortia are proliferating (United Nations, 1988: 3). Satellite stations can broadcast to a number of countries simultaneously, breaking down national attempts to control foreign media access and output. In this context, transnational media companies have significant market power over their national competitors, power which is likely to increase if, as seems likely, more and more nations turn to the widespread use of English as either their first or second language. With the growth of English as the major international means of higher educational communication, the scope for transnational corporations is also immense, particularly if one considers that the major research universities and institutes in the USA already operate in several countries. The scope for these trends to develop is widened by a movement towards a more internationally competitive market in higher education, as well as the media. Proponents of capitalist, especially transnational hegemony, may therefore have an interest in promoting policies favourable to the rapid growth of satellite broad-casting. They are likely to seek to downgrade national public broad-casting institutions, or forge links with them in order to reshape news and advertising output.

THE POWER OF CAPITAL: LIMITS AND CONTRADICTIONS

There are a variety of social forces which may run counter to the interests of capital in general. While we examine some of these, we are particularly interested in those which may serve to limit the rise in the power of transnational capital. Essential to the analysis of these social forces are contradictions which affect the state-civil society relationship at both domestic and global levels.

There is neither stasis nor uniformity in capitalism. In order for capital to reproduce itself it needs profitably to use labour-power: capital is in a dialectical class relationship with labour. As has been noted, this relationship develops within a regime of accumulation which provides the broader conditions which establish the scope and opportunities for investment and growth. In this sense, the form and character of state institutions, in the narrow or extended sense, are a central component of any regime of accumulation. As was noted implicitly in our previous discussion of Lindblom, this raises the issue of the relative autonomy of the state. Lindblom suggests that in a 'polyarchical' capitalist system, the state will tend to serve the interests of capital. What is at issue, therefore, are the dimensions along which this relationship may vary, so as to place limits on the power of capital. One axis of variation is the state's orientation towards national and transnational capital. That is, what is the balance of forces between nationalists and internationalists within the ensemble of state institutions? Which institutions are most associated with internationalist, and which with mercantilist ideas and policies? A state apparatus may be internally divided so that it lacks both cohesion and consistency in its foreign economic policies. This was the case for the USA in the 1920s and 1930s (Frieden, 1988).

The logical corollary of this from the viewpoint of economic liberals who seek to increase the power of capital is to change the orientations and outlook of the bureaucracy, whilst simultaneously dismantling supports for declining industries. For example, incentives encourag-ing efficiency, elements of competition within the public sector, and a reduction in social and job security would serve to weaken the forces which support the forms of welfarist Mercantilism we

113

have noted above. The Japanese method (increasingly used in the UK) is to rotate regularly leadership positions between the private sector and government, so that bureaucrats become more strongly imbued with market values, diluting their distinct professional identity. Years of public service prior to taking up private sector posts may enhance the national orientation of private enterprise: the term 'Japan Incorporated' partly reflects this state of affairs. Hence, under certain conditions, such business-biased corporatism may consolidate cultural and institutional barriers to internationalisation.

In some developing countries similar constellations of state and industrial interests have emerged. These have often coalesced around a concept of 'strategic industries' under national control, sometimes, as in India, based on the Soviet planning model,

> the growth of the public sector was often associated with a nationalist ideology, sometimes born of struggles for independence. In countries like India, nationalist and socialist ideas were fused. Nationalist ideas favoured the growth of military spending and the establishment of arms production. State-sponsored military-industrial development often became a feature of some less-developed countries. . . . However, this may be a transitional phase, reflecting the [economic] backwardness of some countries . . . at independence. (Gill and Law, 1988: 97)

One outcome of the experience of gaining independence, in countries like India, was an entrenched suspicion of foreign capital, and a determination to develop national capital (private or public), if need be, at very high investment outlays, and costs to consumers (Nayar, 1983). Historical experience and the form and quality of the state-civil society relationship are thus major considerations in understanding how far limits to the power of capital, especially transnational capital, will vary between countries. It would be unrealistic to expect the same range and degree of limitations to the power of capital to exist in each country; this is ultimately an empirical question, depending upon the relationship between state and civil society.

At the global level, limits to the power of transnational capital are grounded in contradictions in what, in Gramscian terms, would be called an embryonic international political society, and a still underdeveloped, but more discernible, internationalised civil society. International and domestic aspects of the limits to the power of capital are closely knit. For example, with regard to the political society, the strength of nationalism, concern with security, and of the military/public sector interests are directly related to the intensity of inter-state conflicts. As we have noted, the 1930s saw economic national-ism, militarism, and a pronounced shift towards regional economic blocs. This heightened the tendency towards an international political economy of rival national capitals. By contrast, the more 'orderly' periods of what realists call hegemonic leadership (Britain in the mid nineteenth century, the USA in the twenty-five years after World War II), gave more scope to 'liberal internationalist' elements in domestic political coalitions, and therefore, some extension of dom-estic civil society at the international level. In these more liberal periods, there was a rise in the relative and structural power of internationally mobile capital. In contrast, such structural power declined between the two world wars, as the form of the state–civil society relationship was more nationally circumscribed.

However, the significance of hegemonic leadership for the power of capital depends crucially on the nature of the political economy of the dominant states, and their domestic coalitions which control international economic policy. Both Britain and the USA were not only capitalist, but also in favour of liberal international economic policies. If the hegemonic state after World War II had been the USSR, then the power of capital would have been severely circum-scribed, as it came to be in Eastern Europe. The enlargement of the communist sphere with the 1949 Chinese communist victory extended the political constraints on the international mobility of capital, as well as making communist ideas more appealing, particu-larly in the Third World. Changes in the policies pursued in the communist states in the 1980s, notably in the Soviet Union, Eastern Europe and China towards a more liberal approach to private enterprise, markets, and international trade were, therefore, major enhancements of the power of capital. This is because they gave more scope and potential for foreign investment, and increased the number of states and regions competing to attract foreign capital.

While the power of internationally mobile capital may be weakened when inter-state rivalries are intense (especially among the major powers as in 1914–45), the structural aspect of its power owes much to the division of the world into competing states. Indeed, the relationship between transnational capital and the state has a contra-dictory character. Perhaps the power of internationally-mobile capital would be maximised by a world confederation, with states competing to attract foreign investment (as they do within the EC and the USA), and as the states of the Commonwealth of Independent States (CIS) are likely to do. Cooperation in such a confederation would be easier, the smaller the number of states, since communication would be simplified and the 'free-rider' temptation less pronounced, provided that the leaders in question shared a set of defining concepts of how the world works and a vision of the future. Given the latter, for a large number of states, substantial cooperation is easier if power resources are concentrated in the hands of relatively few states. This point has been developed with respect to the provision of international 'public goods' (Snidal, 1985). What is crucial, therefore, is which forces influence and shape state policy in the small number of key states in the capitalist system: are they 'internationalist' or 'nationalist' in outlook? With respect to the successors to the states of 'existing socialism', are dominant political groups in favour of participation in the structures of global capitalism, or do they wish to pursue autarkic development strategies?

From the viewpoint of capital, the question of the optimal number of states is a dialectical one. It involves tensions between both 'political' and 'economic' dimensions, and direct and structural forms of power, at the domestic and global levels. As has been noted, capital needs the state to provide public goods, including law and order, that is it inevitably requires direct coercive activity by the state. Thus, for capital, structural power is insufficient to sustain its hegemony. At the global level, the precise ways in which these public goods (or, more accurately, quasi-public goods) are provided is a matter for debate: are they to be provided by a hegemonic state, acting, as it were, as a substitute for a global *Leviathan*? Or are there other, emerging forms of international political authority which perform similar, and perhaps more legitimate functions? This is why, although the structural power of internationally mobile capital would be enhanced by having a large number of relatively small states, the problem of political and social order at the global level might be left unsolved.

However, the number of states, be it large or small, in any historical configuration is only one factor influencing the degree to which international co-operation and order is possible. As fundamental is the degree and type of international congruence between different state–civil society complexes (Cox, 1981). Another factor, alluded to above, is the adequacy of theorisations and models of the GPE, and the degree to which these can form the basis for a 'practical consensus' on the directions of policy amongst key states in the system (Cooper, 1985). Even if all these conditions were to be met, successful cooperation would still require massive amounts of accurate, up-to-date information. Much of this is not publicly available: it is either controlled by private institutions or by public agencies operating under conditions of secrecy. Much information is notoriously imperfect. For example, the aggregation of national balance of trade figures by the IMF in 1986 resulted in a world deficit of US $65 billion, instead of the theoretically necessary total of zero.

The general point to be made here is that there is no clear-cut ideal international political society which would promote transnational hegemony on a global scale, since any of the alternatives involves contradictory elements. Moreover, the question is a dynamic and historical one, since the conditions for the creation of hegemonic structures may be very different to those for its maintenance and development. As Cox (1983) has noted, the need for political consent within such structures is most crucial 'at the core', that is at the heart of the system, where capitalist hegemony is at its most intense. What is still an open question is how far this core can be expanded to incorporate more states and interests from the periphery within an emerging transnational historic bloc. Attempts to sketch a strategy of this type have, in fact, been developed in the Trilateral Commission, with its concept of concentric rings of participation, with the major capitalist states at the centre and, in a more redistributive framework, by the Brandt Report (1980).

In the conditions of the late twentieth century, perhaps the best possible situation (for transnational capital) is the one which more-or-less exists in practice for the West, that is where the bulk of transnational capital is headquartered in a small number of economically large nations, ones in which capitalist hegemony is firmly embedded. However, this situation would be only be ideal if a 'restructured' USSR were to become a member of the capitalist inner-group, and was to do so with a reasonably broad based political support at the domestic level for the types of (painful) economic and political restructuring which would go with the transition to capitalism. The historical irony is, of course, that the origins of the current order owed a great deal, not just to US dominance in the West, but to the Soviet challenge from the East, and there is now much debate among Western theoreticians as to whether the eclipse of the USSR will dissolve the 'glue' of Western alliances and allow for a potential return to a quasi-Leninist vision of imperial rivalry between the USA, Japan and Western Europe.

In so far as there are any inhospitable socialist, or strongly nationalist states, pursuing autarkic economic strategies, transnational capital would perhaps prefer them not to be large, nor geographically contiguous. Change in the CIS and China (in the sense of adopting a more welcoming attitude to foreign capital) is

117

therefore of the first importance in this respect. Alternatively, the breakup of a large and relatively autarkic state, particularly one which is reluctant to liberalise its economy would result in an increase in the structural power of transnational capital. India is a possible case, although some limited liberalisation occurred in the 1980s. However, another key consideration for capital is the maintenance of orderly conditions for capital accumulation. Therefore, unrest in a country like India would need to be weighed against the possibility of regional wars in a sub-continent which might be divided into many states. Given this prospect, a more federal Indian state (along US lines) might be most favourable to transnational capital. Similar arguments could be applied to the ethnically diverse CIS, assuming it can sustain an inter-republic political settlement.

In addition, the proliferation of new states since 1947 has tended to increase the level of global militarisation, partly generated by a growing, quasi-capitalist international arms trade and by a more limited spread of arms production. Indeed, these two elements have combined to make possible a more competitive arms market, which is, as a consequence, now much less amenable to the control of the superpowers. Whilst militarisation has gone with the development of the internal security apparatuses of new states, it has also raised the possibility of severe wars, particularly in the Third World. The growth in terrorism is another aspect of these structural changes. One implication is that those interests within the state apparatus which wish to prioritise national security (even at the expense of civil liberties and democracy) are strengthened. They may ally with other statist and nationalist forces and reinforce a nationalist bloc, often protected by a veil of secrecy and other forms of political insulation. In this sense, the need of capital for stable political conditions for accumulation may be at the expense of substantial freedom of enterprise. Thus, whilst the structural power of capital is enhanced by a world of many states, its political conditions of operation may, in some ways, be weakened. Put another way, we are far from a situation in which a global political society is truly in prospect. The persistence of nationalist blocs and security complexes is mainly a problem, in this context, for transnational capital, since concepts of national security are likely to mean that such firms are denied equal access and treatment, when compared with national firms. This is most often the case in the sphere of military production.

The limits and contradictions that affect the formation of a transnational historic bloc and the attainment of transnational hegemony also arise with respect to market structures and economic policy. The internationalisation of production and finance and the spread of consumerism have resulted in an increasingly integrated world economy, as former social structures of accumulation and forms of state either disintegrate or are reconfigured. This means that it is becoming more plausible to apply Gramsci's concept of civil society to world orders (Cox, 1983). However, financial instability and policy perversity associated with what economists call 'fallacies of composition', pose both problems and opportunities for transnational capital. This is not to suggest that such composition effects are confined to economic matters: the search for security by each individual state may generate more insecurity for the world as a whole. In the monetary sphere, this fallacy may be manifested in the macroeconomic policies of governments, and the lending policies of banks. Other spheres where this fallacy can apply are in trade policy and with regard to the environment and ecosphere, as well as in the issue of global migration, which is related intimately to the restructuring of production and widening economic disparities, as well as political violence and instability.

More specifically, a transnational hegemony, involving banks, productive transnationals, highly skilled labour and governments, particularly if it is reflected in policies of 'market monetarism', is invested with contradictions. If all countries compete to prove their 'monetary soundness' their deflationary policies will have negative multiplier effects. World recession is the natural outcome, if all deflate simultaneously. The dangers of the hegemony of a strict financial orthodoxy were illustrated during the 1930s, particularly in the USA and the UK. In these countries a commitment to balanced budgets and monetary discipline made it difficult to reverse the slide into recession. Other countries more rapidly abandoned this orthodoxy, to the point where some capitalist states actively pursued policies to constrain the power of markets. One extreme example of this was Nazi Germany. The wider macroeconomic issue is that what may appear to be 'rational' policy from the point of view of one country, may, if replicated elsewhere, add up to 'collective irrationality' in a single, highly integrated world capitalist economy. This fallacy of composition was involved in the attempts by countries to export their unemployment through competitive depreciation and the restriction of imports during the 1930s. This led to a fall in the level of world trade, exchange rate instability, and a growing climate of international uncertainty which some writers claimed not only discouraged investment, but was one of the conditions which led to the outbreak of World War II (Kindleberger, 1973).

By contrast, in the 1980s there were signs that politicians, bankers and economists, meeting frequently in international conferences and other fora, were aware of the implications of this fallacy, and anxious to avoid them, in part through the international coordination of macroeconomic policies. For example, in 1986–7 a common view was that unless West Germany and Japan took steps to expand their economies, a slowing of world economic growth was inevitable. Such views were aired at the annual economic summits of the Group of Seven (G7) major capitalist countries, and were acted on in 1987 in that the leading capitalist countries allowed more rapid monetary expansion, so boosting demand and imports. This monetary expansion was associated with the large-scale purchase of dollars by the central banks of America's G7 partners. It came early in 1987 and continued after the stock market crash of October 1987. The contrast with the deflationary policies of the 1930s was striking, and it reflected the existence of an internationalised economic policy-making process in the G7, backed up by the IMF, the World Bank, the Bank for International Settlements and the OECD, as well as a perhaps more resilient and integrated world economic structure. However, such co-operation will need to become much greater if a new international regime of accumulation is to be established. This might involve further changes in the functions and resources of the IMF and the World Bank (see Feinberg, 1988).

Nevertheless, it remains the case that, during the 1880s and early 1990s, much of the world's population had endured a long-lasting economic depression with a massive fall in output, living standards and physical destruction of infrastructure and capital (e.g. the 'lost decade' in Latin America since the early 1980s; most of Africa for at least fifteen years; Eastern and Central Europe and the CIS since 1987–8). In many of these countries, decline has gone with the draconian application of IMF and World Bank policies of structural adjustment. The economic outlook for most OECD countries in the early 1990s was also relatively bleak: in Europe, for example, deflationary policies continued to be the norm, partly because of the high real interest rates in Germany to dampen the inflationary effects of rising budget deficits and wage demands in the wake of the unification of the two Germanies. Since the deutschemark is the anchor currency in the European Monetary System, this kept interest rates high in other countries. The USA was experiencing a deep and long-lasting recession, as was Canada, Australia and New Zealand. In Japan, economic growth was slowing. The financial centres in each of these countries appeared more fragile, and were beset by a spate of corruption cases and examples of massive fraud and, so it appeared, the global financial system seemed to lack adequate supervision or oversight.

In this regard, a further contradictory tendency within the GPE stems from the nature of markets, notably financial markets, in so far as they generate economic instability. Competition between banks can and has led to the creation of precarious debt structures and to myopic loans to some less-developed countries (as in the 1970s). There is evidence that in the 1970s, certain borrowing countries used such funds to bolster state capitalist enterprises relative to transnational manufacturing concerns, that is playing off one sector of international capital off against another (Frieden, 1981). This episode suggested both that the power of transnational capital was not sufficiently entrenched in such countries, so as to prevent the use of international finance for nationalist purposes, and that the lack of a collective strategy on the part of the banks had weakened their position. This contradiction is increased when there is a glut of international finance, such that the balance between state capital and transnational capital is tilted more in favour of the former.

At any rate the internationalised policy-process noted above managed, at least by the mid-1980s, to produce an extraordinary amount of co-operation amongst governments and banks in the G7, to manage the crisis, so avoiding the large-scale defaults which occurred in the 1930s. Lessons were not only learned from the 1930s, but also from the 1970s, in a more institutionalised, resilient and perhaps 'organically solid' international financial system (Pfister and Suter, 1987). These recent lessons, then, perhaps have been associated with an enhanced appreciation and analysis of economic interdependence. The significance of market instability, and indeed the estimation of its severity is not a constant. One reason is that the scope and organisation of markets may change. Another is because theoretical knowledge and policy sophistication also varies over time. Yet another is the way in which forms of regulation may prove inadequate to cope with the level of innovation which is generated under capitalism, as in, for example, the field of financial services. Here there is innovation in terms of ideas (e.g. 'rational expectations' models) and techniques (e.g. new financial assets). In the race to keep up with these developments, it is mainly governments, certain international organisations and large-scale private enterprises (rather than trades unions and consumer groups) which have the brainpower and resources to compete, as well as to profit from increased risk and uncertainty.

121

Whilst the developments above (and those in communications and education) may well appear to favour the dominant agents in the GPE, they also open up possibilities for counter-hegemonic forces, particularly at what Gramsci called the ethico-political level. This is because, in Gramscian terms, a global hegemony would need to have not only economic legitimacy and effectiveness, it would also need to have moral credibility. In this context, media images of starving Africans, counterpoised with European butter mountains and wine lakes, are an affront to both moral decency and common sense. In early 1992 the situation in Russia and in many of the former Soviet republics appeared to be one of economic chaos, with widespread criticism of the restructuring policies associated with the IMF, the US government (such as the former Chairman of the US Federal Reserve Board (1979–87), Paul Volcker, who is advising on money and banking institutions in Russia) and academics from Harvard University. Influential in these initiatives on the part of western organic intellectuals has been Professor Jeffrey Sachs of Harvard who was the economic advisor to Solidarity in Poland, where similar levels of disillusionment and opposition now appear to be surfacing following the IMF shock therapy of 1989–90.

An effective counter-hegemonic challenge requires access to large financial resources, knowledge and information, and a degree of control over production and distribution processes. In this respect, co-operatives and groups like the UK-based Intermediate Technology, and the North American RESULTS network are a small beginning (see Bennett with George, 1987: 191–216). However, to mount a significant challenge these groups would need to become much larger, forge more comprehensive transnational links between themselves and mobilise significant support from unions and other producer interests and perhaps from political parties (old and new) who might be sympathetic to these alternatives. Organisations and movements which might form part of a counter-hegemonic bloc include Amnesty International, Green parties and ecological groups, socialist think-tanks like the Transnational Institute, peace groups such as European Nuclear Disarmament, development agencies such as Oxfam, and religious organisations such as the World Council of Churches. Given its size and potential as a vehicle for popular discontent in a range of less-developed countries, Islamic participation in a counter-hegemonic bloc is likely to be essential, although unlikely. One way in which the collective power of such groups could be brought to bear is through the mobilisation of funds at the expense of orthodox capital, for example in the form of 'ethical' investment trusts. In some Moslem countries, such as Egypt, Islamic funds (mutual funds/investment trusts) have been established, to the embarrassment of the authorities, especially since they have gained large numbers of depositors (Walker, 1988). Much more research needs to be done on the ways in which such coalitions might form and become better organised and represented.

Notes

1 We thank Richard Ashley, Robert Cox, Pat McGowan, Craig Murphy, Carlos Parodi, and Kees van der Pijl for comments. A longer version of this essay was published in *International Studies Quarterly*, 33 (1989), 475–99, and in an earlier form, in Gill and Law (1988). Our interpretation of Gramsci has been influenced by Showstack-Sassoon (1980); Larrain (1983); and Cox (1983).

2 On structural power, agency and action, see Knights and Wilmott (1985) and Betts (1986). On the structural power of capital at the domestic level, see Marsh (1983); Lindblom (1977); Ward (1987); and Grant and Sargent (1987). On the agent-structure problem, see Wendt (1987).

3 Kalecki (1943) highlighted business confidence and the wider business climate in the short- and long-term. There is substantial Public Choice literature on the political business cycle (e.g. Alesina and Sachs, 1988) which, however, generally lacks Kalecki's appreciation of the structural requirements of the capitalist system.

4 On supply-side economics and its influence on the Reagan administration, see Canto *et al.* (1983); Evans (1983); Bosworth (1984); Roberts (1984); Stein (1984); and Bartlett and Roth (1985).

5 Intellectuals influencing Thatcherite policies were F.A. von Hayek and Milton Friedman. Institutions active in disseminating liberal economic and social ideas were the Mont Pélèrin Society (founded in 1947 by Hayek); the (British) Institute of Economic Affairs (1955); the British Centre for Policy Studies, CPS, (1974); and the Adam Smith Institute (1977). The 1986 President of the (American) Heritage Foundation, Edwin J. Feulner, Jr., was also Treasurer of the Mont Pélèrin Society (Overbeek, 1987: 184). On conscious advocacy of these ideas, see Seldon *et al.* (1981). Former Thatcher advisor, Sir Alfred Sherman, has defined the purpose of CPS as follows: 'Our object is to reshape the climate of opinion. The Centre proposes to fight vigorously on this front of the battle of ideas' (cited in Overbeek, 1987:185). Mrs Thatcher's stated ambition was, of course, to eradicate socialism in the UK.

6 A sceptical and contrasting view is offered by Gordon (1988). Nevertheless, TNCs loom large in the world economy. The largest 56 TNCs had sales between $10–$100 billion in the late 1980s; 33 TNCs from *developing countries* had sales in excess of $1billion. The largest 600 industrials accounted for between 20–25 per cent of value added in the production of

goods in non-communist countries. Their role as importers and exporters was even greater (United Nations, 1988: 2).

7 Two quotations help capture this. Paul A. Volcker (1985), former US Federal Reserve Board Chairperson (1979–87) summarised what, by the mid-1980s, had become a common policy-making outlook. 'There is [an] element of common strategy . . . [which has been] persistent for some years . . . [it involves] more emphasis on market orientation in economic policies, more concern and effort to reduce the proportion of government in GNP, more emphasis on private initiative. Obviously that matches a lot of rhetoric and oratory in the United States. But what is really startling is the rhetoric and oratory in France that parallels this kind of broad orientation of policies. It is even true in much of the developing world.' (Volcker, 1985). The doyen of American international bankers, Walter Wriston notes: 'there's nothing the politicians can do . . . [about the new] information standard, the information-intensive society moves [political accountability] to a judgement of the way your policies look to the international markets . . . it's a new world and the concept of sovereignty is going to change. Politically, the new world is an integrated market in which . . . [you] can't control what your people hear . . . the value of your currency . . . your capital flows. The idea of fifteenth-century international law has gone . . . It's like the three-mile limit in a world of Inter-Continental Ballistic Missiles' (quoted in Frieden, 1987: 115).

8 Countries with high concentrations of world mineral reserves are special cases. Sooner or later, transnational firms will seek accommodation with the rulers of such nations, whose direct power to control access to indigenous resources has increased since decolonisation. Good examples of this are Libya and Saudi Arabia. The apparent paradox here is that whilst the direct (market) power of some, relatively unusual, Third World states in the minerals sector has tended to rise with political independence, the structural power of transnational capital, relative to Third World states more generally, has become more pronounced. Such structural power affects all Third World states with regard to the bulk of manufacturing.

PART II
PAST, PRESENT AND FUTURE

5 GRAMSCI AND INTERNATIONAL RELATIONS: A GENERAL PERSPECTIVE AND EXAMPLE FROM RECENT US POLICY TOWARD THE THIRD WORLD

ENRICO AUGELLI AND CRAIG N. MURPHY

Gramsci's concepts allow scholars to transcend some of the current debates dividing the field of international relations (IR) while preserving the insights of the major traditions, whether 'realist' or 'idealist', 'structural', or 'historical', at the same time that they help us break the habit of reifying the nation-state by turning our attention toward the deeper sources of social continuity and change. This paper discusses these benefits of employing Gramsci's insights and illustrates them with conclusions from a study of American foreign policy toward the Third World in the Reagan and Bush era.

GRAMSCI'S CONCEPTS AND INTERNATIONAL RELATIONS

The field of international relations studies the consolidation of power over large populations and territories in a world of multiple, territorially separate, power centres. Gramsci's concern in his investigations of 'hegemony' and the broader notion of 'supremacy' was also to understand the dynamics of the consolidation of power, including those dynamics in international relations. Thus, in his commentary on the history of modern Italy, Gramsci is able to treat both the Renaissance state system and politics within the twentieth-century state within the same framework and with the same concepts.

We see Gramsci's sociology of power as beginning with the distinction between rule by 'force' and rule through 'consensus', borrowed from Machiavelli. Gramsci puts this distinction in his own terms by contrasting two ideal types of supremacy: 'domination', the exercise of power without the critical, reflective consent of the

127

governed, and ethical hegemony, i.e., intellectual and moral leadership:

> The supremacy of a social group manifests itself in two ways, as 'domination' and as 'intellectual and moral leadership'. A social group dominates antagonistic groups, which it tends to 'liquidate', or subjugate perhaps even by armed force; it leads kindred and allied groups. (Gramsci, 1971: 57)

Gramsci does not make the two pairs of concepts equivalent. The use of 'force' is not quite the same as 'domination' even though 'consensus' always characterises 'hegemony'. When hegemony is not 'ethical', when it is based upon fraud and deception, Gramsci considers it a form of domination.

Gramsci notes that idealist philosophy, whether of the right (energising what students of IR have come to call 'realism'), or the left (energising what students of international relations have come to call 'idealism', 'liberalism', or 'functionalism'), sees a radical separation between force and consensus, while, in the real world, these two forms of rule are mutually supportive and often combine in ambiguous ways. Force rarely appears as brute force, nor do the representatives of power justify its use by invoking the interests of the dominant social group or dominant social alliance, even though that must always be the ultimate reason why force is used in the place of rule by consensus. To mask the lack of consensus the representatives of power always proclaim grand moral principles to justify the use of force. In parliamentary democracies, Gramsci notes, mobilisation of the 'organs of public opinion' always accompanies the use of force in order to assure wide approval of that choice, even if such consent can only be gained by fraud (Gramsci, 1975: III, 1,638).

Gramsci's three levels of society, the 'economic structure', and the two superstructural levels, 'civil society' and 'political society' locate the domains in which force and consent operate to consolidate power:

> What we can do, for the moment, is to fix two major superstructural 'levels': the one that can be called 'civil society', that is the ensemble of organisms commonly called 'private', and that of 'political society' or 'the State'. These two levels correspond on the one hand to the function of 'hegemony' that the dominant group exercises through society and on the other hand to that of 'direct domination' or command exercised through the State and 'juridical' government (Gramsci, 1971: 12).

128

In our reading, Gramsci's 'civil society' consists of the various forms of voluntary association and it constitutes the moment of transition from economic structure to political society, the social realm in which mere corporate interests (defined by a group's position in the mode of production) can be transformed into broader, more universal, political aspirations. For Gramsci, civil society is the primary political realm, the realm in which all of the dynamics of identity formation, ideological struggle, the activities of intellectuals, and the construction of hegemony (whether 'ethical' or based on fraud) takes place. Civil society is the context in which one becomes conscious and first engages in political action. Civil society is where the aggregation of interests takes place, where narrow interests are transformed into more universal views as ideologies are adopted or amended and alliances formed.

Gramsci locates 'political society', the institutions regulating society, above civil society. What Gramsci calls 'political society' is equivalent to what many 'realists' consider the 'state'. However, in contrast to many realists who assume that force and the threat of force cannot provide the sole basis for the consolidation of power over large territories and populations, Gramsci considers it important to differentiate between 'political society' or the 'state proper' and what he calls the 'state in the organic, wider sense', i.e. what contemporary political theorists often call the 'polity'. By 'state in the organic sense', Gramsci means the overall 'structure of the superstructure', which may include institutions essential to the political life of the community even though they appear to be of a merely private nature, as is the case in contemporary civil society.

Understood thus, the state is neither the external expression of society (merely an 'actor' in international relations), nor is it located above society; the state is a characteristic of society constituted by the articulation of political and civil society. In this sense we even can use Gramsci's concepts to ask to what degree there is a 'state' in the wider sense which characterises *world* society: that 'world state', or 'world polity', or (better) simply 'world political system' involves institutions of 'international civil society' – transnational associations, diplomacy, alliances, and intergovernmental organisations – but includes little or no 'world political society' or 'world state proper'.

Gramsci notes that there is a tendency for there to be a coincidence between force and the realm of the state proper and between rule by consensus and the realm of civil society. But that does not justify the current situation in IR theorising in which 'realists' who focus on force concentrate on the anarchic world of separate states proper while those who look at international economic co-operation and transnational social relations focus on the consolidation of power by consensus. In fact, both force and policies aimed at achieving consent can be applied in any of the three social realms. In particular, force can be applied to national economies as sanctions (changing the 'limits of the possible') or even to the world economy as a whole: consider the impact of the restrictive macroeconomic policies of a great economic power. And force can be applied against institutions of international civil society, thus restricting the possibility of international and transnational cooperation by 'increasing the transaction and information costs' associated with such activity (to use Robert Keohane's (1984a) language).

HYPOTHESES ABOUT SUPREMACY

Gramsci uses these concepts in narratives which recount how consolidated power, what Gramsci calls 'supremacy', has been achieved. This lets him anticipate how power might be consolidated in fundamentally new situations. Gramsci's practical instructions for achieving supremacy can also be thought of as hypotheses that might explain other cases that he did not consider, including, for example, the supremacy of certain states and social forces within world society.

Perhaps the hypothesis that scholars of international affairs most connect with Gramsci's name is this: to achieve supremacy a social group (a corporate actor) must be able to establish 'hegemony' among a group of allies. Gramsci's 'hegemony' is the ability of a social group to exercise a function of 'political and moral direction' in society. Other groups acknowledge the hegemon as having a leading role in society and a relatively wide political consensus supports the hegemon's policy goals. A hegemon leads by responding to its allies' 'interests', their motivations that derive from their positions in the mode of production (one of the two basic motivations of human action recognised by Gramsci), and by both responding to and helping to shape the ideal 'aspirations' (the other basic motivation) that emerge within civil society.

Gramsci argues that in industrial societies only social groups performing an essential role in the mode of production can become hegemonic, unlike, for example, in feudal societies where religious groups have exercised political and moral direction (Gramsci, 1971: 161). This essential role in the world of production is what first confers prestige on a leading social group and makes its dominant social and political role acceptable to others.

Because hegemony involves understanding and responding to interests and aspirations, no group can become hegemonic without first understanding its own interests and developing its own hegemonic aspiration. Members of the potentially hegemonic group must attain self-awareness of the economic role they perform and of the political role that they could fulfill. On the basis of this critical self-understanding, the potential hegemon can make alliances, taking a step beyond defending its economic-corporate interests – i.e., 'immediate and narrowly selfish interests of a particular category' (Gramsci, 1971: 77) – in order to link itself to other groups involved in society's key political struggles. This is the process which Gramsci, using Sorel's language, calls the establishment of a 'historical economic-political bloc' (Gramsci, 1975: III, 1,612) not just an alliance, but a, 'dialectical unity of base and superstructure, of theory and practice, of intellectuals and masses' (Forgacs, 1988: 424).

Here the work of the intellectuals becomes essential. 'The role of intellectuals is to represent the ideas that constitute the terrain where hegemony is exercised' (Gramsci, 1975: II, 1,084). They must supply intellectual and moral support for the hegemon's dominant political role to the point that, 'what is "politics" to the productive [and potentially hegemonic] class becomes "rationality" to the intellectual class' (Gramsci, 1975: I, 134). The intellectuals organically tied to the hegemonic class must demonstrate in every field of knowledge that the aspirations of the group they serve coincide with the interests of society as a whole. The intellectuals of the hegemonic class must produce a philosophy, political theory, and economics which together constitute a coherent world-view, the principles of which can be translated from one discipline to another (Gramsci, 1971: 403). As actors in the ideological struggle, the intellectuals of the dominant class must prevail over the intellectuals of other classes by developing more convincing and sophisticated theories, inculcating other intellectuals with the dominant world-view, and assimilating them to the hegemon's cause. Potential hegemons fail when they are unable to consolidate the support of intellectuals, the way the Italian bourgeoisie of the Communes (analysed by Machiavelli) failed because intellectuals of this new class failed to enlist traditional intellectuals who remained wedded to the ideas and interests of the feudal world.

Finally, Gramsci hypothesises that to further reinforce the solidarity of its immediate bloc of allies and go beyond it to extend the hegemony of the leading social group to the popular masses the potential hegemon must ensure economic development, satisfying the narrower interests of its allies. This is a second reason why hegemons in modern industrial societies can only come from classes that play an essential role in the economy. The central role the hegemonic group plays in production gives it great influence over the economy as a whole, but this potential must be made a reality by conscious political action. Analysing the history of the French bourgeoisie, which had to respond to a series of such crises, Gramsci argues, 'Political consensus is regained (hegemony is retained) by broadening and deepening the economic base with individual and commercial development' (Gramsci, 1975: I, 58). In this process of economic development, which Gramsci sees as one of the progressive functions of the hegemonic social class, the extension of new productive activities and the social ascent of those who are, 'more endowed with energy and spirit of enterprise' (Gramsci, 1975: III, 1,637) take place. Indeed, it was the breakdown of this dynamic process which, according to Gramsci, led to the crisis of bourgeois hegemony in Europe during the great depression after the First World War.

Thus, in Gramsci's view, a corporate actor that wants to achieve hegemony today must take into account all these requirements – developing a critical self-understanding, making alliances, and capturing the ideological realm and, if it intends to extend its hegemony to a larger public, assuring economic development. A society in which any one of these requirements is absent experiences a 'crisis of authority'. And a hegemonic group that fails to maintain at least those requirements that maintain its social alliance, loses its hegemony.

Hegemony, however, is only one side of the consolidation of power. Gramsci sees the supremacy of a corporate actor as based on hegemony over allies within the historical bloc and domination, either by force or fraud, of those social groups outside the alliance. While Gramsci hypothesises that supremacy cannot be achieved by force or domination alone, he does not underestimate the significance of force for maintaining supremacy over groups outside the alliance at the core of the historic bloc. He does, however, suggest that domination based on fraud, domination rooted in a fraudulent hegemony that does not really take into account the interests of allied groups, is eventually bound to fail. In time, it must be replaced either by force (and the exclusion of the group from the historical bloc) or else by a true, 'ethical', hegemony.

APPLYING GRAMSCI'S HYPOTHESES TO
INTERNATIONAL RELATIONS: THE UNITED STATES
AND THE THIRD WORLD

In *America's Quest for Supremacy and the Third World* (Augelli and Murphy, 1988) we applied Gramsci's insights to the Reagan administration's attempts to reassert power over the Third World. We argued that after the Second World War, the dominant classes within the United States had been able to form a coherent international historical bloc: the 'free world', to use the one name most-often applied to it by its supporters. At the centre of this bloc was a hegemonic alliance including some elements of labour in the OECD countries, the dominant classes and (to a surprising extent) the popular masses in much of the dependent Third World, and, of course, the dominant classes in Western Europe and Japan. To a greater or lesser extent, each of these groups was the target of force from the American government throughout the 1980s, especially force directed at the economic level. In the early 1990s only the Third World remains a highly visible target of American force and the Gulf War appears to be a sign of the reconstruction of American supremacy.

We believe that the reconstruction of American world supremacy took place in the 1980s and was primarily the result of the effective use of economic force. American hegemony was ultimately reconstructed by re-establishing the previous, ethical, relationship between the American dominant classes and the dominant classes in Western Europe and Japan. But both within the developed market countries and between them and most of the dependent Third World, the character of American supremacy changed so that today it is based more on domination, through both fraud and force.

To understand the reconstruction of American hegemony it is important to go back the crises to which the US government responded. Perhaps the most important crisis was one of economic development: with the beginning of 'stagflation' in the early 1970s the dominant classes within the US were no longer able to provide the incredible prosperity of the post-war years. This crisis was, in part, a crisis of US relations with the Third World, at least to the extent that stagflation originated in an attempt to pay for both the Vietnam War and Lyndon Johnson's Great Society without raising taxes (see Block, 1977).

In 1973, the one group of Third World states that could claim an essential role in the 'free world' international division of labour, the oil producers, deepened the crisis. For a few years, Third World goverments believed that the first oil crisis gave them an opportunity to change the way in which the international economic system was managed.[1] Western dependence on oil forced the industrial countries to listen to Third World demands and OPEC's price policy revealed potential rifts in the alliance at the core of the Western historic bloc (Miller, 1983).

Nevertheless, OPEC failed to understand its own potential as a world leader. Its refusal to keep the interests of the poorer, oil-dependent Third World nations in mind and its own internal contradictions undermined its ability to enforce a programme of change based on the Third World's New International Economic Order (NIEO) demands. Beyond playing a fundamental role in the world economy and recognising the aspirations of its allies through its support of the NIEO, OPEC lacked all the other characteristics Gramsci identifies as essential for the construction of supremacy. When 1979 oil prices were raised to historically high levels, regardless of the consequences to OPEC's allies, the Third World coalition was shaken, but it continued to exist, thanks to Western disunity and to the illusion of the Third World's poorest countries that the ÑIEO would be established soon.

Given this internal weakness of the challenger to the Western bloc, the policy of force against the Third World that the US employed starting in 1979 quickly destroyed the economic foundation of the alternative bloc. Throughout the Reagan administration, political and military force played mainly a psychological role, reinforcing the US's new verbal assertiveness (Murphy and Augelli, 1988: 180–2; Miller, 1987). The force that really mattered was economic. The cascading monetarist policies initiated by the United States had the combined effects in the Third World of lower export earnings and high interest rates. This caused a catastrophic crisis of liquidity. Even more significantly, the monetarist recession in the industrialised countries and cash-short oil producing nations made oil abundant, thus depriving the Third World of the leverage which gave credibility to the demand for the NIEO (Khader, 1986).

After the Third World bloc was defeated at the end of 1982, the US was free to apply itself to the task of reconstructing its hegemony within the Western bloc, a task completed before the end of Reagan's first term. As Gramsci would have expected, hegemony within the Western social alliance was accompanied by the domination of adversaries, the Third World. The United States not only dominated the Third World by restricting its options indirectly, through the application of force in the world economy, but also the US worked more directly through international civil society. The Western bloc used the leverage of foreign assistance to try to remake Third World economies in a *laissez-faire* image. The United States targeted the intergovernmental organisations (which had been so important in formation of the NIEO consensus within the Third World) and succeeded in making the UN system a more effective conduit of Western policy preferences.[2]

The intergovernmental agencies, especially the IMF and the World Bank, became one of the few power centres in the reconstituted Western bloc concerned with transforming the policy of applying force to the Third World to one of building consensus. The intergovernmental agencies joined some private institutions in international civil society in the ideological struggle against the many versions of global Keynesianism. The anti-Keynesians used the economic success of a few developing countries under the new global regime as evidence in favour of global Reaganomics.

In fact, the success of the east Asian Newly-Industrialising Countries (NICs) may have had more to do with their unusual position in the world economy than with any adherence to the American administration's formulas for the relationship between business and government (Harris, 1987). Moreover, even the economic analysis of those agencies most concerned with promoting the programme of structural adjustments and economic policy reform reveals that the least-advantaged regions and people within the world economy can expect little in a Reaganomic world.[3] For much of the Third World, the new global economic vision of the reconstituted bloc was simply a deception: a fact that both the intergovernmental agencies and those Western scholars who had been supportive of the Third World movement have been increasingly less likely to point out due to their defeat in the ideological struggle.

From 1984 through the end of the Reagan administration, new economic problems put strains on the Western bloc: the overvaluation of the dollar and its subsequent fall, the growing deficit of the US current account and the concomitant rapid increase in foreign ownership of productive assets in the United States, and the continuing instability of world financial markets. The new bases of consensus in the Western bloc constantly had to be tended and secured and it remains an open question whether the American economic policies used to re-establish its world supremacy have increased or undermined its capacity to maintain its hegemony inside the Western bloc in the long run. Nevertheless, in the short run, this task was simplified because the Third World as an independent actor had disappeared from the world scene and it is uncertain if it will ever reappear as an actor whose interests and aspirations must be considered by any supreme power.

In the Gulf War, the Bush Administration was able to go beyond Reagan in cementing the Western alliance and further diminishing the likelihood that any Third World group would be able to use oil as a weapon in the near future. The Bush administration has also moved, to some extent, to try to bring the dominant classes within the Third World back into the alliance at the centre of the Western bloc and, at the same time, has found new and expanded roles for the intergovernmental organisations in building a 'new world order'. The role of the UN Security Council in sanctioning the war against Iraq is only one small part of this new role.

In part the attempt to bring the dominant classes within the Third World back into the Western bloc this has been made by encouraging the replacement of elites. The development crises of the 1970s and 1980s have called into question older elites who developed that whole range of 'populist' economic development strategies aimed at self-reliance which were employed throughout the Third World, often with a great deal of support from intergovernmental organisations, until the late-1970s. In the 1980s, the UN agencies, the World Bank, and the IMF ended their support and increasingly adopted an analysis of Third World economic problems that focused on *domestic policies*, engineered by the same elites, as impediments to prosperity; in the view promulgated by many of the international agencies in the 1980s, Third World governments became the problem rather than the solution.[4]

Many Western donors supported this analysis, and American policy in general, by joining in programmes co-ordinating the increasingly limited aid available to most Third World states through 'policy dialogue' in which preferences for *laissez-faire* policies, and for the abolition of populist welfare-oriented government spending in the Third World, were communicated just as forcefully as they were through the recent 'structural adjustment' programmes of the Bretton Woods institutions (Augelli, 1986).

This delegitimation of 'populist', self-reliance oriented elites occurred not just in the eyes of an international community. The same elites lost their popularity within many Third World states. And that has actually made a difference because the 1980s and early 1990s have been a period of democratisation throughout the Third World. In Latin America, the Caribbean, and Africa, state after state has witnessed the creation or reintroduction of pluralist political systems in which parties really compete for popular support.[5]

In most states where democratisation has taken place in recent years, it has meant the replacement of left-leaning, populist, development- and welfare-oriented governments with those espousing anti-modernist policies (Islamic fundamentalism or ethnic nationalism) or a *laissez-faire* development orientation, or both. The victory of elites dedicated to the vision of the world shared by Reagan and Bush administrations has been far from complete, but it has been significant.

In states where protracted, internationalised conflicts preceded democratisation (Nicaragua, Namibia, Angola, etc.) the UN played a key role in this transition between elites, providing aid in running elections, observing them, and certifying their fairness. This expanded role of the UN may turn out to be more important in the reassertion of American supremacy than the more widely reported role of the UN in the Gulf War. That is, if development can be restored throughout the reconstituted 'free world' system, (which now, with the breakdown of the Soviet empire, may come to include the entire world outside China and India). If that does not occur, we would hazard the guess that the new democratic systems throughout the Third World will turn out to be less permanent than the new governing elites.

This brief account of US policy and the Third World is only one of a number of similar ones that might be derived from applying Gramsci's insights to the problem of 'declining American hegemony' which has preoccupied so many students of international relations for the past decade and a half. Stephen Gill (1986), who focuses more on the crisis inside the Western bloc rather than on North–South relations, for example, reaches slightly different conclusions. But both Gill's account and ours demonstrate, we believe, the advantage of Gramsci's more inclusive framework over the narrower traditions which have dominated the 'declining American hegemony' debate.

Gramsci's framework forced us to consider the role of military and economic force and the accumulation of resources that could be used to threaten such action. Consideration of those 'realist' variables enabled Gill to see that they had played little role, so far, in struggles inside the Western bloc of nation-states and enabled us to see the significant role that economic force had played, as a neo-realist might predict, in North–South relations.

But we could not stop there. Gramsci's framework required us to consider the role that international institutions, both formal and informal, play in maintaining American supremacy and in challenging it. Western institutional innovations, such as the G7 summits, are as essential a part of a Gramscian account of the continuing power of the United States as they are part of an institutionalist account such as Keohane's (1984a). And the destruction of Third World institutions for aggregating interests will be as clearly identified as a significant political factor by a follower of Gramsci as it would be by the 'idealist' who wrote the political analysis at the end of the Brandt Commission's last report (1983).

A GREATER SOCIAL REALISM

So far the claim we have made for applying Gramsci's theory to IR is a very modest one. We have suggested that scholars who work within Gramsci's framework help their colleagues by carrying on some debate within the field as part of their own research programme rather than leaving it up to the longer process of publication and refutation, which can tend to ossify opposing positions as much as to open fruitful debate. We now make a further claim, of greater significance, that Gramsci's theory helps us see a fundamental aspect of the object of our study which would otherwise be obscured.

It should be clear that in employing Gramsci's theory to analyse IR we are forced to learn a great deal about society. The theory offers analysts no sure starting point, no givens like the nation-states that appear as relevantly-similar units of anlaysis in so many traditions. Analysts may start with any concrete relations at any level of analysis; it is Gramsci's questions about society that will begin to make the boundaries of the objects in question clear.

Analysts must define the dynamics and scope of the 'base', the limits of the possible, the productive economy and relationships of human reproduction in which the initial relationship is embedded. They must then use that knowledge to define the classes within the economy, which play fundamental roles, and what the (often contradictory and unconscious) interests of each group might be. Then they are forced to look at the actual ways in which social actors capture these hypothesised interests, in the institutions of civil society and identity groups that operate within it. Their habitual interactions among themselves and with institutions of force become the next problematic. All this before the traditional topics of IR – of force and war and co-operation and peace among states proper – are addressed.

What is the use of all of this preliminary work? To put it succinctly, it makes those who analyse change in international relations more conscious of the more fundamental sources of change in human life and it enables us to think of the boundaries of states more as strategies in social struggles than as preordained social facts.

ATTENTION TO SOURCES OF FUNDAMENTAL CHANGE

That the most fundamental sources of social change are not necessarily visible to someone who concentrates on observing juridical nation-states is not a very contentious proposition. People may fight and die for their nation, but the sources of nationalism, and of every other identity which means more than life can only be found by looking at relations that go on within and across the units upon which international relations analysts sometimes fixate. Equally, the source of the economic interests that people protect (which make threats of economic force work) also arise at levels different from that of the juridical states. Certainly the sources of 'co-operation', in Keohane's sense of untapped, potential material interests, are found at the same level of concrete economies. And the sources of real learning in international relations, of the kind of progress which involves intellectual communities of 'scientists' encouraging 'functionalist' international co-operation can only be understood by identifying the system that generates such intellectuals, a system that cannot be differentiated when one looks at juridical states alone.

In our case, when we set out to understand the reassertion of American supremacy *vis à vis* the Third World in the 1980s the perspective we adopted made us confront the problem of trying to explain the change in American policy which caused the international change we observed. We were taken into the unfamiliar realms of foreign policy analysis, domestic politics, and even cultural history – worlds rarely visited at such length by any of the legion of analysts of the problem of 'declining American hegemony'. Our theory convinced us that to explain US relations to the Third World in the 1980s one had to explain Reagan's rise to power. Others may disagree with that conclusion. They may turn out to be correct, or at least they may be able to convince us that they are. Even so, the insights about American society gained from our excursion into political and social history help illuminate the deeper practical political problems which motivated our research: we do not like the results of current US foreign policy in the Third World and we would like to see it transformed. By delving inside US society we learned a little more about how that might be done.

We became convinced that what is significant about recent American political experience is that apparent solutions to so many problems that its citizens faced could be found in the contradictory agglomeration of ideas that Gramsci calls 'common sense'. Reagan's triumph, after all, did not represent the injection of any new analysis, and new understanding into the organisation of American social life. Rather, the 'right turn' of the 1980s was all about new political organisation around old ideological themes – business pressure groups organising to support their own interests behind a rather superficial view of pre-Keynesian liberalism, the fundamentalist churches that had grown during the social upheaval and economic troubles of the late 1960s and 1970s injecting traditional Puritan themes into the American political process, and Cold War internationalists pushing for technological solutions to the historical battle with the Soviet Union. Surprisingly, despite the fundamentally new problems it faced, Reagan's government, combining all these elements, succeeded in making the public feel a lot better about themselves and their society, for a time.

Other analysts (Edsall, 1984; Ferguson and Rogers, 1987) make the right's triumph look much less significant; as if it only reflected the fact that the Democratic party failed to offer a convincing alternative. But offering as convincing an alternative would be hard, given the prejudice of 'common sense'. The people that Edsall, and Ferguson and Rogers, and we, consider the 'good guys' in American politics – labour rather than business interest groups, the churches and social movements representing the poorest and most disadvantaged rather than the *petit bourgeois* fundamentalists, the peace movement rather than the war movement – cannot simply do the same things that the right did. And the left has no particular advantage just because the general public's attitudes on *concrete* policy issues, as opposed to abstract principles, is far from that of the right. To develop as successful an alternative to Reaganism would require a much greater ideological and intellectual effort. Rather than simply select among prejudices, the anti-Reagans need to help Americans confront their contradictory consciousness and search for the reasons why the abstract principles they accept contradict what Gramsci would call the 'good sense' of their attitudes on specific policies.

140

PROBLEMATISING THE BOUNDARIES OF STATES

In the specific case we examined you might say that responding to Gramsci's theory just made us consider *more* levels of analysis; we looked inside the boundaries of the American polity in the 1980s, but did not challenge its reality. Yet it is, perhaps, that ability to challenge the meaningfulness of apparent social boundaries that most makes applying Gramsci's theories to IR exciting.

Even in our brief study of the history of American political culture we began to see some of the potential of treating the boundaries of the state as problematic. After we had located much of the popular appeal of Ronald Reagan and his message in a historical American political culture which combines elements of Calvinism, classical liberalism, and scientism, we began to look for the things that had helped maintain the unchanging elements of this contradictory consciousness over such a long time. In particular, what accounted for the continued strength of those archaic elements of American consciousness which came from the seventeenth-century religious experience of a relatively tiny handful of 'founders'. The most convincing explanation comes from those historians concerned with understanding the changing boundaries of the American state (in the wider sense). By this we mean not only the shifting westward of the imperial boundaries of the US, but also its changing social boundaries of inclusion and exclusion, partly reflected in US immigration policy. Immigration policy is therefore crucial to explaining both the scale and nature of the US state today. Conformity with an 'Americanism' rooted in Calvinism, so some scholars say, has always been the price of admission of the new immigrant into the US polity.

It takes little imagination to conceive of such a social norm, and the form of the extension of the state that it allowed, as 'functional' in the old discredited sense of being beneficial to someone and thus, if it could be fostered consciously, as a potential weapon in social struggles. And it is not too far from that recognition, to the recognition that the habits of thought and action which maintain and regularly transform the boundaries of other states at other times could be thought of just as fruitfully as representing the results of strategic decisions, as tools in fundamental conflicts, not as givens.

Gramsci, of course, did just that in his examination of the history of modern Italy, the nineteenth-century history of the integration of the contemporary state – one of the central topics of the *Prison Notebooks*. Contemporary IR theorists are willing to problematise state boundaries when studying nineteenth-century Italy or Germany or other cases of juridical integration, or something approaching it, such as the developments within the European Community. International relations might be quite different if the location – between different economic groups as much as different identity groups – were always treated as a problem, if we always had to ask: why is the boundary *here* instead of *there*? Why is this group included and that group not? The critical insight of those who do regularly ask that question – some students of North–South relations of regional conflict, and of the origins of East–West conflict – cannot be denied. And there are significant links to be explored between their conclusion and those few traditions of 'grand' analysis of IR that consistently ask questions about boundaries: the lateral pressure school in the study of great power conflict (Choucri and North, 1975; Ashley, 1980) and certain older schools of thought about international organisation and integration (Deutsch, 1966; Haas, 1964).

BOUNDARIES AND HISTORICAL MATERIALISM

Yet, it is our guess that the critical edge gained from problematising the boundaries of the state which Gramsci provides will have its greatest impact in a different scholarly realm, not among students who raise fundamental questions of IR but fail to be critical about the units of analysis that they employ, but among those who ask the traditional questions of historical materialism yet who are just as apt to reify the juridical state.

The problem has always been a difficult one. Consider Marx and Engels's thoughts on nationalism, internationalism, and the state. In *The German Ideology* of 1846, Marx and Engels wrote that the revolution they championed could only be accomplished by the working classes of the world acting . . . 'all at once' and simultaneously (Marx and Engels, 1947: 46), suggesting that the real unity of the world industrial economy demanded a far more thorough internationalism than socialists have ever demonstrated. Two years later, in the midst of the revolutions of 1848, Marx and Engels amended their analysis, writing in *The Communist Manifesto* that first the proletariat of every nation must deal with their own bourgeoisie (quoted in Anderson, 1983: 13). Benedict Anderson comments that hiding beneath the ambiguity of the pronoun 'their' lie all the problems of national identity that Marxists have never resolved. The same ambiguity also obscures the problem of internationalism that Marx and Engels had exposed in 1846 and the problem of the significance of the juridical state that students of IR have ignored.

142

In 1848, Germans like Marx and Engels were bound to be ambiguous when they referred to the 'nation' or the 'state'. To use those words to imply the existence, or even the likelihood, of a clear bounded state proper, let alone a polity, would have been to invoke as controversial and unproven an idea as the 'internationalism' of the proletariat. In 1848 it may have been harder to identify a concrete 'German nation' than it was to identify a concrete, world-wide industrial working class. The text and historical context of the *Manifesto* give us a good idea of what Marx and Engels might have meant by their own 'nation' in 1848. The revolution triggered the convening of the first parliament of 'all Germans', a constituent assembly made up of representatives from the many independent German states as well as representatives of Germans in the Austro-Hungarian Empire and representative of the German-speaking cantons of Switzerland. It was the interests represented there that Marx and Engels considered the first target of their 'own' proletariat (Draper, 1978: 209–49). But, even so, as Draper says, Marx 'looked upon Germany as one battlefield in a European war, and usually as a secondary one at that' (1978: 241). And the part of the *Manifesto* just before the famous quotation about the need for a national focus of struggles for communism suggests something slightly different. They are the famous ones about capital 'tearing down all Chinese walls', about the bourgeoisie's destruction of the barriers to trade and communication that divided states.

Students of international organisations like to remember that the German Customs Union of the time provided Marx and Engels with a model. It had broken down barriers among some, but not all, of the many states to which the Germans at the 1848 parliament owed allegiance at the same time that the Union integrated the 'German' economy with the economies of those 'non-German' industrialising states that were members. Given the primary emphasis that many contemporary Marxist scholars have placed on the prospects for social transformation within existing juridical nation-states it is worth emphasising that the views of the German nation that were available to Marx and Engels in 1848 were hardly the same thing as 'the state that legitimately ruled all Germans'.

Marx himself was a citizen of a Rhineland province of Prussia, as physically and culturally distant from Berlin as any part of the Union. He worked on the *Manifesto* close to his home, in exile in nearby Belgium, a state that had been recognised as sovereign for little more than a decade and one whose sovereignty was circumscribed by its official status as a 'perpetual neutral'. If we did not know the historical link between the meeting of the German parliament and the drafting of *Manifesto* we might imagine that Marx believed his 'own' proletariat and bourgeoisie to be those of the industrial area then emerging along the Rhine and its tributaries, a capitalist economy that included parts of Germany, the low countries, and a part of northern France.

Marx and Engels were indeed prescient to see that the development of capitalist industry in Rhineland Prussia, and for that matter, in the low countries, northern France, Switzerland, and the parts of the Austrian Empire that industrialised before its dissolution, would be tied to the history of the nation-state that was growing within the German Customs Union in 1848. They erred only by implying that in all places and ever afterward the history of capitalist industry would be bound up with the history of a single nation-state to the extent that the early industrialisation of continental Europe was tied to the history of Germany.

Gramsci's elaboration of historical materialism, particularly in his account of the Italian *Risorgimento*, overcomes the problem Marxists have when they fail to problematise the state and its boundaries. Gramsci does so by examining the concrete historical transformation of the state in its broad sense, the integrated superstructures of civil and political society, from the late Middle Ages onward.

Gramsci sees modern European states as following upon a more encompassing medieval European state, whose fundamental institutions were the Empire and the church. The boundaries of the European state were those of Western Christendom. Gramsci argues that the medieval state began its slow disintegration in the eleventh century as the economic structure of Europe began to change through transformations first of late-medieval agriculture, then of industry in the towns, and finally of trade, with the voyages of discovery and the first establishment of European outposts throughout the world. Along with these changes in the base came concomitant, dialectically related, transformations of culture – humanism and the Renaissance, the Reformation, illuminism, and, finally, liberalism. The historical subject of both sets of changes was the same. It was the new emerging class, the European bourgeoisie, whose power grew as that of the landed aristocracy declined. The birth of the modern state, says Gramsci, took place when the new class succeeded in creating institutional superstructures (states and the state system) which reflected and secured its political and economic interests.

If the process toward the modern state was Europe-wide, why did it end in separate nation-states? Gramsci's analysis suggests the following explanation.

First, while it is true that bourgeois economic expansion needed a larger territory than the municipal areas in which it developed at the beginning, the political consolidation of larger units could not occur simultaneously in the same way all over Europe. The strength of the bourgeoisie and the capacity of resistance of the old class and its allied intellectuals were different in different parts of the continent. Gramsci believed that the change happened first, and in almost a complete form in Holland. In England, and later in Germany, there was a merger between the old and new; in the new superstructure, feudal classes became the intellectuals of the bourgeoisie and kept some privileges on the land, in the management of government, and in the military. France went beyond Holland, but at a later date; the alliance between the bourgeoisie and the masses in the Revolution allowed the old class to be discarded. In Italy, given the weakness of the bourgeoisie, its geographical separation, the uneven development of the country, and, most significantly, the influence of the Church in Rome, the process was much slower. The emergence of separate nations prevented an homogeneous expansion of the European bourgeoisie, leaving national bourgeoisies to prosper inside monarchic shells and, with the help of those states, to expand outside Europe.

Second, the general idea of 'the nation' proved to be a practical and effective ideological weapon against the cosmopolitan and religious conception of the feudal world, which supported the power of the Empire and the Church. Protestantism, which strengthened Protestant princes – ultimately establishing their separate 'sovereignty' – played a similar role.

Finally, the specific content of each nationalism, the promotion of a specific national identity, based as it always was on a people's common culture and on a general distrust of strangers, proved an effective way to channel allegiance toward the new territorial unities, reinforcing the supremacy of the new ruling classes.

Together, these three factors left Europe, at the dawn of its global supremacy, with separate states and the state system. In his own day, Gramsci clearly thought that the boundaries of the separate states of the state system could be treated as the boundaries of separate social systems arguing, 'The historical unity of the ruling classes is realised in the State and their history is essentially the history of States or groups of States' (Gramsci, 1971: 52). Yet, if we follow his method of anlaysis today we may reach a slightly different conclusion because the institutions linking the dominant states in the international system, and their ruling classes have become much more significant (Van der Pijl, 1984; Gill, 1990). Consequently, social actors who oppose the status quo and search for 'their own bourgeoisie' may have to look not just within their own nation-state alone, but within the whole of the more global economic area in which they live, or, if they are from the less industrialised dependent periphery, within the whole of the core market areas to which they are tied.

Nevertheless, we should not exaggerate the degree to which anything approaching a larger 'world' capitalist state has developed. Certainly economic expansion under today's capitalism appears to need larger territories than the national areas in which it developed through Gramsci's day. But this alone would not give us sufficient reason to conclude that the fundamental nature of world politics has changed; in Gramsci's time, too, there was a contradiction between an increasingly global international economy and the policies of many protectionist national governments, as he himself remarked after the economic crisis of 1929. Moreover, Gramsci's work warns us against seeing the evolution of political relations, even at the international level, as a mechanistic outcome of changes in the economy, even at the international level. And, finally, we have little reason to doubt that specific nationalisms remain potent forces securing supremacy even if new, more encompassing, cultural identities – 'Europe', 'the Free World', 'the developed nations' – also may play some role.

Still, Gramsci's method requires us to consider changes in the international economy in light of concrete social actors and the institutions they have built to protect their interests. Today, those institutions include both the most powerful capitalist states, which remain the expressions of the strongest national bourgeoisies, and international institutions: the European Community, the OECD, the IMF, NATO, and so forth. They, along with the ideological identifications which operate at their level, must be considered. Identifying the concrete instruments of power within the changing boundaries within the world economy must be at the core of a Gramscian research programme true to both his sociology of power and the political purpose for which it was developed.

Notes

1 Much of the literature on the Third World economic demands of the 1980s does little to distinguish Third World demands from Third World expecta-

tions, neither of which were fulfilled. Hart (1984) and Murphy (1984) are exceptions.

2 A brief, by no means complete, reading list on the US and the crisis of international organisations in the 1980s, covering a wide range of opinion, would include Adelman (1988), Beigbeder (1987), Cox (1980), Harrod and Schrijver (1988), Puchala and Coate (1989), and Roberts and Kingsbury (1988).

3 We reach this conclusion by comparing the increasingly bleak projections made by the World Bank in its reports on Africa and in the *World Development Report* since 1982.

4 We anlaysed this development (and the accuracy of the analysis) with reference to Africa in Augelli and Murphy (1989b).

5 For those of us with an interest in Africa, the connection between the two phenomena has been especially close. It was hard to watch the recent wave of democratisation sweeping through Africa, with the replacement of so many left, development-oriented, populist governments by political parties espousing Islamic fundamentalism, ethnic nationalism, or *laissez faire* without getting a sense that outgoing parties did so with some sense of relief; 'democratisation' often looked more like 'giving up'.

6 THE THREE HEGEMONIES OF HISTORICAL CAPITALISM

GIOVANNI ARRIGHI

THE CONCEPT OF WORLD HEGEMONY

The decline of US world power in the 1970s and 1980s has occasioned a wave of studies on the rise and decline of 'hegemonies' (Hopkins and Wallerstein, 1979; Bousquet, 1979; 1980; Wallerstein, 1984b), 'world powers' (Modelski, 1978; 1981; 1987), 'cores' (Gilpin, 1975), and 'great powers' (Kennedy, 1987/8). These studies differ considerably from one another in their object of study, methodology, and conclusions but they have two characteristics in common. First, if and when they use the term 'hegemony', they mean 'dominance', and secondly, their focus and emphasis is on an alleged basic invariance of the system within which the power of a state rises and declines.

Most of these studies rely on some concept of 'innovation' and 'leadership' in defining the relative capabilities of states. In the case of Modelski, systemic innovations and leadership in carrying them out are assumed to be the main sources of 'world power'. But in all these studies, including Modelski's, systemic innovations do not change the basic mechanisms through which power in the interstate system rises and declines. As a matter of fact, the invariance of these mechanisms is generally held to be one of the central features of the interstate system.

In this paper I shall attempt to show that by applying Gramsci's concept of hegemony to inter-state relations we can tell a story of the rise and decline of world power that accounts, not just for the invariance, but also for the evolution and supersession of the modern world-system. The concept of 'world hegemony' adopted here refers to the power of a state to exercise governmental functions over a system of sovereign states. In principle, this power may just involve the ordinary management of such a system as instituted at a given time. As we shall see, however, the government of a system of sovereign states in practice always involves some kind of transformative action that changes the mode of operation of the system in a fundamental way.

This power is something more and different than 'dominance' pure and simple. It is the power associated with dominance expanded by the exercise of 'intellectual and moral leadership'. As emphasised by Gramsci with reference to hegemony at the national level,

> the supremacy of a social group manifests itself in two ways, as 'domination' and as 'intellectual and moral leadership'. A social group dominates antagonistic groups, which it tends to 'liquidate', or to subjugate perhaps even by armed force; it leads kindred or allied groups. A social group can, and indeed must, already exercise 'leadership' before winning governmental power (this indeed is one of the principal conditions for winning such power); it subsequently becomes dominant when it exercises power, but even if it holds it firmly in its grasp, it must continue to 'lead' as well. (Gramsci, 1971: 57–8)

This is a reformulation of Machiavelli's image of power as a combination of consent and coercion. Coercion implies the use of force or the credible threat thereof; consent implies moral leadership. When the use of force is too risky and the exercise of moral leadership is problematic, 'corruption' and 'fraud' may temporarily step in as surrogates of power:

> Between consent and force stands corruption/fraud (which is characteristic of certain situations when it is hard to exercise the hegemonic function, and when the use of force is too risky). This consists in procuring the demoralization and paralysis of the antagonist (or antagonists) by buying its leaders – either covertly, or, in case of imminent danger, openly – in order to sow disarray and confusion in its ranks (Gramsci, 1971: 80n).

Corruption and fraud are thus tactical weapons in a rearguard struggle to preserve power. They are the expression, not of power, but of a failure of power.

Hegemony, in contrast, is the *additional* power that accrues to a dominant group in virtue of its capacity to pose on a universal plane all the issues around which conflict rages.

> It is true that the State is seen as the organ of one particular group, destined to create favourable conditions for the latter's maximum expansion. But the development and expansion of the particular group are conceived of, and presented, as being the motor force of a universal expansion, a development of all the 'national' energies. (Gramsci, 1971: 181–2)

To be sure, the claim of the dominant group to represent a universal interest is always more or less fraudulent. Nevertheless, following Gramsci, we shall speak of hegemony only when the claim is at least in part true and adds something to the power of the dominant state. A situation in which the claim of the dominant state to represent a general interest is purely fraudulent will be defined not as a situation of hegemony but as a failure of hegemony.

Since the word hegemony, in its etymological sense of 'leadership' and in its derived sense of 'dominance', normally refers to relations among states, it is entirely possible that Gramsci used the term metaphorically to clarify relations among social groups through an analogy with relations among states. In transposing Gramsci's concept of social hegemony from intra-state relations to inter-state relations – as done implicitly, by myself (Arrighi, 1982) and, explicitly, by Cox (1983; 1987), Keohane (1984a), Gill (1986a), and Gill and Law (1988) among others – we may simply be retracing in reverse Gramsci's mental process. In doing so we are faced with two problems.

The first problem concerns the double meaning of 'leadership', particularly when applied to relations among states. A dominant state exercises a hegemonic function if it leads the *system* of states in a desired direction and, in so doing, is perceived as pursuing a universal interest. It is this kind of leadership that makes the dominant state hegemonic. But a dominant state may lead also in the sense that it draws other states into its path of development. Borrowing an expression from Schumpeter, this second kind of leadership can be designated as 'leadership against one's own will' because over time it enhances competition for power rather than the power of the hegemon (Schumpeter, 1963: 89). These two kinds of leadership may co-exist – at least for a time. But it is only leadership in the former sense that defines a situation as hegemonic.

The second problem concerns the fact that it is more difficult to define a general interest at the level of the interstate system than it is at the level of individual states. At the level of individual states an increase in the power of the state *vis-à-vis* other states is an important component, and in itself a measure, of the successful pursuit of a general (that is, national) interest. But power in this sense cannot increase for the system as a whole, by definition. It can of course increase for a particular group of states at the expense of all other states but the hegemony of the leader of that group is at best 'regional' or 'civilisational' not a world hegemony.

World hegemonies as understood here can only arise if the pursuit of power by states in relation to one another is not the only objective of state action. In fact, the pursuit of power in the interstate system is only one side of the coin that jointly defines the strategy and structure of states qua organisations. The other side of the coin is the maximisation of power *vis-à-vis* subjects. A state may therefore become world hegemonic because it can claim with credibility to be the motor force of a universal expansion of the *collective* power of rulers *vis-à-vis* subjects. Or, conversely, a state may become world hegemonic because it can claim with credibility that the expansion of its power relative to some or even all other states is in the general interest of the subjects of all states.

Claims of these kind are most likely to be truthful and credible in situations of 'systemic chaos'. 'Chaos' is not the same thing as 'anarchy'. Even though the two terms are often used interchangeably, an understanding of the systemic origins of world hegemonies requires that we distinguish between the two.

'Anarchy' designates 'absence of central rule'. In this sense, the modern system of sovereign states as well as the system of rule of medieval Europe out of which the latter emerged, qualify as anarchic systems. Yet, each of these two systems had/has its own implicit and explicit principles, norms, rules, and procedures which justify our referring to them as 'ordered anarchies' or 'anarchic orders'.

The concept of 'ordered anarchy' was first introduced by anthropologists seeking to explicate the observed tendency of 'tribal' systems to produce order out of conflict (Evans-Pritchard, 1940; Gluckman, 1963: ch. 1). This tendency has been at work in the medieval and in the modern systems of rule as well, because also in these systems the 'absence of central rule' has not meant lack of organisation and, within limits, conflict has tended to produce order.

'Chaos' and 'systemic chaos', in contrast, refer to a situation of total and apparently irremediable lack of organisation. It is a situation that arises because conflict escalates beyond the threshold within which it calls forth powerful countervailing tendencies, or because a new set of rules and norms of behaviour is imposed upon, or grows from within an older set of rules and norms without displacing it, or because of a combination of these two circumstances. As systemic chaos increases, the demand for 'order' – the old order, a new order – tends to become more and more general among rulers or among subjects or among both. Whichever state is in a position to satisfy this system-wide demand is thus presented with the opportunity of becoming hegemonic.

THE ORIGINS OF THE MODERN INTER-STATE SYSTEM

World hegemonies are a phenomenon of the modern inter-state system which emerged out of the decay and eventual disintegration of the system of rule of medieval Europe. As argued by Ruggie, there is a fundamental difference between the modern and the medieval (European) systems of rule. Both systems can be characterised as 'anarchic' but anarchy, in the sense of 'absence of central rule', means different things according to the principles on the basis of which the units of the system are separated from one another: 'If anarchy tells us *that* the political system is a segmental realm, differentiation tells us *on what basis* the segments are determined' (Ruggie, 1983: 274, emphasis in the original).

The medieval system of rule consisted of chains of lord-vassal relationships based on an amalgam of conditional property and private authority. As a result, 'different juridical instances were geographically interwoven and stratified, and plural allegiances, asymmetrical suzerainties and anomalous enclaves abounded' (Anderson, 1974: 37–8). In addition, ruling elites were extremely mobile *across* the space of these overlapping political jurisdictions being able 'to travel and assume governance from one end of the continent to the other without hesitation or difficulty'. Finally, this system of rule was 'legitimated by common bodies of law, religion, and custom that expressed inclusive natural rights pertaining to the social totality formed by the constituent units' (Ruggie, 1983: 275).

> In sum, this was quintessentially a system of segmental rule; it was anarchy. But it was a form of segmental territorial rule that had none of the connotations of possessiveness and exclusiveness conveyed by the modern concept of sovereignty. It represented a heteronomous organization of territorial rights and claims – of political space. (Ruggie, 1983: 275)

In contrast to the medieval system of rule, 'the modern system of rule consists of the institutionalisation of public authority within mutually exclusive jurisdictional domains' (Ruggie, 1983: 275). Rights of private property and rights of public government become absolute and separated from one another; political jurisdictions become exclusive and clearly demarcated by boundaries; the mobility of ruling elites across political jurisdictions slows down and eventually ceases; law, religion, and custom become 'national', that is, subject to no political authority other than that of the sovereign.

This 'becoming' of the modern system of rule has been closely associated with the development of capitalism as mode of accumulation on a world scale. This close association is at the heart of Wallerstein's conceptualisation of the modern world-system as a capitalist world-economy. In this conceptualisation, the rise and expansion of the modern inter-state system is held to have been both the main cause and an effect of the endless accumulation of capital: 'Capitalism has been able to flourish precisely because the world-economy has had within its bounds not one but a multiplicity of political systems' (Wallerstein, 1974a: 348). At the same time, the tendency of capitalist accumulators to mobilize their respective states so as to enhance their competitive position in the world-economy has continually reproduced the segmentation of the political realm into separate jurisdictions (Wallerstein, 1974b: 402).

The strength of Wallerstein's conceptualisation is in its emphasis on the fundamental unity of capitalism and the modern system of rule. Its weakness is in its tendency to blur all analytical distinctions between the two terms of this relationship.

In my view, the close historical connection between capitalism and the modern inter-state system does not warrant this blurring of their separate analytical identities. For the relationship between the two is just as much one of contradiction as it is one of unity.

More specifically, the segmentation of the world-economy into competing political jurisdictions does not necessarily benefit capitalist accumulators. It largely depends on the form and intensity of competition. For example, if inter-state competition takes the form of intense and long-drawn-out armed struggles, there is no reason why the costs of interstate competition to capitalist accumulators should not exceed the costs of centralised rule that they would have to bear in a world-empire. On the contrary, under such circumstances the profitability of capitalist enterprise might very well be undermined and eventually destroyed by an ever-increasing diversion of resources of military enterprise and/or by an ever-increasing disruption of the networks of production and exchange through which capitalist enterprises appropriate surpluses and transform such surpluses into profits.

At the same time, competition among capitalist accumulators does not necessarily promote the continual segmentation of the political realm into separate jurisdictions. Again, it largely depends on the form and intensity of competition, in this case among capitalist enterprises. If capitalist accumulators are enmeshed in dense trans-state networks of production and exchange, the segmentation of these networks into separate political jurisdictions may bear negatively on the competitive position of each and every capitalist enterprise relative to non-capitalist enterprises. Under these circumstances, capitalist accumulators may well mobilise their respective states to reduce rather than to increase or reproduce the political segmentation of the world-economy. And this tendency can be expected to be stronger, the more intense is intercapitalist competition.

More generally, inter-state and inter-enterprise competition can take different forms, and the form that they take has important consequences for the way in which the modern world-system – as mode of rule and as mode of accumulation – functions or does not function. It is not enough to emphasise the historical connection between inter-state and inter-enterprise competition. We must also specify the form which they take and how they change over time. Only in this way can we fully appreciate the evolutionary nature of the modern world-system and the role played by successive world hegemonies in making and remaking the system so as to resolve the recurrent contradiction between an endless accumulation of capital and a comparatively stable organisation of political space.

Central to such an understanding is the definition of 'capitalism' and 'territorialism' as opposite modes of rule or logics of power. Territorialist rulers identify power with the extent and populousness of their domains and conceive of wealth/capital as a means or a byproduct of the 'endless' pursuit of territorial expansion. Capitalist rulers, in contrast, identify power with the extent of their command over scarce resources and consider territorial acquisitions as a means and a byproduct of an 'endless' accumulation of capital.

The difference between these two logics can also be expressed in terms of the metaphor that defines states as 'containers of power' (Giddens, 1987). Territorialist rulers tends to increase their power by expanding the size of the container. Capitalist rulers, in contrast, tend to increase their power by piling up wealth within a small container and increase the size of the container only if it is justified by the requirements of the accumulation of capital.

The essential feature of the modern world-system has been the constant opposition of these two logics and the recurrent resolution of their contradictions through the innovative reorganisation of world political-economic space by the leading capitalist state of the epoch. This dialectic between capitalism and territorialism antedates the establishment of the modern inter-state system. Its origins lie in the formation within the medieval system of rule of a regional subsystem of capitalist and protocapitalist states in northern Italy.

154

Initially, this region was nothing but one of the 'anomalous enclaves' that abounded in the political space of the medieval system of rule, as Anderson reminds us in the passage quoted earlier. But as the decay of the medieval system of rule widened and deepened, the northern Italian capitalist enclave became organised into a subsystem of separate and independent political jurisdictions held together by the principle of the balance of power and by dense and extensive networks of residential diplomacy.

As emphasised in different but complementary ways by such authorities as Braudel (1984: ch. 2), Lane (1966; 1979), and McNeill (1984: ch. 3), this subsystem of city-states – centred on Venice, Florence, Genoa, and Milan – anticipated by two centuries or more many of the key features of the modern interstate system. Four such features stand out for comment.

First, this subsystem of city-state constituted a quintessentially capitalist system of war- and state-making. The most powerful and leading state in the subsystem (Venice) is the true prototype of the capitalist state, in the double sense of 'perfect example' and 'model for future instances' of such a state. A merchant capitalist oligarchy firmly held state power in its grip. Territorial acquisitions were subjected to careful cost-benefit analysis and, as a rule, were undertaken only as mere means to the end of enhancing the profitability of the traffics of the capitalist oligarchy that exercised state power (Braudel, 1984: 120–1; Modelski and Modelski, 1988: 19–32).

Pace Sombart, if there has ever been a state whose executive met the *Communist Manifesto's* standards of the capitalist state ('but a committee for managing the common affairs of the whole bourgeoisie' (Marx and Engels, 1967: 82), it was fifteenth-century Venice. From this standpoint, the leading capitalist states of future epochs (the United Provinces, the United Kingdom, the United States) appear as increasingly 'diluted' versions of the ideo-typical standards realised by Venice centuries earlier. As we shall see, this is no accident. Although Genoa, Florence, and Milan (in that order) did not meet the ideo-typical standards of the capitalist state as well as Venice, they all did by the lower standards of later epochs.

Secondly, the operation of the 'balance of power' played a crucial role at three different levels in fostering the development of this enclave of capitalist rule within the medieval system. The balance of power between the central authorities of the medieval system (pope and emperor) was instrumental in the emergence of an organised capitalist enclave in northern Italy – the geopolitical locus of that balance. The balance of power among the northern Italian city-states themselves was instrumental in preserving their mutual separateness and autonomy. And the balance of power among the emerging dynastic states of western Europe was instrumental in preventing the logic of territorialism from nipping in the bud the rise of a capitalist logic within the European system of rule (cf. McNeill, 1984: ch. 3).

The balance of power was thus integral from the start to the development of capitalism as mode of rule. The balance of power can be interpreted as an instrument by means of which capitalist rulers can, individually or as a group, reduce protection costs absolutely and relative to competitors and rivals. For the balance of power to be or become such an instrument, however, the capitalist states(s) must be in a position to manipulate the balance to its (their) advantage instead of being cog(s) in a mechanism which no one or someone else controls. If the balance of power can only be maintained through endless and costly wars, then participation in its working defeats the purpose of the capitalist state(s), because the pecuniary costs of such wars inevitably tend to exceed their pecuniary benefits. The secret of capitalist success is to have one's wars fought by others, if feasible for free and, if not, at the least possible cost.

Thirdly, by developing wage-labour relations in what Lane has aptly called the 'protection-producing industry', that is, war- and state-making, the Italian city-states managed to transform at least part of their protection costs into revenues, and thus make wars pay for themselves.

> [Enough] money circulated in the richer Italian towns to make it possible for citizens to tax themselves and use the proceeds to buy the service of armed strangers. Then, simply by spending their pay, the hired soldiers put these monies back in circulation. Thereby, they intensified the market exchanges that allowed such towns to commercialize armed violence in the first place. The emergent system thus tended to become self-sustaining (McNeill, 1984: 74).

The emergent system could become self-sustaining only up to a point – that is, up to the point where cost inflation and changes in the social composition of the city-state undermined the capability of the dominant capitalist oligarchy to pursue effectively the endless accumulation of capital. In situations of permanent war, the ever-expanding circulation of money within the narrow territorial domains of the city-states sooner or later was bound to, and generally did, raise the price of supplies (means of livelihood, means of protection, means of production) more rapidly than their productivity. Alternatively, or in addition to cost inflation, endless wars tended to increase the social power of artisans (as in Florence) or of military personnel (as in Milan) with negative repercussions on the capitalist predispositions of the city-state.

Fourthly and last, the capitalist rulers of the northern Italian city-states (again, Venice in the first place) took the lead in developing dense and extensive networks of residential diplomacy. Through these networks they acquired the knowledge and information concerning the predispositions and capabilities of other rulers (including the territorialist rulers of the wider medieval system of rule within which they operated) that were necessary to manage the balance of power so as to minimize protection costs. Just as the profitability of long-distance trade depended crucially on a quasi-monopolistic control of information over the largest economic space possible (Braudel, 1982), so the capacity of capitalist rulers to manage the balance of power to their own advantage depended crucially on a quasi-monopolistic knowledge of, and capacity to monitor, the decision-making process of other rulers.

This was the function of residential diplomacy. In comparison with territorialist rulers, capitalist rulers had both stronger motivations and greater opportunities to promote its development. They had stronger motivations because superior knowledge concerning the predisposition and capabilities of rulers was essential to the management of the balance of power which, in turn, was central to an economising behaviour. But they had also greater opportunities because the networks of long-distance trade controlled by the capitalist oligarchies provided a ready made and self-financing foundation on which to build diplomatic networks.

The accumulation of capital through long-distance trade, the management of the balance of power, the commercialisation of war, and the development of residential diplomacy thus complemented one another and, for a century or two, promoted an extraordinary concentration of wealth and power in the hands of the oligarchies that ruled the northern Italian city-states. *Circa* 1420 the leading Italian city-states, not only functioned as great powers in European politics (McNeill, 1984: 78), but also had revenues that compared very favourably with the revenues of the most successful dynastic states of western and north-western Europe (Braudel, 1984: 120). They thereby showed that even small territories could become huge containers of power by pursuing one-sidedly the accumulation of riches rather than the acquisition of territories and subjects. Henceforth, 'considerations of plenty' would become integral and central to 'considerations of power' throughout Europe.

The Italian city-states, however, never attempted individually or collectively a purposive transformation of the medieval system of rule. Two more centuries had to elapse – from *c*. 1450 to *c*. 1650 (the so-called 'long' sixteenth century) – before a new kind of capitalist state (the United Provinces) would actually be presented with, and seize, the opportunity to transform the European system of rule to suit the requirements of the accumulation of capital on a world scale.

DUTCH HEGEMONY AND THE BIRTH OF THE WESTPHALIA SYSTEM

This new situation arose as a result of a quantum leap in the European power struggle precipitated by the attempts of territorialist rulers to incorporate within their domains, or to prevent others from incorporating, the wealth and power of the Italian city-states. As it turned out, outright conquest proved impossible primarily because of the competition among the territorialist rulers themselves. In this struggle for the impossible, however, select territorial states (Spain and France in particular) developed new war-making techniques (the Spanish *tercios*, professional standing armies, mobile siege cannons, new fortification systems, and so on) which gave them a decisive power advantage *vis-à-vis* other rulers, including the supra- and sub-statal authorities of the medieval system of rule (cf. McNeill, 1984: 79–95).

The intensification of the European power struggle was soon followed by its geographical expansion, because some territorialist rulers sought more roundabout ways to incorporate within their domains the wealth and power of the Italian city-states. Instead of, or in addition to, seeking the annexation of the city-states, these rulers tried to conquer the very sources of their wealth and power. These sources were circuits of long-distance trade.

More specifically, the fortunes of the Italian city-states in general and of Venice in particular rested primarily on a monopolistic control over a crucial link in the chain of commercial exchanges that connected western Europe to India and China via the House of Islam. No territorial state was powerful enough to take over the monopoly, but select territorialist rulers could and did attempt to establish a more direct link between western Europe and India/China so as to divert money flows and supplies from the Venetian to their own trade circuits. Portugal and Spain, assisted by Genoese agents crowded out by Venice from the most profitable traffics of the Mediterranean, took the lead in these attempts. While Portugal succeeded in the purpose, Spain failed but stumbled across an entirely new source of wealth and power, the Americas.

The intensification and the global expansion of the European power struggle engendered a vicious/virtuous circle (vicious for its victims, virtuous for its beneficiaries) of more and more massive resources and of increasingly sophisticated and costly techniques of state- and war-making deployed in the power struggle. Techniques which had been developed in the struggle within Europe were deployed to subjugate extra-European states and peoples, and the wealth and power originating from the subjugation of extra-European states and peoples were deployed in the struggle within Europe (McNeill, 1984: 94–5, 100ff.)

The state that initially benefited most from this vicious/virtuous circle was Spain, the only state that was a protagonist of the power struggle simultaneously on the European and on the extra-European fronts. Throughout the sixteenth century, the power of Spain exceeded that of all other European states by a large margin. This power, however, far from being used to oversee a 'smooth' transition to the modern system of rule, became an instrument of the Hapsburg Imperial House and of the Papacy to save what could be saved of the disintegrating medieval system of rule.

In reality, little or nothing could be saved because the quantum leap in the European power struggle since the middle of the fifteenth century had taken the disintegration of the medieval system beyond the point of no return. Out of that struggle new realities of power had emerged in north-western Europe which, to varying degrees, had subsumed the capitalist logic of power within the territorialist logic. The result was the formation of compact mini-empires (best exemplified by the French, English, and Swedish dynastic states) which, individually, could not match the power of Spain, but collectively, could not be subordinated to any old or new central political authority. The attempt of Spain, in conjunction with the Papacy and the Hapsburg Imperial House, to unmake or subordinate these new realities of power, not only failed, but created a situation of systemic chaos that created the conditions for the rise of Dutch hegemony and the final liquidation of the medieval system of rule.

For conflict quickly escalated beyond the regulative capacities of the medieval system of rule and turned its institutions into so many new causes of conflict. As a consequence, the European power struggle became an ever-more-negative-sum game in which all or most of the European rulers began to realise that they had nothing to gain and everything to lose from its continuation. The most important factor in this realisation was the sudden escalation of system-wide social conflict into a serious threat to the collective power of European rulers.

As Marc Bloch once wrote, '[the] peasant revolt was as common in early modern Europe as strikes are in industrial societies today'. But in the late sixteenth century and, above all, in the first half of the seventeeth, this rural unrest was compounded by urban revolts on an unprecedented scale – revolts that were directed not against the 'employers' but against the state. The Puritan Revolution in England was the most dramatic episode of this explosive combination of rural and urban revolts, but almost all European rulers were directly affected or felt seriously threatened by the social upheaval (Parker and Smith, 1985: 12ff).

This system-wide intensification of social conflict was a direct result of the previous and contemporaneous escalation of armed conflicts among rulers. From *c.* 1550 to *c.* 1640, the number of soldiers deployed by the great powers of Europe more than doubled, while from 1530 to 1630 the cost of putting each of these soldiers in the field increased on average by a factor of five (Parker and Smith, 1985: 14). This escalation of protection costs led to a sharp increase in the fiscal pressure on subjects which, in turn, triggered many of the seventeenth-century revolts (Steensgaard, 1985: 42–4).

Alongside this escalation in protection costs, there had been an escalation in the ideological struggle. The progressive breakdown of the medieval system of rule had led to a mixture of religious innovations and of religious restorations from above – following the principle *cuius regio eius religio* – which provoked popular resentments and rebellions against both (Parker and Smith, 1985: 15–18). As rulers turned religion into an instrument of their mutual power struggles, subjects followed suit and turned religion into an instrument of insurrection against rulers.

Last but not least, the escalation of armed conflicts among rulers disrupted the trans-European networks of trade on which rulers depended to obtain means of war and subjects depended to obtain means of livelihood. The costs and risks of moving goods across political jurisdictions increased dramatically and supplies were diverted from the provision of means of livelihood to the provision of means of war. It is plausible to assume that this disruption and diversion of trade flows contributed far more decisively than climatic factors (the Little Ice Age) to the worsening problem of vagrancy and to the 'subsistence crisis' which constitute the social and economic backdrop of the general crisis of legitimacy of the seventeenth century (cf. Braudel and Spooner, 1967).

Whatever the mix of tendencies that caused popular insurgency, the result was a heightened consciousness among European rulers of their common power interest *vis-à-vis* subjects. As James I put it at an early stage of the general crisis, their existed 'an implicit tie amongst kings which obligeth them, though there may be no other interest or particular engagement, to stick unto and right one another upon insurrection of subjects' (Hill, 1958: 126). Under normal circumstances, this 'implicit tie' had little or no influence on the behaviour of rulers. But on those occasions in which the authority of all or most rulers was seriously challenged by their subjects – as it was in the middle of the seventeenth century – the general interest of rulers in preserving their collective power over subjects overshadowed their quarrels and mutual antagonisms.

It was under these circumstances that the United Provinces became hegemonic by leading a large and powerful coalition of dynastic states toward the liquidation of the medieval system of rule and the establishment of the modern inter-state system. In the course of their previous struggle for national independence from Spain, the Dutch had already established a strong intellectual and moral leadership over the dynastic states of north-western Europe, which were among the main beneficiaries of the disintegration of the medieval system of rule. As systemic chaos increased during the Thirty-Year War, Dutch proposals of a major reorganisation of the pan-European system of rule found more and more supporters among European rulers until Spain was isolated completely. With the Peace of Westphalia of 1648, a new system of rule was thus born.

> The idea of an authority or organization about sovereign states is no longer. What takes its place is the notion that all states form a world-wide political system or that, at any rate, the states of Western Europe form a single political system. This new system rests on international law and the balance of power, a law operating between rather than above states and a power operating between rather than above states. (Gross, 1968: 54–5)

The system of rule created at Westphalia had a social purpose as well. As rulers legitimated their respective absolute rights of government over mutually exclusive territories, they also placed under international guarantee the principle of religious equality. Participation in the newly-created inter-state system was thus made conditional upon certain domestic social practices (religious tolerance). A more general principle was thus established which complemented the principle of the separation of political jurisdictions – the principle, that is, that civilians were not included in quarrels among sovereigns.

Beside religious tolerance, the most important application of this principle was in the field of commerce. In the treaties that followed the Settlement of Westphalia a clause was inserted that aimed at restoring freedom of commerce by abolishing barriers to trade which had developed in the course of the Thirty-Year War. Subsequent agreements introduced rules aimed at protecting the property and commerce of noncombatants. An international regime was thus established in which the effects of war-making among sovereigns on the everyday life of subjects were minimised.

> The 18th century witnessed many wars; but in respect of the freedom and friendliness of intercourse between the educated classes in the principal European countries, with French as the recognized common language, it was the most 'international' period of modern history, and civilians could pass to and from and transact their business freely with one another while their respective sovereigns were at war. (Carr, 1945: 4)

The systemic chaos of the early seventeenth century was thus transformed into a new anarchic order. The considerable freedom granted to private enterprise to organise commerce peacefully across political jurisdictions even at times of war reflected, not only the general interest of rulers and subjects in dependable supplies of means of war and means of livelihood, but the particular interests of the Dutch capitalist oligarchy in an unfettered accumulation of capital. This reorganisation of political space in the interest of capital accumulation marks the birth, not just of the modern inter-state system but also of capitalism as world-system. The reasons it took place in the seventeenth century under Dutch leadership instead of in the fifteenth century under Venetian leadership are not far to seek.

The most important reason, which encompasses all the others, is that in the fifteenth century anarchy had not yet turned into systemic chaos so that there was no general interest among European rulers in the liquidation of the medieval system of rule. The Venetian capitalist oligarchy had itself been doing so well within that system as to have no interest whatsoever in its liquidation. In any event, the Italian city-state system was a regional subsystem continually imploded by the greater and lesser powers of the wider world-system to which it belonged. Political rivalries and diplomatic alliances could not be confined to the subsystem. They systematically brought into play, and thereby expanded the powers of, territorialist rulers who kept the capitalist oligarchies of northern Italy permanently on the defensive

By the early seventeenth century, in contrast, increasing systemic chaos had created both a general interest among European rulers in a major rationalisation of the power struggle and a capitalist oligarchy with the motivations and the capabilities necessary to take the lead in serving that general interest. The Dutch capitalist oligarchy was in important respects a replica of the Venetian capitalist oligarchy. Like the latter, it was the bearer of a capitalist logic of power and, as such, a leader in the management of the balance of power and in diplomatic initiatives and innovations. Unlike the latter, however, it was a product rather than a factor of the quantum leap in the European power struggle prompted by the emergence of capitalist states in northern Italy. This difference had several important implications.

First, the scale of operation, and hence the power, of the Dutch capitalist oligarchy in European and world politics was much greater than that of Venice. The wealth and power of Venice rested on a circuit of trade that was itself a link in a much longer circuit which Venice did not control. As we have seen, this local link could be and was superseded by more roundabout and new circuits of trade. The wealth and power of Holland, in contrast, was based on commercial and financial networks that the Dutch capitalist oligarchy had carved out of the seaborne and colonial empires through which the territorialist rulers of Portugal and Spain had superseded the wealth and power of Venice.

These networks encircled the world and could not be easily bypassed or superseded. As a matter of fact, the wealth and power of the Dutch capitalist oligarchy rested more on its control over world financial networks than on commercial networks. This meant that it was less vulnerable than the Venetian capitalist oligarchy to the establishment of competing trade routes or to increased competition on a given route. As competition in long-distance trade intensified, the Dutch oligarchs could recoup their losses and find a new field of profitable investment in financial speculation. The Dutch capitalist oligarchy therefore had the power to rise above the competition and turn it to its own advantage.

Secondly, the interests of the Dutch capitalist oligarchy clashed far more fundamentally with the interests of the central authorities of the medieval system of rule than the interests of the Venetian capitalist oligarchy ever did. As the history of the 'long' sixteenth century demonstrated, the wealth and power of Venice were threatened more fundamentally by the waxing power of the dynastic states of south- and north-western Europe that were emerging out of the disintegration of the medieval system of rule than they were by the waning power of the Papacy and the Imperial House. In contrast, the Dutch capitalist oligarchy had a strong common interest with the emerging dynastic states in the liquidation of the claims of pope and emperor to a suprastatal moral and political authority as embodied in the imperial pretensions of Spain.

As a consequence of its secular struggle for political independence against imperial Spain, the Dutch became a champion and organiser of the proto-nationalist aspirations of dynastic rulers and of popular aspirations for religious self-determination. At the same time, they constantly sought ways and means to prevent conflict from escalating beyond the point where the commercial and financial foundations of their wealth and power would be seriously undermined. In pursuing its own interest, the Dutch capitalist oligarchy thus came to be perceived as the champion not just of independence from the central authorities of the medieval system of rule but also of a general interest in peace which the latter were no longer able to serve.

Thirdly, the war-making capabilities of the Dutch capitalist oligarchy far surpassed those of the Venetian oligarchy. The capabilities of the latter were closely related to the geographical position of Venice and had little use outside that position, particularly after the great leap forward in war-making techniques of the 'long' sixteenth century. The capabilities of the Dutch oligarchy, in contrast, were based on successful front-line participation in that great leap forward. As a matter of fact, the Dutch were leaders not just in the accumulation of capital but also in the rationalisation of military techniques.

By rediscovering and bringing to perfection long-forgotten Roman military techniques, Maurice of Nassau, Prince of Orange, achieved for the Dutch army in the early seventeenth century what scientific management would achieve for US industry two centuries later (McNeill, 1984: 127–39; van Doorn, 1975: 9ff.). Siege techniques were transformed (a) to increase the efficiency of military labour power, (b) to cut costs in terms of casualties, and (c) to facilitate the maintenance of discipline in the army's ranks. Marching and the loading and firing of guns were standardised and drilling was made a regular activity of soldiers. The army was divided into smaller tactical units, the number of officers and noncoms was increased, and lines of command were rationalised so that

> in this way an army became an articulate organism with a central nervous system that allowed sensitive and more or less intelligent

164

> response to unforseen circumstances. Every movement attained a new level of exactitude and speed. The individual movements of soldiers when firing and marching as well as the movements of battalions across the battlefield could be controlled and predicted as never before. A well-drilled unit, by making every motion count, could increase the amount of lead projected against the enemy per minute of battle. The dexterity and resolution of individual infantry men scarcely mattered any more. Prowess and personal courage all but disappeared beneath an armor-plated routine . . . Yet troops drilled in the Maurician fashion automatically exhibited superior effectiveness in battle. (McNeill, 1984: 130)

The significance of this innovation is that it neutralised the advantages of scale enjoyed by Spain and thereby tended to equalise relative military capabilities within Europe. By actively encouraging the propagation of new techniques among its allies, the United Provinces created the conditions of substantive equality among European states that was the premise of the future Westphalia System. And of course, by so doing, it strengthened its intellectual and moral leadership over the dynastic rulers who were seeking the legitimation of their absolute rights of government.

Fourthly and last, the state-making capabilities of the Dutch capitalist oligarchy were far greater than those of the Venetian oligarchy. The exclusiveness of capitalist interests in the organisation and management of the Venetian state was the main source of its power but was also the main limit of that power. For this exclusiveness kept the political horizon of the Venetian oligarchy within the limits set by cost-benefit analysis and double-entry book-keeping. That is to say, it kept Venetian rulers aloof from the political and social issues that were tearing apart the world within which they operated.

The state-making capabilities of the Dutch capitalist oligarchy, in contrast, had been forged in a secular struggle of emancipation from Spanish imperial rule. In order to succeed in this struggle, it had to forge an alliance and share power with dynastic interests (the House of Orange) and had to ride the tiger of popular rebellion (Calvinism). As a consequence, the power of the capitalist oligarchy within the Dutch state was far less absolute than it had been within the Venetian state. But for this very reason the Dutch ruling group developed much greater capabilities than Venetian rulers ever had to pose and solve the problems around which the European power struggle raged. That is to say, the United Provinces became hegemonic in virtue of being less rather than more capitalist than Venice.

165

BRITISH HEGEMONY AND FREE-TRADE IMPERIALISM

The Dutch never governed the system which they had created. As soon as the Westphalia System was in place, the United Provinces lost control of the European balance of power and soon lost their previous world-power status as well. In terms of power, the great beneficiaries of the new system of rule were its former allies France and England. For the next century and a half – from the outbreak of the Anglo-Dutch Wars in 1652 (merely four years after the Settlement of Westphalia) to the end of the Napoleonic Wars in 1815 – the inter-state system came to be dominated by the struggle for world supremacy between these two great powers.

This secular conflict developed in three partly overlapping phases which replicated in some respects the phases of struggle of the 'long' sixteenth century. The first phase was once again characterised by the attempts of territorialist rulers to incorporate within their domains the leading capitalist state. Just as France and Spain had attempted in the late fifteenth century to conquer the northern Italian city-states, so in the late seventeenth century England and France attempted to conquer the United Provinces.

As Colbert emphasised in his advice to Louis XIV, '[if] the king were to subjugate all the United Provinces to his authority, their commerce would become the commerce of the subjects of his majesty, and there would be nothing more to ask' (Anderson, 1974: 36–7). The problem with this piece of advice was in the 'if' clause. Even though the strategic capabilities of seventeenth-century France (or for that matter England) greatly exceeded the capabilities of their fifteenth-century counterparts, the strategic capabilities of the United Provinces exceeded those of the leading capitalist states of the fifteenth century by an even greater margin. Notwithstanding a short-lived joint effort, France and England failed to subjugate the Dutch. Once again, competition between the would-be conquerors proved an insuperable obstacle on the road to conquest.

As these attempts failed, the struggle entered a second phase in which the efforts of the two rivals became increasingly focused on incorporating the sources of the wealth and power of the capitalist state rather than the capitalist state itself. Just as Portugal and Spain had struggled for control over the traffic with the East, so now France and England struggled for control over the Atlantic. Differences between the two struggles, however, are as important as the analogies.

Both France and England were late-comers in the global power struggle. This had some advantages. The most important was that by the time France and England entered the business of territorial expansion in the extra-European world the spread of Maurician 'scientific management' to the European armies had turned their comparative advantage over the armies of extra-European rulers into an unbridgeable gulf. The power of the Ottoman Empire had begun to decline irreversibly.

> Further East, the new style of training soldiers became important when European drillmasters began to create miniature armies by recruiting local manpower for the protection of French, Dutch, and English trading stations on the shores of the Indian Ocean. By the eighteenth century, such forces, however minuscule, exhibited a clear superiority over the unwieldy armies that local rulers were accustomed to bring into the field. (McNeill, 1984: 135)

This comparative advantage *vis-à-vis* extra-European rulers, however, was of little help to the late-comers in displacing the Portuguese, the Spaniards, and, above all, the Dutch from established positions at the crossroads of world commerce. In order to catch up with and overtake the early-comers, the late-comers had to restructure radically the political geography of world commerce. This is precisely what was achieved by the new synthesis of capitalism and territorialism brought into being by French and British mercantilism in the eighteenth century.

This new synthesis had three major and closely interrelated components: settler colonialism, capitalist slavery, and economic nationalism. All three components were essential to the reorganisation of world political-economic space, but settler colonialism was probably the leading element in the combination. British rulers in particular relied heavily on the private initiative of their subjects in countering the advantages of early-comers in overseas expansion.

> Although they could not match the Dutch in financial acumen and in the size and efficiency of their merchant fleet, the English believed in founding settlement colonies and not just ports of call en route to the Indies . . . Besides joint-stock or chartered companies the English developed such expedients for colonization as the proprietory colony analogous to the Portuguese captaincies in Brazil, and Crown colonies nominally under direct royal control. What English colonies in America lacked in natural resources and uniformity they made up for in the number and industriousness of the colonists themselves. (Nadel and Curtis, 1964: 9–10).

Capitalist slavery was partly a condition and partly a result of the success of settler colonialism. For the expansion in the number and industriousness of the colonists was continually limited by, and continually recreated, shortages of labour power that could not be satisfied by relying exclusively, or even primarily, on the supplies engendered spontaneously from within the ranks of the settler populations or extracted forcibly from the indigenous populations. This chronic labour shortage enhanced the profitability of capitalist enterprises engaged in the procurement (primarily in Africa) and transport and productive use (primarily in the Americas) of slave labour. The development of capitalist slavery, in turn, became the leading factor in the expansion of the infrastructure and of the outlets necessary to sustain the settlers' productive efforts.

Settler colonialism and capitalist slavery were necessary but insufficient conditions for the success of French and British mercantilism in radically restructuring the global political economy. The third key ingredient (economic nationalism) had two main aspects. One was the endless accumulation of monetary surpluses in colonial and interstate commerce – an accumulation with which mercantilism is often identified. The other was national – or better, domestic-economy-making. As underscored by Schmoller, 'in its inmost kernel [mercantilism was] nothing but state-making – not state-making in a narrow sense, but state-making and national-economy-making at the same time' (Wilson, 1958: 6).

National-economy-making brought to perfection on a greatly enlarged scale the practices pioneered by the Italian city-states three centuries earlier of making wars pay for themselves by turning protection costs into revenues (see above). Partly through commands to state bureaucracies and partly through incentives to private enterprise, the rulers of France and of the United Kingdom internalised within their domains as many of the growing number of activities that, directly or indirectly, entered as inputs in war-and state-making as was feasible. In this way they managed to turn into tax revenues a much larger share of protection costs than the Italian city-states, or for that matter the United Provinces, ever did or could have done. By spending these greater tax revenues within their domestic economies, they then created new incentives and opportunities to establish ever new linkages between activities and thus make wars pay for themselves more and more.

What was happening, in fact, was not that wars were 'paying for themselves', but that an increasing number of civilians were mobilized to sustain indirectly and often unknowingly the war- and state-making efforts of rulers. War- and state-making were becoming an increasingly roundabout business which involved an ever-growing number, range, and variety of seemingly unrelated activities. The capacity of mercantilist rulers to mobilise the energies of their civilian subjects in undertaking and carrying out these activities was strictly limited by their ability to appropriate the benefits of world commerce, of settler colonialism, and of capitalist slavery, and to turn these benefits into adequate rewards for the entrepreneurship and productive efforts of their metropolitan subjects.

In breaking out of these limits British rulers had a decisive comparative advantage over all competitors, the French included. This comparative advantage was geopolitical and resembled the comparative advantage of Venice at the height of its power.

> Both in overseas trade and in naval strength, Britain gained supremacy, favored, like Venice, by two interacting factors: her island position and the new role which fell into her hands, the role of intermediary between two worlds. Unlike the continental powers, Britain could direct her undivided strength toward the sea; unlike her Dutch competitors, she did not have to man a land front. (Dehio, 1962: 71)

The channelling of British energies and resources toward overseas expansion, while the energies and resources of its European competitors were locked in struggles close at home, generated a process of circular and cumulative causation. British successes in overseas expansion increased the pressure on the states of continental Europe to keep up with Great Britain's growing world power. But these successes also provided Great Britain with the means necessary to manage the balance of power in continental Europe so as to keep its rivals busy close at home. Over time, this virtuous/vicious circle put the United Kingdom in a position to eliminate all competitors from overseas expansion and, at the same time, to become the undisputed master of the European balance of power.

When the United Kingdom won the Seven-Years' War (1756–63), the secular struggle with France for world supremacy was over. But the United Kingdom did not thereby become world-hegemonic. On the contrary, as soon as the struggle for world supremacy was over, conflict entered a third phase characterised by increasing systemic chaos. Like the United Provinces in the early seventeenth century, the United Kingdom became hegemonic by creating a new world order out of this systemic chaos.

As in the early seventeenth century, systemic chaos was the result of the intrusion of social conflict into the power struggles of rulers. There were, however, important differences between the two situations. The most important is the much greater degree of autonomy and effectiveness demonstrated by the rebellious subjects in the late eighteenth and early nineteenth centuries in comparison with the early seventeenth century.

To be sure, the new wave of system-wide rebelliousness had its deeper origins in the struggle for the Atlantic, as we shall presently see. Yet, once it exploded, rebellion created the conditions of a renewal on entirely new foundations for the Anglo-French rivalry, and rebellion continued to rage on for about thirty years after this new rivalry had come to an end. Taking the period 1776–1848 as a whole, this second wave of rebelliousness resulted, one, in a thorough transformation of ruler-subject relations throughout the Americas and in most of Europe and two, in the establishment of an entirely new kind of world-hegemon (British Free-Trade Imperialism) which thoroughly reorganised the inter-state system to accommodate that transformation.

The deeper origins of this wave of rebelliousness can be traced to the previous struggle for the Atlantic because its agents were precisely the social forces that had been brought into being and forged into new communities by that struggle: the colonial settlers, the plantation slaves and the metropolitan middle-classes. Rebellion began in the colonies with the American Declaration of Independence of 1776 and hit the United Kingdom first. French rulers immediately seized the opportunity to initiate a revanchist campaign which, however, quickly backfired with the Revolution of 1789. The energies released by this revolution were channelled under Napoleon into a redoubling of French revanchist efforts which, in turn, led to a generalisation of settler, slave, and middle-class rebelliousness (cf. Hobsbawm, 1962; Wallerstein, 1988; Blackburn, 1988).

In the course of these inter- and intra-state struggles there were widespread violations of the principles, norms, and rules of the Westphalian system. Napoleonic France in particular trampled on the absolute rights of government of European rulers both by fermenting revolt from below and by imposing imperial commands from above. At the same time, it trespassed on the property rights and freedoms of commerce of noncombatants through expropriations, blockades, and a command economy spanning most of continental Europe.

The United Kingdom first became hegemonic by leading a vast array of primarily dynastic forces in the struggle against these infringements upon their absolute rights of government and for the restoration of the Westphalia system. This restoration was successfully accomplished with the Settlement of Vienna of 1815 and the subsequent Congress of Aix-la-Chapelle of 1818. Up to this point British hegemony was a replica of Dutch hegemony. Just as the Dutch had successfully led the about-to-be-born inter-state system in the struggle against the imperial pretensions of Habsburg Spain, so the British had successfully led the about-to-be-destroyed inter-state system in the struggle against the imperial pretensions of Napoleonic France (cf. Dehio, 1962).

Unlike the United Provinces, however, the United Kingdom went on to govern the inter-state system and, in doing so, it undertook a major reorganisation of that system aimed at accommodating the new realities of power released by the ongoing revolutionary upheaval. The system that came into being is what Gallagher and Robinson (1953) have aptly called Free-Trade Imperialism – a world-system of rule which both expanded and superseded the Westphalia System. This expansion and supersession is noticeable at three different but interrelated levels of analysis.

First, the inter-state system came to include a much greater number and variety of states, while the balance of power came to operate above rather than between states. A new group of states joined the group of dynastic and oligarchic states that had formed the original nucleus of the Westphalia System. This new group consisted primarily of states controlled by national communities of property holders which had succeeded in gaining independence from old and new empires. Inter-state relations thus began to be governed not by the personal interests, ambitions, and emotions of monarchs but by the collective interests, ambitions, and emotions of these national communities (Carr, 1945: 8).

This 'democratisation' of nationalism was accompanied by an unprecedented centralisation of world power in the hands of a single state, the United Kingdom. In the expanded inter-state system that emerged out of the revolutionary upheaval of 1776–1948, only the United Kingdom was simultaneously involved in the politics of all the regions of the world and, more importantly, held a commanding position in each and every one of them. For the first time, the objective of all previous capitalist states to be the master rather than the servant of the global balance of power was fully (if temporarily) realised by the leading capitalist state of the epoch.

In order to manage more effectively the global balance of power, the United Kingdom took the lead in tightening the loose system of consultation between the great powers of Europe that had been in operation since the Peace of Westphalia. The result was the Concert

171

of Europe which, from the start, was primarily an instrument of British overrule in continental Europe.

Secondly, the disintegration of colonial empires in the Western world was accompanied and followed by their expansion in the non-Western world. The territorial scope of the modern inter-state system thus expanded manyfold but through a resurgence of imperial rule in its midst. This resurgence of imperial rule is indeed the main reason for designating the new system as Free-Trade *Imperialism*.

No territorialist ruler had ever before incorporated within its domains so many, so populous, and so far-flung territories as the United Kingdom did in the nineteenth century. Nor had any territorialist ruler ever before forcibly extracted in so short a time so much tribute – in labour power, in natural resources, and in means of payments – as the British state and its clients did in the Indian subcontinent in the course of the nineteenth century. Part of this tribute was used to buttress and expand the coercive apparatus through which more and more non-Western subjects were added to the British territorial empire. But another, equally conspicuous part was siphoned off in one form or another to London to be recycled in the circuits of wealth through which British power in the Western world was continually reproduced and expanded. The territorialist and the capitalist logics of power thus cross-fertilised and sustained one another.

The recycling of imperial tribute extracted from the colonies into capital invested all over the world enhanced London's comparative advantage as a world financial centre *vis-à-vis* competing centres such as Amsterdam and Paris. This comparative advantage made London the natural home of *haute finance* – a closely knit body of cosmopolitan financiers whose operations and networks had grown in scale and scope ever since the Westphalia System had placed under international guarantee the property and commerce of noncombatants. And as the organic links between the British government and *haute finance* grew tighter the networks of world finance were turned into yet another instrument of British overrule in the interstate system.

Last and most important, the expansion and supersession of the Westphalia System found expression in an entirely new instrument of world government. The Westphalia System was based on the principle that there was no authority operating above the interstate system. Free-Trade Imperialism, in contrast, established the principle that the laws operating within and between states were subject to the higher authority of a new metaphysical entity – the 'world market' – allegedly endowed with supernatural powers greater than anything pope and emperor had ever mastered in the medieval system of rule. By presenting its world supremacy as the embodiment of this metaphysical entity, the United Kingdom succeeded from the 1820s onward in expanding its power in the interstate system well beyond what was warranted by the extent and effectiveness of its coercive apparatus.

This power was the result of the adoption by the United Kingdom of a free-trade practice and ideology. To be sure, the principle of universal free trade was never applied, nor did the United Kingdom ever try to impose on the inter-state system anything more than a very limited measure of free trade. Nevertheless, by the middle of the nineteenth century the principle became dominant through the progressive opening of the British domestic market.

> The colonization of the empty spaces [sic], the development of the machine driven industry dependent on coal and the opening up of world-wide communications through railways and shipping services proceeded apace under British leadership, and stimulated everywhere the emergence and development of nations and national consciousness; and the counterpart of this 'expansion of England' was the free market provided in Britain from the 1840's onwards for the natural products, foodstuffs and raw materials of the rest of the world. (Carr, 1945: 13–14)

By opening up their domestic market, British rulers thus created world-wide networks of dependence on, and allegiance to, the expansion of wealth and power of the United Kingdom. This control over the world market, combined with mastery of the global balance of power and a close relationship of mutual instrumentality with *haute finance*, enabled the United Kingdom to govern the inter-state system as effectively as a world-empire. The result was 'a phenomenon unheard of in the annals of Western civilization, namely, a hundred years' peace–1815–1914' (Polanyi, 1957: 5).

This unheard of phenomenon reflected the unprecedented hegemonic capabilities of the United Kingdom. Its coercive apparatus (that is, primarily its navy) combined with its island position no doubt endowed the United Kingdom with a decisive comparative advantage relative to all its rivals in the European and global power struggle. But, however great, this advantage cannot possibly account for the extraordinary capacity to restructure the world (not just the European inter-state system) to suit its national interests demonstrated by Great Britain in the central decades of the nineteenth century.

This extraordinary capacity was a manifestation of hegemony –

that is, of the capacity to claim with credibility that the expansion of the power of the United Kingdom served not just its national interest but a 'universal' interest as well. Central to this hegemonic claim was a distinction between the power of rulers and the 'wealth of nations' subtly drawn in the liberal ideology propagated by the British intelligentsia. In this ideology, the expansion of the power of British rulers relative to other rulers was presented as the motor force of a universal expansion of the wealth of nations. Free trade might undermine the sovereignty of rulers but it would at the same time expand the wealth of their subjects, or at least of their propertied subjects.

The appeal and credibility of this claim were based on systemic circumstances created by the revolutionary upheavals of 1776–1848. For the national communities that had risen to power in the Americas and in many parts of Europe in the course of these upheavals were primarily communities of property holders, whose main concern was with the pecuniary value of their assets rather than with the autonomous power of their rulers. It was the ensemble of these communities that formed the 'natural' constituency of British free-trade hegemony.

At the same time, the revolutionary upheavals of 1776–1848 had promoted changes within the United Kingdom itself that enhanced the capabilities of its rulers to satisfy this system-wide demand for 'democratic' wealth. The most important of these changes was the Industrial Revolution which took off after the American Revolution of 1776 and was practically completed during the subsequent renewal of the Anglo-French rivalry. For our present purposes, the main significance of this revolution was two-fold.

On the one hand, it greatly enhanced the relationship of complementarity that linked the enterprises of British subjects to the enterprises of subjects of other states, particularly of the states that had emerged out of the settlers' rebellion against British rule in North America. As a result of this development, British rulers began to realise that their lead in domestic-economy-making gave them a considerable advantage in the use of subject–subject relations across political jurisdictions as invisible instruments of rule over the subjects of other sovereign states. It was this realisation more than anything else that induced British rulers after the end of the Napoleonic Wars to sustain and protect the forces of democratic nationalism against the reactionary predispositions of its former dynastic allies.

On the other hand, the Industrial Revolution transformed the British state by changing its structure of representation and, hence, its predispositions and capabilities in world politics. This transformation was the result of the emergence of a new class of capitalist and protocapitalist entrepreneurs engaged primarily in domestic production, trade, and banking and dependent upon the state and the older and better established class of capitalist merchants and financiers for the procurement of inputs and the distribution of outputs in foreign markets.

This new class of capitalist and proto-capitalist entrepreneurs was an offspring of the successes of eighteenth-century British mercantilism in general, and national-economy-making in particular. The more it grew, however, the more its expansion and prosperity, and hence its very capability of becoming a full-fledged capitalist class, came up against the limits set by the overcrowding of domestic economic space. Rent-inflation, in particular, continually threatened to wipe out the profits of the new entrepreneurs both directly and through its effects on wage rates. Once the Napoleonic Wars were over, the share of tax revenue that came back to these entrepreneurs in the form of war and war-induced demand for their outputs decreased sharply. Competition intensified and so did the rent and wage squeeze on the profits of their enterprises.

It was in this context that the British national bourgeoisie became 'internationalist' and spearheaded a powerful social movement aimed simultaneously at a reform of the structures of representation of the British state and at a more radical opening of the British domestic market to foreign wage goods and raw materials. In struggling for these objectives, the British national bourgeoisie was pursuing its class interest, that is, it was seeking relief from the pressure of overcrowding in the domestic economy. But this interest could be presented truthfully and credibly as being the motor force of the expansion of British world power and of the wealth of all nations. The victory of the British national bourgeoisie in its struggle for representation within the dominant bloc of the United Kingdom thus put the final touch on the making of British world hegemony.

US HEGEMONY AND THE FREE-ENTERPRISE SYSTEM

The United Kingdom exercised world governmental functions up to the end of the nineteenth century. From the 1870s onward, however, it began to lose control of the European balance of power and soon afterward of the global balance of power as well. From both points of view, the rise of Germany to world-power status was the decisive development.

At the same time, the capacity of the United Kingdom to hold the centre of the world market was undermined by the emergence of a new national economy of greater wealth than its own, the United States, which developed into a sort of 'black hole' with a power of attraction for the labour, capital, and entrepreneurship of the world-economy with which the United Kingdom, let alone less wealthy states, had few chances of competing. The German and US challenges to British world power strengthened one another, lessened the capabilities of the UK to govern the inter-state system, and eventually led to a new struggle for world supremacy of unprecedented violence and viciousness.

In the course of this struggle, conflict went through some, but not all, of the phases that had characterised the previous struggle for world supremacy. The initial phase in which territorialist rulers attempted to incorporate the leading capitalist state was skipped altogether. As a matter of fact, the fusion of the territorialist and capitalist logics of power had gone so far among the three main contenders for world supremacy (the UK, Germany, and the US) that it is difficult to say which rulers were capitalist and which were territorialist.

Throughout the confrontation, German rulers showed much stronger territorialist predispositions than the rulers of either the UK or the US, reflecting their late arrival in the business of territorial expansion. As we have seen, the United Kingdom had been all but parsimonious in its territorial acquisitions, and empire-building in the non-Western world had been integral to its world hegemony. As for the US, its development into the main pole of attraction for the labor, capital, and entrepreneurial resources of the world-economy was closely connected with the continental scope attained by its domestic economy in the course of the nineteenth century.

These were the two 'models' that German rulers were trying to imitate with their late territorialism. At first, they tried to follow in the footsteps of the UK. But once the outcome of the First World War had demonstrated the futility of this attempt as well as the superiority of the American model, they tried to follow in the footsteps of the US (Neumann, 1942).

In any event, neither Germany nor the US ever tried to incorporate within their domains the leading capitalist state, as France and Spain had tried in the fifteenth century and France and England in the seventeenth century. The world power of the leading capitalist state had grown so much in comparison to its forerunners and to its contemporary challengers that the struggle could only start with what had previously been the second phase in which the challengers tried to supersede the comparative wealth-and-power advantage of the leading capitalist state. Even though control over world commerce and finance continued to play an important role in determining relative capabilities in the inter-state system, in the course of the nineteenth century the most decisive advantage in the struggle for world power had become the comparative size and growth potential of the domestic market. The larger and the more dynamic the domestic market of a state relative to all others, the better the chances of that state replacing the United Kingdom at the centre of the global networks of patron-client relations that constituted the world market.

From this point of view, the US was far better positioned than Germany. Its continental dimension, its insularity, and its extremely favourable endowment of natural resources, as well as the policy consistently followed by its rulers of keeping the doors of the domestic market closed to foreign products but open to foreign capital, labour and enterprise, had made it the main beneficiary of British Free-Trade Imperialism. By the time the struggle for world supremacy began, the US domestic economy was well on its way to being the new centre of the world-economy, connected to the rest of the world-economy not primarily by trade flows but by more or less unilateral transfers of labour, capital, and entrepreneurship flowing from the rest of the world to its political jurisdiction.

Germany could not compete with the US on this terrain. Its history and geographical position made it a tributary rather than a beneficiary of these flows of labour, capital, and entrepreneurship. At the same time, its secular involvement as a front-liner in the European power struggle endowed its rulers with a comparative advantage in the incipient 'industrialisation of war'. From the 1840s onward, military and industrial innovations began to interact more and more closely within the region that was in the process of becoming Germany. It was precisely this interaction that sustained both the spectacular industrialisation and the ascent to world-power status experienced by Germany in the second half of the nineteenth century (cf. McNeill 1984: chs. 7–8).

The absolute and relative increase in its military-industrial capabilities did not fundamentally change Germany's tributary position in the circuits of wealth of the world-economy. On the contrary, tribute to the UK as the centre of world commerce and finance was compounded by tribute to the US in the form of outflows of labour, capital, and entrepreneurial resources. The growing obsession of German rulers with *Lebensraum* ('vital space') had its systemic origins in this situation of powerlessness in turning rapidly increasing

177

military-industrial capabilities into a commensurate increase in their command over world-economic resources.

As already mentioned, this obsession induced German rulers to follow in the footsteps first of the UK and then of the US. These attempts prompted defensive reactions which made interstate conflict escalate quickly into major confrontations. Right from the start, however, the escalation of inter-state conflict was followed by increasing systemic chaos. Here lies a second important difference between this struggle for world supremacy and the previous one between France and England. In the previous struggle for world supremacy, it took more than a century of armed conflict among the great powers before anarchy provoked a major wave of popular rebellions which, in turn, precipitated systemic chaos. But in the twentieth century anarchy turned into systemic chaos almost as soon as the great powers faced one another in an open confrontation.

As a matter of fact, even before the outbreak of the First World War powerful social movements of protest had begun to develop throughout the Western world and in key locations of the non-Western world. These movements of protest were rooted in, and aimed at, subverting the double exclusion on which Free-Trade Imperialism was based. This double exclusion concerned non-Western peoples, on the one hand, and the propertyless masses of the West, on the other.

Under British hegemony, non-Western peoples did not qualify as national communities in the eyes of the hegemonic power and of its allies, clients, and followers. While the right of Western nations to pursue wealth was elevated above the absolute rights of government of their rulers, non-Western peoples were deprived of their customary rights to self-determination. At the same time, the nations that had become the constituent units of the inter-state system were as a rule communities of property holders from which the propertyless were more or less completely excluded. The right of propertied subjects to pursue wealth was thus elevated, not just above the absolute rights of government of rulers, but also above the customary rights to a livelihood of the propertyless masses (cf. Polanyi, 1957). Like Athenian democracy in the ancient world, nineteenth-century liberal democracy was an 'egalitarian oligarchy' in which 'a ruling class of citizens shared the rights and spoils of political control' (McIver, 1932: 352).

Non-Western peoples and the propertyless masses of the West had from the start resisted those aspects of Free-Trade Imperialism that more directly impinged upon their customary rights to self-determination and to livelihood. By and large, however, this resistance had been ineffectual. This situation of powerlessness began to change for the propertyless masses of the West at the end of the nineteenth century as a direct result of the intensification of interstate competition and of the spread of national-economy-making as an instrument of that competition.

The process of socialization of war- and state-making, which in the previous wave of struggle for world supremacy had led to the 'democratisation' of nationalism, was carried a step further by the industrialisation of war. The productive efforts of the propertyless in general, and of the industrial proletariat in particular, became a central component of the state- and war-making efforts of rulers. The social power of the propertyless increased correspondingly and so did the effectiveness of their struggles for state protection of their livelihoods (cf. Carr, 1945: 19).

Under these circumstances, the outbreak of war among the great powers was bound to have a contradictory impact on ruler-subject relations. On the one hand, it enhanced the social power of the propertyless masses directly or indirectly involved in the military-industrial efforts of rulers. On the other hand, it curtailed the means available to the latter to accommodate that power. This contradiction became evident in the course of the First World War, when a few years of open hostilities were sufficient to release the most severe system-wide wave of popular rebellion ever experienced by the modern world-system.

The focal point of this wave of rebellion was the Soviet Revolution of 1917. By upholding the right of all peoples to self-determination ('anti-imperialism') and the primacy of rights to livelihood over rights of property and rights of government ('proletarian internationalism'), the leaders of the Soviet Revolution raised the spectre of a far more radical interference in the operation of the inter-state system than anything previously experienced. Initially, the impact of the Revolution of 1917 was similar to that of the Revolution of 1776. That is to say, it fostered the revanchism of the great power that had just been defeated in the struggle for world supremacy (Germany, this time) and thereby led to a new round of open conflict among the great powers.

The interstate system came to be polarised into two opposite and antagonistic factions. The dominant faction (headed by the U.K. and France) was conservative, that is, oriented toward the preservation of Free-Trade Imperialism. In opposition to this faction, upstarts in the struggle for world power who had neither a respectable colonial empire nor the right connections in the networks of world commerce and finance, coalesced in a reactionary faction led by Nazi Germany. The rulers who coalesced in this faction had an even greater interest than the rulers of the conservative faction in the annihilation of the Soviet Revolution. Yet, rightly or wrongly they reckoned that their counter-revolutionary objectives were best served by a preliminary or contemporaneous confrontation with the conservative faction.

This confrontation culminated in a complete disintegration of the world market and in new and drastic violations of the principles, norms, and rules of the Westphalia system. What is more, like the Napoleonic Wars 150 years earlier, the Second World War acted as a powerful transmission belt for social revolution, which during and after the War spread to the entire non-Western world in the form of national liberation movements. Under the joint impact of war and revolution, Free-Trade Imperialism collapsed, leaving the inter-state system in a situation of apparently irremediable disorganisation.

Like the UK in the early nineteenth century, the US first became hegemonic by leading the inter-state system toward the restoration of the principles, norms, and rules of the Westphalia System, and then went on to govern and to remake the system it had restored. Once again, this capability to remake the inter-state system was based on a generalised perception among the rulers and subjects of the system that the national interests of the hegemonic power embodied a universal interest.

This perception was fostered by the capacity of US rulers to provide solutions to the problems around which the power struggle among revolutionary, reactionary, and conservative forces had raged since 1917. From the start, the most enlightened factions of the US ruling elite showed a much greater awareness than the ruling elites of the conservative and reactionary great powers of what these issues were:

> In many ways the most significant feature both of Wilson's programme and of Lenin's is that they were not European-centered but world-embracing: that is to say, both set out to appeal to all peoples of the world, irrespective of race and colour. Both implied a negation of the preceding European system, whether it was confined to Europe or whether it spread . . . over the whole world . . . Lenin's summons to world revolution called forth, as a deliberate counterstroke, Wilson's Fourteen Points, the solidarity of the proletariat and the revolt against imperialism were matched by self-determination and the century of the common man. (Barraclough, 1967: 121)

This reformist response to the challenges posed by the Soviet Revolution was well ahead of its time. But once the struggle between the conservative and the reactionary forces of world politics had run its course, resulting in a tremendous increase in the world power of both the US and the USSR, the stage was set for the remaking of the inter-state system to accommodate the demands of non-Western peoples and of the propertyless masses.

After the Second World War every people whether 'Western' or 'non-Western' was granted the right to self-determination, that is to say, to constitute itself into a national community and, once so constituted, to be accepted as a full member of the inter-state system. In this respect, global 'decolonisation' has been the most significant correlate of US hegemony.

At the same time, the provision of a livelihood to all subjects became the most legitimate of objectives for the members of the inter-state system to pursue. Just as the liberal ideology of British hegemony had elevated the pursuit of wealth by propertied subjects above the absolute rights of government of rulers, so the ideology of US hegemony has elevated the welfare of all the subjects ('mass consumption') above absolute rights of property and absolute rights of government. If British hegemony had expanded the inter-state system so as to accommodate the 'democratisation' of nationalism, US hegemony has completed the expansion so as to accommodate the 'proletarianization' of nationalism.

Once again expansion has involved supersession. The supersession of the Westphalia system by Free-Trade Imperialism was real but partial. The principles, norms, and rules of behaviour restored by the Congress of Vienna left considerable leeway to the members of the inter-state system on how to organise their domestic and international relations. Free trade impinged upon the sovereignty of rulers, but their ability to 'delink' from trade networks if they so chose remained considerable. Above all, war and territorial expansion remained legitimate means for members of the interstate system to resort to in the pursuit of their ends.

At the same time, there were no organisations with autonomous capabilities – autonomous, that is, from state power – to rule over the interstate system. Under British hegemony, international law and the balance of power continued to operate, as they had since 1650, between rather than above states. As we have seen, the Concert of Europe, *haute finance*, and the world market all operated above the heads of most states. Nevertheless, they had little if any organisational autonomy from the world power of the United Kingdom. They were instruments of rule of a particular state over the interstate system rather than autonomous organisations overruling the inter-state system.

In comparison with Free-Trade Imperialism, the institutions of US hegemony have considerably restricted the rights and powers of sovereign states. The principles, norms, and rules to which states must submit have increased in number and have become tighter, while a growing number of supranational organisations have acquired an autonomous power to overrule the interstate system.

From the first point of view, sovereign states under US hegemony have been far less free than under British hegemony to organise relations with other states and with their own subjects as they see fit. In particular, sovereign states have been far less free than they ever were to use war and territorial expansion as legitimate means in the pursuit of their ends. From the second point of view, the contemporaneous development of international organisations and transnational corporations has created an extensive and dense network of pecuniary and non-pecuniary exchanges which no single state can control unilaterally and, more importantly, from which no state can 'delink' except at exorbitant costs.

To be sure, from about 1948 to about 1968 these networks were instruments of world government wielded by the US and, as such, they parallel the instruments of world government wielded by the United Kingdom in the nineteenth century. The United Nations, with its assembly, security council, and specialised agencies and bureaucracies, came to perform functions analogous to those performed by the Concert of Europe. The Bank of International Settlements, the IMF, and the World Bank came to perform functions analogous to those performed by *haute finance*. And the organisational networks of US-centred multi-national corporations came to perform functions analogous to those performed by UK-centred commercial networks (cf. Carr, 1945: 49; Gilpin, 1975: ch. 6).

However, the analogies are more formal than substantive. For one thing, the organisational scope and complexity of the institutions of US hegemony are a world apart from those of British hegemony. This greater organisational scope and complexity has in itself been a major factor in enhancing the autonomy of the institutions of US world hegemony from each and every member of the inter-state system, including the hegemonic state itself. In addition, and more decisively, from circa 1968 onward, transnational corporations have developed into an integrated system of production, exchange, and accumulation which is subject to no state authority and has the power to subject to its 'laws' each and every member of the interstate system.

The emergence of this Free Enterprise System – free, that is, from all previous vassalage to state power – has been the most distinctive result of US hegemony as well as its ultimate limit (cf. Arrighi, 1982). It marks the end of the process of supersession of the Westphalia System and the beginning of the withering away of the inter-state system as primary locus of world power.

SOME PRELIMINARY CONCLUSIONS

An analysis of the contradiction of the Free Enterprise System that has come into being under US hegemony falls beyond the scope of the present paper. Yet, what has been said concerning the past recurrence of world hegemonies is sufficient for us to draw some preliminary conclusions concerning the conditions under which new world hegemonies can be expected to rise or not rise. Three main points in particular deserve to be emphasised.

First, what has made the United Provinces, the United Kingdom, and the United States hegemonic in the past has not been their military might or superior command over scarce resources, but their predispositions and capabilities to use either or both to solve the problems over which system-wide conflict raged. These predispositions and capabilities reflected the will and intelligence of the would-be hegemon, but this will and intelligence was itself largely shaped by the systemic chaos that created a general demand for order.

If the past is any guide to the future, we should expect that the future hegemon(s) will emerge out of a new situation of social conflict and systemic chaos, the contours of which, however, are for now still hazy and difficult to predict. In any event, it is not sufficient to focus on the actual or prospective military might and command over scarce resources of the present competitors for world power in order to decide which one(s) is (are) the most likely to become hegemonic and remake the world-system so as to turn future systemic chaos into a new (anarchic?) order. Military might and/or superior command over economic resources may well continue to be necessary conditions of world hegemony, but they are even less likely to be sufficient conditions than they have been in the past.

This brings us to our second point: the pitfalls of excessive reliance on past patterns of hegemonic recurrences to predict future patterns. The modern interstate system has been an essentially evolutionary system, just like its historical correlate – capitalism as world-system of accumulation. This means that world hegemonies have been rising and declining not in an unchanging system, but in a system which they have themselves created, expanded, and superseded. As a consequence of this evolution, the conditions of the rise and decline of world hegemonies have changed from one hegemony to the next in significant ways.

The most important change has been what we may call the 'speeding up of (social) history' as the obverse of Aron's 'slowing down of (political) history'. In all three instances of world hegemony, the intensification of inter-state conflict has engendered system-wide waves of rebelliousness of subjects which, in turn, were instrumental in the transformation of systemic anarchy into systemic chaos. Nevertheless, from one hegemonic cycle to the next it has taken less and less time for inter-state conflict to engender system-wide social conflict, and more and more time to bring social conflict back under control once the acute phase of inter-state conflict has come to an end. This speed-up in the reaction time of popular rebellion to inter-state conflict has been due to the increasing socialisation of the state- and world-making efforts of rulers. As wider and wider circles of subjects have been mobilised directly or indirectly in these efforts, the more quickly has interstate conflict aroused popular rebellions over the distribution of the costs and benefits of these efforts.

The obverse of this speeding-up of social history has been the slowing-down of political history. That is to say, the socialisation of war- and state-making has greatly increased the costs and risks to rulers of their mutual antagonisms. If this is the case, the next struggle for world hegemony may take an even more condensed form than the previous one and skip the phase of armed conflict among the great powers altogether. As a matter of fact, for all we know a new period of struggle for world hegemony may have already begun – a struggle in which systemic chaos is the result, not of heightened inter-state conflict, but of the ongoing crisis of the inter-state system and of its supersession by suprastatal organisations.

In this connection a third and last provisional conclusion can be drawn from the analysis developed in this paper. In all three historical instances of world hegemony, the hegemon was also the leader in the organisation of global processes of capital accumulation and, in this sense, it was the leading capitalist state of its epoch. But the three states were 'leading capitalist states' to different degrees and in different ways. If we focus on the representation of interests within the executive of the three states – as Marx and Engels did in

The Communist Manifesto – then we reach the conclusion that each successive hegemonic state has been less capitalist than the previous one. However, while the hegemonic state has become less and less capitalist in this sense, the inter-state system has become more and more capitalist in the sense that each and every one of its members has been subjected more and more closely to the capitalist logic of power.

If this progression were to continue, the next hegemon would have to be less capitalist in its inner structures of representation than the post-Second World War US, and at the same time it would have to make the world-system even more capitalist than it already is. This sounds very much like world social democracy but could be something quite different. In any event, the road from here to there is quite rough, and it is hard to predict what kind of human race will emerge out of the next round of systemic chaos. Nor is it clear whether the progression of the last 500 years, on which our prediction is based, will continue into the next 50 or 100 years. In order to assess how likely that is, we need to carry our analysis much further than it has been possible here.

7 THE HEGEMONIC TRANSITION IN EAST ASIA: A HISTORICAL PERSPECTIVE
BARRY GILLS

INTRODUCTION

One of the major theoretical challenges today is the formulation of a critical theory of hegemony in international relations. Gramsci's concept of hegemony can be applied at the level of the global political economy. Special attention to the cultural, ideological and political aspects of the hegemonic structure of world order and its dominant class coalitions is enhanced by the Gramscian approach (Cox, 1981; 1983; 1987; and Gill, 1990).

The Gramscian approach to global hegemony re-introduces *politics* into historical materialist analysis of international relations. Such a renewed emphasis on political processes can enrich work on hegemonic and world leadership cycles, undertaken with an emphasis on production, exchange patterns, and military power. The Gramscian approach forces us to examine not only the productive and military capabilities of the state(s) as the motor of hegemonic transition, but also to investigate how class alliances are built and how ideology is employed in order to both construct and legitimate a hegemonic order. The state may be conceptualised as composed of a coalition of classes. Hegemony operates among classes and is historically fluid in composition, much more so than any mistaken anthropomorphic conception of 'the state' would allow. However, in the case of East Asia there is a problem working with the Gramscian concept of consensus. In East Asia, 'consensus' is more constricted than in some other cultures. The state existed for the elite, there were no 'citizens' and no 'rights', only subjects. The ruling classes however, required social legitimacy.

Taking the general Gramscian approach somewhat further, it is possible to view all of international and world history as a perpetual political-economic process of mutual societal penetrations and transformations. Co-existing classes and states interlock in competitive/co-operative relationships of accumulation and rivalry. These relation-

186

ships not only determine shifts in the 'balance of power' or configuration of international hierarchy over time, but equally, if not more importantly, they constantly force restructuring on all of the classes, states, and societies interlocked into these competitive/co-operative relationships. This constant process of societal restructuring should be recognised as the real subject matter of the discipline of international relations. (Palan and Gills, forthcoming)

This chapter sets out to explore the relationship between world order, hegemony, accumulation, and legitimacy, illustrated with examples from East Asian history. Far too often, our theorisations still reflect Eurocentrism, even if unintentionally. A Gramscian approach is equally illuminating when applied to non-Western international history, and when applied to the past as well as to the present. In the case of East Asia, the analysis is greatly enhanced when the region is understood within the overall world context in which it is embedded. Janet Abu-Lughod (1989) has shown that 'the fall of the East preceded the rise of the West'. That is to say, before Europe rose to the predominant hegemonic position in the world-system sometime after the sixteenth century, various Asian powers had held hegemonic power in the world-economy, whilst Western Europe was a relatively backward, or peripheral area. The 'fall' (or rather the relative decline) of Asian hegemonic powers in the world-system, was the historical precondition of the 'rise' (or rather relative ascendance) of the Western powers.

With the shift in power and accumulation came a new global hegemonic order, dominated by Western norms of 'international society', and bearing new ideological, political, and cultural messages to the non-European majority of the world's peoples. However, by the late nineteenth century, the Europeans deliberately co-opted one Asian power, Japan, into the club of global hegemonic powers, primarily in order to utilise it to preserve the regional and global status quo. The incorporation of Japan into the ranks of the global hegemonic powers, initiated almost one century ago, remains a key element in world order today. It continues to pose a dilemma for the Western powers, that of accommodating Japanese expansion, while simultaneously seeking to restrain that expansion so as to preserve overall equilibrium and their own vital interests.

In addition to discussing hegemonic transition in East Asia's historical past, I will discuss the twentieth century, and the current hegemonic transition in the global political economy. As in the past, the current hegemonic transition is part of a fundamental economic and political restructuring brought about by competitive interactions.

187

One of the key elements of this restructuration of the global political economy is shifts in the world accumulation process. There is now, in my view, a tendency for structural tension to intensify between the competing centres of accumulation in the world economy. After a period of American hegemony, in which centralisation of accumulation in one core zone of the world system was the prevailing trend of the world accumulation process, there is now a global hegemony shared by the three principal core zones of the world economy. This trilateral, or G-3/7 hegemony, puts an end to the temporary and somewhat abnormal unipolarism of the *Pax Americana* and returns the global political economy to a situation of tripolarism similar to that which characterised it at the end of the nineteenth century and in the early twentieth century, with new institutional forms.

Among the three core zones, Japan has emerged as potentially the most efficient producer, and on this basis the most successful centraliser of capital accumulation in the world economy. However, it appears very unlikely that Japan will centralise world accumulation or hegemonic power to the extent achieved by the Americans in the early post-war period, or emerge as the sole hegemonic successor to American power. In any event, success in accumulation is not the single attribute of global hegemonic power. The political, ideological, and cultural aspects of hegemony are integral to the transformation of economic power into further political power in the global social formation. Though there is much on-going discussion of how Japan might transform its economic power into further political and military power in the world system, there is a danger of being over-mechanistic, despite the elegance and attractiveness of general descriptions of the historical process of rise and fall of great powers (e.g. Kennedy, 1987/8). A Gramscian analysis of this problem should highlight the limitations to the transformation of Japanese capital's current 'accumulation power' into political, ideological, and cultural and military hegemony at the global level (Rapkin, 1990). Though Japanese structural power (Strange, 1988) has and will continue to increase there is less prospect of a global *Pax Nipponica* on the American model.

In light of the following general historical analysis of the patterns of accumulation and hegemony in East Asia, and particularly the role of East Asian power in the global hegemonic hierarchy during the twentieth century, two substantive hypotheses concerning the limits to Japanese hegemony and the tendencies within the new world order emerge. First, the Japanese state is likely to continue to cultivate the role of a 'co-operative' and ostensibly benign partner within the existing hegemonic coalition of the three core zones. However, it will seek to steadily increase the structural power of the Japanese state and Japanese capital in the flagship institutions of global capitalism. To do otherwise, or especially to seek an obvious passing of the hegemonic baton from the US to Japan, would almost certainly be counter-productive, both economically and politically. In any event this is almost certainly beyond Japan's real political capabilities in the current hegemonic transition.

Secondly, the emerging New World Order is characterised by two structural cross-currents which seem poised to continue throughout the on-going hegemonic transition. Firstly, there is the tendency for increasing integration among the core zones, both in terms of transnationalisation of capital, and political and strategic policy co-ordination. Secondly, there is the countervailing trend toward region-alisation of trade and investment, with the concomitant potential for currency zones to emerge accompanying regionalisation of the world economy. In the coming period of international history, the tension generated by the co-existence of these two trends will be the over-riding characteristic of world order. It will be, therefore, by its very nature, a contradictory age. It is still too early to predict which of these two trends may eventually prevail or even if such an outcome is necessary.

KEY CONCEPTS

Following Stephen Gill (introduction to this volume), an historical materialist analysis should eschew vulgar determinism, while retaining a focus on fundamental economic and class processes. One way of doing this is to privilege the role of capital accumulation in the analysis of historical change. According to Gills and Frank (1990), a *mode of accumulation* consists always of political, ideological, and economic dimensions, which form a unity of inter-linked societal structures. The modes of accumulation require (A) an economic nexus based upon a complex international division of labour in which class relations facilitate extraction of surplus and accumulation; (B) a political apparatus that enforces the rules of surplus extraction and accumulation, with the sanctions of 'legitimate' coercion; and (C) an ideology which conditions historical consciousness to allow accumu-lation, and social order, to occur in that specific historical form. These elements are integral to 'hegemony', in so far as it is exercised domestically between classes, as well as globally between states and classes.

Hegemony may be defined as follows: 'a hierarchical structure of the accumulation of surplus among political entities, and their constituent classes, mediated by force. A hierarchy of centres of accumulation and polities is established that apportions a privileged share of surplus, and the political economic power to this end, to the hegemonic centre/state and its ruling/propertied classes.' (Gills and Frank, 1990: 32) In this hierarchical structuration, the hegemonic centre of accumulation and political power subordinates secondary centres. This pyramidal structure is constituted not merely of states, but of classes also. At the base of the pyramid are the subordinate classes from which surplus is extracted by the elites. At the apex of the pyramid are the classes co-operating in a hegemonic coalition, classes located both in the centre and in the periphery. Inter-elite relations combine elements of competition, cooperation and subordination in all historical hegemonic structures whatever the modes of accumulation.

Rather than conceptualising the *hegemonic transition* as the succession from one single hegemonic state to another, we must take account of the many instances of historical periods without a single all-encompassing hegemon. In fact, the entire global social formation is perhaps better characterised at any time as a set of inter-linking hegemonies. Janet Abu-Lughod (1989: 341) argues that the world system of the thirteenth century was ordered not on the basis of a single hegemon, but rather by 'a number of co-existing "core" powers, that both via conflictual and co-operative relations, became increasingly integrated'. This structuration is analogous to the present tripolar configuration of global hegemony.

Indeed, as Abu-Lughod points out, the cliché 'rise and fall', so indiscriminately applied to nations, civilisations, imperiums, and even historical world systems, is a misleading, imprecise notion. Rather, 'In the course of history, some nations, or at least groups of them, have gained relative power *vis-à-vis* others and have occasionally succeeded in setting the terms of their interactions with subordinates . . . When this happens, it is called a "rise". Conversely, the loss of an advantageous position is referred to as a "decline".' (Abu-Lughod, 1989)

Super-accumulation is a concept which is used to explore how the constituent hegemonies of the over-arching system are linked together through accumulation. Super-accumulation is defined as a process through which one (core) zone of the world system and its constituent ruling/propertied classes is able to accumulate more effectively and thereby centralise accumulation at the expense of other (core) zones. (Gills and Frank, 1990: 1991) Hegemonic power is therefore conceptualised primarily as a means to this end, and the end is accumulation. Yet the political and economic processes of super-accumulation are so integral as to constitute one single historical process.

As a world historical pattern, hegemonic transition can be better understood by relating *cycles of hegemony* to the oscillation between a dominant state, mode of accumulation, and a dominant private mode of accumulation, depending on which class(es) hold(s) hegemony. This oscillation is the expression of a perpetual symbiotic and competitive relationship between the state and private propertied classes, the object of which is the apportionment of shares of social surplus. This formulation is based upon an adaptation of S. N. Eisenstadt's (1963) model of class competition within the pre-industrial empires. Every social formation may be analysed as a combination of public and private modes of accumulation.

When private accumulating classes control a dominant share of the available social surplus at the expense of the state, this constitutes an *entropic phase* of accumulation. In an entropic phase, particularly in pre-industrialised social formations, the structure of accumulation becomes increasingly decentralised and outside the regulation of the state, while social power is more diffused, as the political centre declines, i.e. 'things fall apart'. Thus, entropic, decentralised accumulation is historically associated, particularly before the industrial revolution, with disintegrative tendencies in the state and the disintegration of bureaucratic imperial systems.

The deeper the entropy the more acute the fiscal crisis of the state becomes. As a consequence of both increased concentration of economic power in private hands and fiscal crisis, entropic phases are often associated with an increase in exploitation and immiseration of the producer classes, the growth of social movements, and increased frequency and intensity of rebellion and civil war. In this way, we may directly co-relate the phase of hegemonic order, with the phase of accumulation, and the rhythm of social movements, war, and rebellion.

Geoffrey de Ste Croix's (1981) erudite study of class struggle in the ancient Greek world for instance, argues that the Roman empire in the West fell not simply as a consequence of the barbarian threat and military over-extension, but because of over-concentration of wealth and over-extraction of surplus by the propertied classes and the state. That is, Rome fell in the midst of an entropic phase of accumulation which greatly weakened the imperial state's capacity to resist serious challenges.

Paul Kennedy's (1987/8) widely read study of the rise and fall of great powers puts forward the hypothesis that over-extension of the military and bureaucratic apparatus by great (hegemonic) powers, becomes unsustainable once the economic basis of this military and political power has declined relative to rivals, thus exacerbating their decline. Though largely in agreement with this, I would argue that in the majority of cases in world history, it was more the entropic tendency in the accumulation process, manifested in acute class contradictions, that actually rendered the military and bureaucratic apparatus untenable. That is, the collapse of an over-extended imperial apparatus was symptomatic of underlying structural economic weakness, but this weakness is also expressed through important changes in the class coalitions and class subordinations underlying hegemonic power.

Periods when the state is dominant over private propertied classes in the accumulation structure, and state revenue and power increases in the social formation relative to subordinated private accumulators, is a *centralisation phase* of accumulation. In a centralisation phase, the state and imperial infrastructure expand. The state invests heavily in infrastructure, both productive and administrative. Centralisation phases of accumulation are usually associated with the expansion of hegemonic power and centralised bureaucratic administration, as well as the military apparatus of hegemony. Initially, there is often a period of economic expansion directly related to a new level of political and economic integration. The 'hegemonic peace' within the newly consolidated state or empire, though not necessarily between it and other political entities, further facilitates economic expansion. Thus, in a centralisation phase of accumulation, empire and economic expansion are mutually reinforcing, whereas in an entropic phase of accumulation they are not.

Elsewhere, (Gills, 1989), I have introduced adaptations of the concepts of *synchronisation* and *conjuncture*. Synchronisation occurs when the phases of accumulation in A and B occur in parallel. Conjuncture occurs when they do not. These concepts and the attention given to synchronisation facilitate an analysis of hegemonies that is not merely comparative but which encompasses developmental processes of the whole world system and its constituent 'parts'. When A is in an entropic phase of accumulation and B is in a centralisation phase, the potential exists for a centre-shift and a hegemonic shift. Powers in a centralisation phase of accumulation take advantage of a rival in an entropic phase, and usually seek to subordinate all or part(s) of it. This may take place both as capture of market share, financial control, or seizure of territory and thus of resources, labour and revenue.

In this panoramic process of restructuring that all societies, classes, states, hegemons and cultures undergo, the nature of the mode of accumulation is a constituent element. In the earlier part of the twentieth century, for example, the struggle between the great powers during the Second World War reflected underlying competition between different modes. Nazism and militarism and the modes they represented were defeated in the capitalist core with the defeat of Germany and Japan. In the post-war world order state socialism, democratic liberalism, and neo-mercantilism competed among themselves for supremacy. With the collapse of the former Soviet Union, the state socialist variant has been recognisably defeated, leaving neo-mercantilism – represented by Japan and much of East Asia – to contend for supremacy with the democratic liberalism and *laissez-faire* traditions of the two Western core zones. Japan's specific combination of being the least militarist, the least democratic, and the most mercantilist of the three capitalist cores has made it the most competitive and economically successful – thus posing a direct challenge to Anglo-American orthodoxies about the virtues of 'free enterprise' and the market. As Chalmers Johnson rightly points out, Japan's model calls into question the theory that governmental intervention in the economy is inevitably inefficient and distorting, and undermines the belief that the market mechanism without explicit political direction is sufficient to achieve competitiveness (Johnson, 1982).

THE 'CHINESE' WORLD ORDER?

Michael Mann (1986) and David Wilkinson (1989) have identified the alternation between unitary hegemonic orders and multi-actor systems of states as a key world historical pattern. Historically, all regional international systems appear to have experienced such a pattern over the long term, which is usually calculated in centuries. East Asia is no exception. The contradictions inherent in each form of order generate structural pressures that inexorably produce social and systemic transformation.

Students of East Asian international history have developed an analytical bias by which they view the unitary hegemonic moments as normal or representative. The interregnums between consolidated hegemonies are viewed as somehow abberant from the norm. East Asian history is usually described via a series of imperial dynastic moments, in which, for instance, presumably the same 'Chinese' empire is perpetually reconstituted, albeit by different ruling dynasties. This view of continuity within East Asia is based upon the presumed influence of certain cultural norms and social structures, to which the catch-all term 'Confucian' is usually attached. But we should not view the systems of states in East Asian international history as mere aberrations from the norm of unitary hegemony. Rather, the periodic multi-actor systems of states are just as integral to the overall historical process of alternation between forms of order in East Asia as elsewhere in the world. A brief schematic outline of the hegemonic transitions in continental East Asian history would illustrate this historical process (Gills, 1989).

The Chinese empire was not simply rebuilt again and again. China is a geographical reference, like Europe. No one would argue that Europe was one empire or country, despite its cultural-civilisational continuities. After the collapse of the Chinese power in the last century and the inexorable rise of Japan, we no longer speak of a Chinese world order, but rather of a 'Confucian' civilisation. In reality a succession of very different peoples, classes, states and hegemons ruled in East Asia throughout history. Even when a continental empire was in existence, it co-existed with other powers in a larger East Asian, and Eurasian, international order. Not only were these hegemons different in terms of the ethnic composition of the ruling class, but also in terms of the dominant ideology, and religious cults, utilised and promoted by the elite. They also differed in their organisation of the accumulation process and their approach to linkage with the wider Eurasian economy.

The exaggeration of continuity in the East Asian world order is partly due to a gap between international theory and practice, which is as true of East Asian international history as it is of Western, only more so. For example, official imperial history was typically Orwellian, recorded events being made to conform to the preferred norms, whatever their true character. This marked tendency in Sinic historiography is partly explained by the specific needs of legitimation in that cultural context.

As elsewhere in the world, hegemony was primarily a means to great wealth, as well as power, by the classes wielding it. The state and the imperial dynasty were the largest accumulator, and new imperial orders always paid very close attention to re-organisation of the apparatus of surplus extraction. However, imperial rule by ethnic

Chinese dynasties was as much the exception as the rule. This is illustrated by the recurrent and prolonged periods of rule by Non-Chinese, 'barbarian', or semi-barbarian peoples. In ethnic Chinese eyes, barbarian ruling classes were interested primarily in rapacious extraction, an expectation which the Mongol Yuan dynasty more than lived up to. However, such foreign and greedy rule was difficult to legitimise, given the strong Confucian emphasis on good government defined as due attention to the welfare of the people.

The central hegemonic ideas of East Asian civilisation rested upon a body of social, political, and cosmological doctrine inherited from the formative period of Sinic civilisation, and were ultimately identified with the Chinese as a race or nation. It is partly for this reason that most barbarian ruling dynasties voluntarily chose to undergo self-Sinification, and thereby legitimise their rule. It is also true that whatever the ruling dynasty, the Chinese 'gentry' or the landed class in general, held a uniquely powerful position in society. The state could not function effectively without incorporating this class into the ruling coalition, and this class imbricated itself so thoroughly with the bureaucracy that government itself was to some extent captured by it. But to ally with this class was also to compromise with it, thereby diluting central imperial power and sharing revenue.

Though successive hegemonic states and classes in East Asia made claims to a universal hegemonic role, the real extent of their hegemonic influence was contingent on many other material factors and not mere cultural or ideological influence alone. Hegemony between states is mediated by the use or implied use of force, and recognition of the realities of power by all the players, both great and small. Where conquest was deemed necessary and the means were available, it was employed. But in some cases conquest was not deemed necessary, and in these the consensual, ideological dimension of hegemony was more important. It can be argued that East Asia developed its own distinctive international theory. This international theory was derivative of the views of Mencius in that it downplayed the role of force and upgraded the role of virtue or moral example. In periods of dynastic consolidation the frequency of war seems to be less than in periods of dynastic ascendance. In the two centuries preceding the Meiji restoration of 1868 war seems to have been less a feature of international relations in Confucian East Asia than in the West under the Westphalian system.

In East Asia, the apparent acquiescence of some vassals or tributaries to others' hegemonic claims was not always or necessarily an indication that the claim succeeded on the grounds of genuine assimilation of values, as opposed to self-interest. The compliant 'vassal' could also be acting upon its own calculated material interests in a mutually beneficial relationship while only superficially respecting the obligatory ritual and ideological form of subordination.

For example, Japan was traditionally a 'recalcitrant member' of the Sino-centric hegemonic orders dominated from the continent. Nevertheless, the Ashikaga Shogunate accepted a formal tributary position within the Ming hegemony. The Ashikaga did so in order to facilitate economic exchange, without being fully assimilated into, or dominated by, the overall ideological, political and cultural matrix of the continental system. For several hundred years, the Yi dynasty in Korea conformed outwardly to the demands of the (Manchu) Qing dynasty tributary system as the 'model tributary state', while secretly maintaining a royal shrine to the Ming and despising the barbarian Qing, whom they resented as illegitimate rulers.

The etymology of the terms used for tribute, tax, and domain give us a clue as to the general hierarchical mode of East Asia, and how power and accumulation were linked together in the hegemonic order. Rather than the Westphalian principle of equality among sovereigns, the East Asian norm was more analogous to French feudalism at its highest stage of development. Complex networks of overlapping relationships of 'vassalage' were built up between elites, and between classes. An emperor categorised vassals by various criteria, either cultural, geographical, or otherwise, but the central object was to build up as large a network of dependency by vassals as was possible or useful. Such subordination was not merely formal or symbolic, but also material, since the duties of a vassal invariably included some obligation to provide tribute to the overlord. East Asian hegemonic orders were therefore complex concatenations of bureaucratic-statist and 'feudal' relations of surplus extraction. In practice some entities had vassalage ties to more than one overlord within the same world order. For example, the Ryukyu Islands were long vassal to both the Satsuma Daimyo in Japan and to the Qing on the continent. The island of Tsushima was vassal both to the Tokugawa Shogunate in Edo and to the Korean Yi dynasty in Seoul.

There was a universal discourse of diplomacy in East Asia that applied not only to relations between 'China' and non-Chinese political entities, but also to relations between non-Chinese entities. (Fairbank, 1968; Rossabi, 1983). The forms and the terminology of this 'international society', were ultimately derivative from the archaic Sinic civilisation, but were generalised to the entire East Asian order over many centuries. This discourse was primarily contained within the universe of a shared literary tradition, based on Chinese written characters, much like Latin formed the ultimate basis for the discourse among Europeans in Christendom. The Ming made an exceptional effort to promote far-flung diplomatic contact. The diplomacy of the Ming was possibly motivated by a perceived need to revalidate the principles of traditional Confucian international theory, as distinct from the raw force so often employed by the preceding Mongols (Fairbank, 1968). As a rule, however, the continental empires, relying as they did on the class alliance with the landed gentry, showed little interest in overseas imperialism achieved through naval power projection. The Ming is often singled out as the period when the Chinese navy could have played a key role in the global rivalry process. The fleets of the eunuch admiral Cheng Ho were sailing in the Indian Ocean and the coastal trade ports of East Africa decades before the Portuguese inserted their naval presence into these waters. But China rarely maximised the maritime route to expanding imperial power or seizing rents in the world exchange nexus.

Despite the appearance of an isolated East Asian universe, as in any historical regional system, its internal coherence has been undermined by extensive contact with other systems. There were considerable areas where cultural forms and symbolic discourse overlapped, and inter-regional material exchange took place, often as part of world accumulation processes. One such zone of inter-action was Indo-China, where the influence of Indian civilisation overwhelmed that of China. Even in Roman times this region played a key intermediary role in economic exchange between West and East. Local hegemonic powers arose in the region often on the basis of extracting a rent on this exchange, particularly the maritime powers of the archipelago.

By the seventeenth century the territorial expansion of the Russian empire along the Amur River likewise created a contact point between two regional systems. It is interesting to note that this contact undermined the regulatory efficacy of the Sinic tribute-trade system on the border between the Russian sphere and the Qing. An exceptional example of the effect of inter-regional contact is Japan when it entered into its famous period of 'seclusion' in the seventeenth century. Japan turned its back on the preceding period of extensive contacts with the European trading nations and its failed expansionist bid to conquer Korea. It did this largely to insulate itself from the corrosive ideological influences presented by systemic material exchange with other, and particularly Western powers, and thus safeguard its newly consolidated internal hegemonic order under the Tokugawa. An even more extreme example is British trade in the early nineteenth century, which posed a serious challenge to the entire Sinic socio-political complex. From Britain's point of view, the Qing restrictions on opium trade, imposed through its traditional system of regulation of tributary-trade, conflicted with highly lucrative commodity circuits involving British trade with India as well as China, i.e. accumulation on world scale. To protect this source of profit, the British deployed military force to compel the Qing to allow the trade to continue and expand even though this trade was causing a serious drain of bullion out of China and creating social instability through rampant proliferation of drug addiction.

In terms of its ideology, the East Asian world order is less consistent than is often believed to be the case. Confucianism was not continually the dominant ideological form in East Asian history. Its periods of domination depended on the conditions that favoured it. It was best suited as a doctrine for the legitimation and training of the centralised bureaucracy, and the reproduction of the landed gentry. It functioned well as the doctrine of an already established imperial state, but not so well in periods of rivalry among contending states. Like the dominant ideology of the Roman landed classes, it elevated the status of landed economic pursuits but denigrated commercial or mercantile pursuits. Confucianism was always beset by an incongruence with certain forms of accumulation, especially mercantile ones. Thus merchants had the lowest rating in social status, below a peasant, who at least produces a surplus, while a merchant is 'parasitical'. This prejudice was a reflection of deep-seated class enmity and rivalry in East Asia between the landed oligarchy and the commercial classes. In Japan, where continental style Confucianism was perhaps weakest, the decline of the *samurai* landed ruling class was well advanced by the mid nineteenth century, as was the ascendance of an urban mercantile-commercial class. This situation prepared Japan much better than China or Korea, where the landed class remained overwhelmingly hegemonic, to make the transition to modern industrial-commercial capitalism, and thus to the modern state.

Yet not even Confucianism had a monopoly on the imperial state. By the end of the Han period Taoism, and especially Buddhism, came into prominence, largely at the expense of Confucianism, with official support from new ruling classes. Many of these ruling classes were not ethnic Chinese but rather 'barbarian' people, particularly in the north. Confucianism was not totally eclipsed in this period and retained influence, but structural conditions did not favour its pre-dominance as before under the Han. Even when unitary hegemony was re-constructed under the Tang dynasty, the Tang continued to sponsor Buddhism as the religious cult of the state. However, the Tang faced a powerful Islamic rival in the West. The Tang dynasty's economic linkage with the West through Central Asia led it into direct military conflict with the ascendant Islamic Abbassid dynasty. The Tang defeat in Central Asia by the Abbassids in AD 751 marked the turning point toward imperial decline, entropy and eventual disintegration. Central Asia was lost both to the Tang imperial order and to Buddhist or Confucian culture, and became thereafter a part of the Islamic sphere.

The influence of Buddhism in this period of East Asian international history extended to Korea and Japan as well. Its introduction into East Asia from India was closely related to commercial contracts over the silk roads via Central Asia, and it was first most widely adopted by the merchant class. However, Buddhism also served the state elites' interests. The predominant Mahayana Buddhism promoted a cult of prayer for the security of the state, as well as emphasising individual salvation. In Korea, the landed class was patron of the Buddhist church. In Japan, Buddhism rather than Confucianism was the key ideological agent in early centralisation of the state. The enormous economic power of the Buddhist church, which amassed great estates worked by slaves and tenants, eventually threatened the fiscal health of the state and exacerbated the entropic tendencies in the system. In the mid ninth century the Tang broke the back of the Buddhist church in a great expropriation and dissolution of monasteries. This took place during an entropic phase of accumulation, and reflected the growing damage to state accumulation inflicted by sharing the revenue base with the church. Buddhism as a doctrine of ideological legitimation in a religious rather than a secular form had proven to be untenable. The perils of church–state rivalry inherent in reliance on religious forms of ideological legitimation probably increased the attractiveness of a secular ideology of legitimation, thus preparing the ground for a Confucian restoration.

Neo-confucianism, a synthetic compromise between secularism and religion, was the philosophical and ideological vehicle for the gentry class during the Sung dynasty's centralisation and consolidation phase. It was very different from the Confucianism of the Han dynasty, empowered by a far-reaching reinterpretation of old doctrines, presented as ultra-orthodoxy based on a 'correct' interpretation of classical doctrines. This backward looking reification of archaic authority is an intellectual habit particularly strong in East Asian civilisation. Despite the extreme ideological conservatism of the period, paradoxically, the Sung presided over a period of dramatic economic change. Accumulation in China became increasingly commercialised, the economy increasingly monetised, and science and technology were probably the most advanced in the entire world at that time. Sung maritime commerce was extensive, particularly through South-East Asian channels, and in the seas adjoining Korea and Japan.

The Mongol ruling class which succeeded the Sung had a marked predilection for cosmopolitanism, and penchant for Tibetan (Lamaist) Buddhism. The cosmopolitanism of the Mongols probably reflected the enormous diversity of the lands they ruled in Eurasia. The Mongol hegemony of the thirteenth century comes the closest to being a 'world hegemony' in Eurasian history. The Mongols utilised advisers and officials drawn from all over this ecumene to help them rule, and exploit, China. They promoted commercial transaction and merchant activity among all parts of the empire. However, as a foreign and barbarian ruling class, they lacked legitimacy. They too had to rely on Chinese gentry at the lower levels of the imperial administration to maintain order, but largely excluded them from key posts in the upper echelons. Confucianism also prevailed under the barbarian Qing hegemony, again reflecting the need by the Manchus, who were relatively few in number, to rely on the Chinese gentry for local and provincial administration.

Thus it is clear that any monolithic conception of the so-called 'Chinese' world order, or even the Confucian world order is misplaced. Hegemony in East Asia, as elsewhere, has been exercised by a variety of peoples, classes, states, and empires wielding a variety of cultural and ideological tools. The overall world order has experienced alternation between unitary hegemony and competitive systems of states. Contact with other 'worlds' is very ancient in East Asia and always carried with it the potential for disruption and restructuring, as well as bearing many positive material and cultural messages. The modern history of East Asia is a history of restructuring brought about by interaction with the West.

EAST ASIAN RESTRUCTURING IN THE COLLISION WITH THE WEST

At first the intensifying maritime contact with the expanding powers of the West in the sixteenth and seventeenth centuries involved an accommodation by the 'barbarians' to the East Asian norms. However, as the power of the West grew and the Qing entered an entropic phase, the Western challenge changed in character, and became a superior material force seeking to subordinate the East.

Profound restructuring in East Asia at every level of social existence accompanied this international subordination and the transition to capitalism; throwing the entire social order and the economy into chaos. None of the nations of East Asia has ever been the same since, nor has its culture and national consciousness ever quite recovered from the tremendous shocks of this period. In the end, it was the overwhelming material superiority of the Western powers that determined that their ideas and their economic system emerged victorious.

While conservative oligarchic forces blocked reform in China and Korea, in Japan the rulers of the Choshu and Satsuma domains seized the initiative to destroy the Tokugawa Bakufu in the name of restoring the imperial system. In direct response to the challenge posed by Western imperialism, the new ruling class in Meiji Japan embarked upon radical socio-economic restructuring. Within a short period of time the feudal domains were converted into a modern centralised state, embracing industrialisation, capitalism, and imperialism, including the acceptance of the forms and practices of Western international diplomacy. Japan under the Meiji regime understood the nature of international rivalry far better than the ruling classes of the Qing empire and the Yi dynasty in Korea. The Meiji state's material and ideological restructuring was undertaken as a conscious emulation of its enemies, in order to ensure national survival as a sovereign entity. The extraordinary adaptability of Japanese society to the exigencies of economic and political rivalry in the late nineteenth century and the early twentieth was the key element in its subsequent success. This flexibility was achieved through the *decisive expropriation of the feudal landed class.*

By contrast, in China and Korea the ideological and structural obstacles to reform proved too great to overcome by 'enlightened' revolution from above. In China the entrenched Manchu dynasty and in Korea the powerful landed families, resisted fundamental restructuring as threats both to their vested interests and to the entire civilisation. This obstruction by the conservative landed elite was a decisive influence in the next century of East Asian development. It left only two other possible sources of systemic change: revolution from below, or revolution from outside i.e. peasant revolution or foreign intervention. It was a combination of both of these forces which finally broke the political hold of the Confucian ruling classes, destroyed the old class system, and transformed the state.

The entropic phase of East Asia was ruthlessly exploited by foreign powers seeking to extend their economic interest and to extract surplus from East Asia to fuel their own accumulation processes. Annexation and colonialism were the political means often employed, and Japan quickly outstripped its mentors in its enthusiasm for the use of force, as it illustrated in Taiwan, Korea, and Manchuria, and China itself. Japan abandoned the less coercive norms of East Asian international theory and went from a relatively non-aggressive state to a hyper-aggressive state. The partition and colonisation of China was probably delayed because the strategic effects of a 'scramble' were considered too provocative, with direct strategic implications for the alliance system in Europe. A good analogy is the Ottoman empire, the 'sick man of Europe', which was not partitioned as early as it could have been for similar reasons. None the less, the degradation of China led to a thoroughgoing social revolution in which Confucianism was uprooted as the ideology of the ruling elite, giving way to a period of confusion and intense ideological rivalries. Hegemonic transition is perhaps best understood as always being accompanied by ideological and cultural crisis.

Japan, though an East Asian nation, played a key role in undermining the traditional ideological and social norms of 'Confucian' world order. Japan was the first non-Western nation to demand and win a modern Western style treaty with the Qing, signed in 1871. This was the first time the Qing applied the norms of Western international law to a fellow East Asian state, and as such it was a threat to the traditional tributary system and its ideology.

The intensity of Japan's challenge to the Qing was directly related to its transition to industrial capitalism, its ambitions within the new international order, and the predatory character of imperialism in that era. Japanese capital was admitted to the club of global hegemonic powers via trial by combat. Japan defeated first China, in 1894–5, and then Russia, in 1904–5. During the First World War, Japan, as an ally of Britain, seized German possessions in China and in the Pacific as well as Western market share, and sat at the table in Versailles as one of the victors. Britain relied on Japanese naval power in the Pacific to reduce its own costs of naval power projection to East Asia while simultaneously exercising a guiding and restraining influence on the economic and political ambitions of its junior partner.

However, Japanese ambition in East Asia was a problem for the other hegemonic powers. The question of how to manage the division of China into spheres of influence without allowing the division to alter the relations among the hegemonic powers was of paramount significance in the years after the First World War. The Open Door policy, championed by the United States and supported by several other powers, most notably Britain, was an attempt to maintain an equilibrium among the powers which allowed them to continue to exploit East Asia but did not allow any one power to unilaterally impose monopolistic economic privileges at the expense of others. So long as Japan was satisfied to abide by these restrictions on its own economic and territorial expansion it was incorporated into the hegemonic coalition in the global system. Given that the dominant global powers (post First World War) were democracies: the US, Britain, and France, Japan experimented with democracy during the 'liberal decade' of the 1920s, during which the political parties dominated prime ministerial succession, as opposed to the oligarchs, or the 'genro'. However, even during the heyday of Taisho democracy, repressive legislation set strict parameters on political activity by the left and trade unions.

However, Japanese democracy did not survive the restrictions imposed on Japan by the Washington Treaty system, particularly in the naval sphere, nor the world depression. The Japanese state was usurped by militarists bent on aggressive expansionism as the solution to Japan's economic and security crisis. The ideological and political repercussions were enormous. Not only the Japanese military, but also the Kuomintang regime under Chiang Kai Shek in China, looked to Nazism and Fascism as examples of strong regimes. The ideologies of these new challengers to the status quo appealed to conservative Asian elites, who were both anti-communist and anti-Western. In Japan these ideas resonated with the cult of the emperor and the myth of Japanese uniqueness and racial superiority. Japanese imperialism was not sold to other Asians, however, simply as a divine right to rule. On the contrary, Japanese imperialism was couched in a doctrine of liberation and racial harmony. Japan was presented as the saviour of Asia on a Pan-Asian mission to eliminate the foreign imperialists and construct a new order of economic and racial co-operation.

It might be suggested that the Second World War began in East Asia, and smouldered on there long after stability was re-established in Europe. At stake was the future shape of both regional and global accumulation patterns, class coalitions, and dominant ideologies. In Asia, it was essentially Japan's abrupt disruption of the status quo in

East Asia that produced the Pacific War. Japan's war aims were ambitious: to eliminate all Western imperial presence in Asia and re-structure the economy of the whole region on the model of already existing Japanese colonialism, thus privileging the accumulation of capital by Japan. In Taiwan, and especially Korea in the 1930s, Japanese colonialism was unique in the degree to which it brought capital and technology to the colonial territory and thus developed it industrially. South-East Asia was, however, seized primarily to act as a source of natural resources to feed the Japanese industrial core.

EAST ASIA IN THE POST-WAR GLOBAL POLITICAL ECONOMY

The structure of global power had altered through the success of Japanese capital and Japanese imperialism. Despite defeat in war, Japan was reincorporated into the new global hegemonic coalition. Just as Britain had accommodated Japan in an alliance from 1902, the triumphant United States also accommodated defeated Japan in 1945. Japanese core capital and industry was indispensable to American designs to maintain stability in Asia and to preserve as much of the region as possible for participation in global capitalism. In order to preserve Japanese capitalism, Japan required an Asian periphery, initially held under American political auspices, but ultimately inherited by Japanese capital. The vacuum left by the sudden destruction of the Japanese imperium in the summer of 1945 was tremendously destabilising. The communist revolution in China, the partition of China (into the PRC and the ROC), the partition of Korea and the subsequent Korean War, the partition of Vietnam and the Vietnamese and Indochina wars, all these are to some extent part of the destabilising legacy of the dramatic 'rise and fall' of the Japanese empire and the attempt by the US to fill the vacuum.

After the Pacific War, there was no single hegemonic successor to Japan in Asia. The Cold War and the ascendance of American interests produced deep economic and political changes. The United States played the key role, in alliance with the conservative elite of East Asia, in preserving enclaves of capitalism in China, Korea, and Indochina, and all three were partitioned via American intervention. The fact that the major wars fought by the United States after the Second World War were all in East Asia is an indication of the great importance the United States accorded in its global hegemonic strategy to preserving a capitalist economic sphere in East Asia. The difficulty it faced in doing so by non-military, political means, given the great strength of indigenous communism in East Asia, compelled the US to resort to war. Other potential revolutionary situations, such as in the Philippines and Indonesia, were 'contained' without recourse to full-scale US military intervention.

The preservation of capitalism in East Asia by political-military means was inseparable from the accommodation of a restructured Japanese core into the global capitalist core. However, the political legacy of Japanese militarism made it virtually impossible for Japan itself to undertake the active military-political tasks of counter-revolution in post-war Asia. Nevertheless, the political victories of the United States were shared economically with Japanese capital throughout the region.

Hegemony in the capitalist sphere functions through interpenetrating accumulation processes. Class alliances between the elite of the core and the periphery are struck in order to keep the client countries' economies open to foreign capital and to discipline the domestic work force, by increasing the rate of profit via authoritarian stability. But much of the post-war period's energy was taken up by the monumental political-military task of preserving and stabilising the capitalist sphere in East Asia. It was not until the mid-1960s that the economic miracle in the NICs began to achieve take-off. The war in Indochina effectively prevented any economic miracle there. As Richard Nixon once said, the US had to destroy Vietnam in order to save it! Nevertheless, capitalist South-East Asia was well prepared to take its turn to become the new miracles of the 1980s and 1990s.

The capitalist elite of South Korea, Taiwan and South Vietnam were profoundly anti-democratic and yet supposedly committed to the Free World and its cause of democracy and individual freedom. The elites of these capitalist states saw themselves as part of a natural transnational class alliance. The ideology of anti-communism they adopted was functional to the repression of the domestic left, the military confrontation with rival communist regimes, and domination of the state over civil society and over domestic capital and labour. In this sense these regimes are the direct successors of Japanese militarism. It is not merely coincidental that Korea and Taiwan, former colonies of Japan, emerged as the proto-typical East Asian NICs. Post-war 'guided capitalism', and its neo-mercantilist state-capital alliance, was a legacy of the Japanese militarist neo-mercantilist experience (Johnson, 1982).

The political economy of East Asia can and should be analysed as one coherent development complex. This takes us beyond the debate over the components of the national model, whether it be the 'capitalist developmental state' (Johnson, 1982) or any other national model. While it is true that several NICs and Japan share certain important internal characteristics, the national development model approach has been less able to explain significant differences among them or to adequately capture the overall regional developmental logic. Product cycle theory convincingly explains some of the specific pattern of spatial and temporal restructuring of industry in East Asia in the post-war period (Cumings, 1987). As the Japanese core vacates one tier of technology, it leaves structural space in the regional political economy. The next tier, the 'following geese' exploit this opportunity. Core capital, especially that of Japan, is often an active participant which facilitates, if not drives, the overall process. This integrative dimension of inter-penetrating accumulation has been under-theorised due to the preoccupation with national development models.

The structure of tiers in the East Asian political economy is akin to a pyramid of capital intensity and (high) technology. The existence of sovereignty, i.e. the capitalist states-system, is an integral facet necessary to the reproduction of this regional organisation of capital, technology, and labour (Chase-Dunn, 1989). The Japanese core is the highest tier. Only here has democracy been the predominant political system, though of course in a specific form which has allowed a hegemonic bloc of conservative elites to hold state power in apparent perpetuity (van Wolferen, 1989; Nestor, 1990). Below the core is the intermediate, or alternatively the semi-peripheral tier, consisting of industrialised states like Korea, Taiwan, Singapore, and Hong Kong. Below this is a tier of Neo-NICs occupying the niche of labour-intensive manufacturing previously occupied by the intermediate tier. Below that are zones of the regional political economy which supply primary raw materials and labour reserves.

The competitive pressure from each lower tier upon the tier immediately above it is quite intense, as is the competition between states occupying the same tier. Hence, the structural pressure to continue upgrading each national economy. Rapid national economic growth in this regional complex should not be understood only as a matter of national competitiveness via industrial policy, but rather as a structural-sequential product of the overall developmental logic of the capital accumulation process in the region as a whole. This approach may help explain why Korea and Taiwan were miracles in the 1960s, Thailand and Malaysia in the later 1980s, and Vietnam never. It also helps us to understand the gradual reincorporation of the communist states into the regional political economy despite ideological differences.

Even Vietnam is going out of its way to open up to transnational capital, so much so that it was cautioned by the World Bank not to go overboard to the detriment of its own national entrepreneurs! Given the unrelenting hostility of the US economic embargo, the magnifying glass of transnational capital has not yet been focused on Vietnam, which now has the cheapest labour in the region. When it does Vietnam too may suddenly be tomorrow's miracle.

In relation to the general debate on Third World development, this approach implies no East Asian model of national development which can be successfully emulated by Third World countries from outside the region. Rather, the development of each of the national parts in the regional complex should be analysed within the specific temporal and spatial sequential logic of the whole, while being regarded as highly conjunctural, as opposed to potentially universal. For instance, the first major post-war industrial restructuring wave of this East Asian industrial complex can be identified in the first half of the 1960s when both South Korea and Taiwan went over from import substitution to export orientation. This transition is usually explained as due to the exhaustion of the potential of import-substitution, or to a crisis internal to each state. However, when the overall regional pattern is taken into account, the evidence suggests that the US and Japan used their influence in both Taiwan and South Korea to enlist their elites into a new role in the regional political economy. The overall industrial restructuring this entailed was beneficial to all the participants, though in different ways. Japan was assisted in overcoming business recession and shedding less profitable and more environmentally polluting industries. The United States was able to reduce economic assistance to Korea and Taiwan and thus the costs of maintaining hegemonic power in Asia. Korea and Taiwan were able to more rapidly industrialise by gaining capital, technology, and market access.

Lastly, it is important to characterise accurately the articulation of this East Asian political economy within the global political economy. The industrialisation of the region has been predicated upon and accelerated by the liberal international trading system, of which it is a primary beneficiary. The United States in particular tolerated a flood of manufactured imports from East Asia during the 1960s and 1970s. This may be partly explained by the desire of the US to facilitate rapid industrialisation and capital accumulation in East Asia in order to strengthen and 'stabilise' capitalism there. By the 1980s, however, the colossal trade surpluses of Japan and the Four Tigers constituted an intolerable burden on the American economy. Therefore the US increased bilateral political pressure on the governments of East Asia to redress the disequilibrium and reduce their trade surpluses. The whole East Asian complex was moulded by neo-mercantilism (Nestor, 1990). If East Asian exports to other regions were significantly curtailed by protectionist or extra-GATT managed trade arrangements, it is logical to expect the whole regional political economy to undergo a crisis and possibly profound political and economic restructuring.

JAPANESE SUPER-ACCUMULATION

Economic evidence suggests that during the 1980s Japanese capital attained the super-accumulator position in the world system. Before going on to discuss what this may or may not mean in relation to the question of hegemony in the global political economy, I will first review some of this evidence.

The current account surplus of Japan increased from $4.7 billion in 1981 to $35 billion in 1984, to $79.6 billion in 1988. Japan massively exported capital in the 1980s. For example, according to the Bank of Japan, the deficit in its long term capital account was a mere $9.6 billion in 1981, reached $49.6 billion in 1984, and $130.9 billion in 1988. In 1985 Japan became the largest net creditor in the world, with net overseas assets the largest in the world. In 1988, this was just below $300 billion.

Japanese direct investment overseas increased from $10.8 billion in 1980 to $149.8 billion in 1988. Investment in securities overseas by the Japanese financial institutions increased from a mere $4 billion in 1980 to $102 billion in 1986. Measured in total value of economic assets, the total value of the Japanese economy is now greater than any other state (i.e. Japan is 'number one', not the US).

Japan is also marked by a high ratio of personal financial assets to toal GNP, which in 1987 was 203 per cent of GNP. While the total GNP of Japan grew from Yen 15 trillion in 1960 to Yen 73 trillion in 1970, personal financial assets (excluding corporate assets) grew at the same rate and the same level. This trend toward personal financial asset growth accelerated in the 1970s, when Japan undertook more successful structural adjustment to the oil shocks than its competitors. Nominal GNP expanded to Yen 366 trillion in 1988. This growth and the financial regulatory framework which encouraged a high domestic savings rate, became the fundamental underpinning of a strong Japanese financial position in the world system during the later 1980s. Japanese financial institutions found themselves in possession of mountains of surplus capital to invest in the domestic and international economy. The total of all Banks' banking accounts in 1988 reached Yen 366 trillion, and when other major financial institutions are added to this, such as life insurance and investment trusts, the figure becomes Yen 526 trillion in 1988, according to the Bank of Japan. Japanese insurance companies alone hold over $150 billion in US assets. The Japanese banks financed some 40 per cent of leveraged buy outs in the US in the mid-1980s heyday of corporate merger and takeover mania.

Income from US foreign investments has tended to decline relative to that accruing to Japanese investment. In this sense, Japanese capital is on the opposite trajectory, reinforced by the increase in the level of direct investment abroad by several hundred per cent, which had formerly been only a small part of total foreign assets. Thus, Japanese capital is increasingly exploiting foreign labour and establishing manufacturing plants in foreign locations, thus increasing Japanese structural power in the global production process. This has been made more urgent by the impending economic integration in the EC by 1992, and the introduction of the US Trade Act in 1988, which legitimises formal retaliatory mechanisms against 'unfair' trade partners. Direct foreign investment has the added political benefit of reducing the level of export from Japan proper and thus lessening trade frictions with competitors by reducing its visible trade surplus. For example, in mid-1991 Japan and the EC agreed on new terms for managed trade in the automobile sector. Japan agreed to restrain exports for a few more years, thus allowing the European car industry a breathing space to adjust to increased competition, but Japanese direct investment in car factories inside the EC is set to increase.

Japanese liquidity surplus at home has produced the lowest average domestic interest rates in the world, which is an incentive for Japanese capital to flow abroad seeking higher rates of return. The previous super-accumulators in the world system also had very low levels of domestic interest rates: Britain until the First World War, and the United States until the mid-1970s.

In the Plaza agreement of September, 1985, Japan agreed to co-operate to bring the dollar down. The Maekawa report on structural adjustment in Japan, of April 1986, recommended reforms in the Japanese economy designed to preserve its strength while simultaneously easing tension with trade partners. Nevertheless, all the while Japanese capital was 'internationalising' and expanding its role in global capitalism. When the Bank for International Settlements instituted new capital adequacy regulations in December, 1987, Japan emerged strengthened yet again. The reform, like the pressure on Nakasone to begin the Maekawa process, was originally intended to curtail the expanding structural power of Japanese finance. It had the opposite effect. The concerted moves to force the Yen to appreciate were likewise intended to be more weight thrown on the Japanese thoroughbred, with opposite results. The US Trade Act of 1988 was supposedly another counter-measure, which has had the unintended effect of accelerating Japanese direct investment into global manufacturing thereby transferring even more control of the global production process to Japanese capital.

REFLECTIONS ON JAPAN AND GLOBAL HEGEMONY IN A TRI-POLAR WORLD

The key question is how super-accumulation can be transformed into further political, ideological, military, and cultural power in the global political economy. Throughout this essay I have argued that hegemony is rarely if ever monolithic or one dimensional. Though there is a succession of super-accumulators in the world economy, a single succession of sole hegemons is less easy to demonstrate. Global hegemony is better understood as always being shared among several hegemonic powers and their ruling classes. Before the Pacific War Japan was already incorporated into a trans-national hegemonic coalition. After Japan broke away from the fold and sought to unilaterally extend its imperium in Asia at the expense of its former allies it was eventually brought back into the fold as a necessary and desirable hegemonic partner. Trans-Atlanticism on its own would not be sufficient for the effective exercise of global hegemony in today's world. Therefore, Japan was incorporated into an institutionalised trilateralism among the three core zones of the capitalist world economy. Since the demise of the Soviet Union it has become very clear that the G-3 (acting through the G-7) is attempting to 'run the world' on behalf of core capital.

The question of whether US hegemony is in decline or whether Japan may be the successor leads us in the wrong direction. Since even at the height of US power global hegemony was already extensively shared there is no reason to expect a sole hegemon to succeed a relatively declining US. There is every reason to expect that the institutionalisation of global hegemony so effectively undertaken under American auspices will continue and probably even be strengthened. Japan is now the paramount economic power in several respects. However, that does not necessarily mean it would seek to directly challenge the trilateral institutions of global hegemony that have served its ascent so well in the past. On the contrary, the Japanese state and Japanese capital is likely to want to continue to co-operate within this framework as much as possible for the foreseeable future. In the short term this means prudently supporting continued American military leadership in the global security system and at least professing to take some action to moderate its neo-mercantilist habits. It goes without saying that it is the underlying structural power of Japanese capital that will continue to facilitate a steady increase in Japanese influence in all the flagship institutions of the global political economy.

Japan's rising sun has been on a trajectory toward sharing more and more in global hegemony since it began its transition to modernity in the late nineteenth century. Prime Minister Takeshita's interest in so-called 'power-sharing' arrangements with the US was not a dramatic new departure but rather a continuation of a secular trend. President Bush's humiliation on the tennis court and in the dining room where he fainted after vomiting in Japan at the outset of 1992 is significant. Bush lost a lot more that day than just his dinner. In a very real sense the terms of the relationship within the global hegemonic coalition have changed, and President Bush's momentary incapacity symbolically acknowledged this change. He went to Japan with American captains of ailing industries and asked Japan for help. Prime Minister Miyazawa could offer only an increase in import of car parts, which in effect reinforces the role of the US as 'Japan's subcontractor'. Even that promise had to be qualified a few days later once the ministries had reviewed its implications. In the aftermath of that visit, as recession bit ever deeper into the industrial sinews of the USA, American politics responded with a new debate on 'what to do about Japan', including the proposal for a national industrial policy other than the Pentagon budget.

Be that as it may, the fact remains that Japan is inextricably linked to the other two cores in a shared global hegemony. As I stated at the outset of this essay, the contemporary world order is characterised by two cross-currents of structural change: globalisation and regionalisation. While globalisation has obviated the need for military competition between the three core zones and enhanced their common security interests *vis-à-vis* the Third World, regionalisation has increased the tension within the existing liberal international trade order and fuels further competition between the cores in

211

economic and socio-political terms. As Japan's real power has become greater the terms of the trilateral relationship have changed. Japan will certainly assert itself more in the future within the trilateral institutions of hegemony and its voice shall be heard. The issue of Japan's 'difference', i.e. its neo-mercantilism and superior competitiveness, will continue to dominate the agenda of this relationship, along with the on-going realisation by the other two cores that Japan will continue to increase its wider influence. The era when the white races of Europe and America ruled supreme is over. Japan is no longer a 'junior partner' nor is the Asian race any longer 'second class citizens'. This may be one of the most profound changes of them all.

8 INTERNATIONALISATION AND DEMOCRATISATION: SOUTHERN EUROPE, LATIN AMERICA AND THE WORLD ECONOMIC CRISIS

OTTO HOLMAN

INTRODUCTION

At this particular moment in 'world time'[1] we bear witness to some sweeping changes in state and world-order structures, in part the result of the global economic crisis of the last two decades, in part bound up with the crisis and eventual demise of the bipolar system of superpower politics. The break-up of Soviet dominance and American hegemony has occurred along with an unprecedented renaissance of liberal values, economic and political. This upsurge in liberalism is both the result and cause of changing class, state and world-order structures.

There are two obvious manifestations of this process of liberalisation: first, the rise of neo-liberal politics, initially in Chile after the military coup in 1973, and highlighted in the policies of President Reagan and Prime Minister Thatcher in the 1980s; and, second, the shift from authoritarianism to formal political democracy in a number of developing countries, and particularly in southern Europe in the 1970s and Latin America in the 1980s. Both phenomena are concomitants to the world economic crisis of the 1970s and 1980s.

In comparing the different processes of democratisation in Spain, Portugal and Greece in the mid-1970s and in several Latin American countries in the period thereafter, some questions come to mind. First, to what extent are the transitions to democracy in the three southern European countries interrelated, and can be explained on common grounds, both in terms of timing and content? Second, to what extent are the transitions in such countries as Argentina, Brazil and Uruguay interrelated, and comparable with those in southern Europe? Third, why has political democracy been firmly established and consolidated in Spain, Portugal and Greece while remaining highly unstable and vulnerable in the southern cone of the Western

213

Hemisphere? Fourth, what explains the paradox that two countries with many common characteristics (Spain and Brazil) show such different patterns of political development and world market incorporation? Before moving to these questions we will examine attempts to explain similar characteristics and developments in southern Europe and Latin America. The main body of literature on this subject either foregoes or offers only one-sided explanations. Indeed, only an approach which transcends the implicit or explicit level-of-analysis problem as well as the ongoing question of external versus internal determination, can give us the beginning of an understanding of the processes in both regions. The different positions of southern Europe and Latin America in the post-war system of international or Atlantic Fordism form my basic point of reference, the process of European integration being the decisive element in the divergent directions which Brazil and Spain have been incorporated into, in the global political and economic system in the period in question.

TRANSITIONS TO DEMOCRACY, AND GLOBAL CRISIS: SOME THEORIES

We can categorise the body of literature on southern Europe and Latin America into three groups by drawing a distinction between the following approaches: (i) the 'comparative politics' approach to democratic transition; (ii) the French regulation school, especially the work of Alain Lipietz; and, (iii) the world-system approach, characterised by its radical break with the state-centred interpretations of (i) and (ii). This approach lays stress on an equilibrium model in which the basic units of analysis are geographical: core, semi-peripheral and peripheral zones in the world-economy. We will now briefly review and criticise each of these approaches and then introduce a more integrated political economy perspective to examine the general dynamics of change and the specific cases of Spain and Brazil.

Comparing national efforts of modernisation

The main body of comparativist literature on authoritarian regimes and democratic transition in southern Europe and Latin America shares some common features:

1. Individual countries are analysed from a comparative perspective in an attempt to draw a 'universal' pattern of

214

democratisation, emphasising the similarities rather than the differences between these countries;

2. an abstraction is made from (changes in) internal economic and social structures on the one hand and global structures and developments on the other;

3. the attention is primarily directed to changes in political regimes and forms of interest mediation, resulting in the primacy of political and institutional indicators over social and economic ones;

4. and, finally, political democracy is regarded as a goal in itself, and the counterpart of capitalism as an economic system.

These characteristics give some indication of the shortcomings of a comparative politics approach. From the 'global political economy' point of view, our criticism is initially at the level of analysis used, which is premised on a state-centric perspective. Secondly, economics is in most cases reduced to national rhythms of development and modernisation, resulting in an abstract causal connection with processes of political democratisation.

Thirdly, and of more importance, the comparative approach does not explain common patterns of political development. This is despite being inspired by striking similarities. For example, Spain, Portugal and Greece experienced comparable economic and socio-political developments after World War II (economic liberalisation in the late 1950s and early 1960s; the subsequent internationalisation and accelerated economic growth in the 1960s, and the rise of the so-called new middle classes; the fall of the dictatorships in 1974/75; the coming of power of social-democratic parties; entry into the Common Market). A similar comparison can be made for the Latin America region. Why is it, however, that democratisation in Spain, Portugal and Greece took off in the same period of time? And what about democratic transition in Argentina in 1983, Uruguay in 1984, and (albeit reluctantly) Brazil with the indirect election of Tancredo Neves in 1985? And, again, why in southern Europe has democracy been consolidated, while the Latin American experience is far from stable? The comparative politics approach does not provide the basis for a structural answer to these questions. Explanations have been based upon the assumption that a 'Mediterranean model' of democracy can be discerned, or upon a correlation between majoritarian and consensual patterns of democracy and population size, and their link with the degree of pluralism in national societies (see Pridham, 1984: 26; and Lijphart et al., 1988: 24). This weakness in generating broad-ranging and consistent explanations is an exemplary characteristic of the whole approach.

Inter-state dependency and the globalisation of the crisis of Fordism

As one of the prominent figures of the French regulationist school, Lipietz has established his reputation through his attempt to combine an analysis of the Fordist accumulation regime with the changing pattern of the international division of labour in the 1970s and early 1980s. For Lipietz, Fordism is essentially connected with the socio-economic formations of the old industrial core-areas, where it was introduced in order to regulate the long-established relation between wage labour and capital. When speaking of the eventual extension of Fordism to countries in 'the South', Lipietz argues that their problem is 'the *creation* or establishment of the wage-relation' instead of the *adjustment* of this relation. As a result, the crisis of Fordism in the core-countries and the subsequent transfer of production processes to the 'inner periphery' (the so-called Newly Industrialising Countries) does not and can not include the transfer of the Fordist regime of accumulation. Instead of the global extension of Fordism, one should speak of the extension of the *crisis* of Fordism (Lipietz, 1982). In other words, the overall framework of core-periphery relations necessarily excludes the peripheral countries from adopting similar structures to those of core-countries. Because Fordism originates in the core and is subsequently imported (or 'internalised') in some parts of the periphery, an inferior copy of the original regime – 'peripheral Fordism' – is the necessary outcome.

Lipietz warns us not to use labels applying to the 'old division of labour', in the sense of deducing from the disproven centre-periphery dichotomy to individual social formations. Indeed he argues in favour of the 'primacy of internal causes': the basic unit of analysis is the socio-economic national formation which must be studied in its own right rather than in the context of a single world system of 'world regime of accumulation'. At best we may speak of a 'world configuration' of national regimes of accumulation. None the less, he adds 'if we wish to understand what is happening "in the periphery", we must begin by looking at what is happening in the advanced capitalist world' (Lipietz, 1987: 29–30). Thus, though he stresses the primacy of internal factors, he still pays attention to centre-periphery relations within the 'new international division of labour'. These relations 'are not direct relations between states or territories which are caught up in a single process. They are *relations between processes*, between processes of social struggle and between regimes of accumulation that are to a greater or lesser extent introverted or extraverted' (Lipietz, 1987: 25).

Here we are confronted with the old dilemma between 'internal' and 'external' determination. 'How can our theoretical analysis recognise the primacy of the "internal" productive process in the colonies, and yet reconcile or combine it with the also determinant "external" exchange and other relations of dependence on the capitalist metropolis?' (Frank, 1979: 2–3) This problem of determination or primacy of the 'internal' mode of production and accumulation on the one hand, and the 'external' relations of exchange and capital flows on the other, is clearly reflected in the work of Lipietz. Although he seems well aware of Mao's statement 'that external causes are the condition of change and internal causes are the basis of change, and that external causes become operative through internal causes' (Mao Tse Tung, 1977: 28), it seems that he applies this principle to the socio-economic national formations of the core but much less so to those in the periphery. In the core states internal class structures and regimes of accumulation subordinate external conditions; obversely, in those states where peripheral Fordism is introduced internal structures are subordinated to the global 'relations between processes'. Here the external causes, i.e. the crisis in core Fordism and the subsequent internationalisation of production, are the basis of change, the internal social struggle conditioning the success or otherwise of the implantation.

Several points of critique can be levelled at this thesis. First, Lipietz' implicit analytical distinction between production and accumulation, confined within socio-economic national formations, and international exchange relations may be questioned. It is not that Lipietz denies the internationalisation of productive capital. He does say, however, that 'even if economic interests and transnational ideological pressures do abolish frontiers, it has to be remembered that the form in which those pressures and interests are integrated is still the state form' (Lipietz, 1987: 22). Contrary to this view, in the present article I emphasise the impact of diverse processes of transnationalisation for the development of Atlantic relations. Indeed, it is the analysis of concrete post-World War II *processes*, of which the transnationalisation of production is certainly one of the most important, that enables us to transcend the theoretical and methodological problems of Lipietz' argument. As Robert Cox puts it, referring to the economic component of what he calls the world hegemonic order of the *Pax Americana*, 'a *world* economy of international production emerged within the existing *international* economy of classical trade theory'.[2]

This point of critique is related to a second. Lipietz' analysis of the state is extremely weak, reducing its role to the regulation of national processes of accumulation. While this serves to illustrate the difference between regulationist theory and the literature on democratic transitions (i.e. the primacy of 'regimes of accumulation' versus the primacy of political regimes and institutions) it can not veil the fact that both approaches view the state as the basic if not the only actor in international relations. That this view is so tenacious may surprise us in times of transnationalisation (of production, but also of civil society, of certain state functions, of ideological structures) and the 'internationalisation of domestic politics'.

Thirdly, Lipietz's analysis of the social struggle and the regime of accumulation in a particular peripheral state is 'built-in' to his analysis of the relations between processes, that is the imperialist structure. A major consequence of this kind of analysis is that, as Giovanni Arrighi has argued, it favours generalisation 'and therefore discourages the concrete analyses of concrete situations which is the essence of Marxism'.[3] Lipietz's approach leads him to the erroneous application of the concept of peripheral Fordism to the actual situations in Spain, Portugal and Greece on the one hand, and Brazil, Argentina and Mexico on the other. This is illustrated in the following:

> *Hypothesis*: the same economic causes (the maturation of peripheral Fordism) had the same effects in the early NICs (southern Europe) and, ten years later, in the 'NICs of the seventies'. (Lipietz, 1987: 114)

Intermediate countries and the concept of semi-periphery

Lipietz's hypothesis forms a transition to the third body of comparative literature on southern Europe and Latin America. Although the heterogeneous character of the group of so-called NICs becomes clear when we look in detail at its composition, the very emergence of this group in the 1960s and 1970s has altered discussions within development theory in a substantial way, even leading to the creation of a new concept: the semi-periphery, introduced by Immanuel Wallerstein. It is used in the literature in two ways. First, as a rather loose concept, aimed at distinguishing a particular group of countries from both highly and less developed ones, and frequently accompanied with the explicit statement that the use of this category does not imply any agreement with the views of Frank and Wallerstein on the capitalist world-economy (see, for example, Mouzelis, 1986). Second, it is used as a concept bound up with world-system theory, the theoretical construct we are here concerned with.

World-system theory has radically broken with the idea that the international system is to be explained solely with regard to individual states. It seeks to interpret, for example, the actions of individual states as the result of their operation within a global structure called the world-system. For the first time in the history of social science a relatively homogeneous school of thought (with its own institutions, publications and congresses, and organised around an international network of social scientists) has been able to force the discussion on international relations into a new direction by introducing this 'third level' of analysis, the world-system. However, in overemphasising the importance of global structures the approach is vulnerable to charges of reification and determinism. One body of criticism is directed against the *economic* determinism and functional subordination of political structures to the global economic structure on the one hand, and to a world state-system characterised by its own set of singular, political processes and its own historical dynamics, on the other. Another body of criticism argues against the world-system's definition of capitalism, understood as a network of exchange relations which determines the fate of nations: their structural location in either the core, semi-periphery or periphery. Instead of the maximisation of profits through the production for a mass market, critics of the approach point out that the most important feature of capitalism is to be found in the social relations of production and in class formation, both within and across national frontiers.

Central tenets of world-system theory are reflected in the concept of semi-periphery. One of the main objectives of a common research project developed by world system theorists, was to investigate the reasons for the 'convergence' of Spain, Portugal, Greece, Italy and Turkey 'towards authoritarian regimes and neo-mercantilist policies . . . in the course of the world political-economic crisis of the 1930's, and their convergence 'towards parliamentary regimes and neo-liberal policies . . . during the world political-economic crisis of the 1970's' (quoted in Arrighi, 1985: 12). In explaining why at different periods of time distinctive convergences took place, the impact of both world crises was analysed and compared in order to detect 'an overarching southern Europe pattern of political-economic development'. In his introduction to the first study, Giovanni Arrighi points out that the group's debate centred around the proposition that this

219

southern Europe pattern of 'convergence and transition could be traced to the growing integration of the region in the world-economy as a semi-peripheral zone' (Arrighi, 1985: 14). In other words, socio-political developments in the semi-periphery in general, and, more specifically, the transition to parliamentary democracy and the convergence of neo-liberal policies in the southern European countries, are functions of the positions these countries take within the international *economic* division of labour, i.e. within the global network of exchange relations.

This rather mechanistic explanation received little approval from other participants in the research group. First of all, empirical studies of individual countries showed fundamental differences, which, translated into theoretical consequences, implied the ultimate erosion of the concept of semi-periphery. Secondly, this discrepancy between empiricism and theory is the result of the vagueness of the starting definition, according to which a semi-peripheral state is characterised by an 'overall mix of core-peripheral activities' (Wallerstein, 1985: 35). This implies that there are no semi-peripheral activities as such, which makes the comparative value of this category highly questionable. That is, the quantitative nature of the definition impedes a qualitative comparison of individual countries. One distinguished world-system theorist, Christopher Chase Dunn, attempts to transcend this problem in a recent study. He distinguishes two analytic kinds of semi-peripheries, the one covering Wallerstein's 'balanced mix of core and peripheral activities' within states, and the other covering 'those areas or states in which there is a predominance of activities which are at intermediate levels with regard to the current world-system distribution of capital intensive/labor intensive production' (Chase Dunn, 1989: 212). Though the precise nature of these intermediate activities remains largely unclear, his study seems to indicate he has in mind what Lipietz would call peripheral Fordist activities.

TOWARDS AN INTEGRATED APPROACH

We now seek to go beyond the approaches criticised above, in order to develop a global political economy perspective, after the manner of Cox (1987). This is necessary in order to avoid ahistorical, determinist and idealist explanations, and to locate the transformations in southern Europe and Latin America in the context of 'world time' (see note 1). By conceptualising a global political economy in this way we can avoid the pitfalls of the so-called 'levels of analysis' problem and move towards an integrated, political economy approach.

Atlantic Fordism and different state – civil society configurations

In this section we will look more carefully at the international economic and socio-political context in which the processes of industrialisation and democratisation have taken place in Latin America and southern Europe. We first outline the basic dimensions of the post-war growth model. Starting from a Gramscian interpretation, we call this complex of interrelated national and international, political and economic, features of the post-war growth model international or Atlantic Fordism. This model has three dimensions, which are 'superimposed dimensions of reality, where "facts" pertinent to one dimension only acquire their full meaning if they are considered against the background of the other dimensions' (Overbeek, 1990: 87).

First, Fordism at the national level originates in the factory through the introduction of new productive methods by individual companies, eventually leading to the macroeconomic principle of combined increases in productivity and real wages (that is, the implementation of a macroeconomic growth model, based on mass production and mass consumption). The very introduction of Fordism can be partially dependent on external factors, such as foreign technology and capital. Conversely, the technical superiority of hegemonic states and their national capitals can result in the globalisation of certain production processes and techniques, and modes of labour organisation, through the internationalisation of trade and production. But the successful implantation of Fordism within a country is always inextricably bound up with the existence of a specific level of socio-economic and political development of that country. This, among other things, explains the considerable national differences in time and in content of the eventual emergence and subsequent development of Fordism in the Atlantic area.

Taking this restrictive dimension of Fordism as a point of departure, it is simply not true that the adoption of Fordist production methods in southern Europe and Latin America coincided in time with or was the result of the crisis of Fordism in the core countries of the Atlantic area, as Lipietz for instance argues. Well before the first signs of this crisis, in both regions a restructuring of production along Fordist lines was started, either as the result of domestic (public

221

or private) initiatives, through foreign investments, or a combination of both. In this sense, it is not the timing that was decisive, but the extent to which the introduction of new forms of organisation of production and labour relations changed the conventional economic structure. That is, although Fordism implies the 'rationalisation and extension of (the class relations of capitalism) shorn of all extraneous and precapitalist baggage', it never obtains control over the whole of production (see Cox, 1987: 309ff). Fordist production may become eventually the dominant form, co-existing with other, subordinated forms of organisation of production and labour relations, yet it may not. In this last case a fairly unstable balance between different forms of production (and different forms of social relations of production, for that matter) may persist, leaving regressive and non-productive forces in society considerable room for socio-political manoeuvre.

If we want to know to what extent production has been restructured along Fordist lines in individual Latin American and southern European countries in the post-war period, we should look to the following indicators: the shares of agriculture and industry in total production, and their changes over time, including the labour or capital intensity in both sectors; mutations in the structure of industrial production (for instance, developments in the share of the consumer-goods sector in relation to other sectors); the structural duality in industry, that is the relation between large-scale, modernised enterprises with high productivity rates and relatively high real wages on the one hand, and small factories and shops with backward technology and below-average wages on the other, indicating the heterogenity of industrial production; the size of the respective national populations, showing the potential of the different domestic markets; and, amongst other measures, the extent to which an internal dynamic of growth predominates over export-led growth, both models being reflected in alternative strategies of development.

It goes beyond the scope of this contribution to analyse these indicators in detail for all the relevant countries involved. Besides, such comprehensive measurement of Fordist restructuring would offer us no clear-cut hierarchy of countries, simply because individual countries do not show a linear and uniform pattern with regard to all indicators. Greece, for instance, seems quite comparable with Argentina in some respects, notably with regard to the capital-intensive pattern of industrialisation and the relatively low labour-absorption capacity of the industrial sector (see Mouzelis, 1986: 119). In other respects, Greece shares fundamental characteristics with Spain and Portugal: all three countries showed 'super-Fordist' average annual productivity rises during the 1963–73 period (5.46% in Spain, 6.81% in Portugal, and 7.51% in Greece; see Lipietz, 1987: 127), and experienced a radical change in the composition of the labour force (the percentage of workers employed in the primary sector in Greece declined from 57% in 1960 to 29.7% in 1980, in Portugal from 42.8% to 28.3%, and in Spain from 42.3% to 18.9%; see Holman, 1987–88: 25). Any quantitative analysis of the above indicators should be accompanied therefore by a qualitative assessment of their interconnection. Moreover, no final conclusion can be drawn from such an exercise without taking into account the other two dimensions of what we have labelled Atlantic Fordism.

Nevertheless, an indication is formed by the way individual countries coped with the impact of the global crisis of restructuring of the 1970s and 1980s. Both regions, in a quite different way, have experienced an accelerated incorporation into world market structures. While Latin America has been incorporated dramatically into the international credit economy, Spain, Portugal and Greece have realised their integration into the Common Market in the 1980s. Looking more closely to the Latin American region, we must conclude that the authoritarian regimes of countries like Argentina, Chile and Uruguay have implemented harsh neo-liberal policies, eventually leading to a deindustrialisation of the national economy. The military regimes which came to power in these countries in the 1970s synthesised neo-liberalism with the doctrine of national security, blaming the previous process of industrialisation and the subsequent strengthening of the labour movement for all socio-political evils. A forced restructuring towards an export economy based on the predominance of primary production was the ultimate outcome, creating a power bloc of rural bourgeoisies, urban financial institutions and military bureaucracies (see Fernandez Jilberto, 1989; and Cortazar *et al.*, 1984).

In Brazil and Mexico a model of 'bank debt-financed, government-led industrialisation', the so-called indebted industrialisation, was implemented in the 1970s, aimed at counteracting the excessive influence of foreign transnational companies in their national economies by attempting to increase local public and private sector participation in industrial growth, and using state intervention, debt-financing and export-promotion of manufactured consumer-goods as its principal methods. With exports beginning to slacken in the early 1980s, this growth-model collapsed, leading to a shift from transnational corporations to international banks as the principal suppliers of foreign capital to these countries (see Frieden, 1981; and also

223

Harris, 1987). Ironically, this has led to a situation in which the countries who have restructured their economies to a greater extent along Fordist lines in the 1960s and 1970s, based on an apparently stable alliance between local private and public capital and transnational productive capital, are more and more forced to implement neo-liberal principles in order to deal with their dazzling debt-burden. In fact, Brazil and Mexico seem to be the main victims in Latin America of the restructuring impact of the world economic crisis and changing world order structures. And indeed, it looks like the recent turn to democracy in Brazil and the 1989-election of the neo-liberal Fernando Collor de Mello as president must be interpreted in this context, a U-turn in economic policy forced upon the social classes under the banner of democratic legitimacy.

In the southern European countries, finally, the impact of the international economic crisis has been severe, especially in the later half of the 1970s and early 1980s. What is more, this economic crisis coincided with the first years of democratic transition in these three countries, postponing at least initially, a full implantation of 'austerity measures' in order not to threaten the young and vulnerable democracies. Later, after social-democratic parties had come to power in the early 1980s (therewith consolidating the respective democratic systems), a full-scale crisis management was directed at restructuring and modernising the national economies in the light of full entrance into the Common Market, especially in Spain and Portugal. That is, neither a neo-liberal destruction of industrial capacity, as in the case of Chile and Argentina, nor an indebted industrialisation followed by an externally induced check on sustained economic growth, as in the case of Brazil and Mexico, took place. Instead, the Spanish and Portuguese economies experienced average annual rates of growth that were the highest within the Common Market during the late 1980s, showing a remarkable capacity of industrial reconversion and modernisation (see Holman, 1989a; and *The Economist*, 28 May 1988).

The second dimension of Atlantic Fordism refers to the state and its relation to civil society. We are referring here to Keynesianism as an economic policy, with the interventionist state and the 'mixed economy' as its concomitants, on the one hand, and 'modes of social relations of production' on the other.

Whereas Fordism in its restrictive meaning is characterised by a specific form of organisation of production and labour relations, eventually leading to a compromise between the main social forces (a compromise based on the combination of increasing productivity and rising real wages), Keynesianism is the reflection of a particular balance of power in economic *policy*, in a determinate, Fordist conjuncture. Or, in other words, ideal-typical Keynesianism 'implies the use of government to influence and direct decisions made in the private sector' (Wolfe, 1981: 54). In those countries in which a strong labour movement existed, a Keynesianist economic policy could be effectively pursued in order to 'save capitalism from the capitalists'. In most cases, social democracy functioned as the obvious political medium of such a policy. On the other hand, in those countries without a strong socialist or social-democratic tradition, post-war macroeconomic planning implied 'the use of the private sector to influence the scope and activities of government'. In this case we should rather speak of 'counter-Keynesianism' (Wolfe, 1981: 54). But although counter-Keynesianism 'presupposes an interventionist political authority [whose] economic administration fulfils the expectations of groups or classes that dominate it', the policies of such an authority 'serve to legitimate the authority of the hegemonic power inasmuch as the achievements due to them correspond to the promises propagated within the dominant ideology' (Keyder, 1985: 140).[4] That is, even in the cases of counter-Keynesianism the interests of the dominated groups or classes have to be fulfilled to some extent.

Obviously, neither the above description of Keynesianism or (and even less so) that of counter-Keynesianism is applicable to the post-war situation in Latin America and southern Europe. It is one thing to speak of the social confrontation between dominant and subordinated groups in society, resulting from an unequal division in wealth and income and eventually leading to spontaneous upheavals and strikes in an overall and continuous climate of social unrest; it is quite another to speak of the existence of a well-organised labour movement, institutionalised in strong trade-unions and political level in order to obtain their goals. It may be clear that the latter situation is one of the concomitants of relatively advanced class societies, a reflection of a particular level of economic and socio-political development on the basis of which in Western Europe in the immediate post-war period, a restructuring of production along Fordist lines could take place. That is, previous industrialisation confined within national economic systems provided the economic and socio-political structures within which the introduction of Fordist and the subsequent transnationalisation of productive capital could be realised during the era which came to be known as the *Pax Americana*. In Latin America and southern Europe such basic structures were almost completely absent before World War II, and, therefore, had to be constructed in an international, Atlantic setting into which the most advanced countries had moved at a new stage of their development. The impact of the post-war industrialisation in both regions had to be necessarily a different one than the one the 'old industrial heartland' had experienced previously. One of the most striking examples of this structural deficiency was the absence of considerable middle strata, the so-called new middle classes, on the basis of which in Western Europe social democracy became the obvious political medium of Keynesian economic policy.

The main difference between both regions is, however, that in southern Europe authoritarian regimes came to the fore during the inter-war period and stayed continuously in power until well into the 1970s, while in Latin America a cyclical pattern of transitions from authoritarianism to formal democracy, and vice versa, became the characteristic feature of political development. This difference has had some important consequences.

First, regime continuity in southern Europe formed the political framework in which relatively smooth and linear social and economic developments have broken the 'vicious circle' (i.e. involving the pattern of a weak state which foments individualism and particularism, leaving the field open for the so-called 'poderes facticos' – 'oligarchy, army and church – who tend to counterbalance any strengthening of the state), gradually replacing it for a 'virtuous circle' (i.e. a strong state which foments a civil culture based on socio-political mass participation, strengthening interest groups within civil society who tend to counterbalance excessive state centralism and tend to insist upon a less hypertrophic state) (Tortosa, 1985: 20–1). In Latin America, structural socio-political instability, characterised by a continuous struggle for power between rival economic and political elites, and an ever present warfare between social classes, impeded such a gradual shift towards a state-civil society configuration in which civil society has achieved a degree of self-sustaining cohesion that democracy no longer forms a threat to the dominant classes.

Second, and related to the first point, in southern Europe a fairly stable system of interest mediation (or 'mode of social relations of production') was implemented over time, a system of 'state corporatism' (and in the Greek case of 'state clientelism'). Though the harmonisation of interests became a general principle of organisation for society (in Spain even affecting student organisations), in all three countries this authoritarian mode of interest mediation was primarily directed at managing social and political conflict, 'the conditioning of the development of the social forces in struggle' (Foweraker, 1987: 58), through the hierarchical, non-representational and exclusive institutionalisation of labour relations. In Spain, this took the concrete form of the Vertical Syndicate within the Franquist organic state (see below), in Portugal decisions on wages, prices and production were channeled through the various corporations (organised by sector of production) and the Corporative Chamber in Salazar's Estado Novo, and in Greece trade-unions were state-controlled and labour interests mediated through a 'vertical incorporative mode of inclusion' (Mouzelis, 1986). In Latin America, attempts to superimpose such state corporatist structures 'from above' were frustrated by the continuous resurrection of populism, to a certain extent overlapping with the alternation of dictatorships and democratic regimes. Here, the recurrent mobilisation of the popular classes by charismatic leaders has been both cause and effect of the lack of (authoritarian) institutionalisation of society, especially in the field of labour relations.

Of crucial importance is, then, that in southern Europe state corporatism created the preconditions for the eventual transition to *and* consolidation of democracy in the 1970s and 1980s. To understand this paradox, we first have to refute the characterisation of democratisation as the turning over of state functions to the institutions of an incipient but reinforcing civil society, as if civil society and the state are separate spheres, and the strengthening of the one necessarily implies the weakening of the other.

In our view, a 'weak' state is *inter alia* characterised by the virtual amalgamation of political and economic power within an oligarchical ruling class, a class-divided society separating this oligarchic or aristocratic class (or estate) from the dominated classes (or lowest estate), an all-embracing network of patron-client relations serving as a mechanism to contain popular uprisings at an individual level. Thus in such states there is an absence of nationalism and a lack of societal vertebration and incorporation, that is, civil society is virtually non-existent. In southern Europe and Latin America such 'weak' states existed during the greater part of the first half of this century.

A 'strong' state on the other hand does not have to rely on direct or indirect military intervention in domestic politics in order to safeguard regime stability, making possible the effective subordination of the military apparatus to civil institutions. At the socio-political level, a strong state is characterised by a formal separation or insulation of economic and political power leading to the emergence of a political ruling class which obtains a relative autonomy *vis à vis* the social classes at the political level while at the same time safeguarding class-domination at the socio-economic level. Finally, a

227

strong state is characterised by a high degree of societal incorporation making clientelist, populist, oligarchic or authoritarian modes of political domination not only increasingly unnecessary but more important, also highly undesirable and counter-productive. In this sense, a strong civil society is the concomitant of a strong state. As a matter of fact, it is in this configuration of strong states and strong civil societies that the Gramscian notion of hegemony becomes relevant (see Holman, 1989b).

A final note has to be made to fully understand this last argument. When talking about 'strong' states, we always have to keep in mind the relative meaning of this notion in respect to the outside world, that is in comparison with other states. This also applies to the degree of economic development within a state. A 'strong' state is not characterised only by its relatively developed economic structure. As Wallerstein has stated, 'a state is stronger than another state to the extent that it can maximise the conditions for profit-making by its enterprises (including state corporations) within the world-economy' (Wallerstein, 1984a: 5). This includes also the position of strength of a state *vis à vis* foreign capital operating or aspiring to operate within its territory. In the following section we will look at this point more closely, raising the discussion at the third dimension of Atlantic Fordism, the overall political and economic organisation of capitalist relations in the Atlantic area. Brazil and Spain, though apparently comparable, show totally different patterns of adaptation to changing world order structures in the late 1970s and 1980s, and are as such good examples from which we can extrapolate general patterns for both regions.

The different impact of changing world order structures on Brazil and Spain

As we have mentioned, state corporatism created the conditions for the eventual transition and consolidation of democracy in southern Europe. In the case of Spain, state corporatism, forced upon the social classes by a bloody class war, helped to generate unprecedented economic growth. The implementation of this system not only saved capitalism from revolutionary counterforces through physical extermination and severe repression, but also offered the institutional framework for the deepening of capitalist relations of production (and a total restructuring of the Spanish economy). Paradoxically, by implementing this very framework, the dictatorship set into motion its own internal erosion and prepared its own collapse.

But what, then, accounts for the differences between Spain and Brazil? If we restrict the impact of state corporatism to the economic developments it generated some apparent similarities between both countries can not be ignored (Holman and Fernandez, 1989: 17–18):

1. Both countries have experienced a preliminary phase of industrialisation in the first half of the present century, as a direct consequence of an 'import-substitution-industri-alisation strategy' under the ideological banner of econ-omic nationalism. This first phase laid the foundation for;

2. an acceleration and deepening of the respective processes of industrialisation from the late 1950s (Spain) and early 1960s (Brazil) onwards, resulting in high average annual rates of growth and the denomination of the two econ-omies as the 'economic miracles' of the Western world;

3. In both countries a model of development was implemented in the 1960s, based on a combination of Keynesian economic policies and cautious economic liber-alisation, and resulting in the opening of the respective economies towards the outside world and the subsequent 'internationalistion of capital'. In both countries a fairly well balanced alliance came into existence between local private and public capital and foreign transnational capi-tal. Moreover, this liberalisation was accompanied by a certain degree of selective protectionism and took place under the continued presence of the Franquist political system in Spain and the Brazilian military dictatorship that came into existence in 1964.

At the socio-economic level, as a direct consequence of these econ-omic developments, in both countries a structural transformation took place which resulted in an increasing discrepancy between a societal demand for democracy and the vertical political structures of the authoritarian states. A loss of legitimacy of the two regimes was not only reflected in increasing popular discontent, but also, and more importantly, in a changing attitude of the economic elites. These elites had traditionally benefited most from the authoritarian systems, but began increasingly to extricate themselves from the regimes once they perceived a turn to democracy as the best way to continue their class dominance under changed socio-economic conditions.

In Brazil, the ultimate consequence of these developments was a gradual opening of the regime, starting with the 'deliberate

decompression' during the Geisel administration (1974–8) and cul-
minating in the indirect election of Tancredo Neves in 1985 and the
first free presidential elections since the 1964 military coup, held in
November and December 1989 (see Lamounier, 1989). In Spain the
death of Francisco Franco in 1975 was the prelude to a process of
democratic transition, involving the principal governmental and
oppositional forces and strongly supported by both trade-unions and
employer's organisations. This resulted in the final consolidation of
democracy when the socialist party (PSOE) obtained an absolute
majority in the 1982 elections.

Thus, in Brazil the political opening took place from within the
military regime and was forced upon the extra-parliamentary and
illegal opposition 'from above', whereas in Spain the transition from
dictatorship to democracy was from the beginning negotiated with
all major societal forces, the so-called *ruptura pactada*. And it is
precisely here that our comparison between Brazil and Spain must
shift from apparent similarities to striking differences. In order to
show this, we have to return to the impact of state corporatism on
Spanish society.

A second major consequence of the authoritarian system was that
it channelled the transformations in Spanish society through the
creation of state institutions and corporations, which showed a
remarkable capacity to adapt to changing circumstances, especially
in the field of labour relations. An example of this is the Franquist
Vertical Syndicate, created to control and order the whole of national
production according to vertical lines of command. Already in the
1940s syndical elections were held at the factory level, and at the
local, provincial and national levels, though the electorate became
smaller and less representative as the posts to be filled increased in
importance. Initially, the hierarchical lines from the Ministry of Labour
downwards were far more important. During the liberalisation and
internationalisation of the Spanish economy in the 1960s, this Syndicate provided the space for collective bargaining and the organisation
of the labour force 'from below', a space which was in due course
filled up by the Spanish Communist Party through the so-called
Comisiones Obreras. These workers' commissions infiltrated the Syndicate through the syndical elections at factory level and eventually
came to play an increasingly important role in decentralised negotiations on production and labour conditions, especially after their
transformation into an autonomous national labour organisation in
1966. As Foweraker puts it, 'Franco's corporatist strategy represented
a fixed and exclusive mode of mediating the capital-labour relation,

and its exclusivity, not its intrinsic qualities, proved to be its fatal historical flaw' (Foweraker, 1987: 60). It is in this context that we can understand the smooth transition from state to societal corporatism after the death of Franco (see Holman, 1989b). This transition contributed to the stable character of the overall process of democratisation. And it is from this that we can explain partially the changing attitude of the Spanish bourgeoisie towards the Franco-regime, in favour of democracy.

One of the determinants not only of the transition to democracy as such, but also of its very success in the long run, is the coalescence of this political project with dominant concepts of control, or 'modes of economic behaviour', in the cupola of the bourgeoisie. Concepts of control are long-term strategies, related to particular fractions of the bourgeoisie, formulated in comprehensive terms and dealing with such areas as labour relations, socio-economic policies and the international socio-economic and political order (van der Pijl, 1984). When opting for democracy, then, (fractions of) the bourgeoisie developed a clear perception of the nation's role in present and future economic and political relations at the global level.

In this sense it is important to note that the liberalisation and opening of the Spanish economy in the 1960s, and the subsequent internationalisation of capital in Spain, generated an outward-looking mentality in the Spanish business community, which for obvious reasons was first and foremost directed at Western Europe, notably at integration into the Common Market. But in order to realise this option Spain had to establish democratic politics, an additional reason for the Spanish bourgeoisie to support democratic transition. During the period of transition, especially after the Socialist Party had come to power, this European option was confirmed as the only realistic alternative for Spanish capital. The increasing transnationalisation of the Spanish economy in conjunction with its growing orientation to the Common Market formed an important reason for the successful transition and consolidation of democracy: this was as important as the impact of state corporatism. In fact, from the perspective of the Spanish state-civil society configuration in the 1970s and 1980s, these two phenomena can not be separated.

During this period Spanish civil society has obtained a relative strength, by which we mean to say that it has achieved a certain degree of autonomy and self-sustaining cohesion *vis à vis* the state. In order to understand this fully, we may use one of the Gramscian conceptions of civil society, quoted in the editors introduction to the chapter on 'State and civil society' in the *Prison Notebooks*:

> Between the economic structure and the State with its legislation and its coercion stands civil society . . . The State is the instrument for conforming civil society to the economic structure, but it is necessary for the State to "be willing" to do this; i.e. for the representatives of the change that has taken place in the economic structure to be in control of the State. (Gramsci, 1971: 208)

The editors rightly state that Gramsci in effect is equating here the notion of civil society with 'mode of economic behaviour'. In Spain, the 'representatives of the change that has taken place in the economic structure', i.e. the Spanish Socialist Party in co-operation with the transnationalised, Europeanist bourgeoisie, have effectively used the Spanish state for 'conforming civil society'. On the other hand, however, the Spanish bourgeoisie still depends on the Spanish state with regard to the policy needed to prepare Spanish business for full competition in 1992. The socialist policy of industrial reconversion and modernisation on the one hand, and anti-cyclical macroeconomic adjustment on the other, implies 'the use of government to influence and direct decisions made in the private sector'. If a state 'is stronger than another state to the extent that it can maximise the conditions for profit-making by its enterprises within the world-economy', as suggested by Wallerstein, our evaluation of the strength of the Spanish state will also depend on the degree in which it succeeds in neutralising demands of the trade-unions and in giving direction to the modernisation of Spanish industry.

Turning back to our comparison, we can state the following: both the role of state corporatism in the creation of an autonomous and relatively strong Spanish civil society, and the impact of the process of European integration on the consolidation of Spanish democracy impedes us from carrying any further the analogy between these two countries. In his excellent analysis of the Brazilian transition to democracy, seen from the historical perspective of the process of Hobbesian state building, Lamounier argues that Brazilian institutional development was pre-eminently state-centred, in a continuous attempt to curtail intra-elite conflict and to repress popular uprising or mere organised opposition. Although generating sustained and accelerated industrial growth, the military regime which came to power in 1964 did not improve living conditions of a substantial part of the Brazilian population, leaving structural socioeconomic inequality and absolute poverty largely intact (Lamounier, 1989). In 1960 the poorest 50% of the active population earned 17.7% of the national income, and only 11.8% in 1976. In the same period, the richest 5% saw their share in national income increase from

27.7% to 39%. Other social indicators (the infant mortality rate for instance) confirm that the Brazilian distribution of wealth is amongst the most unequal in the world (Roett, 1988: 113). In this context, clientelism, populism and particularism remain ever persistent features of Brazilian society, leaving space for the unexpected and obstructing a 'universalisation of policy'. It may be clear that this situation has been aggravated as a result of the present debt position of Brazil. Drawing our parallel with Spain once more, this implies that the nascent democratic state in Brazil 'has to influence and direct decisions made in the private sector' by implementing a neo-liberal policy of deregulation and trade liberalisation, while at the same time being fully incorporated in the international credit economy. Curbing hyper-inflation and meeting the burden of foreign debt seems incompatible with reassuming the path of industrial growth. After more than a year of economic tricks and quick solutions, the Collor de Melo government has realised absolute, social, economic and political chaos.

Another option for the near future is offered by the possibility of reinforcing the process of regional integration in Latin America within the context of the Latin American Integration Association (LAIA). Unsuccessful attempts in this direction in the 1950s and 1960s may be renewed in the light of changing world order structures, and more particularly the change in the political and economic relations of the region with the United States. In a crude and perhaps oversimplified way, we can state that during the *Pax Americana* US dominance in the inter-American system was generally accepted by the politico-military and economic elites in Latin America, while to a greater or lesser extent rejected by large parts of the Latin American populations. A network of bilateral relations between the US and individual Latin America countries secured the internal cohesion of this inter-American system, on the implicit premise of divide and rule. This situation seems to have come to an end, somewhere beginning with the US–Latin American collision in the Falkland Islands crisis of 1982 and more recently illustrated by the overt Latin American protest against the US intervention in Panama in December 1989.

This changed situation may well form the prelude to increasing political independence from the United States and growing inter-regional co-operation, certainly if the other two alternatives are likely to be either national introvertion and democracy breakdown, or sustained incorporation in the international credit economy and forced adjustment to the principles of global neo-liberalism. In this context recent discussions within the RIO-group with respect to the viability of a 'Latin America 1995' project, and the establishment of the Mercosur, the Common Market between Argentina, Brazil, Paraguay and Uruguay, are first steps in this direction. This scenario gains further weight if we note the accelerating investments of foreign capital from other countries, notably Japan, which emerged during the 1980s and which may continue during the 1990s. On the other hand, the enthusiastic reactions in Latin America after the launching of the 'Enterprise for the Americas' by President Bush in the summer of 1990 seems to indicate that most Latin American leaders still tend to rely heavily on US hegemony in the region if (and only if) the United States are prepared to play the 'universal interest' card.

CONCLUSIONS

One of the main conclusions we must draw from the above analysis, is that the processes of democracy transition in southern Europe and Latin America can not be interpreted separately from their historical origins, from the inalienable connection of long-term economic and socio-political developments in both regions, and from the global context in which structural changes have taken place in individual countries. In this sense, we analytically distinguished three dimensions: the transforming impact Atlantic Fordism has had on economic structures; the articulation of changing class and state structures in state – civil society configurations; and the impact of changing world-order structures on national economic and socio-political developments. It is this historical materialist interrelationship between the three dimensions of Atlantic Fordism which count for the theoretical differences with comparativist literature, Lipietz' analysis of peripheral Fordism and world system approaches suggests the innovative character of a Gramscian theory of international relations.

Moreover, in comparing Spain and Brazil, we have stressed the importance of the growing orientation of Spain towards Western Europe. In Gramscian terms, this 'Europeanisation', as alternative to political isolationism and mercantilism, has been the mediating force in the historical transition from the economic-corporate level of consciousness to the hegemonic level of consciousness, 'bringing about not only a unison of economic and political aims, but also intellectual and moral unity, posing all the questions around which the struggle rages not on a corporate but on a 'universal plane', and thus creating the hegemony of a fundamental social group over a series of subordinate groups' (Gramsci, 1971: 181–2). The option of European integration, materialised through the links between the Spanish bourgeoisie and its European counterparts, has united the economic and political aims of the principal social groups, therewith creating the framework for the 'universalisation' of Spanish politics, while preserving bourgeois hegemony. In the context of this 'European consciousness', Spanish social democracy fulfils the political task of making transnational capitalism more acceptable to the subordinated classes.

The acceleration of the process of European integration in the second half of the 1980s, itself a concomitant to changing world order structures, has furthermore reinforced the need for Spain to adopt its economic and socio-political structures to the ones prevailing in the most advanced member states. The transferring of resources from northern European countries to the south has been and will be an essential factor in making this process of modernisation a success. Hence recent fears of Spanish politicians and industrialists that the opening up of Eastern Europe will divert German investment to countries like Poland, Hungary and Czechoslavakia, in due course followed by companies from other northern European countries.

In the case of Brazil, an alternative option like the one European integration represented for Spain has been absent during the period in question. As a result, the adaption of Brazilian economic structures to the mechanisms of Atlantic Fordism have had dissimilar effects on social, political and ideological structures. Notably in respect to the state-civil society configuration in Brazil it can be concluded that the Brazilian civil society has not obtained as yet a considerable degree of self-sustaining cohesion, leaving bourgeois hegemony and nascent democracy highly vulnerable to continuing inter- and intra-class struggle. It may be clear that in this context the accelerated incorporation of Brazil into the international credit economy in the late 1970s and early 1980s have had the opposite effect of what Gramsci called the 'unison of economic and political aims'.

In attempting to curtail its traditional dependence on the United States, Brazil is recently following a strategy of diversifying its economic relations. This can be illustrated by the strengthening of Brazilian–Japanese trade relations, and by the growth of Japanese investment in Brazil. In fact, given the importance Japanese analysts attach to Brazil as an outlet for Japanese firms, ranking the country with an 'AA' rating for resource industries, and an 'A' rating for mass market industry opportunities (Nester, 1989: 395), Japanese investment in Brazil is likely to increase in the 1990s. This in turn may form the prelude to a further economic and, eventually, political estrangement from the United States, giving *inter alia* the option of Latin American regional integration new impetus.

Notes

1 By 'world time' I mean, following Anthony Giddens, 'that an apparently similar sequence of events, or formally similar social processes, may have quite dissimilar implications or consequences in different phases of world development' (Giddens, 1981: 167).
2 See Cox, 1987: 244ff. 'Where the international-economy model focuses on exchange', Cox continues, 'the world-economy model focuses on production'. In the next section we will see that what Cox labels as *'world-economy'*, in the era of the *Pax Americana* was restricted to the Atlantic area.
3 From a personal communication of Arrighi in which he comments on the early work of Frank (quoted in Frank, 1979: 6–7).
4 Note that Keyder in his contribution to the volume edited by Arrighi (1985) is referring to *international* Keynesianism, and the post-war hegemony of the United States in the international system. Although it may be doubted that such a system of international *Keynesianism* ever existed, we do believe that Keyder's remarks apply to Keynesianism at the national level.

9 STATE SOCIALISM AND PASSIVE REVOLUTION

KEES VAN DER PIJL

The thesis of this chapter is that the demise of Soviet socialism and the collapse of the USSR have to be interpreted in terms of a transition of one particular state/society configuration to another. The passing of a Hobbesian Leviathan rather than a crisis of socialism as much marks its *dénouement*. Meanwhile, it is not only Gramsci's notes on the importance of civil society as a sphere separate from formal state power that warrants a reference to the author of the *Prison Notebooks* in this connection. Gramsci also sketched a theory of 'molecular' class formation governed by the relations between different types of state which is particularly relevant in the Soviet case.

We will first briefly outline this theory and then interpret the various phases of the USSR's history in light of it, up to the Yanayev coup attempt of August 1991, the moment which catalysed the final dissolution of the USSR.

PASSIVE REVOLUTION AND INTERNATIONAL RELATIONS

We proceed from the premise that international relations are an aspect of global social development, in which states function to articulate the conditions of social production and power between rulers and ruled, and between states as such. As each political unit combines within itself a historically concrete array of social forces, reflecting the unequal development of different fragements of an immanent world society, state formation and international relations reflect the friction on the road to global integration in a most acute way, as war linked to social revolution (Rosenstock-Huessy, 1961).

Along with the growth of capital, with which modern state formation interacts, social structures will become more similar and foster horizontal integration in the heartland of capitalism. This development is favoured by the tendency of the most developed capitalist states to allow civil society a wider margin of self-regulation.

Hence, in the nineteenth and twentieth centuries, a transnational civil society grafted on the cultural bonds between Britain and the white English-speaking settler colonies, exploiting its periphery via the world market, developed into what may be termed a *Lockian heartland*.

The formation of this integrated core of Western imperialism passed through a critical phase when at the close of World War I the United States added its weight to it. Thus, at the outset Bolshevik power was confronted with the unified strength of the victorious Entente. Gramsci, writing in 1919, had this configuration of forces in mind when judging the prospects of the October revolution.

> During the war, to meet the demands of the struggle against imperial Germany, the states making up the Entente formed a reactionary coalition with its economic functions powerfully central-ized in London and its demagogy choreographed in Paris . . . The enormous administrative and political apparatus that was set up at that time is still in existence; it has been further strengthened and perfected, and is now effectively the instrument of Anglo-Saxon world hegemony. With Imperial Germany prostrated, and the Social-Democratic *Reich* incorporated into the global politico-econ-omic system controlled by Anglo-Saxon capitalism, capitalism has now forged its own unity and turned all its forces to the destruction of the Communist Republics. (Gramsci, 1977:81)

The interaction between a Lockian state/society configuration and transnationalisation can also be reconstructed from Gramsci's work. Thus, in the *Prison Notebooks* we find scattered remarks on, for example, the Anglo-Saxon Lockian state (1971: 261–2, 293); on the tradition of self-government in England and the rule of law (1971: 46, 186n, 195); and on transnational social forces (such as the Roman Catholic Church, Rotarianism, and the Jews), which function to 'mediat[e] the extremes [and] 'socialis[e]' the technical discoveries which provide the impetus for all activities of leadership, of devising compromise between, and ways out of, extreme solutions' (1971: 182n).

Yet on the above issues concerning the state, law and the role of the Church and religion, Gramsci's reflections are still incomplete and sometimes contradictory, as they are on, for instance, the actual directive role of the USA (1978: 284; 1971: 317).

It is on the borderline between the Lockian heartland and its immediate periphery, however, that Gramsci's thought becomes most pertinent as far as the interaction between international rela-tions and class formation is concerned. From his notes on the French

Revolution and its effects in Italy and central Europe, we can deduce a model for the relationship between the expansion of the Lockian heartland (in the sense of the state/society configuration progressively adjusting to the class structure generated by the capitalist mode of production) and the less developed states facing it. To Gramsci, the historical relationship between the modern French state born in the revolution and the states of continental Europe should be understood in terms of four elements (1971: 114):

1. The revolutionary explosion in France;
2. European opposition to the French Revolution and its extension abroad;
3. war between France, under the republic and Napoleon, and the rest of Europe – initially, in order to avoid being stifled at birth, and subsequently with the aim of establishing a permanent French hegemony tending toward the creation of a universal empire; and
4. national revolts against French hegemony, and birth of the modern European states by successive small waves of reform rather than by revolutionary explosions like the original French one. The 'successive waves' were made up of a combination of social struggles, interventions from above of the enlightened monarchy type, and national wars – with the two latter phenomena predominating.

Element 4 is the key component in this enumeration. It refers to the concept Gramsci uses to analyse the impact of an original revolution in a society resisting it on the political plane, *passive revolution*. Passive revolution combines the notions of (a) a 'revolution from above', without mass participation (the 'successive small waves of reform' and 'interventions from above of the enlightened monarchy type'), and (b) a creeping, 'molecular' social transformation, in which the progressive class finds itself compelled to advance in a more or less surreptitious, 'compromised' fashion. Its political strategy has to be adequate to this situation in the sense that where in a mass revolution, the revolutionary class may pose the question of power openly and directly, and adopt ways of action summarised by Gramsci's notion of 'war of manoeuvre' (or war of movement), under the conditions of passive revolution it can only hope to conquer the terrain by a more protracted 'war of position' (Gramsci, 1971: 108).

The limits of Gramsci's analysis lie in its one-sided concentration on political struggle and relative neglect of the development of capital on the international plane. The French revolution, we would hold, was itself an expression of the failure of late-feudal, absolutist France to sustain its mercantilist strategy of catching up with British world market supremacy. Whereas the English ruling class could allow the regulation of exploitation and authority to devolve from the state to civil society, reflecting the social cohesion sustained by the more developed market economy and ideology of industrial capitalism, in France and other continental states, state power and economic exploitation were still much more directly entwined. Thus at close distance in time and space from the Anglo-Saxon centre of the global social development, a configuration of state and society persisted that had been idealised in Hobbes's *Leviathan*, a text no longer relevant to English bourgeois self-consciousness by the time of the Glorious Revolution. But precisely because of the immediacy of the confrontation, the Hobbesian state tended to turn into what Gramsci (1971: 117) calls 'a rational absolute'.

The emancipation of self-regulating civil society from the state under these conditions was postponed by the concentration of all social forces in the state. Not only in France, but in all subsequent late-comer states, the protracted Hobbesian phase typical of passive revolution hampered the transition to, and integration into, the Lockian configuration (Cohen-Tanugi, 1987: 6). The process of original accumulation on which the transformation of agrarian society and eventually, capital accumulation, are premised, in the Hobbesian setting becomes a state task turning the domestic countryside into the functional equivalent of overseas markets and colonies (Lefebvre, 1976: II, 35–6). Gramsci even estimated – exaggerating perhaps – that 'self-government has only been possible in England, where the class of landowners, in addition to its condition of economic independence, had never been in savage conflict with the population (as happened in France) and had not had great corporate military traditions (as in Germany) with the separateness and the authoritarian attitude which derive from these' (1971: 186n; see, however, Moore, 1977).

Thus we arrive at the following schema. A revolution may be checked by counter-revolution in neighbouring countries, but the very need to contain the revolutionary forces (combining states and a given mode of production) compels the counter-revolution to anticipate the changes it seeks to resist politically. This in turn allows or invites the progressive class to develop in a molecular fashion, by means of a 'war of position'. The Russian revolution occurred in a complex configuration of forces as this pattern had repeated itself already several times: England/France; France/Continental Europe; the US and Europe *vis à vis* Japan; Western Europe/Russia, etc., while capital accumulation had fostered the autonomisation of the state in the English-speaking world as a corollary to integration. Thus, while the Bolshevik revolution posed a revolutionary threat to the capitalist world (generating a passive revolution in which Social Democracy in particular could advance 'in a molecular fashion'); the integration of Anglo-American imperialism reinvigorated the bourgeois revolution. The new vitality of capitalism put the USSR on the defensive, paradoxically generating a passive revolution within 'Socialism in One Country' that reproduced aspects of previous 'Hobbesian' experiences, notably nineteenth century Germany, but also allowed a progressive class to develop in the context of the planned economy.

In the remainder of this chapter, we will concentrate on the Russian side of the equation. We will discuss, first, the state-led process of original accumulation that led to October; second, the turn to Socialism in One Country, which placed the Soviet Union again in the position of a state resisting the dynamic of a superior civilisation; third, the internationalisation of Stalinism; and finally, the perestroika episode which was terminated by the Yanayev coup attempt and the collapse of the old order.

CZARIST RUSSIA FROM PASSIVE REVOLUTION TO SOCIALIST EXPLOSION

The theory of revolution of Marx and Engels held that a transformation would begin with the collapse of unstable political structures 'in the extremities of the bourgeois body', sparking off a series of transformations ultimately reaching the heartland of developed capitalism. In 1850, when he first formulated this scenario, Marx thought of France and Germany as the periphery, England as the central area (*MEW*: 7; 97). As the sphere of capital expanded across Europe, Russia increasingly was identified as the 'extremity of the bourgeois body' in this perspective. Here the dislocations inherent in original accumulation were most acute, the Czar's absolutism highly unstable. The corrupt Russian state, held together, in Engel's words, 'with great difficulty, by an oriental despotism . . . which in its present embodiment has become internally confused', presided over a country rapidly transforming itself into a capitalist-industrial country. Mass proletarianisation of the peasants and the disintegration of the village communities were the landmarks of this metamorphosis (*MEW*: 18, 567; see also 19; 115).

Once the defeat in the Crimean War had destroyed the complacency that had been allowed to persist after the struggle with

Napoleon, the autocracy began a belated process of modernisation from above. The emancipation of the serfs in 1861 and the abolition of the administrative power of the landlords served proletarianisation and the differentiation of state and society (Berend and Ránki, 1982: 40–1). However, the weakness of the indigenous Russian bourgeoisie turned Social Democracy into the vanguard of the progressive forces, although orthodox Marxism, including Lenin, stuck to the idea of a radical democratic rather than a socialist revolution in Russia (Löwy, 1981: 36–8).

The working class itself was still in its formative phase. Around 1899, migrant workers living on the land during summer, and actually going back to their villages during winter weekends as well, were still peasants in their outlook. Peasant-workers organised in *artels*, led by a foreman who sold their labour power to an employer, formed the next slice. They were housed in barracks, with their families still in the villages and the companionship of the *artel* replacing to some extent the household community. In the third stage, workers were in direct contact with factory-owners, lived with their families near the factory, and went back to the village only in old age. Textile workers lived like this. Only those employed in the metal and machine industries could be considered a full-blown proletariat, living with their families in factory towns in separate quarters.

> Generally speaking, there were many more peasants than workers in the common trek to the factories, but the movement also had its proletarian vanguard, though one barely strong enough to substantiate the Marxist contention. (Von Laue, 1967: 74–5)

For the greater part of the emerging working class (to which some 10 million villagers were added for war purposes after 1914) the shock of being drawn from their seventeenth century living conditions was the primary experience. This tended to produce the typical state of collapse of the former sense of identity and community, *anomie*, which radical ideologies may transform into a new sense of community but which hardly can be equated to advanced class consciousness (Anderson, 1983; Vieille, 1988: 233–4).

The 'rational absolute' which the state represents in the area of passive revolution also shaped the general attitude and political programme of Social Democracy, and the German experience was paradigmatic in this respect. Commenting on the Lassallean tenets of the 1875 Gotha Programme, Marx emphasised that the majority of 'working people' in Germany were still living on the land. While the party declared all other classes a single reactionary mass, it placed all its hopes in the national state. This in Marx's view was a self-defeating strategy. How could the German workers resist the international bourgeoisie already unified against them if their internationalism was more timid than that of the free-traders in the bourgeoisie? His conclusion was that by their assumption that the state was 'an autonomous entity, which possesses its own '*spiritual, moral, and libertarian foundations*', rather than being the concrete state form of a given society, the demands of the German socialists remained within the limits of the demands of the bourgeoisie elsewhere (*MEW*: 19; 18).

In Russia, the demands of social democracy *were* the demands of the 'bourgeoisie elsewhere'. Lenin's concept of the vanguard party was already prescribed by the small proletarian frontline facing the universe of semi-proletarianised peasants in Russia to begin with. Lenin's tactical genius lay in his understanding of the complexity of the social forces the Bolshevik party was supposed to lead, including the national minorities. Criticising doctrinaire revolutionaries who wanted only pure socialists to take part in the revolution, he wrote that 'To imagine that social revolution is *conceivable* without revolts by small nations in the colonies and in Europe, without revolutionary outbursts by a section of the petty bourgeoisie *with all its prejudices*, without a movement of the politically non-conscious proletarian masses and semi-proletarian masses against oppression by the landowners, the church, and the monarchy, against national oppression, etc. – to imagine all this is to *repudiate social revolution*' (*MEW*: 22, 355).

The revolt of the masses in 1917 was eventually phrased in religious terms, directed against a state-monitored process of original accumulation uprooting the people's traditional existence, exacerbated by the horrors of war. Socially, the Russian revolution, as Moshe Lewin writes, was a 'movement of Christian indignation against the state' rooted in a 'spontaneous anti-statism felt by the rural masses' (Lewin, 1985: 269). Original accumulation and its dislocations, not class struggle against a bourgeoisie provided the critical mass to the Bolshevik-led insurrection. 'The social base of the Bolshevik Revolution', Hough notes, 'as of the Khomeini revolution in Iran, was provided by former peasants streaming into the city,' and this migrant worker component gave a xenophobic undercurrent to the revolt (Hough, 1990: 48).

The need to maintain the proletarian nature of the revolution required breaking out of the Russian context. 'The real obstacle to the implementation of a socialist programme by a workers' government in Russia would not be economic so much – that is, the backwardness of the technical and productive structures of the country – as *political*: the isolation of the working class and the inevitable rupture with its peasant and petty-bourgeois allies. Only international solidarity could save the socialist Russian revolution . . .' (Löwy, 1981: 56).

Following the revolution's defeat in Central Europe (Hungary, Germany), the Russian revolution was thrown back onto itself and forced to entrench behind a unified state power. This also implied revoking the rights previously granted to the nationalities in the perspective of advancing revolution. Civil war and foreign intervention brought home to the Bolsheviks that they were, as Lenin put it in 1919, 'living not merely in a state, but *in a system of states*' (*MEW*: 29; 153). But at the root of the centralised state was the undeveloped relation between state and society. Lacking the pluralism of an emancipated civil society, in which fractions of the ruling class can regroup (transnationally as well as nationally) into hegemonic blocs without necessarily bringing state power into play, the undifferentiated state/society configuration can allow only one, fixed political order and a single (political) *state class*, i.e. a class owing its unity primarily to the state and therefore, strictly speaking, an estate rather than a class (Fernández, 1988; Cox, 1987).

While a revolution in such a context may break through to state power directly by a 'war of manoeuvre', it lacks the preconditions to articulate interests and aspirations into the organic social compromise underlying a hegemonic concept of control. Hence the unifying theme which tends to remain what Gramsci terms a 'revolutionary myth' at once ceases to exist, scattering into an infinity of individual wills which in the positive phase then follow separate and conflicting paths' (1971: 128).

After the Civil War, in which the peasants still had sided with the Bolsheviks against the Whites and their Western backers, the retreat to the New Economic Policy had the effect of setting free these 'separate and conflicting' forces. The contrast, notably, between the 'socialist' industrial centres and an anarcho-liberal countryside rapidly increased (Laird and Laird, 1970: 37).

STALINISM AS PASSIVE REVOLUTION

The consolidation of Soviet power on what could be held of the territory of formerly Czarist Russia left the Bolsheviks in a defensive position *vis à vis* the Western bourgeoisie. The Comintern remained committed to the notion of the 'general crisis of capitalism', but Gramsci (although entertaining the idea of the Russian revolution generating a passive revolution in Italy – 1971: 118) considered the conclusion of the Soviet-British trade agreement of 1921 as a set-back for the revolution. Even if it represented a political victory for the workers' government in Moscow, the agreement allowed capitalism to become the factor restoring production for the peasants. 'The very foundations of the workers' state are damaged and corroded by this fact . . . the strength of the Russian proletariat has been diminished economically by the agreement,' Gramsci commented (1978: 27–8).

The reinforcement of the state, tactical at first, increasingly became defined by the objective dependence on the West. The formation of a state class typical of the Hobbesian state, the 'confiscation' of the civil sphere (Carrère d'Encausse, 1980), and the transformation of internationalist vanguardism into a national (i.e. USSR-wide) mass mobilisation of the uprooted population, developed hand in hand.

As to the state class, in 1920, departments of the Central Committee and of the regional committees were created, responsible for the registration and appointment of officials, the *Uchraspreds*. In 1922, the year when Stalin became Secretary-General, 'Uchraspred had made more than ten thousand appointments, and it expanded its activities in 1923' (Voslensky, 1984: 48–9). The *nomenklatura* system that evolved on this basis coincided with the rise of Stalin as the exponent of (1) the administrative side of Bolshevik power, (2) the shift from world revolution to consolidating the revolution in the former Czarist empire and the need to control centrifugal tendencies in that context, and (3) the need to employ and control bourgeois specialists (compare Stalin's three functions: Secretary-General of the Party, People's Commissar for the Nationalities, and head of the Peasants' and Workers' Inspection).

The transformation of the Bolshevik party into an organisation of the state class began in the mid-20s. While abroad, Communist party membership halved between 1922 and 1931, the Soviet party grew by record numbers even though the sociological working class had largely dissipated in the civil war (Elleinstein 1975: 13–14; Claudin 1975: 112). The transformed party's task shifted to the domestic front, where it served as a command chain in the resumption of the process of original accumulation under the auspices of the Hobbesian state after 1927–8. Of the internationalist Bolsheviks, Bukharin saw the connection most clearly. 'It was he who used, in the Central Committee, the strong and provocative term 'Leviathan state', which was going to result from the system of 'military-feudal exploitation of the peasantry' that Stalin and his supporters were employing in order to industrialise' (Lewin, 1985: 19–20).

Partly because it was encircled by imperialism and partly because of the threat from the fascist spearhead of counter-revolution, the confiscation and domination of Soviet society by the state was without precedent:

> The state engaged in a hectic, hasty, and compulsive shaping of the social structure, forcing its groups and classes into a mold where the administrative-and-coercive machinery retained its superiority and autonomy. Instead of 'serving' its basis, the state, using the powerful means at its disposal (central planning, modern communications and controlling mechanisms, monopoly of information, freedom to use coercion at will), was able to press the social body into service under its own *diktat*. (Lewin, 1985: 265)

Yet, as in previous experiences of this kind, the isolated USSR was frantically trying to emulate the enemy in key respects. The autarkic drift inherent in the economic policy of the period (foreign trade after an initial rise dramatically fell again to about half of the 1929 volume in 1937, van der Pijl, 1982: 72, table 1) did not cut off Soviet economic development from patterns laid down by advanced capitalism. As a typical passive revolution, Soviet industrialisation was a state-monitored emulation of a more advanced type of social and productive relations, in this case Taylorism and Fordist mass production.

Abandoning their initial reliance on German technology, Soviet planners in the late 1920s turned to a US engineering firm, the A. Kahn Organisation. For fees totalling US $2bn between 1928 and 1930, Kahn wrote the blueprints for the first two plans, conducted management training programmes and directly controlled (in the case of military installations through foreign engineers who were Communist Party members) the development of the entire range of Soviet light and heavy industry. 'Western assistance', A. C. Sutton writes, 'was focused by the Soviets upon single, clearcut objectives to build new, gigantic, mass-production units to manufacture large quantities of simplified standard models based on proven Western designs without design changes over a long period. Thus after the transfer of Western technology, simplification, standardisation, and duplication became the operational aspects of Soviet industrial strategy' (quoted in Spohn, 1975: 240).

The resumption of original accumulation under state auspices and the nationalistion of the original revolutionary 'myth' created a contradiction between the Soviet state class and the internationalists in the Comintern and the CPSU. This contradiction was solved by the purges after 1934, highlighted in the Moscow trials; the dissolution of the Comintern in 1943; and the purges and show trials in Eastern Europe in the early 1950s. Simultaneously, these were moments in the struggle by which the Soviet class destroyed the internationalist revolutionaries, first the actual Bolsheviks, subsequently the Popular Front generation in Eastern Europe.

Stalin's purges and the demonisation of Trotsky as the emblematic exponent of world revolutions served to galvanise the unity and class consciousness of the ascendant state class. It also drove beyond it in the sense that the state class itself was subjected to a terror reflecting the impossibility of breaking the speed of construction to a more tolerable pace, an impossibility subjectively interpreted as treason.

This second dimension of the terror of high Stalinism reflected the configuration of the new political terrain following the destruction of the internationalist Bolsheviks, when the main contradiction in the Soviet ruling elite was shifted to the *nomenklatura* itself. In the 1920s, this had already become apparent in frictions between the party bureaucracy and the professional elite of the State Plan Commission (Konrád and Szelényi, 1981: 283). As the frenzied pace of construction, coinciding with the culmination of autarky and political closure, reached its apogee however, technical requirements were entirely subordinated to universalising teleology. Legitimised in terms of a quasi-Hegelian dialectic, the terror at its height indeed became entirely 'spiritual', autonomised from the real parameters of the society it sought to transform.

Marx's qualification of the terrorism of the French Revolution as 'nothing but a *plebeian way* of dealing with the *enemies of the bourgeoisie*, absolutism, feudalism and philistinism' (quoted in Blishchenko and Zhdanov, 1984: 20) can be extrapolated to the Stalinist terror. This time directed against those resisting the policy of Socialism in One Country or merely failing to keep in step with its forced marches, it presented the issues to the populace in terms of a struggle between the forces of progress and wreckers seeking to plot against them. Such imagery was congenial to a people in the grips of an *anomie* engendered by original accumulation; not only to those embracing a revolutionary myth turned into state doctrine, but more generally to 'minds trained in and by beliefs in witches, demons, and the "evil force"' on the Russian land, where 'in the 1920s the rural sects were expanding vigorously at the expense of the official Orthodox Church' (Lewin, 1985: 17).

Beginning with the opening stages of the Second World War, a periodic relaxation became necessary to allow the technocratic element to function at all, a process entering a qualitatively new stage with de-Stalinisation. Henceforth, Soviet socialism in the USSR and elsewhere became characterised by a 'pulsating alternation of concessions and repression' on the part of the ideological *vis à vis* the technocratic element in the *nomenklatura* and the state class at large (Konrád and Szelényi, 1981: 289). To the degree this evolved into a structural class compromise, a differentiation of state and society developed that created opportunities for a technocratic and democratic *cadre class* of managers, educators and specialists of all sorts (Bihr, 1989). Until very recently, however, their advance in the sense of a 'progressive class' in the context of passive revolution remained surreptitious, based on molecular changes dependent on initiative 'from above'.

INTERNATIONALISATION OF STALINISM

Lenin on his death-bed redrafted the blue-print for world revolution by shifting the co-ordinates of the 'extremities of the bourgeois body' further to the periphery. India and China had become the terrain of original accumulation and the war had drawn them out of their former complacency. 'The general European ferment has begun to affect them, and it is now clear to the whole world that they have been drawn into a process of development that must lead to a crisis in the whole of world capitalism' (*MEW*: 33, 498–501).

The particular traits of Stalin's USSR – a strong state, confiscation of the civil sphere, extremist forms of political mobilisation and terror to drive forward and control the technical executive element in the passive revolution while providing an 'imagined community' to the masses – were as functional in the periphery as they restricted Communist influence in the Lockian heartland. Like Lenin in his critique of 'Left Communism', Gramsci concluded that 'a change was necessary from the war of manoeuvre applied victoriously in the East in 1917, to a war of position which was the only form possible in the West . . . In Russia, the state was everything, civil society was primordial and gelatinous; in the West, there was a proper relation between state and society, and when the state trembled a sturdy structure of civil society was at once revealed' (Gramsci, 1971: 237–8).

The Bolshevisation of the Communist parties abroad, interacting with Comintern centralisation, served to impose the Soviet pattern also in Europe. But the Hobbesian profile of the Stalinist party, combining authoritarianism and a manipulative attitude to social forces, only appealed to workers in the early stages of industrialisation, who were beyond the anarchism congenial to first-generation peasant-turned workers, but not yet fully integrated into the universe of the commodity where all social relations are perceived in terms of exchange value. In semi-industrial sectors like mining or dock work; in construction, where workers are organised in teams selling their labour power collectively and on a seasonal basis, and more generally in countries like pre-fascist Germany, France, and Italy where they could recruit a second-generation constituency with an anarcho-syndicalist background, Communist parties gained a foothold (Lorwin, 1967: 66–9). In modern capitalist industry, Soviet theses on a decaying capitalism lacked credibility in light of the spectacular development of the productive forces in the US in the 1920s and subsequently in north-west Europe. Social imperialism and ideological mechanisms, effective notably where direct exploitative mechanisms are hidden, further marginalised the Communist parties.

Yet even when the shock-waves of the October Revolution and the epoch-making concessions it brought in the West such as general suffrage and social legislation had ebbed, the Soviet model continued to exert a pressure within advanced capitalism. This influence interacted with the process of socialisation of production and reproduction generated by capital accumulation. The cadre class associated with this process, 'advancing surreptitiously' in support of economic planning, full employment and social legislation, constituted a force 'between bourgeoisie and proletariat' (Bihr, 1989). In the context of the Cold War, the technocratic and managerial cadre class in Europe achieved political representation primarily in Social Democracy. The Socialist parties, rather than the Communists, thus developed into the party negotiating 'molecular' change in advanced capitalism (Bahro, 1980: 157).

Objectively, there were substantial similarities between the Western and Eastern cadre class or technocracy, both in terms of roles and in terms of social consciousness. The Soviet-type cadre class, too, in a sense was situated between the (international) bourgeoisie and the proletariat. Therefore, the shift in party labels from Communism to Social Democracry in the perestroika period was not just tactical and cosmetic, but reflected a real process of emancipation of the technocratic cadre class (see Szelényi and Szetenyi, 1991).

From Moscow, the failure of the revolution to advance in Europe was interpreted as treason and, subsequently, as complicity with fascism. But Stalin had little interest in world revolution to begin with. 'His lack of enthusiasm for Comintern and for foreign communists was notorious', Carr writes; except for the Fifth Comintern Congress of 1924, when he was active in the corridors but did not show up in the plenary sessions, he never attended a Comintern Congress (Carr, 1982: 403–4). Following the fall of Zinoviev and the demotion from Comintern affairs of Bukharin after its Sixth Congress in 1928 had promulgated the Stalinist ultra-left line of 'class against class' that reflected the collectivisation and industrialisation drive, the correction of this self-defeating course following Hitler's rise to power fell to non-Soviet Communist leaders. Dimitrov, who had defied Nazi judges in the Reichstag trial, became the hero of the VIIth Comintern Congress in 1935.

Although apparently retreating to a national state format (the American party in 1939 even disaffiliated from the Comintern to emphasise this, and the organisation itself was dissolved by Stalin in 1943), the VIIth Congress in the struggle with fascism spawned a new internationalism that briefly after would be tested on the battlefields of Spain and in the Resistance during the Second World War. The Moscow trials already served to destroy the basis these internationalists still had in Moscow, and the hunt for Trotskyites soon extended to the Spanish front-lines and later, the anti-fascist resistance.

After the Second World War, the goal of the Soviet leadership remained set on consolidating the recognition it had won in the wartime alliance, confirmed at Yalta and Potsdam. But a surge of popular aspirations threatened from below the diplomatic status quo thus achieved. Stalin, therefore, was intent on eliminating this threat, but the formulas of 1935, reinforced by the democratic patriotism nourished in the Resistance to Fascism, still animated Communist parties in Europe. In Asia, the Chinese, Korean, and Vietnamese revolutions, too, were advancing irrespective of great power agreement.

The economic embargo that accompanied the Marshall Plan, and the free world ideological offensive of which it was part, drew a sharp line between Eastern and Western Europe and threatened to roll back Soviet control of Eastern Europe within two years after VE-day. Communist-led coalitions in the Soviet sphere-of- influence were now put to the test and were replaced, most dramatically in Prague, by Communist one-party rule, whether formally or de facto. The looming conflict between Stalinism and a hegemonic type of rule, preferred by Eastern European internationalists in the 1935 spirit; between a centrally planned, autarkic economy subordinated to a fixed ideology or an economy also inserted into the capitalist international division of labour, now came to a head. The struggles of the pre-war USSR – internationalists versus the state class and within the latter, ideologists versus technocrats – resurfaced and with them, the 'plebeian' forms of acting them out, however inappropriate in light of the often more advanced political development of the population.

Agents operating through party channels, in Eastern Europe backed up by force (secret service, police, army – Soviet Marshall Rokossovski became Minister of Defence of Poland) served to impose Soviet control. Only in the case of Yugoslavia, the attempt to force Tito to accelerate the liquidation of capitalism and to break off his links with the West had to be made by mail, since the Yugoslav Communists alone had been able to keep control of their own security apparatus.

Tito was excommunicated and a struggle was launched against the East European survivors of the VIIth Comintern Congress, who had made a name for themselves in Spain, the Resistance, and post-war reconstruction. Show trials led to their elimination in Hungary, Bulgaria (Dimitrov died a natural death before things came to a head), and Czechoslovakia. 'Men like you, with your past, your ideas, your concepts, your international contacts are not made for countries in the process of constructing socialism,' Artur London, a veteran of the Spanish Civil War and State Secretary in Prague, was told upon his arrest. 'We must get rid of you' (London, 1970: 59).

Simultaneously, ideology triumphed over technical expertise within the state class, also in the USSR itself. The head of Gosplan, N. Voznesenskii, who was considering a relaxation of extreme centralism, was removed in 1949 and perished a year later; while it was in 1948 that Lysenko's theory of genetics triumphed over its critics (Nove, 1978: 298). Central planning and a command economy were now transposed to the East European countries, and the pattern of original accumulation geared to autarkic economic development was introduced as well, even though several countries were more developed than the USSR. The failure to switch trade to the USSR was a key part of the indictment of Slansky, the Czech party's General Secretary, and his co-defendants (London, 1970: 267).

In spite of US embargo policies which hurt Western exports but were not effective in the field of technical literature and licences, technical development in the socialist countries remained modelled on the Western example (Boot, 1982: 32). The logic of the arms race, however, kept Soviet military technology roughly within the matrix created by the US lead, albeit on a lower basic level (Holloway, 1984: 152–7). Eventually, their fundamental dependence on the capitalist model would force the socialist states to turn directly, and independently from each other, to the West to obtain the technology for the next higher stage of economic development; this led them into the debt trap, and ultimately, into direct dependence on world capital (van Zon, 1991).

Stalin himself hailed the prospects of a unified 'socialist world market', created, by default, by the Marshall Plan (Stalin, 1972: 31). But the typical Hobbesian state/society configuration established in Eastern Europe and replicated in China, North Vietnam, and North Korea, militated against the division of labour between them. Comecon, the East European economic bloc established in 1949, was based on heavy-industry centred state economies. However, they had little inclination to mutual trade, apart from their need to obtain imports of raw materials from the Soviet Union.

The conflict with Rumania was a clear example of a Socialism in One Country resisting a planned division of labour in the framework of Comecon. In 1962, Gheorghiu-Dej, engaged in a strategy of forced industrialisation, refused to co-operate with Krushchev's plan for supra-national planning, a plan 'which would have transformed Rumania into a reservoir of oil, a granary, and a supplier of raw materials' (Marcou, 1979: 116). Any social forces within Rumania – or in the USSR, for that matter – willing to establish transnational economic ties would have found themselves constrained by the reality of the Hobbesian state and its foreign trade monopoly. Thereafter, conflicts between socialist states tended to result from the different stages they had reached in the process of economic development and from the means employed to speed up this primary or original accumulation, partly by creating links with the capitalist world market.

In Stalin's last days, the ascendancy of the technocratic element forced corrections or modifications of the highly politicised line last attempted from 1949 on, if only as a consequence of the need to develop the productive forces. This shift was exemplified by the critique of extremist theories in linguistics (represented by the Lysenko of that field, Marr). Such theories, Marcuse writes, 'may have fulfilled a useful function in the 'magical' utilisation of Marxian theory. But with the technological and industrial progress of Soviet society . . . they came into conflict with more fundamental objectives [and] . . . had to give way to more universalist, 'normal', and internationalist conceptions' (Marcuse, 1971: 31). Conceding a class compromise to the technocratic element in the state class (i.e. de-Stalinisation) led to the resurgence of the '1935' orientation in several East European countries such as Hungary and Poland. In the less-developed countries, such decentralisation was impossible. In China, Albania, and Rumania, the 'mobilisation of internal resources' which coincides with the initial formation of a state class, generated the extreme forms of confiscating the social sphere and the 'spiritualisation' of social life that had accompanied the process of original accumulation and the subordination of the technocratic, professional elite in USSR earlier on. In these countries, state-led original accumulation tended to reproduce features of Stalinism.

Conflicts among socialist states, then, were not simply the proof of international anarchy or of eternal nationalism (although ethnic conflict was a compounding factor with a history of its own). They represented the unequal development between states committed to the construction of a socialism by means of a passive revolution and the concomitant differences in terms of the emancipation of a more outward-looking 'progressive class', that is, a technocratic cadre class, from the ideological constraints of the initial closure. Henceforth, this structural aspect of 'fraternal' conflict was compounded by the different attitudes to state-led original accumulation elsewhere: for the USSR from Krushchev on, socialist division of labour was seen as the preferable strategy; while China stuck to self-reliance until the modernisation policies of Deng Hsiao-ping put the country on the road to a 'New Economic Policy' sliding to capitalism.[1]

PERESTROIKA AND COLLAPSE

The history of the USSR illustrates in a dramatic fashion Marx's concept of historic social formations, which Gramsci (1971: 106) summarised as 'the two fundamental principles of political science: 1. that no social formation disappears as long as the productive forces which have developed within it still find room for further forward movement; 2. that a society does not set itself tasks for whose solution the necessary conditions have not already been incubated, etc.'

The drama of premature socialism was that while capitalism still had untapped resources for expansion, the forced marches of 'Socialism in One Country' pressed the USSR into the mold of a conservative power facing the still advancing bourgeois revolution. The Soviet bloc never transcended the position of a collection of states held together by coercion, while Anglo-American capitalism evolved towards transnational civil society, integrated politically at various levels yet leaving the state intact. The 'Cold War' was a crude way of denoting the unequal struggle between the Lockean heartland of

253

capital controlling a global field of operation and the bloc of 'Social-isms in One Country' led by or, as in the case of China, even arrayed against the Soviet Union. Only the tremendous demographic and natural resources controlled by the USSR and its continuing links to the advancing process of political and economic decolonisation could sustain Soviet military parity and the myth of overtaking capitalism.

In the early 1970s, the – in hindsight – final phase of this 'Cold War' began when decolonisation in the Third World assumed revolutionary proportions and the metropolitan working classes and youth assumed militant postures. The state classes of the Third World states against the background of this global revolt unfurled the banner of a New International Economic Order, raising oil and other raw material prices to press their demands; while the cadre class and Social Democracy in the West, and the USSR in the global political balance, each could reinforce their position in the fact of an apparently retreating and disorganised US-led imperialism. For a time, it may have seemed as if the liberal principles of the capitalist world were to give way to a global 'regime' based on what Krasner (1985) calls authoritative allocation.

In response to this challenge, however, an initially disparate but gradually more systematic redeployment of the capitalist ruling class began, involving a restructuring of capital towards integrated world market production, reorganising bourgeois hegemony around a neo-liberal concept of control, and recapturing the initiative from socialist and reformist forces on a world scale (van der Pijl, 1987; Overbeek, ed., forthcoming). Stepping up the arms race was seen as a key element in defeating the motley NIEO coalition and its hangers-on (Gerbier, 1987). In 1978–9, NATO began to raise pressure on the USSR by INF and other missile deployment and punitive embargoes. The latter, imposed in retaliation over the intervention in Afghanistan and martial law in Poland, were pinpointed at two projected pillars of Soviet growth, computer technology and fodder grains for raising meat consumption.

The restructuring of capital in the West involved both an intensification of the international division of labour and shop-floor exploitation, and the introduction of a new generation of production technology. The embargoes merely accentuated the fact that the USSR, for structural reasons, was unable to match these developments. East–West trade had still boomed in the 1970s as a consequence of high energy prices. It already lost its momentum at the beginning of the next decade, but when after 1985, oil prices fell, the USSR lost about 40 per cent of its export earnings in convertible currencies. The Soviet bloc was marginalised from the restructured world economy also in other respects. The Comecon states, which in 1973 still accounted for 22.7 per cent of machinery imports into the OECD area, by 1985 found their share reduced to 4.9 per cent (van Zon, 1987: 11).

Under the Reagan Administration, a counter-revolution on a global scale was launched, subsequently framed into a 'Reagan Doctrine' but entwined with private business ventures involving arms and drugs dealers and military zealots as well as assorted sheiks and sultans. With respect to the Soviet bloc in Europe, the US by 1984 had moved from recognising the territorial status quo (at Helsinki in 1975), via Carter's human rights campaign directed primarily at the USSR, to an explicit rejection of 'the artificially imposed division of Europe' by Secretary Shultz (US Department of State, 1984).

In March 1981, Richard Pipes, former head of the 'Team B' installed by CIA director George Bush in 1976 to upgrade agency estimates of Soviet military power, and National Security Council official in charge of Soviet affairs under Reagan, in an interview declared that the USSR would have to change its system or go to war. Within a year, documents from the RAND Corporation and actual Administration material led the US press to report that the USA had apparently declared economic and technical war on the Soviet Union. By 1984–5, pressure meant to 'spend the Soviet Union into bankruptcy' by introducing weapon systems the Soviets could not match (such as SDI), was complemented by the creation of a National Endowment for Democracy meant to support the agents of change *within* the hard-pressed 'Evil Empire' (Gervasi, 1990: 22–5).

Pipes at a Washington conference in 1982 (devoted to the upgrading of Slavic Studies programmes in the US) predicted that Reagan's policy of intensified pressure would eventually force a new NEP on the Soviet Union, entailing a reallocation of scarce resources away from the military sector (*Neue Züricher Zeitung*, 10 November 1982). After an initial Soviet attempt to respond in kind to NATO's acceleration of the arms race and emulate new US departures in weapons technology (causing conflict within the Soviet military about the need to introduce high-tech non-nuclear arms), Gorbachev upon his coming to power shifted gear to a policy of unilateral disarmament, discarding with the previous 'parity cult' (Izyumov and Kortunov, 1988). Thus Pipes' prediction was confirmed, albeit at tremendous cost to the US itself.

Under Gorbachev's perestroika, the last phase in the Soviet passive revolution became entangled with the emancipation of civil society from the state. Soviet sociologists were discussing the need to prove a 'social strategy' which would galvanise the modernising forces and neutralise the hypertrophy of intermediaries in ministries and regional administrations. Gorbachev in this connection spoke of a struggle between 'Bolshevik professionalism' and the forces of conversatism and lethargy. In a key address to Leningrad Polytechnic in May 1985, he called for a breakthrough in the 'scientific-technical revolution', backed up in the same month by a salary increase for the more than 13 million academic specialists in the USSR (*Neue Züricher Zeitung*, 28 September 1985).

Whether perestroika still began as a revolution from above, or already, as Hough (1990: 178) writes, was 'a middle-class revolt -- a revolt supported most strongly by the bureaucrats, the professionals, and the intelligentsia' is less important than its dynamic as a process of emancipating civil society from the Hobbesian state.

Gorbachev, like the ascendant cadre class saw Soviet society as part of an emerging global civil society, which was still contradictory in class terms but nevertheless subject to common interest which foreign policies could no longer ignore. Gorbachev therefore sought to define the tasks of the Soviet Union in terms of a planetary struggle to deal with a comprehensive crisis of civilisation gripping both capitalism and Soviet socialism (Collective, 1988: 564). However, in the eyes of many in the westernmost parts of the USSR and the East European countries, especially the younger generation, it was only Soviet-style communism that was the problem, indeed an anomaly standing in the way between them and the coveted West. There was the universe of the commodity, its generous abundance, and the joy of living embodied by capitalism. Like Pop-Art in the 1950s in the West, images and sounds conveying Western life-style fed into the East in the early 1980s and gripped a mass public in the Soviet orbit with the promises of consumerism (Menand, 1990: 106; Hough, 1990: 122).

Much of the attention given in the Soviet Union to the concept of civil society (*grazhdanskoe obshchestvo*, Flaherty, 1988: 27) in effect tended to express a creeping integration into the hegemonic structures of Western capitalism as much as the actual emancipation from state control. To deal with this tendency, Gorbachev developed an essentially Social Democratic strategy including a mixed economy, attempting to strike a compromise between the *nomenklatura* and the cadre class. But centrifugal forces, national and otherwise, multiplied to the point that in 1990 the power of the party passed to various parliamentary bodies, while private property was recognised in addition to collective property. This effectively buried the socialist option and initiated a struggle between various fractions of the *nomenklatura* itself over the spoils of privatisation; compounded by ideological cleavages carried over from the 1985–9 period but now located firmly in a capitalist frame of reference (Chauvier, 1991b).

As Gramsci put it in his prison notes, 'One may apply to the concept of passive revolution . . . the interpretative criterion of molecular changes which in fact progressively modify the pre-existing composition of forces, and hence become the matrix of new changes' (1971: 109). In the Soviet crisis, cumulative changes had reached a point where they were changing the situation qualitatively. With civil society available as the new terrain of overt class and national struggles, these now assumed the characteristics of a 'war of manoeuvre' again, waged primarily by the forces led by Boris Yeltsin. Gorbachev had sought to transform the Soviet Union by means of compromise, allowing a gradual metamorphosis of the *nomenklatura* state class into a state bourgeoisie in addition to upgrading the social status of technocratic cadre class. By contrast, the Yeltsin forces favoured a more radical break with the past. Allying with new strata of entrepreneurs, traders and intellectuals, as well as with foreign investors active notably in the media, Yeltsin embraced neo-liberal tenets and like his counterparts in other republics, fostered the overhaul of the All-Union structures in order to entirely alter the terrain of struggle. To this end, he courted Russian nationalism including its fascist wing, *Pamyat* (Chauvier, 1991a; 1991b).

With the demise of state control and sovereignty, political struggle inevitably becomes entangled in transnational networks of power operating from the Lockian heartland. Whereas Gorbachev attempted to forge links with the Socialist International, the Yeltsin forces, like the Baltic and other nationalists, established intimate connections with such bastions of Atlantic neo-liberalism and anti-Communism as the Heritage Foundation, the German Konrad Adenauer Foundation, as well as with Cuban exiles in Miami (Bellant and Wolf, 1990: 29–31); Chauvier, 1991b; *Volkskrant*, 14 September 1991).

Clearly, the Yanayev coup attempt played entirely into the hands of the neo-liberal forces already ascendant. The tentative social-democratisation of the USSR was already disintegrating in key respects: the democratic system of workers' self-management, enacted in 1988, was rescinded in 1990. Neo-liberalism wants to orient the workers to money gains and privileged positions rather than going for 'populism' (Chauvier, 1991a: 7). Likewise, the initially encouraged, but politically conservative petty bourgeoisie emerging from the 'second economy' was marginalised after having first been considered an essential intermediary in the transformation to a mixed economy (Hough, 1990: 191). The leader of the agrarian co-operatives movement, Starodubtsev, was even among the 1991 putschists.

Commenting on plans in the Soviet Union (then still ascribed to Trotsky), to 'give supremacy in national life to industry and industrial methods, to accelerate, through coercion imposed from the outside, the growth of discipline and order in production, and to adapt customs to the necessities of work', Gramsci wrote that 'given the general way in which all the problems connected with this tendency were conceived, it was destined to end up in a form of Bonapartism' (1971: 301). As the Soviet Union collapses into the 'extremity of the bourgeois body' it was on the eve of the Bolshevik revolution and its perspective dims to becoming a collection of economies comparable to that of Nigeria today or of France fifty to sixty years ago (Chauvier, 1991b), the dilemma of the strong state versus the free society in peripheral capitalism cannot fail to be posed anew.

Note

1 Where Soviet 'fraternal aid' and the moderating, if often high-handed presence of advisers were allowed to operate, as in Cuba, excesses inherent in rapid transformation were largely avoided; where they were not, as in Kampuchea, frenzied 'self-reliance' in the process of original accumulation could turn into massacre. For Soviet theoretical views on these issues, see Hough (1986).

10 STRUCTURAL ISSUES OF GLOBAL GOVERNANCE: IMPLICATIONS FOR EUROPE

ROBERT W. COX

In a period of fundamental changes in global and national structures, the conventional separations of politics, economics, and society become inadequate for the understanding of change. These are aspects that in relatively stable times can conveniently be selected out for particular examination on an assumption of *ceteris paribus*. Fundamental changes have to be grasped as a whole. This whole is the configuration of social forces, its economic basis, its ideological expression, and its form of political authority as an interactive whole. Antonio Gramsci called this the *blocco storico* or historic bloc (Gramsci, 1971). We can think of the historic bloc, as Gramsci did, at the level of a particular country. We can also think of it at the level of Europe, and at the world in so far as there is evidence of the existence of a global social structure and global processes of structural change.

This chapter will focus on three broad issues of global governance in the transition from the twentieth century to the twenty-first: (1) the globalisation of the world economy and the reactions it may provoke; (2) the transformation of the inter-state system as it has been known since the Westphalian era; and (3) the problematic of a post-hegemonic world order.[1] In discussing these issues, three levels of human organisation have to be considered in their interrelationships: the level of social forces, the level of states and national societies, and the level of world order and global society. The aim of the chapter, adopting the perspective of historic blocs, is to sketch out a framework for understanding the problem of global governance, using these three issues and three levels, and then to consider its implications for Europe, and for Europe's choices in relation to the world.

GLOBALISATION

The two principal aspects of globalisation are (1) global organisations of production (complex transnational networks of production which source the various components of the product in places offering the most advantage on costs, markets, taxes, and access to suitable labour, and also the advantages of political security and predictability); and (2) global finance (a very largely unregulated system of transactions in money, credit, and equities). These developments together constitute a *global economy*, i.e. an economic space transcending all country borders, which co-exists still with an *international economy* based on transactions across country borders and which is regulated by inter-state agreements and practices.[2] The growth of the global economy and the progressive subordination to it of the international economy are widely seen among liberal economists and politicians as the wave of the future – on the whole a 'good' thing to which everyone sooner or later must adapt through the pressure of global competition.

Globalisation has certain consequences, which are less often pointed out, but which have serious implications for the future structure of world order.

One of these consequences is a process that can be called the internationalisation of the state. If you think back to the inter-war period and especially the depression years of the 1930s, the role of states was primarily to protect national economic space from disturbances coming from outside. The Bretton Woods system moved towards a different balance. It sought to achieve a compromise: states still had a primary responsibility to safeguard domestic welfare and levels of employment and economic activity; but they were to do this within rules that precluded economic aggression against others and aimed at a harmonisation of different national economic policies. Since the mid-1970s, with the demise of Bretton Woods, a new doctrine has achieved preeminence: states must become the instruments for adjusting national economic activities to the exigencies of the global economy – states are becoming transmission belts from the global into the national economic spheres. Adjustment to global competitiveness is the new categorical imperative.

The effect of this tendency is differentiated by the relative power of states. Indebted Third World states are in the weakest position. Here, states that are weak in relation to external pressures must become strong enough internally to enforce punitive adjustment measures on vulnerable social groups. States in 'developed' countries discover that sensitivity to foreign bond markets, fiscal crisis, and the transnational mobility of capital have effectively diminished their autonomy in making national policy. The United States, despite being the world's biggest debtor, nevertheless retains a relative autonomy in determining national economic policy. Germany and Japan have some autonomy when they are prepared to risk exercising it. Other states must adjust their economic policies to situations very largely determined by the United States.

Another consequence of globalisation is the restructuring of national societies and the emergence of a global social structure. Globalisation is led by a transnational managerial class that consists of distinct fractions (American, European, Japanese) but which as a whole constitutes the heart of what Susan Strange (1990) has called the 'business civilization.' The restructuring of production is changing the pattern of organisation of production from what has been called 'Fordism' to 'post-Fordism'.[3] That is to say, the age of the large integrated mass-production factory is passing; the new model is a core/periphery structure of production with a relatively small control-centre core and numerous subsidiary component-producing and servicing units linked as required to the core. Economies of scale have given place to economies of flexibility. More flexibly decentralised production facilitates border-crossing relationships in organising production systems; it also segments the labour force into groups segregated by nationality, ethnicity, religion, gender, etc. such that this labour force lacks the natural cohesion of the large concentrated workforces of the old mass production industries. Power has shifted dramatically from labour to capital in the process of restructuring production.

The geographical distinction of First and Third Worlds is becoming somewhat blurred. Third World conditions are being reproduced within 'developed' countries. Mass migrations from South to North combine with the re-emergence of 'putting out' production, sometimes of a 'sweatshop' variety, and the expansion of low-wage employment in services in the 'developed' countries of the North, to produce a phenomenon called the 'peripheralisation of the core'. The terms 'core' and 'periphery' are losing their earlier exclusively geographical meaning to acquire gradually the meaning of social differentiation within a globalising society – a differentiation produced in large measure by the restructuring of production.

Karl Polanyi's (1957) analysis of nineteenth-century Britain suggests a paradigm for present-day global changes. Polanyi wrote of a 'double movement'. The first phase of this movement was the imposition upon society of the concept of the self-regulating market. To Polanyi, as economic historian and anthropologist, the notion of an economic process disembedded from society and set over and above society was an historical aberration, a utopian idea that could not endure. The disintegrating effects that the attempt to impose the self-regulating market had upon society generated during the later nineteenth century the second phase of the double movement: a self-protective response from society through the political system re-asserting the primacy of the social. This second phase took form with the legalising of trade unions and collective bargaining, the construction of social security systems, the introduction of factory legislation, and ultimately recognition of government's responsibility to maintain satisfactory levels of employment and welfare.

One can well hypothesise today that the present trend of deregulation and privatisation which appears to carry all before it in global economics will encounter a global response. This response will endeavour once again to bring economic process under social control, to re-embed the economy, now at the global level, in society and to subordinate enhanced economic capacities to globally endorsed social purposes.

TRANSFORMATION OF THE STATE SYSTEM?

Economic globalisation has placed constraints upon the autonomy of states. More and more, national debts are foreign debts, so that states have to be attentive to external bond markets and to externally-influenced interest rates in determining their own economic policies. The level of national economic activity also depends upon access to foreign markets. Participation in various international 'regimes' channels the activities of states in developed capitalist countries into conformity with global economy processes, tending toward a stabilisation of the world capitalist economy.[4]

Apart from these constraints inherent in the existing global economic order, there are new tendencies within this order producing two new levels of participation, one above and one below the level of existing states. These new levels can be named macro- and micro-regionalism.

As counterweights to the dominance of the US economy and its prolongation into a North American economic sphere, two other macro-regional economic spheres are emerging, one in Europe and the other in eastern Asia centred on Japan. Europe and Japan confront separately the challenge of enlarging their autonomy in the global economy in relation to the dominance of US economic power.

At the same time, the opening of larger economic spaces, both global and macro-regional, coupled with the weakening autonomy of existing states, has given scope for sub-state entities to aspire to greater autonomy or independence, to seek direct relationship to the larger economic spaces, escaping subordination to a weakened existing state. Catalan and Lombard micro-regionalists aspire to a more affluent future in the Europe of post-1992, free from Spanish or Italian central governmental controls and redistributive policies. Quebec *independentistes* are the most enthusiastic supporters of a North American economic space. The Soviet empire and Yugoslavia have collapsed into a multiplicity of political entities most of which can hardly hope to control their own destinies but all of which will seek some form of relationship with the large economic spaces now in formation.

Globalisation is generating a more complex multi-level world political system, which implicitly challenges the old Westphalian assumption that a state is a state is a state. Structures of authority comprise not one but at at least three levels: the macro-regional level, the old state (or Westphalian) level, and the micro-regional level. All three levels are limited in their possibilities by a global economy which has means of exerting its pressures without formally authoritative political structures.

There is an increasingly marked duality and tension between the principles of interdependence and territorially based power. Interdependence (most often a euphemism for relationships of dominance and dependence) is manifested in the economic sphere. Territorial power is ultimately military. The United States is at the heart of the tension between the two principles. Global economic interdependence requires an enforcer of the rules – just as the self-regulating market of the nineteenth century had as enforcers at the local and global levels Robert Peel's police force and British sea power. Today the United States plays the role of global enforcer; but at the same time the US economy is losing its lead in productivity.

The trade deficit and budget deficit in the United States have been bridged by foreign borrowing, mainly in recent years from Japan, The internal reforms that would be necessary to reverse this process by reducing the deficits are blocked by the rigidity of the US political system and the unwillingness of politicians to confront the public with unpleasant choices. For the time being, foreign finance sustains in the United States a level of military and civilian consumption that US production would otherwise not allow.

The Gulf War underlined on the military side (as Germany, Japan, Saudi Arabia and Kuwait were obliged to pay for a war decided and directed by the United States) what has quietly become the case on the civilian side for some years. The United States does not pay its way in the world, while its structural power, resting increasingly on its military strength, continues to bias the global system in its favour. This is a far cry from the post-World War II world in which the United States provided the resources for recovery and the model of productivity for the rest of the world.[5] What was a system of hegemonic leadership has become a tributary system.

HEGEMONY AND AFTER[6]

There is an active debate about whether or not the hegemony of *Pax Americana* is in decline.[7] What remains unclear in this debate is a failure to distinguish between two meanings of 'hegemony'. One meaning, which is conventional in international relations literature, is the dominance of one state over others, the ability of the dominant state to determine the conditions in which interstate relations are conducted and to determine the outcomes in these relations. The other meaning, informed by the thought of Antonio Gramsci, is a special case of dominance: it defines the condition of a world society and state system in which the dominant state and dominant social forces sustain their position through adherence to universalised principles which are accepted or acquiesced in by a sufficient proportion of subordinate states and social forces (Cox, 1983). This second meaning of hegemony implies intellectual and moral leadership. The strong make certain concessions to obtain the consent of the weaker.

The *Pax Americana* of the post-World War II era had the characteristics of this Gramscian meaning of hegemony. The United States was the dominant power and its dominance was expressed in leadership enshrined in certain principles of conduct that became broadly acceptable. The economic 'regimes' established under US aegis during this period had the appearance of consensual arrangements. They did not look either like the crude exploitation of a power position or like a hard bargain arrived at among rival interests.

The recourse of US policy during the 1980s to unilateralism and the more manifest divergencies of interest among the United States, Europe, and Japan, together with the more open subordination of Third World countries to Western economic and military pressures have changed the nature of global relationships. US power may not have declined either absolutely or relatively, but the nature of the world system can no longer be described as hegemonic in the earlier sense.

Past hegemonies – the *Pax Britannica* of the mid-nineteenth century and the *Pax Americana* of the mid twentieth – have been based on universal principles projected from one form of Western civilisation. A civilisation is an intersubjective order, that is to say, people understand the entities and principles upon which it is based in roughly the same way. Their understandings are stimulated and confirmed by their own experiences of material life. By understanding their world in the same way, they reproduce it by their actions. Intersubjective meanings construct the objective world of the state system and the economy.[8] The fashionable prediction that we have arrived at the 'end of history'[9] (a notion stimulated by the collapse of Soviet power and the end of the Cold War) celebrates the apotheosis of a late Western capitalism. It is, however, in the nature of history not to have an end, but to move ahead in zig-zag manner by action and reaction. If the consensual basis of *Pax Americana* is no longer so firm as it was in the 1950s and 60s, then we must ask what intersubjective basis there could be for a future world order.

A post-hegemonic era would be one in which different traditions of civilisation could co-exist, each based on a different intersubjectivity defining a distinct set of values and a distinct path towards development. This is a difficult challenge to common ways of thinking. It would imply building a mental picture of a future world order through a mutual recognition and mutual understanding of different images of world order deriving from distinct cultural and historical roots, as a first step. Then, as a second step, working out the basis for the co-existence of these images – creating a supra-intersubjectivity that would connect or reconcile these culturally distinct intersubjectivities.

EUROPE'S CHOICES: FORMS OF STATE AND SOCIETY

How do these global tendencies and issues appear in the European context? How will Europeans respond in shaping their society and their form or forms of state?

It has become a commonplace on both left and right of the political spectrum that the capitalist state has both to support capital in its drive to accumulate and to legitimate this accumulation in the minds of the public by moderating the negative effects of accumulation on welfare and employment. During the post-war years, a neo-liberal form of state took shape in countries of advanced capitalism based on a negotiated consensus among the major industrial interests, organised labour, and government – the neo-liberal historic bloc. It was 'neo' in the sense that classical liberalism was modified by

Keynesian practice to make market behaviour consistent with social protection of the more disadvantaged groups.[10]

During the 1970s, governments in advanced capitalist countries in effect denounced the social contract worked out with capital and labour during the post-war economic boom. Governments had to balance the fear of political unrest from rising unemployment and exhaustion of welfare reserves against the fear that business would refrain from leading a recovery that would both revive employment and enlarge the tax base. In this circumstance they leaned towards the interests of capital.

In the neo-liberal consensus it had become accepted wisdom that society would not tolerate high unemployment or any dismantling of the welfare state. If these things were to occur, it would, it was said, cost the state the loss of its legitimacy. The truth of this statement has not been demonstrated uniformly. Indeed, it would more generally seem to be the case that the legitimacy of state welfare and of labour movements has been undermined in public opinion, not the legitimacy of the state. Large-scale unemployment has produced fear and concern for personal survival rather than collective protest. The unions are in strategic retreat, losing members, and unable, in general, to appeal to public opinion for support.

The disintegration of the neo-liberal historic bloc was facilitated by a collective effort of ideological revision undertaken through various unofficial agencies – the Trilateral Commission, the Bilderberg conferences, the Club of Rome, the more esoteric Mont Pélèrin Society among others – and then endorsed through official consensus-making agencies like the OECD. A new doctrine defined the tasks of states in relaunching capitalist development out of the depression of the 1970s. There was, in the words of a blue-ribbon OECD committee, a 'narrow path to growth', bounded on one side by the need to encourage private investment by increasing profit margins, and bounded on the other by the need to avoid rekindling inflation.[11]

The government – business alliance formed to advance along this narrow path ruled out corporative-type solutions like negotiated wage and price policies and also the expansion of public investment. It placed primary emphasis on restoring the confidence of business in government and in practice acknowledged that welfare and employment commitments made in the framework of the post-war social contract would have to take second place.

The restructuring of production has accentuated segmentation and divisions within the working class, but this tendency has not been uniform. In many Western European countries, a long history of ideological education has maintained a sense of solidarity. In both Italy and France there have been instances where unions have maintained solidarity of action between migrant workers and local established workers, but xenophobic agitation has also found resonance among workers and unemployed. Segmentation has been the underlying trend that explains the weakness of labour in opposing the disintegration of the post-war social consensus and the programme put in its place by the government-business alliance.[12]

It would be premature to define the outlines of a new historic bloc likely to achieve a certain durability as the foundation of a new form of state. Two principal directions of change in political structures are visible in the erstwhile neo-liberal states of Western Europe: one is exemplified by the confrontational tactics of Thatcherism in Britain (analogous to those of Reaganism in the United States) toward removing internal obstacles to economic liberalism; the other by a more consensus-based adjustment process that has been characteristic of West Germany and some of the smaller European countries. Whether by confrontation or consensual movement, Western European practice has been moving from Keynesianism to free markets.

HYPER-LIBERALISM

The Thatcher-Reagan model can be treated ideologically as the anticipation of a hyper-liberal form of state – in the sense that it seems to envisage a return to nineteenth-century economic liberalism and a rejection of the neo-liberal attempt to adapt economic liberalism to the socio-political reactions that classical liberalism produced. It takes the 'neo' out of neo-liberalism. The whole paraphernalia of Keynesian demand-support and redistributionist tools of policy are regarded with the deepest suspicion in the hyper-liberal approach.

Hyper-liberalism actively facilitates a restructuring, not only of the labour force, but also of the social relations of production. It renounces tripartite corporatism. It also weakens bipartism by its attack on unions in the state sector and its support and encouragement to employers to resist union demands in the oligopolistic sector. Indirectly, the state encourages the consolidation of enterprise corporatist relations for the scientific-technical-managerial workers in the oligopolistic sector. State policies are geared to an expansion of employment in short-term, low-skill, high-turnover jobs that contribute to further labour-market segmentation.

The political implications are a complete reversal of the coalition that sustained the neo-liberal state. That state rested on its relationship with trade unions in the oligopolistic sector (the social contract), an expanding and increasingly unionised state sector, readiness to support major businesses in difficulty (from agricultural price supports to bail-outs of industrial giants), and transfer payments and services for a range of disadvantaged groups. The neo-liberal state played a hegemonic role by making capital accumulation on a world scale appear to be compatible with a wide range of interests of subordinate groups. It founded its legitimacy on consensual politics.

The government-business alliance of hyper-liberalism generates an imposing list of disadvantaged and excluded groups. State-sector employees made great gains as regards their collective bargaining status and their wages during the years of expansion and have now become front-line targets for budgetary restraint. Welfare recipients and non-established workers, socially contiguous categories, are hit by reduced state expenditure and unemployment. Farmers and small businessmen are angry with banks and with governments as affordable finance becomes unavailable to them. Established workers in industries confronting severe problems in a changing international division of labour – textiles, automobiles, steel, shipbuilding, for example – face unemployment or reduced real wages.

So long as the excluded groups lack strong organisation and political cohesion, then ideological mystification, success in remote foreign wars, measures to broaden identification with the middle class and to entrench middle-class interests, and a focus in common discourse on personal survival rather than collective action, maintain the momentum of the new policy orthodoxy. If at least a small majority of the population remains relatively satisfied, or even a politically participant minority, it can be mobilised to maintain these policies against the dissatisfaction of an even very large minority or slim majority that is passive, divided and incoherent.

STATE CAPITALISM

While the hyper-liberal model reasserts the separation of state and economy, the alternative state form that contends for relaunching capitalist development promotes a fusion of state and economy. The visible hand of this state capitalism operates through a conscious industrial policy. Such a policy can be achieved only through a negotiated understanding among the principal social forces, mediated by the state in a corporative process. This process aims to produce agreement on the strategic goals of the economy and also on the sharing of burdens and benefits in the effort to reach those goals.

The state-capitalist approach is grounded in an acceptance of the world market as the ultimate determinant of development. Unlike the neo-liberal approach, the state-capitalist approach does not posit any consensual regulation of the world market as regards multilateral trade and financial practices. 'Regimes' may survive from the neo-liberal era, but state capitalism is not the most fertile ground for the formation of new regimes or the reform of old ones. States are assumed to intervene not only to enhance the competitiveness of their nations' industries but also to negotiate or dictate advantages for their nations' exporters. The world market is the state of nature from which state-capitalist theory deduces specific policy.

The broad lines of this policy consist of, in the first place, development of the leading sectors of national production so as to give them a competitive edge in world markets, and in the second place, protection of the principal social groups so that their welfare can be perceived as linked to the success of the national productive effort.

The first aspect of this policy – industrial competitiveness – is to be achieved by a combination of opening these industrial sectors to the stimulus of world competition, together with state subsidisation and orientation of innovation. Critical to the capacity for innovation is the condition of the knowledge industry; the state will have a major responsibility for funding scientific and technological research and development.

The second policy aspect – balancing the welfare of social groups – has to be linked to the pursuit of competitiveness. Protection of disadvantaged groups and sectors (industries or regions) would be envisaged as transitional assistance for their transfer to more profitable economic activities. Thus training, skill upgrading, and relocation assistance would have a pre-eminent place in social policy. The state would not indefinitely protect declining or inefficient industries but would provide incentives for the people concerned to become more efficient according to market criteria. The state would, however, intervene between the market pressures and the groups concerned so that the latter did not bear the full burden of adjustment.

Where internally generated savings were deemed to be essential to enhanced competitiveness, both investors and workers would have to be persuaded to accept an equitable sharing of sacrifice, in anticipation of a future equitable sharing of benefits. Thus incomes policy would become an indispensable counterpart to industrial policy. Similarly, the managerial initiative required to facilitate innovation and quick response to market changes might be balanced by forms of worker participation in the process of introducing technological changes. The effectiveness of such a state-capitalist approach would, accordingly, depend on the existence of corporative institutions and processes, not only at the level of enterprises and industries, but also of a more centralised kind capable of organising inter-industry, inter-sectoral and inter-regional shifts of resources for production and welfare.

The state-capitalist form involves a dualism between, on the one hand, a competitively efficient world-market-oriented sector, and, on the other, a protected welfare sector. The success of the former must provide the resources for the latter; the sense of solidarity implicit in the latter would provide the drive and legitimacy for the former. State capitalism thus proposes a means of reconciling the accumulation and legitimation functions brought into conflict by the economic and fiscal crises of the 1970s and by hyper-liberal politics. It remains an open question whether the expansion of the world-market-oriented sector in the form of transnational corporations may not develop the autonomy of this sector in relation both to the home state and the domestic welfare sector. This would make the balance in dualism difficult to maintain. The claims of international competitiveness would tend to outweigh those of domestic welfare.

In its most radical form, state capitalism beckons toward the prospect of an internal socialism sustained by capitalist success in world-market competition. This would be a socialism dependent on capitalist development, i.e. on success in the production of exchange values. But, so its proponents argue, it would be less vulnerable to external destabilisation than were socialist strategies in economically weak countries (Allende's Chile or post-revolutionary Portugal). The more radical form of state-capitalist strategy presents itself as an alternative to defensive, quasi-autarkic prescriptions for the construction of socialism which aim to reduce dependency on the world economy and to emphasise the production of use values for internal consumption.[13]

Different countries are more or less well equipped by their historical experience for the adoption of the state-capitalist developmental path with or without the socialist colouration.[14] Those best equipped are countries in which the state (as in France) or a centralised but autonomous financial system (as in Germany) has played a major role in mobilising capital for industrial development. Institutions and ideology in these countries have facilitated a close co-ordination of state and private capital in the pursuit of common goals. Those least

270

well equipped are the erstwhile industrial leaders, Britain and the United States, countries in which hegemonic institutions and ideology kept the state by and large out of specific economic initiatives, confining its role to guaranteeing and enforcing market rules and to macroeconomic management of market conditions. The lagging effects of past hegemonic leadership may thus be a deterrent to the adoption of state-capitalist strategies. The state's role, especially in the United States, is mainly to use political leverage in foreign trade to support industries unable to succeed in foreign markets.

The corporatist process underpinning state-capitalist development, which would include business and labour in the world-market-oriented sector and workers in the tertiary welfare-services sector, would at the same time exclude certain marginal groups. These groups have a frequently passive relationship to the welfare services and lack influence in the making of policy. They are disproportionately to be found among the young, women, immigrant or minority groups, and the unemployed. The number of the marginalised tends to increase with the restructuring of production. Since these groups are fragmented and relatively powerless, their exclusion has generally passed unchallenged. It does, however, contain a latent threat to corporatist processes. This threat could take the form either of anomic explosions of violence among the young male alienated element or, more seriously, of political mobilisation among the marginals, which would pit democratic legitimacy against corporatist economic efficiency. These dangers are foreshadowed in the writings of neo-liberal ideologues about the 'ungovernability' problem of modern democracies (see Crozier et al. 1975). The implication is that the corporatist processes required to make state-capitalist development succeed may have to be insulated from democratic pressures. To the extent this becomes true, the prospects of internal socialism sustained by world-market state capitalism would be an illusion. In the medium term, state-capitalist structures of some kind seem a feasible alternative to the hyper-liberal impasse. The long-term viability of these forms is a more open question.

Western Europe has, in its different national antecedents, propensities tending toward each of these forms of state and society.[15] It might be said that in its present power structure, the dominance of capital in the opening of the Europe of 1992 favours hyper-liberalism. However, the social corporativist tradition is strong, especially in continental Europe, and may compensate in politics for the dominance of hyper-liberalism in economic power. The concept of 'social Europe', anathema to Thatcherism and more covertly rejected by some elements of continental capital, is sustained by a social democracy more deeply rooted than in other major world regions (Spyropoulos, 1990). The issue between hyper-liberalism and state capitalism will be tested first in Europe, and Europe's answer will serve as a model or at least as an alternative for North America, Japan, and perhaps other regions in a future world.

SOCIAL FORCES COUNTERACTING GLOBALISATION

Hyper-liberalism is the ideology of globalisation in its most extreme form. State capitalism is an adaptation to globalisation that responds at least in part to society's reaction to the negative effects of globalisation. We must ask ourselves whether there are longer-term prospects that might come to fruition following a medium-term experiment with state capitalism. This is best approached by enquiring how the conditions created by globalisation could generate a *prise de conscience* among those elements of societies that are made more vulnerable by it.

If the state-capitalist solution were to be but an interim stage, the prospect of turning around the segmenting, socially disintegrating, and polarising effects of globalisation rests upon the possibility of the emergence of an alternative political culture that would give greater scope to collective action and place a greater value on collective goods.[16] For this to come about, whole segments of societies would have to become attached, through active participation and developed loyalties, to social institutions engaged in collective activities. They would have to be prepared to defend these institutions in times of adversity.

The condition for a restructuring of society and polity in this sense would be to build a new historic bloc capable of sustaining a long war of position until it is strong enough to become an alternative basis of polity. This effort would have to be grounded in the popular strata. The activities that comprise it will not likely initially be directed to the state because of the degree of depoliticisation and alienation from the state among these strata. They will more likely be directed to local authorities and to collective self-help. They will in many cases be local responses to global problems – to problems of the environment, of organising production, of providing welfare, of migration. If they are ultimately to result in new kinds of state, these forms of state will arise from the practice of non-state popular collective action rather than from extensions of existing types of administrative control.

Europe's social history has known such movements. They have marginally influenced the shaping of society and state, though they have never fulfilled their own initial aims. These aims could in any event hardly be achieved in one national society alone; movements of this kind would have to grow simultaneously in several countries. The merging of European political processes inherent in the project of 1992 could provide a broad arena in which this struggle might be pursued. Economic globalisation, however, suggests that such movements could not succeed in one macro-region alone. It would have to draw sufficient support in the world system to protect its regional base or face the consequences of a relative military and economic weakening if competing macro-regions did not experience comparable developments. The existing globalisation grounded in the economic logic of markets would have to be countered by a new globalisation reembedding the economy in global society.

THE SEQUEL TO 'REAL SOCIALISM'[17]

If the options for the Europe of Western capitalism can be expressed in relatively clear terms, the situation of the countries of erstwhile 'real socialism' approaching the threshold of the twenty-first century is more complex. Yet the long-term future of Europe implies an accommodation between these two regions. It is easy in the early 1990s to proclaim real socialism a failure. It is more difficult to envisage the effacing of the history of two generations through which social structures have been formed. Eastern Europe is not a *tabula rasa* on which Western capitalism may be simply inscribed. The options for that region, whether for that part that may anticipate total integration within the West (the former GDR), closer association with the European Communities, or an autonomous evolution with a greater degree of integration into the world economy, have realistically to take account of existing social structures.

Both capitalist and socialist societies have grown by extracting a surplus from the producers. In market-driven capitalist societies, this surplus is invested in whatever individual capitalists think is likely to produce a further profit. In socialist societies, investment decisions have been politically determined according to whatever criteria are salient at the time for the decision-makers, e.g. welfare or state power. The social structure of accumulation is the particular configuration of social power through which the accumulation process takes place. This configuration delineates a relationship among social groups in the production process through which surplus is extracted.

This power relationship underpins the institutional arrangements through which the process works.[18] It also shapes the real form of political authority.

To grasp the nature of the social structure of accumulation at the moment of the crisis of existing socialism in the late 1980s, one must go back to the transformation in the working class that began some three decades earlier. The new working class composed largely of ex-peasants that carried through the industrialisation drive of the 1930s in the Soviet Union and the war effort of the 1940s worked under an iron discipline of strict regulation and tough task masters recruited from the shop floor. During the 1950s a new mentality reshaped industrial practices. Regulations were relaxed and their modes of application gave more scope for the protection of individual workers' interests. Managerial cadres began to be recruited mainly from professional schools and were more disposed to the methods of manipulation and persuasion than to coercion. The factory regime passed from the despotic to the hegemonic type.[19]

An historic compromise worked out by the Party leadership included a *de facto* social contract in which workers were implicitly guaranteed job security, stable consumer prices, and control over the pace of work, in return for their passive acquiescence in the rule of the political leadership. Workers had considerable structural power, i.e. their interests had to be anticipated and taken into account by the leadership, though they had little instrumental power through direct representation. This arrangement of passive acquiescence in time generated the cynicism expressed as: 'You pretend to pay us. We pretend to work.'

The working class comprised an established and a non-established segment. One group of workers, the established worker segment, were more permanent in their jobs, had skills more directly applied in their work, were more involved in the enterprise as a social institution and in other political and civic activities. The other group, the non-established worker segment, changed jobs more frequently, experienced no career development in their employment, and were non-participant in enterprise or other social and political activities. The modalities of this segmentation varied among the different socialist countries.

Hungarian sociologists discerned a more complex categorization of non-established workers; 'workhorses' willing to exploit themselves for private accumulation (newly marrieds for instance); 'hedonists' or single workers interested only in the wage as the means of having a good time; and 'internal guest workers' mainly women, or part-time peasant workers, or members of ethnic minorities allocated to the dirty work.[20] In practice, labour segmentation under 'real socialism' bore a striking similarity to labour segmentation under capitalism.

This differentiation within the working class had a particular importance in the framework of central planning. Central planning can be thought of in abstract terms as a system comprising (a) redistributors in central agencies of the state who plan according to some decision-making rationality, i.e. maximising certain defined goals and allocating resources accordingly; and (b) direct producers who carry out the plans with the resources provided them. In practice, central planning developed an internal dynamic that defied the rationality of planners. It became a complex bargaining process from enterprise to central levels in which different groups have different levels of power. One of the more significant theoretical efforts of recent years has been to analyse the real nature of central planning so as to discern its inherent laws or regularities.[21]

Capital is understood in Marxist terms as a form of alienation; people through their labour create something that becomes a power over themselves and their work. Central planning also became a form of alienation: instead of being a system of rational human control over economic processes, it too became a system that no one controlled but which came to control planners and producers alike.

A salient characteristic of central planning as it had evolved in the decades just prior to the changes that began to be introduced during the late 1980s was a tendency to overinvest. Enterprises sought to get new projects included in the plan and thus to increase their sources of supply through allocations within it. Increased supplies made it easier to fulfil existing obligations but at the same time raised future obligations. The centrally planned economy was an economy of shortages; it was supply constrained, in contrast to the capitalist economy which was demand constrained. The economy of shortages generated uncertainties of supply, and these uncertainties were transmitted from enterprise to enterprise along the chain of inputs and outputs.

Enterprise managers became highly dependent upon core workers to cope with uncertainties. The core workers, familiar with the installed equipment, were the only ones able to improvise when bottlenecks occurred. They could, if necessary, improvise to cope with absence of replacement parts, repair obsolescent equipment, or make use of substitute materials. Managers also had an incentive to hoard workers, to maintain an internal enterprise labour reserve that could be mobilised for 'storming' at the end of a plan period.

Managers also came to rely on their relations with local Party officials to secure needed inputs when shortages impeded the enterprise's ability to meet its plan target.

These factors combined to make the key structure at the heart of the system one of management dependence on local Party cadres together with a close interrelationship between management and core workers in a form of enterprise corporatism. From this point, there were downward linkages with subordinate groups of non-established workers, with rural cooperatives, and with household production. There were upward linkages with the ministries of industries and the state plan. And there was a parallel relationship with the 'second economy' which, together with political connections, helped to bypass some of the bottlenecks inherent in the formal economy.

Several things can be inferred from this social structure of accumulation. One is that those constituting its core – management, established workers, and local Party officials – were well entrenched in the production system. They knew how to make it work and they were likely to be apprehensive about changes that would introduce further uncertainties beyond those that they had learned to cope with. Motivation for change was most likely to come from those at the top who were aware that production was less efficient than it might have been, and who wanted to eliminate excess labour and to introduce more productive technology. (Those at the core of the system had a vested interest in existing obsolescent technology because their particular skills made it work.) Motivation for change might also arise among the general population in the form of dissatisfaction with declining standards of public services and consumer goods; and among a portion of the growing 'middle class' of white-collar service workers. The more peripheral of the non-established workers – those most alienated within the system – were unlikely to be highly motivated for change. There was, in fact, no coherent social basis for change but rather a diffuse dissatisfaction with the way the system was performing. There was, however, likely to be a coherent social basis at the heart of the system that could be mobilised to resist change.

ECONOMIC REFORM AND DEMOCRATISATION

Socialist systems, beginning with the Soviet Union, have been preoccupied with reform of the economic mechanism since the 1960s. The problem was posed in terms of a transition from the extensive pattern of growth that was producing diminishing returns from the mid-1960s onward, to a pattern of growth that would be more intensive in the use of capital and technology. Perception of the problem came from the top of the political-economic hierarchy and was expressed through a sequence of on-again off-again experiments. Piece-meal reform proved difficult because of the very coherence of the system of power that constituted central planning. Movement in one direction, e.g. granting more decision-making powers to managers, ran up against obstacles in other parts of the system, e.g. in the powers of central ministries and in the acquired job rights of workers.

Frustrations with piece-meal reforms encouraged espousal of more radical reform; and radical reform was associated with giving much broader scope to the market mechanism. The market was an attractive concept insofar as it promised a more effective and less cumbersome means of allocating material inputs to enterprises and of distributing consumer goods. It was consistent with decentralisation of management to enterprises and with a stimulus to consumer-goods production. The market, however, was also suspect in so far as it would create prices (and thus inflation in an economy of shortages), bring about greater disparities in incomes, and undermine the power of the centre to direct the overall development of the economy. Some combination of markets with central direction of the economy seemed to be the optimum solution, if it could be done.

Following in the tracks of the reform movement came pressures for democratisation. These came from a variety of sources: a series of movements sequentially repressed but cumulatively infectious in East Germany, Poland, Hungary, and Czechoslovakia; the rejection of Stalinism and the ultimate weakening of the repressive apparatus installed by Stalinism; and the consequences of the rebirth of civil society and of the recognition by the ruling cadres that the intelligentsia was entitled to greater autonomy. Indeed, the intelligentsia required access to the ideas and research of advanced capitalist societies if it was to be able to help real socialism out of its impasse. The two movements – perestroika and glasnost in their Soviet form – encountered and interacted in the late 1980s. Would they reinforce each other or work against each other? We do not yet know the answer.

Some economic reformers saw democratisation as a means of loosening up society which could strengthen decentralisation. Some of these same people also saw worker self-management as supporting enterprise autonomy and the liberalising of markets. Humanist intellectuals tended to see economic reform as limiting the state's coercive apparatus and as encouraging a more pluralist society. For these groups, economic reform and democratisation went together.

Other economic reformers recognised that reform measures would place new burdens on people before the reforms showed any benefits. There would be inflation, shortages, and unemployment. The social contract of mature real socialism would be discarded in the process of introducing flexibility into the labour market and the management of enterprises. The skills of existing managers would be rendered obsolete, together with those of many state and Party officials engaged in the central planning process. Anticipating the backlash from all these groups, 'realist' reformers could well conclude that an authoritarian power would be needed to implement reform successfully. Without it, reform would just be compromised and rendered ineffective, disrupting the present system without being able to replace it.[22] The economic Thatcherites of real socialism could become its political Pinochets.

The initial effects of both economic reform and democratisation have produced some troublesome consequences. Relaxing economic controls towards encouraging a shift to market mechanisms has resulted in a breakdown of the distribution system with a channelling of goods into free markets and black markets, rampant gangsterisms, and a dramatic polarisation of new rich and poor. Among the new rich are members of the old *nomenklatura*, well placed to adapt their knowledge of how enterprises worked to the new opportunities of market capitalism. The relaxing of political controls gave vent to conflicts long suppressed, mobilising people around ethnic nationalisms, various forms of populism, and, at the extreme, right-wing fascist movements. Furthermore, the outburst of public debate, while it demolished the legitimacy of the socialist state and its sustaining myths, has also demonstrated an inability to come to grips with the practical reorganization of economy and society. The reform process has itself made things worse, not better. The understandings among social groups on which the old system was based have been disrupted, revealing a state of nature in which predatory primitive capitalists thrive.

The legitimacy of real socialism was destroyed by Stalinism and the anti-Stalinist backlash. Civil society is re-emergent but its component groups have not achieved any articulate organised expression. This is a condition Gramsci called an organic crisis; and the solution to an organic crisis is the reconstitution of a hegemony around a social group which is capable of leading and acquiring the support or acquiescence of other groups. What does our analysis of the social structure of real socialism tell us about the prospects of this happening?

There are three distinct meanings that can be given to 'democracy' in the context of the collapse of real socialism. One is the conventional 'bourgeois' meaning of liberal pluralism. It has a strong demonstration effect in Eastern Europe. Liberal pluralism has a history and many examples. Two other meanings arise out of socialist aspirations.

One is producer self-management. It has been expressed in spontaneous action by workers in many different revolutionary situations – in the original Russian soviets, in the *Ordine nuovo* movement of northern Italy in 1919, in workers' control of factories during the Algerian revolution, in the works councils set up in Poland following the events of 1956, and in factory movements in Hungary during the 1956 revolution and Czechoslovakia in 1968. These experiences were all short-lived. The only long experience with worker self-management is the Yugoslav one and, despite much analysis and debate, it cannot be considered persuasive. There is a strong point about producers being able to determine their own conditions; but there is also evidence of a tendency for such experiences, assuming they survive repression by a higher political authority, to turn in the direction of self-serving corporatism.

The other socialist meaning is popular participation in central planning. No historical experience can be cited; it would have to be invented. And yet it is perhaps the most attractive prospect in the spirit of socialism. Alec Nove (1983: 199) suggested a form of compromise between democratic planning and producer self-government: consumers would decide what to produce; producers would decide how.[23]

George Lukács (1985) wrote a text that was posthumously published in Hungary as *Demokratisierung Heute und Morgen*.[24] Rejecting both the Stalinist past and the liberal concept of democracy, he speculated about the conditions in which a democratisation of socialism might be possible.

A first condition, for Lukács, was a reduction in socially necessary labour time that would shift the balance in human activity from the realm of necessity to the realm of freedom. Society would have to be able to produce sufficient to satisfy the necessities of material existence without absorbing all the time and effort of its people This condition is recognised also by others who have thought about the problem. Janos Kornai (1971) (before he embraced the capitalist alternative) posited that sufficient slack in production would be necessary to undertake reform in an economy of shortage. Rudolf Bahro (1978) argued that a state of 'surplus consciousness', i.e. the existence of a margin of time and effort over and above the satisfaction of basic wants, was requisite for the pursuit of 'emancipatory interests' as an alternative to the 'compensatory interests' of consumerism.

The next condition would be a coalition of social forces upon which the structure of democratic socialism might be based. At this point, Lukács' prescription becomes obscure. Like Bahro and like Gorz in the West, he did not, in this last phase of his thought, look to the workers as the leading social class around which democratic socialism could take form. He spoke rather of liberating the 'underground tendencies' hitherto repressed. The Party could, he hoped, reconstitute itself to achieve this.

This was a hope inspired by the reform movement led by the intelligentsia in Czechoslovakia in 1968. It had a brief revival again in the GDR during the time *Neues Forum* and similar groups were building the popular movement that overturned the Honecker regime. The project lives on, though its plausibility is diminished.

Two other routes towards democratisation in recent Eastern European experience have been, first, a movement from outside a moribund Party led by an independent workers' movement to which an intelligentsia attached itself (Poland); and second, an enlargement of scope for independent decision-making in the economy through a strategic withdrawal by the Party from direct control over certain aspects of civil society (Hungary). Both of these routes now in retrospect seem to have led towards restoration of capitalism. The former GDR shows a third route to capitalism: total collapse of the political structures of real socialism and full incorporation of its economy into West German capitalism.

For the remaining European countries of erstwhile real socialism, options for the future can be grouped broadly into three scenarios. Each of these should be examined in terms of the relationship of the projected form of state and economy with the social structure of accumulation of real socialism.

The first scenario is economic liberalisation leading towards market capitalism and the integration of the national economy into the global capitalist economy. In its 'pure' form, this project is favoured by some segments of the intelligentsia who think that a 'shock therapy' in the Polish mode will be necessary to carry through privatisation and the freeing of market forces. They would argue that popular support for political liberalisation creates the conditions in which people are ready to put up with the hardships of 'shock therapy' – the bankruptcies of enterprises, massive unemployment, rampant inflation, shortages of vital necessities, and the polarisation of new rich and poor that occurs as the accompaniment to radical market reform.

This is the option encouraged by the Western consultants pullulating through the world of collapsing real socialism as the whiz-kid offspring of prestigious universities, private consulting firms and agencies of the world economy. It is encouraged paradoxically by the revival of von Hayek's ideas in Eastern Europe and by the mythology of capitalism and of a pre-environmentalist fascination with Western consumerism.

The beneficent mood of political liberalisation is, however, vulnerable to the reality of unprecedented deprivation and collective humiliation. The choice then would become which to sacrifice, democracy or the free market? The historical record, as Karl Polanyi (1957) presented it in his analysis of Central Europe in the 1930s, suggests that democracy is first sacrificed but the market is not ultimately saved. This setting was, for Polanyi, the opening of the path towards fascism; and some observers from Eastern Europe raise again this spectre as a not unlikely outcome of the social convulsions following the breakdown of real socialism.[25]

More moderate and mature political leadership might hesitate before enforcing the full measure of market-driven adjustments upon the resistant and the vulnerable elements of civil society. The compromise envisaged by this leadership would likely be a form of corporatism that would aim at co-opting core workers into the transition to capitalism, separating the more articulate and more strategically placed segments of the working class from the less articulate and less powerful majority. The enterprise-corporatist core of real socialism's social structure of accumulation would thus lend itself to facilitating the transition to capitalism – to something like the state-capitalist option for Western Europe discussed above with a possibly more authoritarian political aspect.[26]

The second scenario is political authoritarianism together with a command-administrative economic centre incorporating some subordinate market features and some bureaucratic reform. This would leave basically intact the enterprise-corporatist heart of the existing planning system, which would also constitute its main political roots in civil society and its continuing source of legitimation in the 'working class'. The 'conservatives' of the Soviet Union (with the backing of some influentials in the military and the KGB) may be counted among its supporters. The long-term problem for this course would be in the continuing exclusion of the more peripheral segments of the labour force from any effective participation in the system, though these elements might be calmed in the short run if the revival of authority in central planning were to lift the economy out of the chaos resulting from the collapse of authority in both economic planning and political structures.[27]

The third scenario is the possibility of democratisation plus socialist reform. As suggested above, this could take the form either of producer self-management, or of a democratisation of the central planning process, or conceivably of some combination of the two. Of the three scenarios, this one, with its two variants, is the least clearly spelled out. It has been passed over in the domestic debate and in the injection of foreign prescriptions for reform. The power of the media has been monopolised by the adherents of the first two scenarios and especially by the radical market reformers (Mandell, 1990).

Self-management has been claimed by both economic liberals and socialists. It has lost ground among the liberals without noticeably gaining conviction among socialists. Some of those economic reformers who once thought of self-management as a support to economic liberalisation, now appear to have drawn back from this option.[28] Nevertheless, from a socialist perspective, the possibility must remain that self-management, in the absence of some larger socialist economic framework, is likely to evolve towards a form of enterprise corporatism within a capitalist market, i.e. the moderate variant of the first scenario.

The prospect of democratising central planning has all but been removed from the current agenda of public debate, yet it retains some support among those intellectuals who, pessimistic about the viability of the crude market orientation of present policies, envisage a coming backlash. They hope for a social market economy building upon Michal Kalecki's idea of a planning mechanism activated from below and the achievements of Western social democracy. 'Socialism' has become an almost unpronounceable word in Eastern Europe, but the values of socialism survive without the word and could give substance to the coming reaction against the socially devastating consequences of unbridled market behaviour. The great fear of those supporting this alternative is that it will be pre-empted by a descent into chaos that engenders a fascist-type populist regime.[29]

The position of workers in relation to these three scenarios remains ambiguous and fragmented. In this there is a striking resemblance to the position of workers under capitalism since the economic crisis of the 1970s. The same question is to be raised in each case: does the unqualified term 'working class' still correspond to a coherent identifiable social force? The potential for an autonomous workers' movement was demonstrated in Poland by *Solidarnosc*; but in the hour of its triumph that movement fragmented. The Soviet miners' strike of July 1989 revived credibility in a workers' movement; but it was not sufficient to make a trend.

Projects for managing and reorienting the working class that emanate from members of the intelligentsia are more readily to be found than clear evidence of autonomous working-class choice. It would appear that the Soviet government tried to channel the miners' strike towards demands for enterprise autonomy, only subsequently to abandon self-management as part of market reform (Davies, 1990: 18). Academician Zaslavskaya, in a now famous internal Party document, advocated a policy of manipulating worker attitudes 'in an oblique fashion' through incentives.[30] Some economic liberal reformers, no longer interested in self-management, entertain the notion of collective bargaining by independent trade unions as a counterpart to a capitalist economy.

Workers, it seems, may not have very much of an active, initiating voice in the reform process. They may continue as previously to be an important passive structural force that reforming intelligentsia will have to take into account. Their attitudes might be remoulded over time as Zaslavskaya and others would envisage. For the present workers, as a structural presence, are likely to remain committed to some of the basic ideas of socialism: egalitarianism in opportunities and incomes, the responsibility of the state to produce basic services of health and education, price stability and availability of basic wage goods. 'In this respect, they would have to be classified, in the new vocabulary with which perestroika is discussed, as 'conservatives'.) Workers like other groups are critical of bureaucracy and irritating instances of privilege. These are the basic sentiments that future options for socialism could most feasibly be built upon.

EUROPE AND THE WORLD

The future of Europe has been considered here in terms of the options for forms of state and society as they are conditioned by existing social forces within Europe – forces which are the European manifestation of global tendencies discussed in the first part of this chapter. Europe's relationship to the rest of the world will depend upon how Europeans define their own social and political identity by making their choices among these options; but at the same time external influences from the world system are affecting the internal European balance of social forces in the making of these choices.

The emerging European macro-region will have a formal political structure different from the more informal authority structure of the other two macro-regions, the US and Japanese spheres. Whereas the United States and Japan are economically and politically dominant in their spheres, the European core area in economic terms is a corridor running from Turin and Milan in the south through Stuttgart in the east and Lyons in the west up to the low countries and the southeast of England, spanning seven states. In political terms authority rests in a consultative confederalism in which participant states have often differing policy preferences and micro-regions are asserting their autonomy. This makes it less likely that Europe can speak in a unified way, especially on foreign policy matters – witness the divergences over the Gulf War and over a common response to Yugoslavia's disintegration – although pressure from the other macro-regions could become a recurrently unifying force.

The central issue in defining the future European identity will be the extent to which it is based on a separation of the economy from politics. Strong forces urge that this separation become the basic ontology of the new European order; and that a European-level political system be constructed that would limit popular pressures for political and social control of economic processes. These processes would then be left to a combination of the market and a Brussels-based technocracy which would, in turn, reflect the dominance of big capital and the 'core' states, especially Germany. These forces have the initiative within Europe, and they have the external backing of the United States as the enforcer of global economic liberalism.[31] Europe has, however, a deeply rooted tradition of political and social control over economic processes, both in Western social democracy and in Eastern real socialism. This is why the transformation of Eastern European societies can be so important, despite their current weakness, in the overall balance of social forces shaping the future. East and West are no longer isolated compartments. Political processes will flow from one to the other; and although now the dominant flow is from West to East, a counterflow may be anticipated in migration and in political movements. Despair generating right-wing extremism in the East could both challenge and encourage right-wing extremism in the West. The emergence of a firmly based and clearly articulated democratic socialism from the transformation of real socialism in the East could likewise strengthen western social democracy.

Europe's relation with the United States will in the long run be redefined as Europeans recreate their own identity. The Gulf War and President Bush's 'new world order' placed Europe in an ambiguous position. Britain and France followed the US lead, intent on regaining a position near the centre of global politics as these were envisaged in the 1940s. Neither country appears to have gained status or other rewards as a consequence. Germany held back, conscious of a divided domestic opinion and of the overwhelming need to give priority to absorbing the impact of the collapse of real socialism in the east. Italy, in a certain manner, followed both courses.

Will Europe continue to accept the role of the United States as enforcer of global-economy liberalism? Will Japan continue to subscribe to the US deficit? The United States, despite its unquestioned economic and political power, is moving into the same kind of difficulties as beset the Soviet economy – declining rates of productivity, high military costs, and an intractable budgetary deficit. The role of enforcer is not sustainable by the United States alone; and there is a real question whether Europeans and Japanese would want to perpetuate and to subsidise this role for long.

Reconsidering Europe's relationship to the United States links directly to Europe's relationship to the Third World. The Gulf War was, in one of its manifold aspects, an object lesson to the Third World that the global political economy was capable of mustering sufficient military force to discipline and punish a Third World country that sought to become an autonomous military power and to deviate from acceptable economic behaviour. The subsequent decision by NATO to establish a European rapid deployment force under British command can be read as a reaffirmation of this lesson.

This is consistent with a view that sees the Third World from the perspective of the dominant forces in the global economy: some segments of the Third World become integrated into the globalisation process; other segments which remain outside must be handled by a combination of global poor relief and riot control. Poor relief is designed to avoid conditions of desperation arising from impoverishment which could threaten to politically destabilise the integrated segments. Riot control takes the form of military-political support for regimes that will abide by and enforce global economy practices, and, in the last instance, of the rapid deployment force to discipline those that will not.

Europe, in historical and in geopolitical terms, has a particular relationship to the Third World: the relationship of Islamic to Christian civilizations. Europe's vocation for unity can be traced to the medieval *Respublica Christiana*, a concept of unity that had no corresponding political authority. Islam's vocation for unity looks to an equally distant past and to the ephemeral political authority of the caliphate. Its unity also transcends states. Islam is for Christendom the great 'Other'. In contemporary terms, Islam also appears as a metaphor for the rejection of Western capitalism as a developmental mode.

The cancelling of the schism between East and West in Christendom, symbolised by the collapse of 'real socialism' but reappearing in the war between Serbs and Croats, leaves unresolved the European confrontation with Islam. The global economy perspective sees the Third World as a residual, marginal factor, a non-identity. The historical experience and perspective of Europe confronts Islam as a real identity, a different civilisation. Islam returned to Europe's lost origins in Greek philosophy, taught Europe science and medicine, and showed Europe a cultivated style of living, yet remained fundamentally alien and never, unlike Europe, germinated its own capitalism.

The confrontation with Islam is not only external, across borders and the Mediterranean sea. It is also becoming internalised within European societies, in migration and in the responses to migration by such political phenomena such as the Front National in France. The new Europe is challenged to free itself from the residual, marginalised view of the Third World and to confront directly the cultural as well as economic and political issues in a recognised co-existence of two different civilisations.[32]

Europe, in sum, can be a proving ground for a new form of world order: post-hegemonic in its recognition of co-existing universalistic civilisations; post-Westphalian in its restructuring of political authority into a multi-level system; and post-globalisation in its acceptance of the legitimacy of different paths towards the satisfaction of human needs.

Notes

1 This text is a revised version of a paper originally prepared for a Conference on 'A new Europe in the changing global system', convened

in September 1991 in Velence, Hungary, under the auspices of the United Nations University and the Hungarian Academy of Sciences. I am indebted to Stephen Gill and Susan Strange for their close critical reading of the original text and their suggestions. I doubt that either will be satisfied with my revisions.

2 On this distinction between international and global economies, see Madeuf and Michalet (1978)

3 These terms have been used by the French *régulation* school of economists, e.g. Boyer (1990). A similar approach to the transformation of industrial organisation has been taken by some US economists, e.g. Piore and Sabel (1984).

4 On the role of 'regimes', see especially, Keohane (1984a). Of course, factors that escape regime regulation like swings in bank lending can have disruptive consequences.

5 See in this regard the perceptive essay by Maier (1977).

6 I am borrowing from the titles of two very different books, each of which have nevertheless something relevant to say: E. H. Carr's *Nationalism and After* (1945) and Robert O. Keohane's *After Hegemony* (1984)

7 In addition to Keohane, 1984a; see Kennedy, 1987/8; Nye, 1990; Strange 1987; Gill 1990.

8 On intersubjective meanings in politics, see Taylor (1976).

9 Francis Fukuyama, in *The National Interest*, summer 1989.

10 This section is based on chapter 8 of Cox (1987); and also Cox (1991a).

11 The McCracken Report, *Towards Full Employment and Price Stability*. Paris, OECD, 1977.

12 On the segmentation trend, *inter alia*: Wilkinson (1981).

13 Some French writers have probed these questions, e.g. Stoffaes (1978); and Kolm (1977).

14 Some recent US studies that have compared the institutional characteristics of leading capitalist countries include Katzenstein (1978); and Zysman (1983).

15 Aubert (1991) contrasts two types of rival capitalisms which approximate the hyper-liberal/state capitalist contrast made here. One he presents as an American type based on individualism and short-term financial profit, the other a north European type based on long-term collective success and consensus. The first, he sees as present in Thatcherite Britain, the second more characteristic of Germany, the Netherlands, Switzerland and Japan. Aubert's inference is that Europe's capitalism should be built on the second model.

16 One has to be careful about the meanings of words here. The discourse of globalisation represents the main features of economic globalisation as 'public goods', i.e. the maintenance of the preconditions for a global capitalist economy. By 'collective action' and 'collective goods' I mean here the moderating of individualism in favour of community action and the production or conservation of use values that can be directly enjoyed by people, like public transport and a healthy environment. Other terms that have been appropriated by the hegemonic discourse with a change

of meaning are 'basic needs' as used by the World Bank and 'structural adjustment' (replacing the more critical 'structural change') as used by the IMF. The list can probably be extended.

17 This section is largely based on Cox (1991b).

18 I have taken the concept of social structure of accumulation from Gordon (1980). My use of it focuses more specifically on the relationship of social forces, whereas Gordon uses it more broadly to encompass, e.g., the institutions of the world economy. I have applied the concept to the capitalist world economy in Cox (1987), chapter 9.

19 The terms are taken from Michael Burawoy's use of Gramsci's concept of hegemony. See Burawoy (1985).

20 See Hungarian Academy of Sciences, 1984.

21 Prominent among those who have opened up this line of theoretical enquiry are Brus (1973); Kornai (1980, 1982).

22 The positions of various groups in Soviet society with regard to reforms are reviewed in Davies (1990).

23 Stafford Beer went to Chile in the time of Allende to put into practice a computer-based interactive planning system in which signals would come from the base as well as from the summit, using modern micro-processing technology to democratise socialist planning. Of course, the scheme did not come to anything because of the Pinochet coup. See Beer (1974).

24 See Lukács (1985). I am indebted to Dr. A. Bródy, Institute of Economics, Hungarian Academy of Sciences, for drawing this text to my attention.

25 E. g. Vojinovic (1990). Ralf Dahrendorf (1990: 115–6), while arguing the possibility of capitalism with liberal pluralism, is also concerned by the possibility of a fascist revival.

A symposium edited by Antoni Kuklinski (1991) for the Polish Association for the Club of Rome, *Globality versus Locality*, vols. 1 & 2, examines this scenario. A contribution by Zdzislaw Sadowski assesses the public support for market reforms and willingness to endure hardships that would not have been tolerated under the former regime as turning into disillusionment around May 1990, leading towards an openness to crude populism. This would, he argues, further diminish the possibility of a long-term rational strategy of economic recovery. Jan Szczepanski, in an analysis of Polish political history, argues that political stability would have to be based on political parties that represented well-organised social classes (workers, peasants, and middle class) but this did not exist either in communist or post-communist Poland. *Solidarnosc'* anti-communism presented no coherent socially-based alternative. It disintegrated into a multiplicity of parties that would likely lead to political immobilism and disillusion people with parliamentary politics. These analyses all point towards some kind of populist authoritarianism. Even the observation (e.g. by Sadowski) that authoritarianism has often been more efficient than democracy in making the transition to capitalism (cases like South Korea and Taiwan) does not validate the kind of populist authoritarianism that could arise in Poland.

26 In an interview for *Le Monde* (11 September 1991) Lech Walesa, the Polish chief of state, said:

> En Pologne, dans nos réformes, nous avons commis une erreur: on a choisi d'aller vite, pour aller à votre rencontre. Résultat: aujourd'hui on a des problèmes terribles, énormément de chomage, des machines arrêtées. Si on était allé plus lentement, on aurait moitié moins de chômeurs. Ce n'est pas d'argent qu'on a besoin, mais de la réponse à la question: comment faire fonctionner le potentiel existant?

27 This was written prior to the aborted putsch of August 1991 in Moscow. The scenario is not for that reason to be discarded as *déjà vu*. The putsch may have been a premature, poorly planned, badly led, and generally botched event. A sequel, following society's descent into chaos, could have unpredictable consequences.

28 Davies (1990:23) reports this of, e.g., the economist Aganbegyan.

29 This seems to be the hope and fear of contributors to Kuklinski (1990).

30 Novosibirsk Report, 1984. *Survey* 128 (1): 88–108. This point is made on pp. 95–96.

31 Stephen Gill, 'The Emerging World Order and European Change: The Political Economy of European Union', paper presented to the XVth World Congress of the International Political Science Association, Buenos Aires, July 1991.

32 A thoughtful introduction to such a perspective can be found in Lacoste (1984). First published in French by Maspero, Paris, 1966.

REFERENCES

Abu-Lughod, J. (1989) *Before European Hegemony. The World System A.D. 1250–1350.* New York: Oxford University Press.

Adamson, W. (1980) *Hegemony and Revolution: A Study of Antonio Gramsci's Political and Cultural Theory.* Berkeley: University of California Press.

Adelman, C. C. (1988). *International Regulation: New Rules in a Changing World Order.* San Francisco: ICS Press.

Alesina, A. and Sachs, J. (1988) 'Political Parties and the Business Cycle in the United States, 1948–1984'. *Journal of Money, Credit and Banking*, (20) 65–80.

Althusser, L. (1977) *For Marx.* London: New Left Books.

Althusser, L. and Balibar, E. (1979) [1969] *Reading Capital.* London: Verso.

Amsden, A. (1990) 'Third World Industrialization: 'Global Fordism' or a New Model?' *New Left Review*, (182) 5–31.

Anderson, B. (1983) *Imagined Communities. Reflections on the Origin and Spread of Nationalism.* London: Verso.

Anderson, I. H. (1981) *Aramco, the United States and Saudi Arabia: A Study of the Dynamics of Foreign Policy, 1933–50.* Princeton NJ: Princeton University Press.

Anderson, P. (1974) *Lineages of the Absolutist State.* London: New LeftBooks.

(1976) *Considerations on Western Marxism.* London: Verso.

Arblaster, A. (1984) *The Rise and Decline of Western Liberalism.* Oxford: Blackwell.

Arrighi, G. (1982) 'A Crisis of Hegemony,' in S. Amin, G. Arrighi, A. G. Frank & I. Wallerstein (eds.) *Dynamics of Global Crisis.* New York: Monthly Review.

(1985) 'Introduction' in G. Arrighi (ed.) *Semiperipheral Development. The Politics of Southern Europe in the Twentieth Century.* Beverly Hills: Sage, 11–27.

Arthur, C. J. (1986) *Dialectics of Labour: Marx and his Relation to Hegel.* Oxford: Blackwell.

Ashley, R. K. (1980) *The Political Economy of War and Peace.* London: Frances Pinter.

(1988) 'Untying the Sovereign State: A Double Reading of the Anarchy Problématique'. *Millennium*, (17) 227–62.

Aubert, M. (1991) *Capitalisme contre capitalisme.* Paris: Seuil.

Augelli, E. (1986) 'Il 'dialogo sulle politche' secondo Washington'. *Politica Internationale*, (14) 108–11.

Augelli, E. and Murphy, C. (1988) *America's Quest for Supremacy and the Third World*. London: Pinter.

—— (1989a) 'Gramsci and International Relations', paper presented at the annual meetings of the *International Studies Association*. London.

—— (1989b) 'The International Economy and the Development of Sub-Saharan Africa', in E. Caputo (ed.) *Which Cooperation with Africa in the Nineties?* Rome: Instituto Italo-Africano.

Avineri, S. (1968) *The Social and Political Thought of Karl Marx*. Cambridge: Cambridge University Press.

Bachrach, P. and Baratz, M. S. (1962) 'The Two Faces of Power'. *American Political Science Review*, (56) 947–52.

—— (1963) 'Decisions and Non-Decisions: An Analytical Framework'. *American Political Science Review*, (57) 631–42.

Bahro, R. (1978) *The Alternative in Eastern Europe*. London: New Left Books.

—— (1980) [1977] *Die Alternative*. Reinbek: Rowohlt.

Barraclough, G. (1967) *An Introduction to Contemporary History*. Harmondsworth: Penguin.

Bartlett B. and Roth, T. P. (eds.) (1985) *The Supply-Side Revolution*. London: Macmillan.

Beer, S. (1974) *Designing Freedom*. Toronto: CBC Publications.

Beigbeder, Y. (1987) *Management Problems in United Nations Organizations: Reform or Decline?* London: Pinter Publishers.

Bellant, R., and Wolf, L. (1990) 'The Free Congress Foundation Goes East'. *Covert Action Information Bulletin*, (35).

Berend, I.T. and Ranki, G. (1982) *The European Periphery and Industrialization, 1780–1914*. Budapest: Akadémiai Kiadó.

Berki, R. N. (1984) 'On Marxian Thought and the Problem of International Relations', in R. B. J. Walker (ed.) *Culture, Ideology, and World Order*. Boulder : Westview, 217–42.

Bernstein, R. J. (1971) *Praxis and Action*. Philadelphia: University of Pennsylvania Press.

Betts, K. (1986) 'The Conditions of Action, Power and the Problem of Interests'. *The Sociological Review*, (34) 39–64.

Bihr, A. (1989) *Entre bourgeoisie et prolétariat. L'encadrement capitaliste*. Paris: l'Harmattan.

Blackburn, R. (1988) *The Overthrow of Colonial Slavery, 1776–1848*. London: Verso.

Blair, J. (1976) *The Control of Oil*. New York: Pantheon.

Blishchenko, I., and Zhdanov, N. (1984) *Terrorism and International Law*. Moscow: Progress.

Block, F. (1977) *The Origins of International Economic Disorder: A Study of United States International Monetary Policy from World War II to the Present*. Berkeley: University of California Press.

Bluestone, B. and Harrison, B. (1982) *The Deindustrialization of America*. New York: Basic Books.

Boot, P. (1982) *De Sovjet-Unie en Oost-Europa*. Amsterdam: SUA.

Bosworth, B. (1984) *Tax Incentives and Economic Growth*. Washington DC: Brookings Institution.

Bousquet, N. (1979) 'Esquisse d'une théorie de l'alternance de périodes de concurrence et d'hégémonie au centre de l'économie-monde capitaliste'. *Review*, (2) 501–18.

(1980) 'From Hegemony to Competition: Cycles of the Core?' in T. K. Hopkins & I. Wallerstein (eds.) *Processes of the World-System*. Beverly Hills: Sage.

Boyer, R. (1990) *The Theory of Regulation: A Critical Analysis*. New York: Columbia University Press.

Bradford, C. I. Jr. (1987) 'Trade and Structural Change: NICs and Next Tier NICs as Transitional Economies'. *World Development*, (15) 299–316.

Brandt Commission (1983) *Common Crisis*. Cambridge, MA: MIT Press.

Braudel, F. (1981) [1979] *The Structures of Everyday Life: The Limits of the Possible*. Vol. I of *Civilisation and Capitalism, 15th–18th Centuries*. Translated by Siân Reynolds. New York: Harper and Row.

(1982) *The Wheels of Commerce*. Vol. II of *Civilization and Capitalism, 15th–18th Centuries*. New York: Harper & Row.

(1984) *The Perspective of the World*. Vol. III of *Civilization and Capitalism, 15th–18th Centuries*. New York: Harper & Row.

Braudel, F. and Spooner, F. (1967) 'Prices in Europe from 1450 to 1750', in E. E. Rich & C. H. Wilson (eds.) *The Cambridge Economic History of Europe*, Vol. IV. London: Cambridge University Press.

Brenner, R.(1977) 'The Origins of Capitalist Development: A Critique of Neo-Smithian Marxism'. *New Left Review*, (104) 25–92.

(1986) 'The Social Basis of Economic Development', in J. Roemer (ed.) *Analytical Marxism*. Cambridge: Cambridge University Press, 23–53.

Brewer, A. (1980) *Marxist Theories of Imperialism*. London: Routledge and Kegan Paul.

Brus, W. (1973) *The Economics and Politics of Socialism*. London: Routledge and Kegan Paul.

Buci-Glucksmann, C. (1982) 'Hegemony and Consent: A Political Strategy', in A. S. Sassoon (ed.) *Approaches to Gramsci*. London: Writers and Readers Publishing Cooperative, 116–26.

Bukharin, N. (1976) [1915] *Imperialism and World Economy*. London: Merlin Press.

Burawoy, M. (1985) *The Politics of Production*. London: Verso.

Calchi Novati, G. (1989) 'Comment on "The International Economy and the Development of Sub-Saharan Africa"' in E. Caputo (ed.) *Which Cooperation with Africa in the Nineties*. Rome: Instituto Italo-Africano.

Callinicos, A. (1983) *Marxism and Philosophy*. Oxford: Clarendon.

Canto, V. A., Joines, D. H. and Laffer, A. (1983) *Foundations of Supply-Side Economics: Theory and Evidence*. New York: Academic Press.

Carnoy, M. (1984) *The State and Political Theory*. Princeton: Princeton University Press.

Carr, E. H . (1945) *Nationalism and After*. London: Macmillan.

(1982) *Twilight of the Comintern 1930–1935*. New York: Pantheon.

Carrère d'Encausse, J. (1980) *Le Pouvoir confisqué. Gouvernants et gouvernés en U.R.S.S.* Paris: Flammarion.

Chase–Dunn, C. (1989) *Global Formation: Structures of the World Economy.* Oxford: Basil Blackwell.

Chauvier, J. M. (1991a) 'les réels enjeux de la rivalitè entre MM. Eltsine et Gorbatchev'. *Le Monde Diplomatique* (April).

(1991b) 'Les batailles à venir', *Le Monde Diplomatique* (September).

Choucri, N. and North, R. C. (1975) *Nations in Conflict.* San Francisco: W. H. Freeman.

Claudin, F. 1975 [1970] *The Communist Movement. From Comintern to Cominform.* Harmondsworth: Pelican.

Cobham, D. (1984) 'French Macro-economic Policy under President Mitterand: An Assessment'. *National Westminster Bank Review*, February.

Cohen-Tanugi, L. (1987) *Le droit sans l'état. Sur la démocratie en France et en Amérique.* Paris: PUF.

Collective 1988, 'Der soziale Fortschritt in der Welt von heute. Thesen zur Diskussion. *Gesellschaftswissenschaftliche Beiträge*, (6).

Colletti, L. (1975) 'Introduction', in K. Marx, *Early Writings*. New York: Vintage, 7–56.

Cortazar, R., Foxley, A. and Tokman, V. E. (1984) *Legados del Monetarismo.* Buenos Aires: Solar.

Cox, R. W. (1977) 'Labour and Hegemony'. *International Organization*, (31) 385–424.

(1979) 'Ideologies and the NIEO: Reflections on Some Recent Literature'. *International Organisation*, (33) 257–302.

(1980) 'The Crisis of World Order and the Problem of International Organization in the 1980s'. *International Journal*, (35) 370–95.

(1981) 'Social Forces, States and World Orders: Beyond International Relations Theory'. *Millennium*, (10) 127–55.

(1982) 'Production and Hegemony: Toward a Political Economy of World Order', in H. K. Jacobson and D. Sidjanski (eds.) *The Emerging International Economic Order.* Beverly Hills: Sage, 37–58.

(1983) 'Gramsci, Hegemony and International Relations: An Essay in Method'. *Millennium*, (12) 162–75.

(1986) 'Social Forces, States and World Orders'. Revised version, in R. O. Keohane (ed.) *Neorealism and its Critics.* New York: Columbia University Press.

(1987) *Production, Power and World Order: Social Forces in the Making of History.* New York: Columbia University Press.

(1989) 'Middlepowersmanship, Japan and Future World Order'. *International Journal*, (44) 823–62.

(1990) 'Towards a Counterhegemonic Conceptualisation of World Order'. Notes prepared for the *Governance-without-Government Workshop.* Ojai California, February, Mimeo.

(1991a) 'The Global Political Economy and Social Choice', in Daniel Drache and Meric S. Gertler (eds.) *The New Era of Global Competition*. Montreal: McGill/Queen's University Press.

(1991b) '"Real Socialism" in Historical Perspective', in Ralph Miliband and Leo Panitch (eds.) *Communist Regimes: The Aftermath. The Socialist Register 1991*. London: Merlin Press.

Crick, M. (1985) *Scargill and the Miners*. Harmondsworth: Penguin.

Crozier M., Huntingdon, S. P., and Watanuki, J. (1975) *The Crisis of Democracy. Report on the Governability of Democracies to the Trilateral Commission*. New York: New York University Press.

Cumings, B. (1987) 'The Origins and Development of the Northeast Asian Political Economy: Industrial Sectors, Product Cycles, and Political Consequences', in F. Deyo (ed.) *The Political Economy of the New Asian Industrialism*. Ithaca: Cornell University Press.

Dahrendorf, R. (1990) *Reflections on the Revolution in Europe*. New York: Random House.

Davies, R. W. (1990) 'Gorbachev's Socialism in Historical Perspective'. *New Left Review*, (179) 5–27.

Dehio, L. (1962) *The Precarious Balance: Four Centuries of the European Power Struggle*. New York: Vintage.

Der Derian, J. (1987) 'Mediating Estrangement: A Theory of Diplomacy'. *Review of International Studies*, (13) 91–110.

Deutsch, K. (1966) *Nationalism and Social Communication*. Cambridge, MA: MIT Press.

De Vroey, M. (1984) 'A Regulation Approach to the Interpretation of the Contemporary Crisis'. *Capital and Class*, (23) 45–6.

Draper, H. (1978) *Karl Marx's Theory of Revolution*. Vol. II. New York: Monthly Review Press.

Edsall, T. B. (1984) *The New Politics of Inequality*. New York: W. W. Norton.

Eisenstadt, S. N. (1963) *The Political Systems of Empires*. Glencoe, Illinois: The Free Press.

Elleinstein, J. (1975) *Histoire du phénomène stalinien*. Paris: Grasset.

Evans, M. K. (1983) *The Truth About Supply-Side Economics*. New York: Basic Books.

Evans-Pritchard, E. (1940) *The Nuer: A Description of the Modes of Livelihood and Political Institutions of the Nilotic People*. Oxford: Clarendon.

Fairbanks, J. K. (1968) *The Chinese World Order: Traditional China's Foreign Relations*. Cambridge: Harvard University Press.

Ferguson, T. (1984) 'From Normalcy to New Deal: Industrial Structure, Party Competition, and American Public Policy in the Great Depression'. *International Organization*, (38) 41–94.

Ferguson, T., and Rogers, J. (1987) *Right Turn*. New York: Hill and Wang.

Fernandez Jilberto, A. E. (1988) 'El debate sociologico-politico sobre casi dos siglos de estado nacional en America Latina: un intento de reinterpretacion'. *Afers Internacionals*, 12/13.

(1989) 'La derrota politica de la burocracia militar y del neoliberalismo en Chile'. *Sistema*, (92) 55–77.

Flaherty, P. (1988) 'Perestroika Radicals: The Origins and Ideology of the Soviet New Left'. *Monthly Review*, (40) 4: 19–33.

Forgacs, D. (1988) *An Antonio Gramsci Reader*. New York: Schocken.

Foweraker, J. (1987) 'Corporatist Strategies and the Transition to Democracy in Spain'. *Comparative Politics*, (20) 57–72.

Frank, A. G. (1979) *Dependent Accumulation and Underdevelopment*. New York: Monthly Review Press.

Frey, B. S. (1984) *International Political Economics*. Oxford: Basil Blackwell.

Frieden, J. (1981) 'Third World Indebted Industrialisation: International Finance and State Capitalism in Mexico, Brazil, Algeria and South Korea'. *International Organisation*, (35) 407–31.

Friedman, M. (1962) *Capitalism and Freedom*. Chicago: University of Chicago Press.

Friedman, M. and Friedman, R. (1980) *Free to Choose*. Harmondsworth: Pelican.

Froebel, F. et al. (1980) *The New International Division of Labour: Structural Unemployment in Industrialised Countries and Industrialisation in Developing Countries*. Cambridge: Cambridge University Press.

Gallagher, J. & Robinson, R. (1953) 'The Imperialism of Free Trade'. *Economic History Review*, (6) 1–15.

Gerbier, B. (1987) 'La course aux armements: l'impérialisme face au nouvel ordre international'. *Cahiers de la Faculté des Sciences Economiques de Grenoble*, (6).

Gervasi, S. (1990) 'A Full Court Press: The Destabilization of the Soviet Union'. *Covert Action Information Bulletin*, (35).

Giddens, A. (1979) *Central Problems in Social Theory: Action, Structure and Contradiction in Social Analysis*. London: Macmillan.

(1981) *A Contemporary Critique of Historical Materialism*. London: Macmillan.

(1985) *The Nation-State and Violence: Volume II of a Contemporary Critique of Historical Materialism*. Berkeley: University of California Press.

(1987) *The Nation State and Violence*. Cambridge: Polity Press.

Gill, S. R. (1986a) 'Hegemony, Consensus and Trilateralism'. *Review of International Studies*, (12) 205–21.

(1986b) 'American Hegemony: Its Limits and Prospects in the Reagan Era.' *Millennium*, (15) 311–39.

(1988) 'The Rise and Decline of Great Powers: The American Case'. *Politics*, (8) 3–9.

(1990) *American Hegemony and the Trilateral Commission*. Cambridge: Cambridge University Press.

(1991a) 'Gramsci, Historical Materialism and International Political Economy', in Murphy and Tooze (eds.), *The New International Political Economy*.

(1991b) 'Reflections on Global Order and Sociohistorical Time'. *Alternatives*, (16) 275–314.

(1992) 'The Emerging World Order and European Change', in R. Miliband and L. Panitch (eds.) *The New World Order. Socialist Register 1992*. London: Merlin Press.

Gill, S. R. and Law, D. (1986) 'Power, Hegemony and International Theory: Recessions and Restructuring in the Global Political Economy'. *International Studies Association*. Annual Congress, Anaheim, California.

—— (1988) *The Global Political Economy: Perspectives, Problems and Policies*. Brighton: Wheatsheaf; Baltimore: Johns Hopkins University Press.

—— (1989) 'Global Hegemony and the Structural Power of Capital'. *International Studies Quarterly*, (33) 475–99.

Gills, B. K. (1989) 'Synchronisation, Conjecture and Centre-Shift in East Asian International History'. *International Studies Association*. Annual Congress, London.

Gills, B. K. and Frank, A. G. (1990) 'The Cumulation of Accumulation: Theses and Research Agenda for 5000 Years of World System History'. *Dialectical Anthropology*, (15) 19–42.

Gilpin, R. (1975) *U.S. Power and the Multinational Corporation: The Political Economy of Foreign Direct Investment*. New York: Basic Books.

—— (1977) 'Economic Interdependence and National Security in Historical Perspective', in K. Knorr and F.Trager (eds.) *Economic Issues and National Security*. Lawrence, Kansas: Allen Press.

—— (1981) *War and Change in World Politics*. Cambridge: Cambridge University Press.

—— (1984) 'The Richness of the Tradition of Political Realism'. *International Organisation*, (38) 287–304.

—— (1987) *The Political Economy of International Relations*. Cambridge: Cambridge University Press.

Gluckman, M. (1963) *Custom and Conflict in Africa*. Oxford: Basil Blackwell.

Gordon, D. (1980) 'Stages of Accumulation and Long Economic Cycles', in Terence K. Hopkins and Immanuel Wallerstein (eds.) *Processes of the World System*. Beverly Hills: Sage.

Gould, C. (1978) *Marx's Social Ontology*. Cambridge: MIT Press.

Gramsci, A. (1971) *Selections from the Prison Notebooks of Antonio Gramsci*. Translated by Q. Hoare and G. Nowell Smith. New York: International Publishers; London: Lawrence and Wishart

—— (1975) *Quaderni del Carcere*. Torino: Einaudi.

—— (1977) *Selections from Political Writings 1910–1920*. Q. Hoare (ed.). Translated by John Matthews. New York: International Publishers.

—— (1978) *Selections from Political Writings 1921–1926* Q. Hoare (ed.). New York: International Publishers.

—— (1988) *An Antonio Gramsci Reader*. D. Forgacs (ed.). New York: Schocken Books.

Grant, W. with Sargent, J. (1987) *Business and Politics in Britain*. London: Macmillan.

Gross, L. (1968) 'The Peace of Westphalia, 1648–1948', in R. A. Falk and W. H. Hanrieder (eds.) *International Law and Organization*. Philadelphia: Lippincott.

Gunnell, J. G. (1968) 'Social Science and Political Reality: The Problem of Explanation'. *Social Research*, (35) 159–201.

Habermas, J. (1975) *Legitimation Crisis*. London: Heinemann.

Haas, E. (1964) *Beyond the Nation-State*. Stanford: Stanford University Press.

Hall, S. (1982) 'The Rediscovery of Ideology', in M. Gurevitch et al. (eds.) *Culture, Society and the Media*. London: Methuen.

Hamelink, C. (1983) *Cultural Autonomy in Global Communication*. London: Longman.

Harris, N. (1987) *The End of the Third World: the newly industrializing countries and the decline of an Ideology*. Harmondsworth: Penguin.

Harrod, J. and Schrijver, N. (eds.) (1988) *The U.N. Under Attack*. Aldershot: Gower.

Hart, J. A. (1984) *The New International Economic Order*. New York: St Martins Press.

Hill, C. (1958) *Puritanism and Revolution*. New York: Schocken.

Hobsbawm, E. (1962) *The Age of Revolution 1789–1848*. New York: New American Library.

Holloway, D. (1984) *De Sovjet-Unie en de bewapeningswedloop*. Amsterdam: Mets.

Holman, O. (1989a) 'Het Spaanse voorzitterschap van de Europese Gemeenschappen'. *Internationale Spectator*, (43) 627–633.

(1989b) 'In Search of Hegemony: Socialist Government and the Internationalization of Domestic Politics in Spain'. *International Journal of Political Economy*, (19) 76–101.

Holman, O. and Fernandez Jilberto, A. E. (1989) 'Clases sociales, crisis del régimen autoritario y transición democrática: los casos de Brasil y España en una perspectiva comparativa'. *Afers Internacionals*, (16) 5–22.

Hopkins, T. K. and Wallerstein, I. [with the Research Working Group on Cyclical Rhythms and Secular Trends] (1979) 'Cyclical Rhythms and Secular Trends of the Capitalist World-Economy: Some Premises, Hypotheses and Questions'. *Review*, (2) 483–500.

Hough, J. F. (1986) *The Struggle for the Third World. Soviet Debates and American Options*. Washington: Brookings.

(1990) *Russia and the West. Gorbachev and the Politics of Reform*. New York: Simon and Schuster.

Hungarian Academy of Sciences, Institute of Economics (1984) *Studies*, 23 & 24, *Wage Bargaining in Hungarian Firms*.

Hymer, S. (1979) *The Multinational Corporation: A Radical Approach*. Cambridge: Cambridge University Press.

Inayatullah, N. and Rupert, M. (1990) 'Hobbes, Smith, and the Problem of Mixed Ontologies in Neorealist Political Economy'. *International Studies Association*. Annual Congress, Washington, D.C.

Isaak, J. (1987) *Power and Marxist Theory: A Realist View*. Ithaca: Cornell University Press.

Izyumov, A. and Kortunov, A. (1988) 'The Soviet Union in the Changing World.' *International Affairs* (Moscow), (8) 46–56.

Jacoby, R. (1981) *Dialectic of Defeat: Contours of Western Marxism*. Cambridge: Cambridge University Press.

Jay, M. (1984) *Marxism and Totality*. Berkeley: University of California Press.

Jessop, B. (1982) *The Capitalist State: Marxist Theories and Methods*. New York: New York University Press.

Johnson, C. (1982) *MITI and the Japanese Miracle: The Growth of Industrial Policy, 1925–1975*. Stanford: Stanford University Press.

Joll, J. (1977) *Gramsci*. Glasgow: Fontana.

Kalecki, M. (1943) 'Political Aspects of Full Employment'. *Political Quarterly*, (14) 322–31.

Katzenstein, P. (Ed.) (1978) *Between Power and Plenty: Foreign Economic Policies of Advanced Industrial States*. Madison: University of Wisconsin Press.

Keat, R. and Urry, J. (1982) *Social Theory as Science*. (2nd ed.). London: Routledge and Kegan Paul.

Keegan, W. (1985) *Mrs Thatcher's Economic Experiment*. Harmondsworth: Pelican.

Kennedy, P. (1987/88) *The Rise and Fall of the Great Powers: Economic Change and Military Conflict from 1500 to 2000*. New York: Random House.

Keohane, R. (1984a) *After Hegemony: Cooperation and Discord in the World Political Economy*. Princeton NJ: Princeton University Press.

(1984b) 'The World Political Economy and the Crisis of Embedded Liberalism', in John Goldthorpe (ed.) *Order and Conflict in Contemporary Capitalism*. Oxford: Oxford University Press.

(1986) 'Theory of World Politics: Structural Realism and Beyond', in R. Keohane (ed.) *Neorealism and its Critics*. New York: Columbia University Press.

Keohane, R. and Nye, J. (1977) *Power and Interdependence*. Boston: Little, Brown.

(1983) 'Power and Interdependence revisited'. *International Organizations*, (41) 725–53.

Keyder, C. (1985) 'The American Recovery of Southern Europe: Aid and Hegemony', in G. Arrighi (ed.) *Semiperipheral Development. The Politics of Southern Europe in the Twentieth Century*. Beverly Hills: Sage.

Khader, B. (1986) 'Oil for Peace'. *Strutture Ambientali*, (75) 2.

Kindleberger, C. P. (1973) *The World in Depression, 1929–39*. London: Allen Lane.

Knights, D. and Wilmott, H. (1985) 'Power and Identity in Theory and Practice.' *The Sociological Review*, (33) 22–47.

Kolakowski, L. (1968) 'Karl Marx and the Classical Definition of Truth', in L. Kolakowski *Toward a Marxist Humanism*. New York: Grove Press.

(1981) *Main Currents of Marxism*. 3 volumes. Oxford: Oxford University Press.

Kolm, S. C. (1977) *La transition socialiste. La politique économique de la gauche*. Paris: Editions du cerf.

Konrad, G., and Szelenyi, I. (1981) [1978] *Die Intelligenz auf dem Weg zur Klassenmacht*. Frankfurt: Suhrkamp.

Kornai, J. (1971) *Anti-Equilibrium. On Economic Systems Theory and the Tasks of Research*. Amsterdam: North Holland.

(1980) *Economics of Shortage*. Amsterdam: North-Holland.

(1982) *Growth, Shortage and Efficiency: A Macrodynamic Model of the Socialist Economy*. Berkeley: University of California Press.

(1986) *Contradictions and Dilemmas*. London: MIT Press.

Krasner, S. D. (1985) *Structural Conflict. The Third World against Global Liberalism*. Berkeley: University of California Press.

Kuklinski, A. (ed.) (1991) *Globality versus Locality* Vols. 1 & 2. Warsaw: Polish Association for the Club of Rome.

Laclau, E. (1975) 'The Specificity of the Political: The Poulantzas-Miliband Debate.' *Economy and Society*, (5) 87–110.

(1977) *Politics and Ideology in Marxist Theory*. London: New Left Books.

Lacoste, Y. (1984) *Ibn Khaldun. The Birth of History and the Past of the Third World*. London: Verso. (First published in French by Maspero, Paris, 1966).

Laird, R. D., and Laird, B. A. (1970) *Soviet Communism and Agrarian Revolution*. Harmondsworth: Pelican.

Lamounier, B. (1989) 'Brazil: Inequality Against Democracy', in Diamond et al. (eds.) *Democracy in Developing Countries. Volume Four: Latin America*. Boulder and London: Lynne Rienner Publishers.

Lane, F. (1966) *Venice and History*. Baltimore: Johns Hopkins University Press.

(1979) *Profits from Power. Readings in Protection, Rent and Violence-Controlling Enterprises*. Albany: State University of New York Press.

Larrain, J. (1979) *The Concept of Ideology*. London: Hutchinson.

(1983) *Marxist Theories of Ideology*. London: Hutchinson.

Lefebvre, H. (1976) *De l'État* (Paris: 10/18), 4 volumes

Lenin, V. I. (various years) *Collected Works*. Moscow: Progress.

(1939) [1917] *Imperialism: The Highest Stage of Capitalism*. New York: International Publishers.

Levine, R. (1988) *Class Struggle and the New Deal*. Lawrence: University of Kansas Press.

Levinson, C. (1972) *International Trade Unionism*. London: Allen and Unwin.

Lewin, M. (1985) *The Making of the Soviet System. Essays in the Social History of Interwar Russia*. London: Methuen.

Lijphart, A, et al. (1988) 'A Mediterranean Model of Democracy? The Southern European Democracies in Comparative Perspective'. *West European Politics*, (11) 7–25.

Lindblom, C. (1977) *Politics and Markets*. New York: Basic Books.

Linklater, A. (1986) 'Realism, Marxism and Critical International Theory'. *Review of International Studies*, (12) 301–12.

Lipietz, A. (1982) 'Towards Global Fordism?' *New Left Review*, (132) 33–47.

(1987) *Mirages and Miracles. The Crises of Global Fordism*. London: Verso.

Lipson, C. (1981) 'The International Organisation of Third World Debt'. *International Organisation*, (35) 603–31.

Lloyd, J. (1985) 'Understanding the Miners' Strike'. *Fabian Society Tract*, 504. London: Fabian Society.

London, A. 1970 [1968] *The Confession*. New York: Morrow.

Longstreeh, F. (1979) 'The City, Industry and the State', in Colin Crouch (ed.) *State and Economy in Contemporary Capitalism*. London: Croom Helm.

Lorwin, V. R. (1967) 'Working Class Politics and Economic Development in Western Europe' [1958] in Lorwin (ed.) *Labor and Working Conditions in Modern Europe*. New York: Macmillan.

Lukes, S. (1970) 'Power and Structure', in Steven Lukes (ed.) *Essays in Social Theory*. London: Macmillan.

Löwy, M. (1981) *The Politics of Combined and Uneven Development. The Theory of Permanent Revolution*. London: Verso.

Lukács, G. (1985) *Demokratisierung Heute und Morgen*. Budapest: Akadémiai Kiadó.

Lukes, S. (1973) *Individualism*. Oxford: Blackwell.

McCracken Report (1977) *Towards Full Employment and Price Stability*. Paris, OECD.

McGovern, A. F. (1970) 'The Young Marx on the State'. *Science and Society*, (34) 430–66.

MacIver, R. M. (1932) *The Modern State*. London: Oxford University Press.

McNeill, W. (1984) *The Pursuit of Power: Technology, Armed Forces, and Society since A. D. 1000*. Chicago: University of Chicago Press.

Madeuf, B. & Michalet, C. A. (1978) 'A New Approach to International Economics'. *International Social Science Journal*, (30).

Maier, C. (1977) 'The Politics of Productivity: Foundations of American International Economic Policy after World War II'. *International Organization*, (31).

(1988) *In Search of Stability*. Cambridge: Cambridge University Press. Chapters 3 and 5.

Mandell, D. (1990) '"A Market without Thorns": The Ideological Struggle for the Soviet Working Class'. *Studies in Political Economy*, (33) 7–38.

Mann, M. (1986) *The Sources of Social Power, Vol. I: A History of Power from the Beginning to A.D. 1760*. Cambridge: Cambridge University Press.

Mao tse-tung. (1977) *Five Essays on Philosophy*. Peking: Foreign Languages Press.

Marcou, L. (1979) *L'Internationale après Staline*. Paris: Grasset.

Marcuse, H. (1971) [1958] *Soviet Marxism*. Harmondsworth: Pelican.

Marsh, D. (1983) 'Interest Group Activity and Structural Power', in David Marsh (ed.) *Capital and Politics in Western Europe*. London: Frank Cass.

Marx, K. (1971) *Grundrisse*. Edited by McLellan, D. Harmondsworth: Penguin.

(1975a) 'Economic and Philosophical Manuscripts', in *Early Writings*. New York: Vintage Books.

(1975b) 'Critique of Hegel's Doctrine of the State', in *Early Writings*.

(1975c) 'On the Jewish Question' in *Early Writings*.

(1975d) 'Theses on Feuerbach', in *Early Writings*.

(1977a) *Capital, Volume I*. New York: Vintage Books.

(1977b) 'Appendix: result of the Immediate Process of Production'. in *Capital, Volume I*.

Marx, K. and Engels, F. (various years). *Marx–Engles Werke*. (Collected Works). Cited in this volume as *MEW*. Berlin: Dietz.

(1947) *The German Ideology*. C. J. Arthur (ed. and trans.). New York: International Publishers.

(1967) *The Communist Manifesto*. Harmondsworth: Penguin.

(1970) *The German Ideology*. C. J. Arthur (ed.) New York: International Publishers.

Mattelart, A. (1979) *Multinational Corporations and the Control of Culture*. Brighton: Harvester.

Mayer, T. F. (1989) 'In Defense of Analytical Marxism'. *Science and Society*, (53) 416–41.

Mearsheimer, J. (1990) 'Why We shall soon miss the Cold War'. *Atlantic Monthly*, August.

Menand, L. (1990) 'Pop Goes the Proletariat'. *Esquire* September.

Meszaros, I. (1975) *Marx's Theory of Alienation* (4th edn). London: Merlin Press.

Miliband, R. (1969) *The State in Capitalist Society*. New York: Basic Books.

Miller, J. D. B. (1981) *The World of States: Connected Essays*. London: Croom Helm.

Miller, L. B. (1983) 'Energy and Alliance Politics: Lessons of a Decade'. *The World Today*, (39) 477–82.

(1987)'Innocence Abroad? Congress, the President, and Foreign Policy'. *The World Today* (43) 62–5.

Milliken, J. (1990) 'Praxis and Structuration in International Relations', Master's thesis, Maxwell School of Citizenship and Public Affairs, Syracuse University.

Modelski, G. (1978) 'The Long Cycle of Global Politics and the Nation-state'. *Comparative Studies in Society and History*, (20) 214–38.

(1981) 'Long Cycles, Kondratieffs and Alternating Innovations: Implications for U.S. Foreign Policy', in C. W. Kegley & P. McGowan (eds.) *The Political Economy of Foreign Policy Behavior*. Beverly Hills: Sage.

(1987) *Long Cycles in World Politics*. Seattle: University of Washington Press.

Modelski, G. and Modelski, S. (eds.) (1988) *Documenting Global Leadership*. Seattle: University of Washington Press.

Moore, B., Jr. (1977) [1966] *Social Origins of Democracy and Dicatorship*. Harmondsworth: Pelican.

Morera, E. (1990) *Gramsci's Historicism*. London: Routledge.

Mouffe, C. (ed.) (1979) *Gramsci and Marxist Theory*. London: Routledge and Kegan Paul.

Mouzelis, N. (1986) *Politics in the Semi-Periphery. Early Parliamentarism and Late Industrialization in the Balkans and Latin America*. London: Macmillan.

Murphy, C. N. (1984) *The Emergence of the NIEO Ideology*. Boulder: Westview Press.

Murphy, C. N. and R. Tooze (eds.) (1991) *The New International Political Economy*. London: Macmillan.

Nadel, G. and Curtis, P. (eds.) (1964) *Imperialism and Colonialism*. New York: Macmillan.

Nayar, B. R. (1983) *India's Quest for Technological Independence. Vol II: The Results of Policy*. London: Lancers.

Nester, W. (1989) 'The Third World in Japanese Foreign Policy'. *Millennium*, (18) 377–98.

Neuman, S. (1984) 'International Stratification and Third World Military Industries'. *International Organisation*, (38) 167–98.

Neumann, F. (1942) *Behemoth: The Structure and Practice of National Socialism*. London: Gollancz.

Noel, A. (1987). 'Accumulation, Regulation and Social Change: An Essay on French Political Economy'. *International Organization*, (41) 303–33.

Nove, A. (1978) [1969] *An Economic History of the U.S.S.R.* Harmondsworth: Pelican.

(1983) *The Economics of Feasible Socialism*. London: George Allen & Unwin.

Novosibirsk Report (1984) Trans. published in *Survey*, (128) 1: 88–108.

Nye, J. S. Jr. (1990) *Bound to Lead. The Changing Nature of American Power*. New York: Basic Books.

Ollman, B. (1976) *Alienation: Marx's Conception of Man in Capitalist Society* (2nd edn). New York: Cambridge University Press.

(1990) 'Putting Dialectics to Work: The Process of Abstraction in Marx's Method'. *Rethinking Marxism*, (3) 26–74.

Overbeek, H. (1987) 'Global Capitalism and Britain's Decline', PhD thesis, University of Amsterdam, Netherlands.

(1990) *Global Capitalism and National Decline. The Thatcher Decade in Perspective*. London: Routledge.

Overbeek, H. W. (ed.) (forthcoming) *Neo-Liberalism and Global Hegemony: Concepts of Control in the Global Political Economy*. London: Routledge.

Palan, R. and Gills, B. (eds.) (forthcoming) *Transcending the State/Global Divide: The Neo-Structuralist Agenda in International Relations*. Boulder: Lynne Reinner.

Parker, G. and Smith, L. (eds.) (1985) *The General Crisis of the Seventeenth Century*. London: Routledge & Kegan Paul.

Payer, C. (1982) *The World Bank: A Critical Analysis*. New York: Monthly Review Press.

Petrovic, G. (1983) 'Alienation', in T. Bottomore (ed.) *A Dictionary of Marxist Thought*. Cambridge: Harvard University Press.

Pfister, U. and Suter, C. (1987) 'International Financial Relations as Part of the World System'. *International Studies Quarterly*, (31) 239–72.

Pinder, J. et al. (1977) *Industrial Policy and the International Economy*. New York, Trilateral Commission.

Piore, M. and Sabel, C. (1984) *The Second Industrial Divide*. New York: Basic Books.

Poggi, G. (1978) *The Development of the Modern State*. Stanford: Stanford University Press.

Polanyi, K. 1957 [1944] *The Great Transformation: The Political and Economic Origins of Our Time*. Boston: Beacon.

Poulantzas, N. (1969) 'The Problem of the Capitalist State'. *New Left Review*, (58) 67–78.

(1973) *Political Power and Social Classes*. London: New Left Books.

Pridham, G. (1984) 'Comparative Perspectives on the New Mediterranean

Democracies: A Model of Regime Transition?', in Pridham (ed.) *The New Mediterranean Democracies: Regime Transition in Spain, Greece and Portugal.* London: Frank Cass.

Puchala, D. J. and Coate, R. (1989) *The Challenge of Relevance: The United Nations in a Changing World Environment.* Hanover, NH: Academic Council on the United Nations System.

Putnam, R. D. and Bayne, N. (1984) *Hanging Together: The Seven-Power Summits.* London: Heinemann for the Royal Institute of International Affairs.

Radice, H. (Ed.) (1975) *International Firms and Modern Imperialism.* Harmondsworth: Penguin.

Rapkin, D. P. (1990) 'Japan and World Leadership', in David P. Rapkin (ed.) *World Leadership and Hegemony.* Boulder: Lynne Reinner Publishers.

Resnick, S. A. and Wolff, R. D. (1987) *Knowlege and Class.* Chicago: University of Chicago Press.

Roberts, P. C. (1984) *The Supply-side Revolution.* Cambridge MA: Harvard University Press.

Roberts, A. and Kingsbury, B. (eds.) (1988) *United Nations, Divided World: The U.N.'s Role in International Relations.* Oxford: Clarendon Press.

Roemer, J. (1982) *A General Theory of Exploitation and Class.* Cambridge: Cambridge University Press.

Roett, R. (1988) 'Brazil: Economic Crisis and Policy Options', in J. M. Chacel, P. S. Falk and D. V. Fleischer (eds.) *Brazil's Economic and Political Future.* Boulder and London: Westview Press.

Romano, R. (1983) 'Between the Sixteenth and the Seventeenth Centuries: The Economic Crisis of 1619–22', in G. Parker & L. M. Smith (eds.) *The General Crisis of the Seventeenth Century.* London: Routledge & Kegan Paul.

Rosenstock–Huessy, E. (1961) [1931] *Die europäischen Revolutionen und der Character der Nationen.* Stuttgart: Kohlhammer.

Rossabi, M. (1983) *China Among Equals: The Middle Kingdom and Its Neighbours 10th–14th centuries.* Berkeley: University of California Press.

Ruggie, J. G. (1982) 'International Regimes, Transactions and Change – Embedded Liberalism in the Post-War Order'. *International Organisation,* (36) 379–415.

Ruggie, J. (1983) 'Continuity and Transformation in the World Polity: Toward a Neorealist Synthesis'. *World Politics,* (35) 261–85.

Rupert, M. (1990) 'Producing Hegemony: State/Society Relations and the Politics of Productivity in the United States'. *International Studies Quarterly,* (34) 427–56.

Sampson, A. (1975) *The Seven Sisters: The Great Oil Companies and the World They Made.* London: Hodder and Stoughton.

Sassoon, A. S. (1982) 'Hegemony, War of Position and Political Intervention', in A. S. Sassoon (ed.) *Approaches to Gramsci.* London: Writers and Readers Publishing Cooperative.

Sayer, D. (1983) *Marx's Method: Ideology, Science and Critique in 'Capital'* (2nd edn). Atlantic Highlands: Humanities Press.

(1985) 'The Critique of Politics and Political Economy: Capitalism, Communism and the State in Marx's Writings of the mid-1840's.' *Sociological Review*, (33) 221–53.

(1987) *The Violence of Abstraction: The Analytic Foundations of Historical Materialism*. Oxford: Blackwell.

Schmiegelow, H. and Schmiegelow, M. (1975) 'The New Mercantilism in International Relations: the Case of France's External Policy'. *International Organisation*, (29) 367–92.

Schollhamer, H. (1978) 'Identification, Evaluation and Prediction of Political Risks from an International Business Perspective', in M. Ghertman and J. Leontiades (eds.) *European Research in International Business*. Amsterdam: North Holland.

Schumpeter, J. (1963) *The Theory of Economic Development*. New York: Oxford University Press.

Seldon, A. (1981) *Whither the Welfare State?* London: Institute of Economic Affairs.

Seldon, A. et al. (1981) *The Emerging Consensus? Essays on the Interplay Between Ideas, Interests and Circumstances in the first 25 Years of the Institute of Economic Affairs*. London: Institute of Economic Affairs.

Senin, M. (1973) *Socialist Integration*. Moscow: Progress.

Short, K. (Ed.) (1986) *Western Broadcasting over the Iron Curtain*. London: Croom Helm.

Showstack–Sassoon, A. (1980/87) *Gramsci's Politics*. London: Croom Helm.

Skidelsky, R. (1979) 'The Decline of Keynesian Politics', in Colin Crouch (ed.) *State and Economy in Contemporary Capitalism*. London: Croom Helm.

Skocpol, T. (1979) *States and Social Revolutions*. Cambridge: Cambridge University Press.

Spohn, W. (1975) 'Die technologische Abhängigkeit der Sowjetunion vom Weltmarkt'. *Probleme des Klassenkampfs*, 5 (October) [summary and commentary on Sutton's three-volume study, *Western Technology and Soviet Economic Development 1917–65*, Stanford 1968–73].

Spyropoulos, G. (1990) 'Labour Law and Labour Relations in Tomorrow's Social Europe.' *International Labour Review*, (129) 733–50.

Stalin, J. 1972 [1952] *Economic Problems of Socialism in the U.S.S.R.* Peking: Foreign Languages Press.

Sté Croix, B.E.M. de (1981) *The Class Struggle in the Ancient Greek World*. London: Duckworth.

Steensgaard, N. (1985) 'The Seventeenth-Century Crisis', in G. Parker & L. M. Smith (eds.) *The General Crisis of the Seventeenth Century*. London: Routledge & Kegan Paul.

Stein, H. (1984) *Presidential Economics*. New York: Simon and Schuster.

Stoffaes, C. (1978) *La grande menace industrielle*. Paris: Calmann-Levy.

Strange, S. (1987) 'The Persistent Myth of Lost Hegemony'. *International Organization*, (41) 551–74.

(1988) *States and Markets*. London: Pinter.

(1990) 'The Name of the Game', in N. X. Rizopoulos (ed.) *Sea Changes*. New York: Council on Foreign Relations Press.

Strange, S. (Ed.) (1984) *Paths to International Political Economy*. London: Frances Pinter.

Szelenyi, I. and Szelenyi, S. (1991) 'The Vacuum in Hungarian Politics: Classes and Parties'. *New Left Review*. (187) 121–37.

Taylor, C. (1976) 'Hermeneutics and Politics', in Paul Connerton (ed.) *Critical Sociology* Harmondsworth: Penguin.

Texier, J. (1979) 'Gramsci, Theoretician of the Superstructures: On the Concept of Civil Society', in C. Mouffe (ed.) *Gramsci and Marxist Theory*. London: Routledge and Kegan Paul.

Thompson, E. P. (1978) 'The Poverty of Theory or an Orrery of Errors', in *The Poverty of Theory and Other Essays*. New York: Monthly Review.

Tickner, J. A. (1991) 'On the Fringes of the World Economy: A Feminist Perspective', in C. Murphy and R. Tooze (eds.) *The New International Political Economy*.

Tortosa, J. M. (1985) *El 'Cambio' y la modernización. OTAN, CEE y nuevas tecnologías*. Alicante: Juan Gil-Albert.

Tunstall, J. (1977) *The Media are American*. London: Constable.

Turner, L. (1980) *The Oil Companies in the International System*. London: Heinemann for the Royal Institute of International Affairs.

United Nations Center on Transnational Corporations (1988) *Transnational Corporations in World Development*. New York.

US Department of State. (1984) 'Secretary Shultz: Building Confidence and Security in Europe' [January 17]. *US Department of State*. Washington.

Van der pijl, K. (1982) *Marxisme en internationale politiek*. Amsterdam: IPSO.

(1984) *The Making of an Atlantic Ruling Class*. London: Verso.

(1987) 'Neoliberalism versus Planned Interdependence. Concepts of Control and the Struggle for Hegemony', in J. N. Rosenau and H. Tromp (eds.) *Interdependence and Conflict in World Politics*. Aldershott: Avebury.

(1988) 'The Socialist International and the Internationalisation of Capital.' *After the Crisis: Occasional Papers*. University of Amsterdam, Faculty of Political and Social Sciences.

(1989) 'Ruling Classes, Hegemony, and the State System'. *International Journal of Political Economy*, (Fall) 7–35.

Van Doorn, J. (ed.) (1975) *Armed Forces and Society*. The Hague: Mouton.

Van Wolferen, K. (1989) *The Enigma of Japanese Power: People and Politics in a Stateless Nation*. London: Macmillan.

Van Zon, H. (1987) 'Planeconomieën en de wereldmarkt in de jaren tachtig'. Mimeo, University of Amsterdam, Department of International Relations.

(1991) 'East European Debt: A Comparative Perspective', in J. Michie (ed.) *The Economics of Restructuring and Intervention*. Aldershot and Brookfield: Edward Elgar.

Verba, S. (1970) 'The Silent Majority: Myth and Reality'. *University of Chicago Magazine*, (63) 13–14.

Vielle, P. (1988) 'The World's Chaos and the New Paradigms of the Social Movement', in Lelio Basso Foundation (eds.) *Theory and Practice of Liberation at the End of the Twentieth Century*. Bruxelles: Bruylant.

Vojinovic, M. (1990) 'Will there be a Palingenesis of Extreme Rightist Movements?' Paper for the conference *After the Crisis*, University of Amsterdam, 18–20 April.

Von Hayek, F. A. (1960) *The Constitution of Liberty*. London: Routledge and Kegan Paul.

(1967) *Studies in Philosophy, Politics and Economics*. London: Routledge and Kegan Paul.

(1976) [1944] *The Road to Serfdom*. London: Routledge and Kegan Paul.

Von Laue, T. H. (1967) [1961] 'Russian Peasants in the Factory', in V. R. Lorwin (ed.) *Labor and Working Conditions in Modern Europe*. New York: Macmillan, London: Collier/Macmillan.

Voslensky, M. (1984) *Nomenklatura. Anatomy of the Soviet Ruling Class*. London: Bodley Head.

Walker, T. (1988) 'Islamic Funds: A Liquidation Threat'. *Financial Times*, June. Supplement on Egypt.

Wallerstein, I. (1974a) *The Modern World System, I: Capitalist Agriculture and the Origins of the European World-Economy in the Sixteenth Century*. New York: Academic Press.

(1974b) 'The Rise and Future Demise of the World Capitalist System: Concepts for Comparative Analysis'. *Comparative Studies in Society and History*, (16) 387–415.

(1979) *The Capitalist World-Economy*. Cambridge: Cambridge University Press.

(1980) *The Modern World-System II: Mercantilism and the consolidation of the European World-Economy, 1600–1750*. New York: Academic Press.

(1984a) *The Politics of the World-Economy*. Cambridge: Cambridge University Press.

(1984b) 'The Three Instances of Hegemony in the History of the Capitalist World-Economy'. *International Journal of Comparative Sociology*, (24) 100–8.

(1985) 'The Relevance of the Concept of Semiperiphery to Southern Europe', in G. Arrighi (ed.) *Semiperipheral Development. The Politics of Southern Europe in the Twentieth Century*. Beverly Hills: Sage.

(1988) *The Modern World-System, III: The Second Era of Great Expansion of the Capitalist World-Economy, 1730–1840*. New York: Academic.

Waltz, K. N. (1979) *Theory of International Politics*. Reading, MA.: Addison-Wesley.

Ward, H. (1986) 'Structural Power – A Contradiction in Terms?' *Essex Papers in Politics and Government*, Department of Government, Essex University, England.

Weber, M. (1946) 'Bureaucracy', in H. H. Gerth and C. W. Mills (eds.) *From Max Weber*. Oxford: Oxford University Press.

Wendt, A. (1987) 'The Agent-Structure Problem in International Relations Theory'. *International Organization*, (41) 335–70.

Wilkinson, D. (1989) 'The Future of the World State: From Civilization Theory to World Politics', *International Studies Association*, Annual Conference, London.

Wilkinson, F. (ed.) (1981) *The Dynamics of Labour Market Segmentation*. London: Academic Press.

Wilson, C. (1958) *Mercantilism*. London: Routledge Kegan & Paul.

Wolfe, A. (1981) *America's Impasse. The Rise and Fall of the Politics of Growth*. New York: Pantheon.

Wood, E. M. (1981) 'The Separation of the Economic and the Political in Capitalism'. *New Left Review*, (127) 66–95.

Young, S. et al. (1988) *Multinationals and the British Economy*. London: Croom Helm.

Zysman, J. (1983) *Governments, Markets, and Growth*. Ithaca: Cornell University Press.

NAME INDEX

A. Khan Organisation, 246
Abbassids, 199
Abu-Lughod, Janet, 187, 190
Afghanistan, 254
Africa, 136
Africa, east, 197
Albania, 253
Alker, Hayward, 84
Allende, Salvador, 270
Althusser, Louis, 22
American Declaration of Independence, 170
American Revolution, 174
Amnesty International, 122
Amsterdam School of International Relations, 1
Anderson, Benedict, 142, 155
Anglo-Dutch Wars, 166
Argentina, 213, 215, 218, 222-4, 234
Aron, Raymond, 184
Arrighi, Giovanni; 42-3, 218-19
Ashikaga Shogunate, 196
Ashley, Richard, 30
Asia, 14,210, 250, 262
Asia, central, 199
Asia, east, 187-8, 193-6, 198-208
Athenian democracy, 178
Augelli, Enrico, 47
Australia, 10, 120
Austro-Hungarian Empire, 143-4

Bahro, Rudolf, 280
Balibar, Etienne, 22
Baltic Sea, 257
Bank for International Settlements, 8, 103, 120, 182, 210
Bank of Japan, 208-9
Beethoven, Ludwig von, 36
Belgium, 143
Berki, R. N., 86
Berlin, 143
Bilderberg meetings, 103, 266
Birmingham University Centre for Contemporary Cultural Studies, 3

Bismarck, Otto von, 93
Bloch, Marc, 160
Bolshevik party, 238, 243-4, 247, 256
Bolshevik Revolution, 50, 52, 241, 243, 258
Bosch, Hieronymous, 12
Brandt Commission, 117, 138
Braudel, Fernand, 1, 9,15, 36, 44, 155
Brazil, 12, 167, 213-15, 218, 223-4, 228-30, 233-6
Bretton Woods, 32, 34, 35, 62, 96, 136, 260
Britain see Subject index
British Petroleum, 103
British Commonwealth, 39
Bukharin, Nicolai, 29, 45, 245, 250
Bulgaria, 251
Bundesbank, 36
Bush administration, 136-7
Bush, George, 8, 127, 211, 234, 255, 285

Canada, 8, 10, 120
Carr, E. H., 249
Carter, Jimmy, 255
Ceaucescu, Nicolai, 39
Central America, 65
Chase-Dunn, Christopher, 220
Cheng Ho, 197
Chiang Kai Shek, 203
Chile, 213, 223-4, 270
China, 6, 40, 96, 105, 115, 117, 137, 158, 194, 196-8, 200-4, 248, 252-4
Chinese Communist Party, 57
Choshu Daimyo, 201
CIA, 103, 255
Club of Rome, 266
Colbert, Jean-Baptiste, 166
Cold War, 5, 6, 31, 32, 34, 40, 96, 140, 204, 249, 254, 265
Collor de Mello, Fernando, 224, 233
Comecon, 255
Comintern, 244, 246-9
Common Market see European Community

308

SUBJECT INDEX

Lightning Source UK Ltd.
Milton Keynes UK
UKOW04f2308190615

253793UK00001B/75/P